Rhymes in the Flow

Rhymes in the Flow

How Rappers Flip the Beat

Macklin Smith and Aurko Joshi

University of Michigan Press
Ann Arbor

Published in the United States of America by
the University of Michigan Press
Manufactured in the United States of America
Printed on acid-free paper

First published June 2020

A CIP catalog record for this book is available from the British Library.

Library of Congress Cataloging-in-Publication Data

Names: Smith, Macklin, 1944– author. | Joshi, Aurko, 1993– author.
Title: Rhymes in the flow : how rappers flip the beat / Macklin Smith and
    Aurko Joshi.
Description: Ann Arbor : University of Michigan Press, 2020. | Includes
    bibliographical references and index.
Identifiers: LCCN 2020004449 (print) | LCCN 2020004450 (ebook) |
    ISBN 9780472073894 (hardcover) | ISBN 9780472053896 (paperback) |
    ISBN 9780472124046 (ebook)
Subjects: LCSH: Rhyme. | Rap (Music)—History and criticism. | Musical
    meter and rhythm. | Performance poetry—History and criticism. | Poetics.
Classification: LCC PN1059.R5 S66 2020 (print) | LCC PN1059.R5 (ebook) |
    DDC 808.1—dc23
LC record available at https://lccn.loc.gov/2020004449
LC ebook record available at https://lccn.loc.gov/2020004450

Contents

Digital materials related to this title can be found on the Fulcrum platform via the following citable URL: https://doi.org/10.3998/mpub.9450148

Preface

We are two nerds with a passion for rap music, a retired professor and a former undergraduate student from the University of Michigan. In his first term, Aurko came to Macklin's office looking for insights about how poetic rhythms and meanings interacted. He walked in carrying a *King Lear* paperback defaced with scansion marks, and he'd just been listening to Nas's *Illmatic* out in the hall. We immediately realized that we shared similar questions about sounds and beats—especially in rap music. We've been collaborating ever since, examining rap lines, exploring the dynamics of style, and every now and then texting battle verses back and forth.

We are staunch hip hop proponents, recognizing it both as a sophisticated forum for the systematically suppressed and as music to party to. Macklin was for years the only University of Michigan teacher who included rap in his Intro to Poetry sections. Some colleagues challenged this: "Do you really think it qualifies as poetry?" He would reply, "Yes, it's always metrical and has amazing rhymes, but it's performance poetry, not literature. It can be as intricate as *Sir Gawain*, as biting as Shakespeare, and a lot more fun than Byron."

We both know that, and we've been studying rap rhythms for the last six years, but we are nevertheless hip hop outsiders. Macklin's white. A sometime poet and an expert in medieval four-beat poetics, he's been listening and engaging with rap since "Rapper's Delight." Aurko's brown, a millennial immigrant who grew up the United Kingdom and Michigan, who caught the hip hop bug when he came stateside. Neither of us has lived in an urban black ghetto. We enjoy and admire hip hop because we like its beats, its flows, and its messages—how they play off against each other. We conceived this book as a thorough exposition of rap poetics, as a kind of explanation for its global appeal and relevance. We also wanted to give credit where credit is due. Our analyses and insights suggest that rap, so often disparaged as monotonous and silly or crude, is far more complex and complicated, far more versatile, far more nuanced, and far more important than has been widely realized. If others agree, then our book will have helped the cause of critical justice.

Acknowledgments

I, *I'm*, *me*, and *mine* are spoken several hundred times on N. W. A.'s *Straight Outta Compton*, an album-length brag from '88. But the vinyl's sold in a cardboard sleeve crowded with fine-print thank-yous, acknowledging all that *I*, *I'm*, and *mine* owe cops, rappers, God, the Dodgers and 256 named others. Def—*and* debt—be not proud We, too, owe.

—Mark Costello and David Foster Wallace, *Signifying Rappers*

We, too, owe. This book honors and engages with forty years of rap music, ranging from The Sugarhill Gang's "Rapper's Delight" to Kendrick Lamar's *DAMN.*, each song belonging to a community whose members form an endless list of artists, listeners, fans, and intellectuals whose influence has extended far beyond popular culture and into theaters like politics and fashion.

Much of our work—be it the formulation of our framework, the analysis of our data, the support to follow our intuition, or the historical context we needed—would not be possible without this community. Many insights came from undergraduate and graduate students in Macklin's classes at the University of Michigan, as well as from friends with special musical talents, from family, from the freestylers in Ypsi, and from commentators on Genius.

And while we owe our primary debt to the community, we mustn't neglect those who gave us skills, support, and, most of all, their time. Without astute, meticulous commentaries on our early drafts from Tessa Brown, Michael Schoenfeldt, Gil Scott Chapman, and David Manley; without the analytical savvy of Shashank Joshi (Aurko's father), Richard Price, Kevin Just, Bopeng Li, and Nandi Tawani; without musical and aesthetic consultations with Amy and Rebecca Smith (Macklin's daughters), Dexter Kaufmann, Yuma Uesaka, and MC M. T. Z.; and without the encouragement of Adam

Bradley, David Kelly (aka Capital D), Lynette Smith, and John Whittier-Ferguson, this book would have been plainly impossible.

We are especially grateful to LeAnn Fields, our editor, as well as to our anonymous external reviewers and to the members of the University of Michigan Press Editorial Board, for suggesting many improvements in the book's scope, argument, and style.

To the artists and producers who created the lyrics, music, and traditions we researched, studied, and comment upon in this book, we owe our biggest debt. We quote and analyze beats, verses, and choruses from many rap songs—themselves a subset of our broader research, whose sources are listed in the Discography. Here we name and thank the DJs, MCs, and other vocalists whose artistry we discuss in the chapters that follow:

Aesop Rock, Afrika Bambaataa, André 3000, Anthony Ramos, AZ the Visualiza, B.o.B., Big Bank Hank, Big Boi, Big Daddy Kane, Big Youth, Bizzy Bone, Black Thought, Busta Rhymes, Capital D, CeeLo Green, Christopher Jackson, Chuck D, Common, Cosmic Force, Danny Brown, Daveed Diggs, Debra Killings, Del (The Funky Homosapien), Dido, DJ Jazzy Jay, DJ Premier, DMC, Dr. Dre, Drake, Duke Bootee, E. D. I. Mean, Easy A.D., Eazy-E, Eminem, Eric B., Eve, Faith Evans, Gemini, Ghostface Killah, Gil Scott-Heron, Grandmaster Caz, Guru, Hussein Fatal, Ice Cube, Ice-T, Immortal Technique, Inspectah Deck, Iomas, J. Cole, Jay Dee, Jay-Z, JDL, Jr., Justin Vernon, Kanye West, Kay Gee, Kendrick Lamar, KG, Khia, Khujo Goodie, Kid Cudi, Krayzie Bone, KRS-One, Kurtis Blow, Lauryn Hill, Leslie Odom Jr., Lightnin' Rod, Lil Wayne, Lil' Kim, Lin-Manuel Miranda, Liz Rodrigues, Lupe Fiasco, Mac Miller, Mannie Fresh, Master Gee, MC Ren, MCA, Melle Mel, Method Man, Mike D, Missy Elliott, Mr. Biggs, Nas, Nicki Minaj, Okieriete Onaodowan, Ol' Dirty Bastard, Pepa, Pharoahe Monch, Phife Dawg, Pop, Pow Wow, Q-Tip, Queen Latifah, Raekwon, Rakim, Renée Elise Goldsberry, Richie Rich, Rick Ross, Run, RZA, Salt, Sam Adams, ScHoolboy Q, Senim Silla, Shaheed, Slick Rick, Slug, Snoop Dogg, Stro, T-Pain, Talib Kweli, Tekniq, The Genius, The GLOBE, The Notorious B. I. G., Tupac, U-God, Umar Bin Hassan, Vast Aire Kramer, Vin Jay, Vordul Megallah, Wiz Khalifa, Wonder Mike, Woody Guthrie, Yaki Kadafi, and Yasiin Bey (Mos Def).

MS/AJ
UNIVERSITY OF MICHIGAN

Introduction

We got to understand rap been here a long time
—Afrika Bambaataa, "Rap History"

When we hear rap, we recognize it from the feel of the beat, the non-melodic (spoken, shouted, declaimed) delivery of the poetic lines, and the rhythmic interplay of the beat and the lines. If we are hip hop heads, we can identify the flow of particular rappers, or the beat contours of particular producers, or the regional style or historical period of unfamiliar rap songs. Rap music, then, like many other genres, is both deeply coherent and widely differentiated.

Early rap can be characterized variously as loud party-blasting street poetry, as catchy disco-club poetry, as protest poetry, as poetry representing African American communities, and as poetry expressing black masculinity. Today, rap has successfully occupied Broadway (*Hamilton*) and has vastly influenced the beats and prosodies of American pop music, but it remains a powerful voice of the historically disenfranchised—as witnessed by Kendrick Lamar's *DAMN*. Rap's message and style continue to challenge traditional American musical norms. Its non-melodic (or, at most, semi-melodic) voices accompany beats constructed from percussive and harmonic musical fragments, which may in turn be infused with urban noises (traffic, shouts, police sirens) or sampled verbal tags. Rap may be playful, seductive, smooth, ironic, grandiose, angry, aggressive, prophetic, or spiritually wise, but it always tends to be edgy. Its modes may be lyric, narrative, or dramatic; collaborative or combative. It innovates out of artistic competition and social disruption and dissolution (Urban Renewal, redlining, poverty, the War on Drugs, systematically racist incarceration, family trauma), articulating a new African American sound.

Although rap's basic beat, accommodating a four-stress line in 4/4 time, is globally common and, in point of fact, replicates the oldest English meter poetry, the *sound quality* of the musical composition embodying this beat is revolutionary. It's an extraordinarily complex musical collage of sampled sounds—also called the beat—appropriated (flipped) from other compositions. What is also revolutionary, in parallel to the composition of the hip hop beat, is the way rappers engage with its simple, utterly ordinary rhythmic 4/4 foundation so as to accommodate extraordinarily complex vocal rhythms. Busta Rhyme's Conglomerate—formerly, the Flipmode Squad—comes to mind here, as does Nas's classic battle boast: "Rappers, I monkey flip 'em with the funky rhythm / I be kickin', musician, inflictin' composition." Our title's key word is of course *flow*, the ongoing and continually variable rhythm through which each rapper *flips* his or her 4/4 beat into an individually styled message.[1]

Yet after forty years of recorded rap music, we can hear its rhythmic flow(s) as both new and renewed. We can hear recurrences and cross-references, ideas and attitudes. Jay-Z's flow stands out as distinctly his, and he capitalizes on this exclusivity, translating it into superiority. "You got starch in your flow," he boasts, "I got a arch in my flow."[2] But Jay also claims representation, inclusion, and universality. His flow incorporates Marvin Gaye and a Rucker Park pickup game, and it never stays the same: "I evolve with the flow." He's the best, of course—"I'm off the charts with the flow / Actually I'm number one on the charts with the flow"—and he doesn't mind noting that in some places they say that, "I am God with the flow." But his emcee (MC) ego also channels the community spirit of hip hop culture, perhaps even its histories and ongoing futures: "I am the youth spirit, I am y'all with the flow."

This spirit is already invoked in the opening lines of "Rapper's Delight" (1979), the first rap radio hit. Although a studio production, "Rapper's Delight" had a live feel to it, and although in fact a test of rap's viability for a broad listening audience, what we thought we heard was a real disco party with a new poetry groove. Before Wonder Mike even introduces himself on the mic, he defines his performance as rapping to the beat, as collaborative, and as meant to get the audience up and moving. It is still these things.

Now what you hear is not a test,
I'm rappin' to the **beat**,
And me, the **groove**, and my friends
Are gonna try to **move** your **feet**.[3]

Wonder Mike's "friends" on the fourteen-minute EP were Big Bank Hank and Master Gee, and there were already some much more talented rappers out there—most notably Grandmaster Caz—who weren't in the studio that day; but once the genre took off, these "friends" would include hundreds and then thousands of MCs, worldwide. Their art remained the same, but it became more commercial, more lucrative, more competitive, more differentiated.

This book accounts for the basic but underappreciated complexity of rap's interplay of beat and poetry—the mix of rhythmic components recognized as rap by all audiences—and traces the range of variation within this mix, offering insights into the constituents of individual and regional rap styles. It will explain what the Jay-Z and Wonder Mike passages share in common and how each of them represents an outlier tendency in rap history. There hasn't been a lot of attention given to rap's poetic features, in part because rap is relatively new on the world poetry scene; in part because rap is so demonstrative and powerful and entertaining that it seems perhaps inappropriate to analyze it systematically; in part because students and teachers of poetry, academic and otherwise, have often been unwilling or unable to recognize rap's poetic worth, or even its legitimacy as a form of poetry. We need to acknowledge what rap is and isn't, how it's special, and how it relates to other verse traditions.

Rap is oral performance poetry made to be heard. We can easily find, read, and study rap lyrics on the internet, appreciating their style and meaning, their complexity, denseness, allusiveness, and intelligence; but rap is not literature. Beat by beat, word by word, rap blasts right through our ears into our minds and bodies—a poetic listening experience predating literature by thousands of years. As Afrika Bambaataa puts it in the epigraph to this chapter, "We got to understand rap been here a long time." Indeed, rap has a lot in common with the verses chanted by oral poets like Homer,[4] the Old English bards,[5] and the West African griots.[6] At the same time, rap is always up to date. Even the best freestylers, like Black Thought or Eminem, whose memory for phrases, lines, and rhyme formulas can be said to rival analogous skills in oral poets like Homer, typically write and rewrite their lyrics with attention to the currency of their craft. Although rap's literate orality reaches far back to Africa, the Delta blues, the dozens, Harlem Renaissance and BAM poetry (and more recently to pre-Rap rappers like The Last Poets, Funk, and Jamaican DJing over dub tracks),[7] it tracks the ongoing, multitudinous expressions of contemporary culture. Although rap's aesthetics arose from social clashes in the Bronx in the 1970s, its topics and styles are constantly shifting with the times, like any vital art.

Essentially African American, compounded and complicated, rap is an underclass expression largely managed by corporate interests and infused with a capitalist ethos featuring competition and success, hustling the game, and the self-made man.[8] Rap accommodates broken glass and trash, traffic noise, crime and addiction, street jive, and barbershop jokes, but it infuses these everyday realities with hyperbolic, fantasy-zone artistry indebted to break dancing, subway graffiti, Marvel Comics, and Ninja mythologies. Although black, it can also be white, or yellow, or brown. It's local, regional, cosmopolitan, and global. Although originally and still performed in African American English dialect(s) enriched with urban slang, sophisticated vocabulary, and self-referential allusions, rap is now also performed in Spanish and Spanglish, French Creole and French, German, Arabic, Hebrew, Japanese, Korean, and countless other languages, where it may sound like a linguistic hybrid, retaining English stress accents.[9] Poetically, it sounds like nothing else in the world while sharing features with chanting traditions all over the world. Its meter is almost identical to that of four-beat alliterative verse from the English Middle Ages, but its rhymes behave like no other rhymes anywhere, anytime.

Six decades after the emergence of blues and jazz, hip hop burst forth as the last great African American musical innovation of the twentieth century, and is now, like its predecessors, established as an international art. Like blues singing, hip hop rapping—as distinct from earlier Beat and BAM-style rapping—is formed of rhythmically regulated lines. As in blues, these lines conform to a four-beat meter: they contain four stressed syllables falling on or near the musical beats and typically arranged two and two. But these fettered lines are also free. They may contain extra stresses, various pauses, and any manageable number of unstressed syllables. Although rap's beated stresses are strictly timed, the syllable-stream running through them flows relatively freely. As in blues and jazz, rap's syllable-notes, even including those on the beat, may be syncopated, blue, or otherwise unruly.

Unlike sung blues lines, rap lines are spoken percussively: *rapped*. And rather than being bundled into stanzas, rap lines occur in longer sequences. The lines are typically grouped into rhyming pairs, or *couplets*, which in turn are sequenced into indeterminate series known as *verses*. Rap lines and couplets fit within beat loops, and rap verses also usually satisfy musical expectations,[10] corresponding for example to a sixteen-bar unit; but the ongoing form of rap is the rhyming four-beat line. Rap's line-by-line (or *stichic*) verse form contrasts with the stanzaic (or *strophic*) form of the optional but frequent *choruses* in rap songs. Anyone familiar with Salt-N-Pepa's "Let's Talk

About Sex," The Notorious B. I. G.'s "Hypnotize," Eminem's "Stan," or Lil Wayne's "This Is The Carter" will recognize that their choruses differ from their relentlessly ongoing, varied verses in being repetitive, shorter-lined, and grouped into traditional song quatrains. In this regard, hip hop songs can act like hybrids. They merge the two archetypal modes of world poetry, which are stichic or strophic, chanted or sung. Homer, the *Beowulf*-poet, and West African griots chanted continuous verses to the *rhythmic* strumming of a harp or kora, or to drumming; Sappho and Woody Guthrie sang series of discrete stanzas to the *melodic* plucking of a lyre or guitar, or to flute, piano, or orchestral accompaniment. In "Stan," Eminem chants (raps) the dramatic parts of Stan and Slim Shady, between which Dido sings a sad lyric commentary in the voice of a bereaved woman.

Four-beat meter was the original meter of English poetry. It's the meter of the earliest known poem in English, "Caedmon's Hymn," composed by an illiterate cowherd in the seventh century. It's the meter also of *Beowulf,* whose final, tenth-century version was written by a learned monk, but which contains many earlier lines composed (as were Homer's) by one or more illiterate bard. Whether written or composed mentally, *all* of the thousands of lines surviving from the Anglo-Saxon era were performed aloud, whether to monks seated in monastery dining halls, to beer- or mead-drinking warriors gathered in the court of a regional king, or to common folk assembled at a fairground. Four-beat meter arose within a culture which listened to poetry rather than reading it—when *to read* meant to sound out written words.

After the French Conquest (1066), the English four-beat tradition persisted underground, eventually flowering spectacularly in the fourteenth century, when many of the poets using it were well-educated clerics. All along, however, poetry had remained an oral performance art. Books had to be copied by hand, so they were rare and valuable. Few people owned or studied books, but everyone listened socially to poetry being read or improvised aloud. Meanwhile, a new kind of English poetry derived from French and Latin models had come on the scene. Its meter, which counted syllables rather than beats, challenged and eventually supplanted our native four-beat meter as the vehicle for "serious poetry." But four-beat never died. It's in Shakespeare's songs, English ballads, and Appalachian Old Folk music. It shows up in jingles, in nursery rhymes, in jive rhymes, and in the "ABC Song." And it shows up, of course, in blues and rap. Like a powerful underground stream, four-beat meter keeps bubbling up into open, available channels. It suits our stress-timed language perfectly, and there's something basically appealing about its regular beat pattern. It feels as natural as walking, breathing, or a heartbeat, and it makes us want to hear and engage with it rhythmically.

If it hadn't emerged as what Wonder Mike in "Rapper's Delight" called "rapping to the beat," if it hadn't had a danceable and head-bobbing sound, it if had retained the cool, urbane, outspoken, but *prose-like* form of its immediate predecessors (The Last Poets and Gil Scott-Heron), rap would never have had the traction and longevity and popularity it has enjoyed. Its success and sustained creativity are due in part to its more "universal" features, in particular its rhyming and meter—features which make it, as well as African American, fundamentally English and human.

Despite its metrical commonality, hip hop poetry, historically speaking, belongs to a rare subset. Almost all of the other four-beat verse we hear or know about exists in old songs, jingles, or blues—that is, in stanzas. Rap is only the third manifestation ever of successful line-by-line four-beat poetry in English. The first was during the Anglo-Saxon era, from the seventh to the eleventh centuries, when *all* poetry took this form. The second was during the fourteenth and fifteenth centuries, when the two competing English poetic meters briefly coexisted as cultural equals. The third is now. Those early manifestations engaged small local English audiences totaling at most several thousand individuals. Ours began with small local audiences in the Bronx, Brooklyn, Queens, Compton, and Atlanta, but, propelled by vinyl, radio, TV, and digital media, now engages a global audience of billions.

Being fundamentally African American, rap is a product of the African diaspora, so it may seem irrelevant or even disrespectful to relate it to the long history of English poetry. But just as rap survived white hegemony, four-beat English poetry survived the French invasion and the brutalizing policies of French feudal masters. The French took away England's schools and literature, implemented serfdom, and denigrated the status of the English language. Meanwhile, English four-beat poetry survived in folk music. It briefly resurfaced as a viable, sophisticated literary medium in the fourteenth century—as attested by poems like *Piers Plowman* and *Sir Gawain and the Green Knight*—but even then it was ridiculed as crude and uncultivated in contrast to French-inspired metrical verse. And since then, four-beat songs and poems have commonly been stigmatized as non-literary and un-poetic.

For the African victims of colonialism, the brutalizing forces were, of course, much, much worse. Centuries after the English had survived French oppression, English, French, Portuguese, and Belgian invaders occupied and exploited vast areas of West Africa, enslaving many of the inhabitants and shipping them to the Americas, where they were essentially worked to death by Spanish, Portuguese, French, English, and Dutch colonialists in the production of sugar and other commodities. Those who survived this ordeal invariably were required to adopt the language, religion, and cultural forms of their masters, retaining little else but their own music, their poetic roots.

West African music was grounded in four-beat rhythm. If we listen to YouTube samples of Griot chanting in any of several contemporary languages, we may not detect any clear four-beat metrical structure, but the musical scaffolding of this poetry is clearly four-beat in its phrasing.[11] Each bar consists of two-beat phrases around a strong medial pause. Historical records confirm this tradition. As early as 1688 and 1730, English observers of Jamaican and Barbadian slave commerce noted musical rituals bearing strong resemblance to the Kumina tradition still preserved in Jamaica today.[12] Rap beats and rap poetry were decisively influenced by Afro-Caribbean music while also continuing in the four-beat traditions of American field songs and blues. Fittingly, a little over one century after the Emancipation Proclamation, after having already given blues, jazz, and (yes) rock and roll to American music, African Americans created hip hop, revitalizing the power of four-beat meter.

Rap started out in the United States as street-party and dance-club poetry. Eventually it became studio-recorded and vinyl-pressed poetry, and simultaneously, radio poetry and record-store poetry, and later, MTV poetry. Today, it is electronically produced iPod poetry. All along, it has remained poetry to be heard, danced to, and head-bobbed to. Its themes may be complex and complicated, emotionally powerful and socially or politically or spiritually urgent, but its actual artistry, beat by beat and rhyme by rhyme, is always meant to grab a listener's attention and to entertain. Most rappers write their lyrics although some, like Common, Jay-Z, and Lil Wayne, compose mentally. But all competent rappers, whether they stopped at ninth grade like Eminem, were college drop-outs like Common, or earned advanced degrees like Capital D, are highly talented, rhetorically clever, intelligent, thoughtful, deliberate wordsmiths with huge vocabularies. Still, we would insist that this often highly literate art is essentially non-literary. However it's composed, it's designed to *feel* spontaneous, needs to be appealing on first hearing, and thus demands immediate sensory comprehension. Even such lexical gymnasts as Nas, Yasiin Bey (Mos Def), Eminem, Pharoahe Monch, Lil Wayne, Lupe Fiasco, Black Thought, and Kendrick Lamar, whose songs may seem to demand a second, third, or fourth hearing, have mastered the delivery of the first hearing. Meanwhile, modern freestylers really can and do improvise on the spot. Interestingly, the best freestylers are often the very same people (e.g., Eminem) who can also write lyrically dense lines for studio production, and the fact that freestyle rap can sound a lot like studio rap offers further evidence that the poetics of hip hop are those of an oral performance art.

For that reason, even though we sometimes use the analytical methods of literary criticism in this book, we remain relatively uninterested in the textuality of rap lyrics. Certainly rap has arisen within a literate culture and is composed by literate members of that culture, but it's not literary. Some rap is comparable to some literary poetry in the complexity, nuance, and allusiveness of its meaning—conveyed through extraordinary rhythmic craft—but rap poetry has never been intended to be read on the page—except originally by the MCs themselves, for their exclusive use, and now by innumerable fans who want to study and annotate digital rap wikis.

In researching this book, we have often consulted internet-published lyrics, using these texts to verify our transcriptions prior to scanning rap lines for rhythmic patterns. In many cases, we have needed to reconstruct these lines so as to fit the metrical and rhyme structures heard in the songs themselves.[13] We have also consulted the *Anthology of Rap*, edited by Adam Bradley and Andrew DuBois, where the lyrics are, we feel, almost always accurately lineated. We have benefitted from critical commentaries in other books and articles, as well as in Genius. Some of the most useful explications of rap's rhythmic dynamics have been by professionals: Kool Moe Dee's *There's a God on the Mic* (2003) and Jay-Z's *Decoded* (2011) offer thoughtful reflections both on the art of particular MCs and on the genre generally; these are nicely supplemented by the numerous testimonials from rappers, presented in Paul Edwards's *How to Rap* (2009) and *How to Rap 2* (2013).

Our book attempts a comprehensive poetics for rap—a poetics directed by empirical investigation, responsive to the theory and practice of rappers themselves, and respectful of rap's actual marriage of beat and poetry. Buckshot comments on this fusion: "Why my flows and my rhythms come out the way they come out is because I become an instrument. If there are five pieces on that beat, I'm gonna be the sixth piece." Or as Q-Tip puts it: "Musically you could write it out . . . write out the beats in a bar in pauses and triplets and all that stuff, show it musically and theoretically, you could apply that to it."[14]

A desire to introduce debates and theories that had yet to be raised in published work drove much of our inquiry. Being interested in bridging the gap between musicology and poetics, we felt that a thorough study of rap stylistics necessitated a metrical model accountable to the rhythmic components of the beat, captured in a database of coded rap lyrics from diverse MCs. On the one hand, Adam Krims's impressive and still relevant musicological approach in *Rap Music and the Poetics of Identity* (2000) is dated with respect to rap styles and unwieldy with respect to the analysis of the poetry, while Joseph G. Schloss's *Making Beats: The Art of Sample-based Hip-Hop* (2004) offers insights into the production of the rap beat but avoids the poetry altogether. On the other hand, Adam Bradley's *Book of Rhymes: The Poetics of Hip Hop* (2009), a pioneering work on rap poetics,[15] glosses over the interplay of poetry and beat, reduces poetic rhythm to its stress patterns, and fails to account for rhyme's rhythmic function. David Caplan's *Rhyme's Challenge: Hip Hop, Poetry, and Contemporary Rhyming Culture* (2014) addresses rap only peripherally, attending to the cultural semantics and rhetoric of rhyme, not its poetic function in relation to the beat, syntax, or meter of rap music. Meanwhile, the vast majority of rap scholarship is devoted to historical and cultural studies, and if and when rap poetry is quoted in such works it is used as evidence for social attitudes and issues and themes, not to illustrate or evaluate how it works. Particularly useful to us in thinking about the early history of rap styles—and in particular about rap's indebtedness to Caribbean sources—has been Jeff Chang's *Can't Stop Won't Stop: A History of the Hip-Hop Generation* (2005). More generally useful have been Dan Charnas's *The Big Payback: The History of the Business of Hip-Hop* (2010), Cheryl L. Keyes's *Rap Music and Street Consciousness* (2002), and *That's the Joint: The Hip-Hop Studies Reader* (2004), edited by Murray Forman and Mark Anthony Neal.

We first came to this book project, however, not as scholars of rap music but as avid listeners—as rap fans who were also interested in poetics. We wanted to understand how the rhythmic structures of the rap beat determined yet were complemented by the rhythmic structures of the poetry. Most of our research has involved *listening*—listening to discover as much as possible about the regional and individual variety within the genre, listening for the fun of it, and listening systematically to create a statistical database. To construct the database, we selected material covering rap's known recorded history, and in doing so we attempted to represent regional and racial diversity and to include meaningfully weighted samples of work by male and female MCs. Because we were committed to an analytical approach that considered not just rap's fundamental units, the line and the couplet, but also whole verses, songs, and even albums, we rejected random sampling in favor of a conscious and necessarily subjective selection of songs. Here our primary criterion was *success*, applied for example in the use of "Rapper's Delight,"

"The Breaks," and "The Message" from the very early years; groups and rappers like Rakim, N. W. A., Snoop Dogg, Tupac Shakur, Salt-N-Pepa, Queen Latifah, The Notorious B. I. G., Guru, Lauryn Hill, Black Star, Eminem, Lupe Fiasco, and Lil Wayne from the pantheon as a whole; and particularly successful songs like "Gin and Juice," representing Snoop, "Let's Talk About Sex," representing Salt-N-Pepa, and "Stan," representing Eminem.

We then methodically scanned over 10,000 lines from such songs, marking their stresses, rhymes, pauses, and internal phrasal patterns, coding individual rap and chorus lines as a sequence of vocal events. In conceiving a statistical code for analyzing the patterns of rhythm and rhyme in rap lines, we tried to account for all—and only—its basic verse components. Rap's phrasal units—its half lines and lines and couplets—depend on segmenting pauses of two kinds, so we distinguished between expected short pauses at mid-line and at end-line, further coding for the occasional absence of pauses at these positions. We distinguished further between these structural (metrical) short pauses and those occurring unexpectedly in other positions. And we created another code for long pauses taking up the space of a quarter line. We also coded for different kinds of syllables: those of normal length spoken by the rapper, imported sample sounds (like the trumpeting elephant in Missy Elliott's "Work It"), and abnormally prolonged syllables (like the "Ssssshhhhhhh" in Lil Wayne's "This Is The Carter," which lasts three beats). Normal rap syllables behave like normal English syllables generally in that they are either stressed or unstressed; but rapping does two things that ordinary English doesn't do, and neither of these is optional. Rap isn't rap unless it coordinates stressed syllables to a musical beat, and rap isn't rap unless it rhymes. So for syllables we distinguished between those stressed and those unstressed, on the beat and not on the beat, and rhymed or unrhymed. Our variables for pauses and syllables can never capture the amazing rhythmic variety and rich sound textures heard in hip hop, but they can account for its basic vocal categories.

Note that our coding system deals with syntax only insofar as the rap line's expected pauses normally mark phrasal junctures as well as musical boundaries, bar to bar and beat to beat. And our coding system deals with content only abstractly, in that rap stresses and rhymes tend to fall on grammatically prominent words. We view rap poetics, then, primarily as a musical system.[16] Not that content is irrelevant. The best MCs, it is widely agreed, are those who can rap an extraordinary message with exemplary flow.[17] But rap isn't really rap unless it's musically right. Evidence from Dilated Peoples makes this point:

I would say ultimately, the flow is more important in rap music than the message. And that sounds disgusting and shitty and shallow to say, but I'm going to take a stand and say it. Because I don't care how good [your message is], if I can't feel the way you're saying it, then you should find a different means to translate that message. That's my personal opinion. I mean, think about it—what if a singer had the greatest message but couldn't hit a fucking note? It just doesn't make sense. It's sad to say that "yeah, you have this great message, but no, I don't want to hear you," but it's sad but true.[18]

The chapters that follow explain how rap poetry relates to the hip hop beat. We account for every listener's common experience of rap music—its beat, meter, phrasing, rhythmic complexity, rhyme patterns, and larger formal structures. We also explore the poetic continuums between modern freestyle and scripted rapping and among regional styles, and we ask tough questions about what constitutes artistic quality in rap. We want to advance the listening community's understanding of hip hop poetics, but we know we don't have all the answers. Why, for example, do rappers use more similes than metaphors? Are similes easier to compose? Easier to grasp? Are they rhythmically useful? A lot of early rap lines end with "like a Y that's Z" phrases. Was this a rhythm we wanted to hear, a syntactic formula, or a little of both? Or: how to explain the frequency of "motherfucking X" in rap? This phrase, at once offensive and meaningless, lends authenticating slang to many a line, but it also contains a catchy guttural rhyme and exhibits a long-beloved rhythm, the three-syllable dip of **L-M-N-O-P**. Perhaps its main utility, then, is to embody a common musical sequence in rap flow.

Still, it means what it means, raising the vexed issue of "explicit content."[19] For the rap corpus, this umbrella term covers sexual innuendo (common) and obscenity[20] (rare), threats or depictions of gun violence, and taboo or merely crude language. Although purposefully coarse, offensive speech has probably been common since the evolution of language itself, its place in artistic expression, such as satire or Low Comedy (from Aristophanes to *South Park*), has often been controversial. Rap's linguistic indecencies range from formulaic f-word qualifiers such as *motherfucking* to the n-word *nigga*, flipped from a racist insult to a badge of community, gang, or crew identity—positive and often exclusively male. Many male MCs articulate "nigga" personas whose style is "real" as well as dominant, whose skills may include hustling, and whose attitudes may embody misogyny and homophobia.[21] In this context, the word *ho* is never endearing and rarely literal; it is used figuratively through synecdoche to denigrate women generally as sex-objects or to sustain male superiority with respect to sexual transactions, including pimping. *Bitch*, used by male MCs, may be a near-synonym for *ho*, but it more often refers to (and objectifies as such) any sexually attractive woman, and may also be a term of endearment[22]; the semantic continuum between extreme misogyny and normal desire is fluid. Used by female MCs, *bitch* may be a neutral descriptor or even a compliment. In other words, the term is complexly gendered in the African American community.[23] Lil Wayne, with his extraordinary mastery of lexical wit, manages to give the word multiple and additional resonances, playful, and even possibly spiritual: "Karma is a bitch? Well, just make sure that bitch is beautiful." Although explicit homophobic statements are relatively rare in rap generally, *faggot* is a pervasive formulaic insult in early battle rap—one insult among many.[24]

Yet when rap first hit the scene as funky street-party and disco-club poetry, no one seems to have found its language particularly offensive compared to, say, that of African American styles like R&B, Motown, or funk, or to predominantly white styles like acid rock. Rap's performance trope of male posturing differed little from that in rock and roll.[25] Although the early MCs' delight in sexual innuendo—genealogically descended not just from the African American tradition toasting,[26] but from blackface minstrel-show hokum, vaudeville, and "dirty" blues[27] distributed on "race records"—may be rightly characterized as both racial and racialized, this cultural tradition had already been appropriated by white rock musicians like Elvis Presley and Keith Richards well before the rise of hip hop.[28] And the early MCs' occasional braggadocio tended to emulate the comedic spirit of the dozens, not its raunchiness or hostility. What was potentially transgressive about rap, however, was lurking in it from the very start, in the sampled beat and in the MC's voice. Rap rhythm overrode melody, and rapping wasn't song. The beat could turn fun into furious. A smooth, party voice could be switched out for a voice that smoothly hustled; or a voice that shouted over the police sirens; or a voice that yelled protest slogans; or, eventually, a voice that bragged about gun possession or criminal success, and that demeaned women.

What caused this tonal evolution? Certainly rappers played no part at all in the initial liberalization of American standards for sexual explicitness and profanity. This change—as well as its backlash—predated rap music. In 1972, Chuck Berry's "My Ding A Ling" became his only #1 single; *Last Tango in Paris* and *Deep Throat*, released through different distribution venues, were each widely viewed and discussed; and George Carlin's stand-up comedy album *Class Clown* included the track, "Seven Words You Can Never

Say on Television," namely *cocksucker, cunt, fuck, motherfucker, piss, shit,* and *tits*. In short sequence, Richard Pryor broke the n-word taboo with *That Nigger's Crazy* (1974), *Is It Something I Said?* (1975), and *Bicentennial Nigger* (1976). Meanwhile, real-life precursors and preconditions for later expressions of violence were the televised Vietnam War, the assassinations of JFK (1963), Malcolm X (1965), and MLK (1968); nationwide anti-war protests; the emergence of the openly armed Black Panther Party, claiming equality in Second Amendment rights; and the Detroit Riot (1967).

Considering that rap was almost devoid of "explicit content" during its first decade on vinyl and radio (1979–1988), the cultural models for sexual and profane expression and for political activism listed above cannot have been as causally important as the objective and subjective realities of American life for African Americans. On the one hand, after the defeat of Jim Crow laws and the hibernation of the Ku Klux Klan in the face of the Civil Rights Movement, the Civil Rights Act (1964), and the Voting Rights Act (1965), it had become possible if not utterly prudent for black males to express their sexuality without fear of being lynched. On the other hand, the normalized yet increasingly severe economic oppression of African Americans through job discrimination, educational inequality, redlining, and ghettoization continued unabated, enhanced by Reaganomics. Meanwhile the War on Drugs, initiated by Richard Nixon, codified in the Rockefeller Drug Laws (1973), and escalated during the Reagan years (1981–1989), with newly militarized police policies, produced a drastic increase in the incarceration of black and Latino men.[29] Deepening despair, anger, and civil strife, perhaps inevitable, were exacerbated by the intra-community gun violence that accompanied the crack cocaine epidemic during the 1980s, further intensifying gang violence and police brutality in the urban ghettos of Los Angeles, New York City, and elsewhere. Hence the hostile explicitness of songs like "Fuck tha Police."

Today, such content has become normalized as a generic marker of rap,[30] a component of its "realness" as well as, to some degree, an instrument of provocation or defiance directed against white cultural norms. However, when MCs express crass, cruel, or otherwise offensive thoughts, the boundaries between community and individual norms, between persona and personality, are often unclear. Nas can be Nas, Nasir, or Nasty Nas. With a few exceptions, female MCs emulate male MCs in their mastery of raunchy speech, but they may also deploy this speech to battle misogyny. Freedom of expression merges with free transgression, all of it constrained by convention. This dynamic is further influenced—and controlled—by market interests. In the late 1980s, millions of record sales were generated by two musical/ poetic mixes: West Coast hard funk with the gangsta rap of N. W. A., Snoop Dogg, and others; Miami bass with the freaknik rap of 2 Live Crew. Spurred not only by cultural backlash but by cultural success, the record industry was only too happy to let consumers choose between "parental guidance" and "explicitness." The downside of having a "clean" version is that the missing words are marked as rhythmic skips, evidencing their inauthenticity, so most listeners opt for "explicit content." It goes without saying that explicit lyrics have been widely condemned as such at times by racists, at times by religious moralists, at times by academics, at times by everyday listeners, and at times by "conscious rappers" themselves, who are often Muslims.[31]

Like many other listeners and commentators, we have wrestled with our personal distaste for rap's occasional celebration of gang violence and drug-dealing, degradation of women, and homophobia, but we've never stopped loving the music and the poetry. We may cringe at the weapon-toting brag-gadocio of N. W. A. (Niggaz Wit Attitudes) and the all-too-entertainingly blunt misogyny of Snoop Dogg, but meanwhile we respect the moral force of so-called "gangsta rap" as a response to and symptom of police brutality and systemic environmental racism and sexism, and we know that N. W. A.'s innovations within West Coast flow helped lift the entire game out of its stylistic rut in the mid-1980s, enabling the brilliant innovations of the decade to come.

Acknowledging that rap sometimes contains objectionable statements, we believe on principle, as authors and critics, in the imperative that art is a protected environment where an inhibited freedom of expression is an existential risk. We would note, too, that while expressions of obscenity, sexism, and aggression by black artists have become a nearly obsessional— and politicized—concern of the American media, comparatively little concern has been directed against similarly objectionable (often masked) speech by white artists. A racialized and racist linguistic divide is evident in our national culture's general tolerance of *chick* versus its intolerance of *bitch*— each term equally misogynistic, but in different ways. A good corrective commentary on *bitch* in rap songs comes from the rapper Lupe Fiasco, who in "Bitch Bad" (2012) not only details this word's deleterious impact on boys, girls, and boys and girls together, but understands the nuanced seman-tics of this word among African American speakers.[32]

In this book, we sometimes quote "explicit" rap lyrics without comment; at other times we may call attention to their normalized or commercially motivated offensiveness—or to their ironic or mimetic utility. Misogyny, violence, and the pervasive rhetorical deployment of shock and raunchiness in rap have all been well documented by other scholars, are the topic of an extensive apologia in Adam Bradley's book, and inform much of the cultural studies work on hip hop. Our primary focus, by contrast, is on the stylistic range and complexity of formal features like rhythm and rhyme. Although we pay a lot of attention to the ways in which various rhythms and rhymes relate to thematic expressiveness, our interest is less evaluative than descriptive. As formal critics interested in particular rap lyrics, we don't feel well positioned to judge rappers (or rap music generally) morally, partly because moral judgments of the lyrics often require iffy judgments of artistic intent, partly because rap's content is itself informed by irony, narrative didacticism, or dramatic voice.

Hot Vinyl

Takes a long time to happen so fast
To realize your future is somebody else's past
—Lupe Fiasco, "Old School Love"

If you were an American rock fan living in the 1960s and 1970s, you might have attended a Rolling Stones concert, you might also have had albums by Howlin' Wolf and Buddy Guy in your record collection, and you might have seen Son House or Skip James perform at the Newport Folk Festival. If you were white, you might have been unaware of Elvis Presley's unpaid debt to black artists, but if you were reading music magazines you would certainly have learned from the top British guitarists about their indebtedness to and reverence for the Delta blues tradition. Anyone into music or some other art form will have some idea of its tradition and will make evaluative judgments based on it. If you are the coauthors of this book and have been indulging in hip hop ranking games, you are pretty sure that the two greatest ever MC poets are Melle Mel and Kendrick Lamar.

This chapter explores the beginnings of the rap tradition, but what is tradition? A true history? A myth? A genealogy? A 100-Best selection? A validation? Retro reverence? In "Old School Love," Lupe Fiasco names Melle Mel along with the Fat Boys, Juice Crew, Ice-T, Kool Moe Dee, and LL Cool J. He refers to his predecessors generally as OGs and presents himself as a now established MC willing to guide others coming up. Lupe's paradoxes suggest that the rap tradition is both a foreshortened version of time and an ongoing mentorship: "Takes a long time to happen so fast / To realize your future is somebody else's past."

We can't track the birth of hip hop music and rap poetry by mythologizing or even quoting DJ Kool Herc, Grandmaster Flash, Kurtis Blow, or

Grandmaster Caz, because we lack recordings of their earliest performances. But we can imagine them. It helps to listen *backwards* from 1979, the date of the first rap vinyl celebrated as such. To orient the birth of rap music, it helps to listen to pre-hip hop rappers such as the talking blues artists Woody Guthrie and Bob Dylan; Gil Scott-Heron and The Last Poets, influenced by Black Arts Movement poetics; and especially to the work of Jalal Nuriddin, a. k. a. Lightnin' Rod, in *Hustler's Convention.* It also helps to listen to hard funk, epitomized by James Brown, electronic music such as Kraftwerk, punk, and especially Jamaican artists like Big Youth, whose dub mixes and overlaid verses strongly influenced what emerged in the South Bronx as unrecorded street and club music. This was the range of music that inspired Herc, Caz, and the other pioneers to create breaks and sampled beats and to rap verses over them. This, along with bebop, cool jazz, blues, disco, and even Top 40 pop, represented vinyl to these emerging, still unrecorded artists—locally famous, yet nationally and internationally unknown. Vinyl meant authorship and legitimacy beyond the corner, the borough, the city. Vinyl meant radio play. Vinyl meant fame that could be monetized, and it meant the means to broadcast an important social message. More familiarly, vinyl meant your parents' or friend's or, better yet, your own record collection; it meant digging through crates of used LPs for rare material. Vinyl meant a vast archive of riffs, bass lines, drum solos, and song phrases ready to be sampled and reassembled into hip hop beats.

And vinyl would mean entering into an entirely new performance medium, one potentially capable of recreating the spontaneity of a street or club atmosphere, yes, but a medium whose musical norms would inevitably be redefined by emerging technologies of recording, mixing, and digital sampling.[1] This did not happen overnight. In point of fact, all of even the earliest hip hop hits—The Sugarhill Gang's "Rapper's Delight" (1979), Kurtis Blow's "Christmas Rappin'" (1979) and "The Breaks" (1980), Afrika Bambaataa and the Soul Sonic Force's "Planet Rock" and "Looking for the Perfect Beat" (1982), and Grandmaster Flash and the Furious Five's "The Message" (1982)—featured studio musicians.[2] "Rapper's Delight" involved three MCs rapping to prerecorded live music. After recreating Blondie and Chic's "Good Times," The Sugarhill Gang chopped and mixed in Love De-Luxe's "Here Comes That Sound Again" to capture the wheels-of-steel aesthetic within a synthesized studio beat.

Vinyl would also inevitably condition song length. Not counting the then-defunct 78 rpm records, vinyl came in three models: 45 rpm, for radio singles (A-side, B-side), designed for popular use on portable lo-fi record players; 33⅓ LP, for albums, suitable for hi-fi systems; and the specialty 33⅓ EP, to package songs longer than the radio norm. Theoretically, songs on vinyl might emulate the eighteen-minute B-side cut on John Coltrane's *A Love Supreme*, but the vast majority of cuts on LPs ran from four to seven minutes—radio length or a couple minutes longer—and many LPs were in effect packages of 45-length songs.

With regard to the commercial and aesthetic importance of song length, some factoids re "Rapper's Delight" may be revealing. Its original version of fourteen and a half minutes, released as a 33⅓ 12" EP, was not only the first hip hop hit; it was the first ever Top 40 song marketed as an EP. In this version of 348 verse lines, Wonder Mike, Big Bank Hank, and Master Gee work in successive relays, each MC rapping three long verses. The entire song is upbeat, entertaining, and frequently funny, but it has no discernable thematic or formal structure except that of nonstop rapping. In the signature words of Master Gee, "Well it's on n on n on on n on, / The beat don't stop until the break of dawn." Despite its phenomenal success in the United States, it fared even better internationally: #1 on the Canadian singles chart, #3 on the UK singles chart, and #1 on the Dutch Top 40—where it was released as a five-minute 45.

After "Rapper's Delight," the major hits were all considerably shorter, and each of them attempted in various ways to introduce some degree of thematic coherence from verse to verse and to use choruses to introduce, repeat, and finally summarize the song's main themes. "The Breaks" (1980) runs to 7:52 minutes; "Planet Rock" and "Looking for the Perfect Beat" (1982), 7:32 and 6:57, respectively; and "The Message" (1982), 6:05. Although these figures show a trend toward economy of length, none of the earliest rap hits approached the four-minute 45 rpm norm already established for popular genres and built into radio scheduling. Nor do any of these songs adopt the tight pop formula of hook> verse 1> chorus> verse 2> bridge> verse 3> chorus. All three songs preserve a live street-and-club feel, a tendency toward structural looseness grounded in improvisation and audience engagement. Kurtis Blow inserts lengthy dance breaks (as "The Breaks," in effect, promises) between his verses, and he structures some of these verses with alternating call-and-response bars—a format suited to encourage audience participation, even though the "audience" is in the studio and consists of his crew.[3] Afrika Bambaataa also packs his songs with a lot of breaks, alternating them with choruses "about" the music itself ("Looking for the perfect beat"), and his verses also often include call and response, half line to half line, or are else rapped in unison—a format likewise suited to audience participation.

Unlike Kurtis Blow and unlike almost all later MCs, Bambaataa never raps these verses solo.

Of all the post-1979 hits, "The Message" was truly the breakaway song, the first song that realized the potential of vinyl without attempting to import and preserve street-and-club performance experiences. Like Wonder Mike, Big Bank Hank, and Master Gee in "Rapper's Delight," Melle Mel and Duke Bootee rap each of their verses solo, avoiding unison rapping and call and response altogether. But unlike The Sugarhill Gang, whose professed goal is quite simply to engage and delight the audience directly (albeit *via* vinyl) and to get them up dancing—

> Now what you hear is not a test,
>   I'm rappin' to the beat,
> And me, the groove, and my friends
>   Are gonna try to move your feet.

—the Grandmaster Flash release articulates a message *adapted* to vinyl replay, that is, a thematically tight message worth hearing again and again:

> Don't push me 'cause I'm close to the edge
> I'm trying not to lose my head,
> Ah huh-huh-huh, ah huh-huh-huh—
> It's like a jungle sometimes, it makes me wonder
> How I keep from going under.

With slight variations, Mel's chorus alternates with five verses in which the two collaborating MCs offer thematically coherent and progressively grim depictions of the ghetto "jungle" and how its social constrictions induce crazy, destructive, and self-destructive behavior. The message comes with a powerful beat, and its artistry is thoroughly engaging, but the point is more to instruct than to delight. It's not party-and-bullshit rap anymore, it's rap *representing* the community. It's the emergence of the MC as solo poet *and* collective voice, the emergence of style in the service of truth-telling.

What Was All the Buzz About?

With the phenomenal and unexpected success of "Rapper's Delight" in 1979, there was a lot of media buzz about rap, what it was and wasn't, where it came from, whether it really *was* delightful or kind of annoying. Was it an exclusively black genre? Was it an entirely new kind of music? Some people said it was nothing new, that Bob Dylan had already been rapping in the sixties and Woody Guthrie before him; others said that Gil Scott-Heron and The Last Poets had already done it, but in a political way, not as party music; still others said that Lightnin' Rod was the first true rapper because he *did* the party, rapping about hustlers in what we would later call a mack style.

If we define rapping as authoritatively declaimed speech, as a kind of demonstrative discourse which shares certain commonalities with literary poetry, oratory, preaching, prophesy, marketing, sloganeering, and boasting, then rapping has been around for a long, long time. But it isn't the same as rap. Rap music deploys spoken word in lieu of song, but its linguistic features, as with song, are linked definitively with music. This music is emphatically rhythmical. A bass line marks strong beats, and the onset and closure of its four-beat bar are formalized by the bass drum on the down beat and by snares on the two off beats. Rap lines coincide with musical bars. The lines' stressed syllables correspond with musical beats, and the rhymes accentuate key stresses to create timed phrasal closures. Regularly, line after line, four-stressed units of speech are superimposed over four-beat, 4/4 rhythmic intervals, and these speech units and rhythmic intervals are in turn divided in two, with medial pauses in the line timed to the bars' on-beat off-beat || on-beat off-beat rhythm.

In this context, none of the counter-cultural, political rappers named above were doing what we now call rap. The primary proof of this is experiential, relating to the essential musical grounding of all hip hop rap: a powerful beat. We may tap our feet when we listen to Woody Guthrie's "Talking Dust Bowl Blues" (1940) or to Bob Dylan's "Talking World War III Blues" (1962), each accompanied by acoustic guitar; or to Gil Scott-Heron's "The Revolution Will Not Be Televised" (1970) or to The Last Poets' "When the Revolution Comes" (1970), each accompanied by African drumming; or to the series of rapped skits in Lightnin' Rod's *Hustler's Convention*, accompanied by jazz and club music. But none of these captivating, witty, talking-to-music performances moves us to get up and dance. In all five cases, the beat is too weak to support rap. It's not delineated into the strong, discrete bars needed to support four-beat rap lines and to induce a head-bobbing response.

And in most of these tracks, the poetry itself is not sufficiently formalized to be overlaid over a strong beat, even assuming such a beat were present. Woody Guthrie's talking blues is exceptional in this regard, and the rhyth-

mic behavior of the lines in its six-line stanzas has a lot in common with that
in Golden Age rap:

Way up **yon**der on a **moun**tain **road**, |	9
I had a **hot** | **mo**tor and a **heavy load**, |	11
I's a-**go***in'* pretty **fast**, || I **wasn't** even **stop***pin'*, |	14
I's a **boun***cin'* up and **down** like ***pop***corn a-**pop***pin'*	12
Had a **break***down*, || sort of a **ner**vous **bust***down* |	11
Of the uh | **mech**anism there | some **kind**, || **en**-*gine* **trou**ble.	13

The lines display an appealing mix of rhythmic stability and rhythmic varia-
tion. All of them have four primary **stress**es, most have medial pauses (\|\|),
and all but one are end-stopped (\|); but lines 1 and 4 flow right through
the expected medial pause, line 4 also flows over the expected end-stop, line
2 has an off-center pause (\|), and line 6 has *two* of these. Meanwhile the
syllable count per line varies from nine to fourteen. In addition, while all of
the lines have end rhymes, marking couplets, there is also quite a bit of extra
internal rhyme. Over all, the rhythmic (and sonic) stability lends a sense of
integrity to the passage's lines, while all of the variations play well thematically and add enjoyment to the listening experience. If Woody Guthrie had
teamed up with DJ Kool Herc or Eric B., "Talking Dust Bowl Blues" would
be hip hop rap.

Three of the other four pre-hip hop rappers have poetic performance
styles incompatible with rap. In Dylan's "Talking World War III Blues,"
there are typically four emphatic stresses in the line, but medial pauses occur
rarely, as do end-stops. Dylan's poetry, then, behaves very much like his
continuous guitar-strumming beat: propulsive and dynamic, but lacking the
kind of formal scaffolding which can provide a context for expressive rhythmic variation. Rather than a series of bars, we sense an incessant forward
momentum.

In The Last Poets' "When the Revolution Comes," each section begins
and ends with the title clause. This two-beat frame is repeated up front in
a call-and-response manner, with the beats and stresses of "when the revolution comes" falling in different places. Between these often-syncopated
framing clauses, however, there occurs a long main clause during which,
as in Dylan's talking blues, there are often none or few decisive phrasal
breaks—just the ongoing syllable stream. This main clause describes some

humorously ironic ("some of us will probably catch it on TV, with chicken hanging from our mouths—you'll know its revolution because there won't be no commercials") or violently ironic ("transit cops will be crushed by the trains after losing their guns and blood will run through the streets of Harlem drowning anything without substance") event impossible in today's reality.[4] The syntax sprawls. It's as if free verse long lines from Ginsberg's "Howl" were being recited. The longest such clause, also the most politically strident, occupies six bars of drumming:

> I hope pearly white teeth froth the mouths that speak of revolution without reverence, the cost of revolution is 360 degrees understand the cycle that never ends, understand the beginning to be the end and nothing is in between but space and time that I make or you make to relate or not to relate to the world outside my mind your mind, speak not of revolution until you are willing to eat rats to survive.

This is brilliant, powerful, emotionally charged rapping. It careens wildly, almost metaphysically, toward the desperate revolutionary willingness to "eat rats to survive." But the style is unsustainable for easy comprehension or for any active audience response, such as dancing. Its musical and formal properties are about as far from hip hop rap as rapping can be.

The same is true of Gil Scott-Heron's "The Revolution Will Not Be Televised" (1971). The title assertion tags the end of every section, and although these sections sometimes begin with what *might* be four-stress lines they invariably devolve into long free verse lines or prose:

> Green Acres, The Beverly Hillbillies, and Hooterville Junction will no longer be so damn relevant, and women will not care if Dick finally got down with Jane on Search for Tomorrow because Black people will be in the street looking for a brighter day.
> The revolution will not be televised.
> There will be no highlights on the eleven o'clock news and no pictures of hairy armed women liberationists and Jackie Onassis blowing her nose. The theme song will not be written by Jim Webb or Francis Scott Key, nor sung by Glen Campbell, Tom Jones, Johnny Cash or Englebert Humperdink, or the Rare Earth.
> The revolution will not be televised.

You had to have been there. The song is an acerbic yet hilarious critique of corporate-sponsored (white) popular culture, riddled with overt and subtle allusions to TV shows, public personalities, and commercial products. It's not hip hop, for sure, but it does anticipate the fun and the sometimes arcane allusiveness that has typified rap culture ever since 1979.

Just three years after the release of "When the Revolution Comes," Jalaluddin Mansur Nuriddin, a member of The Last Poets, independently released *Hustler's Convention* under the pseudonym Lightnin' Rod. In this 31:35 LP, he presents a series of rapped skits, each of which is tied to the next either by spoken poetry, sound effects, or live background (funk and jazz) music. As with the earlier rapping output of Woody Guthrie, Bob Dylan, The Last Poets, and Gil Scott-Heron, *Hustler's Convention* lacks the emphatic pulse that gets us nodding our heads, and ultimately, dancing. It was for listening entertainment.

Diverging from precedent, in which an MC would adopt a stage persona in order to facilitate and enliven the show, Lightnin' Rod never speaks in "his own" lyric voice; instead, he impersonates the two main hustlers, Sport and Spoon, as well as others they game against, several different cops, and a few extras. Acting multiple parts over multiple episodes, Lightnin' Rod projects his characters' attitudes, stories, and tropes through jingle-like quatrains delivered over background music. In each successive setting, the music changes in genre, style, tempo, and key; and is enhanced, in turn, by appropriate sampled sounds such as crowd noise, shuffled cards, a broken pool rack, sirens, or gunshots. Always in the forefront, however, are the ballad quatrains, each alternating between lines of four and three stresses, with end rhymes linking the three-stress lines (2 and 4). The four-stress lines (1 and 3) are further formalized by internal rhyme on the second and fourth stresses. Loosely aligned to the beat of the background music, emphases on rhyme and stress are further marked by exaggerated intonations appropriate to each speaker. The scenes and characters keep changing, and the never-changing stanzas are delivered with ever-changing nuance. It's a masterful dramatic performance.

Although much of the variation in stanza performance relates to impersonated voice quality, including intonations, Lightnin' Rod deploys a large range of line length and often varies away from expected end-line pauses. His syllable-count can tally as many as nineteen in a single four-stress line, as in this stanza, where pauses are also "missing" after lines 1 and 3:

It had cost me 12 years of my time || to realize what a nickel and dime
Hustler I had really been
While the real hustlers were rippin' off Bens || from the unsuspecting mens
Who are programmed to think they can win

Overall, *Hustler's Convention* is an instructive comedy caricaturing hood personas. The content is both memorable and fun, so its plot is populated by fabulous characters and sweetened by hyperbole and other fabrications—distancing Nuriddin from his performance and setting a new precedent for *topicality* within vinyl rapping. More than a noteworthy poetic expression, far more ambitious than a typical short skit, the album resembled a full-length radio play. It offered morals to be remembered when making life choices.

As a devout Muslim, Jalal Nuriddin hardly endorsed the lifestyle of hustling and pimping, but working as Lightnin' Rod he could enthusiastically embody a kind of satirical romanticism, allowing that lifestyle to seem glamorous and outrageously successful—until, bang bang, it's all over. Ironically, the figures he represents in *Hustler's Convention* would inspire the mack personas of later rappers, from Grandmaster Caz to The Notorious B. I. G., among many others, whose real-life self-promotions could be equivalently lucrative and fatal.

Beginning with descriptions of Sport, an ordinary hustler, and Spoon, who has just been released from prison, Lightnin' Rod goes on to present the lead-up, duration, and aftermath of the Hustler's Convention itself. By the LP's fourth track, Hominy Grit,[5] a fellow hustler and supposed friend of theirs, alerts them to the convention at the Café Black Rose. That event, he says, will be replete with fine women, cash, and drugs, and will offer the consummate test of hustling prowess: all competitors must either continue to out-hustle their rivals or be excluded from the premises. At the winner-take-all event, our protagonist team of Sport and Spoon outmaneuver everyone else at craps, pool, and poker till they have collected over $165,000 in winnings.

But just as they are about to leave, Grit betrays them, demanding a sixty-percent cut of their winnings and threatening them with bodily harm should they not deliver. The duo, hardly ready to part with their hard-earned cash, starts a gunfight and attempts to escape. Speeding off, they attract the attention of the police, ending up in a junkyard where they hope to stash their winnings. Now sure they will be subjected to police racism, Sport and Spoon begin a second shootout, during which their worst fears are confirmed. The police mercilessly shoot Spoon and beat up Sport before he ends up in the prison hospital. He is sentenced to the electric chair, but fortunately the death penalty is abolished by the time his case is resolved, and he is eventually freed. Sport realizes that he has learned the whole truth while imprisoned.

This plot trajectory, with its sequence to progressive success, crash, and eventual moral epiphany, can be traced along formalized tropes and motifs supported by rhymes—a foretaste of later, thematically expressive rap such as would be inaugurated by Melle Mel in "The Message." The great Grandmaster Caz himself would cite *Hustler's Convention* as one of the earliest instances of rapping. It was an LP he revered and knew by heart. Nevertheless, while its latent ideologies would come to define several later rappers, and while its stanza form would cameo in "Rapper's Delight" and in Kurtis Blow's "The Breaks," *Hustler's Convention* doesn't behave like normative rap, and this is because its rapping is performed against a musical backdrop, not in time with a musical beat. The album does inherit the jocular narrative properties of toasting—an inmate chanting tradition accompanied by ad hoc percussion and believed to have preserved African tribal traditions in toasts like "The Signifying Monkey"—and these would live on in hip hop rap, although the quatrain form and continuous skit structure would fade as rappers chose to present albums consisting of verses *and* skits. Content-wise, *Hustler's Convention* keeps it real while keeping it art, but it isn't rap: it's just missing that brazen street aesthetic rooted in the 4/4 beat.

The above examples of pre-rap rapping all illustrate a defining negative quality: rap is not just poetry, it's part of a *song*. In rap songs, the beat assumes maximal importance. Without that strong beat, without a clear sense of its looped construction into bars, it is relatively easy to rap long strings of words and phrases but relatively difficult to rap rhythmically integral lines—although Woody Guthrie could do it even to the beats of his acoustic guitar and Lightnin' Rod could do it to background jazz grooves. In the pre-hip hop era, musical beats and linguistic stresses may align, but the irregularity or even lack of pauses gives the listener no way to hierarchize information from a continuous stream of words. The listener can understand their meaning, but since this meaning is not formally regulated it can feel chaotic, inconsistent, or unsettling—therefore less immediately engaging and not so much fun. Finally, we don't respond to rap mainly for its meaning, but for its ability to get us moving rhythmically, to experience a message concordant with bodily movement.

"Rapper's Delight" (1979)

Early rap captured, as well as a new musical aesthetic, a different attitude from the political militancy and social satire of its predecessors. In contrast to "When the Revolution Comes," which characterized apathetic ghetto consciousness as "party and bullshit,"[6] "Rapper's Delight" called *for* a party, and everybody—of all races and classes—was invited. In Wonder Mike's memorable shout-out, he forecasts the wide appeal "rapping to the beat" would have:

> See | I am Wonder Mike,
> And I'd like to say hel-lo
> Uh to the black, to the white || the red, and the brown,
> The purple and yellow

Everyone knows who the black, white, red, brown, and yellow were, ethnically, but what about the *purple*? Possibly alluding to Sheb Wooley's "Purple People Eater" (1958) and Jimi Hendrix's "Purple Haze" (1967), the word injects some light discord and could refer to gays, acid-heads, or nonconformists generally.[7] Either way, the song was meant to draw an inclusive crowd using a catchy beat that everybody could vibe to, and what that meant was that the poetry couldn't dominate, as in political rapping. It had to subordinate itself to the musical beat. It was for the discos.

The beat of the 14:45 minute track merges a studio bass line, drums, and clapping with Chic's disco hit "Good Times" (1979).[8] The rapping is mostly non-stop, an MC relay of nine verses totaling 364 lines. This includes four repetitions of Wonder Mike's signature chorus ("I said a hip | hop || the hippie | the hippie / To the hip hip hop || a you don't stop the rock it / To the bang bang boogie") and analogous riffs by Big Bank Hank ("Hotel | motel || Holiday Inn") and Master Gee ("Well it's on n on || n on on n on / The beat don't stop until the break of dawn"). Mike and Hank rap some lines in four-line stanzas, which Master Gee never does, but most of "Rapper's Delight" consists of couplets. As we'll see, there are actually three forms of poetry in this song. One would very soon disappear from rap, one would persist from then till now, and one would lie dormant till the emergence of a new style with Rakim and others.

All of the rapping is upbeat entertainment. MC cheerleading, cajoling, and joking are interspersed with boasts[9] about sexual prowess, possessions, style, and rhyming skill, as well as anecdotes, scatting, and commentary on the ongoing performance. Some of the best material is that of Grandmaster Caz, who had generously (in a weak moment he would come to regret) lent Hank some of his own rhymes. So "Rapper's Delight" also channels a lot of Caz's superior wit, sound play, and self-confidence, as well as—seemingly oblivious to the irony—some moralizing on biting, a. k. a. plagiarism, the unacknowledged use of another MC's rhymes.[10]

Focusing now on the poetics, here are four of Master Gee's couplets dealing with rap's affect:

Now I'm **fee**lin' the **highs** ‖ and ya **fee**lin' the **lows**		12
The **beat** starts gettin'in ‖ **to** your **toes**		8
Ya start **pop**pin' ya **fingers** ‖ and **stomp**in' your **feet**		12
And **mo**vin' your **bo**dy ‖ while you're sittin' in your **seat**		13
Then **damn** | ya **start** . **do**in' the **freak**		8
I said **damn** | a-**right** . **out**ta your **seat**		9
Then ya **throw** your *hands* **high** ‖ in the **air**		9
Ya **rock**in' to the **rhythm** ‖ *shake* your **der**ri**ere**		11

Here all the lines are end-stopped (\|), and all but two have a medial pause, or caesura (‖). With thematic appropriateness, each of the two lines with "damn" at first-beat position, describing how the music gets people out of their seats and up dancing, has an early pause (\|), then glides over (.) the expected caesura. The only other rhythmic variations in these lines occur in the final couplet, where each line contains one *secondary* stress, for a total of five stresses. All of the lines have end-rhyme, giving line closure and bonding the couplets. There's a lot of internal line as well, most importantly on the array of *feeling, beat, feet, seat,* and *freak,* but also effectively on the parallel *damn* exclamations.

Three features typical of Old School rap show up here. First, the average line length is short, about ten syllables. Second, almost all the stressed syllables mark content words (nouns, verbs, adjectives, and adverbs), that is, semantically important words; and in fact, all of the content words here take stresses. There happen to be five such words in each of the last two lines, so that both of these contain a secondary stress, but the majority of couplet lines have four and only four stresses. Third, especially in the second half lines, the rhythm (as well as the syntax) tends to be formulaic. A few phrasal patterns predominate. One is the triadic /x/ rhythm evident in "**to** your **toes**" and "**in** the **air**," also present with an intro in xx/x/ or \x/x/ ("*shake* your **derriere**"). Another of these is /xx/, evident in "**do**in' the **freak**" and "**out**ta your **seat**," as well as, with an intro, in x/xx/ ("and **stomp**in' your **feet**") and xx/xx/ ("and ya **fee**lin' the **lows**").[11] To a certain degree, there is tension between the line's normal array of four stressed content words in time with the beat, and the second half line's formulaic phrasal patterns. In effect, rhythm trumps grammar, and this is evident three times in our passage: the weak prepositions *out* and *-to* each take "unnatural" stress, as does the first syllable of "derriere." Experientially, however, the net impact of this tension is minimal. After listening to eighty or a hundred lines of "Rapper's Delight," the rapping becomes very predictable.

Yet "Rapper's Delight" sounds anything but predictable at the outset. Wonder Mike's first verse (and Big Bank Hank's too) starts off in a poetic form that is not at all expected even though it sounds very familiar. Once upon a time, and only then, rap poetry could sound like an Old Folk ballad, *The Rime of the Ancient Mariner*, many a hymn or jingle, or the theme some from *Gilligan's Island*, set to a disco beat:

Now **what** you **hear** ‖ is **not** a **test**	8
I'm **rappin'** | **to** the **beat** [**B**]	6
And **me** | the **groove** ‖ **and** my **friends**	7
Are gonna **try** | to **move** your **feet** [**B**]	8
See **I** | **am** ‖ **Won**der **Mike**	7
And I **like** to **say** hello [**B**]	7
Uh to the **black** | to the **white** ‖ the **red** and the **brown**	12
The **pur**ple | **and** yellow [**B**]	6

As in the couplets from "Rapper's Delight," stressed content words determine the flow, such as it is—except when the prescribed rhythm promotes little words (*to, and, am, and*). This is still four-beat poetry, but the fourth beat in the stanza's even lines is a *virtual beat*, heard in the music and felt in the body, but not realized in a fourth stress. The average syllable count, then, is less than in couplets, and the *abcb* rhyme scheme reduces the rhyme frequency as well. It's catchy, but there's not much for an ambitious MC to work with—except to vary the line length, as Wonder Mike does very effectively in the third line of the second stanza.

As we've seen, this venerable, centuries-old *abca* ballad stanza was used— more extravagantly—by Lightnin' Rod, a huge influence on Grandmaster Caz.[12] Presumably Hank got his quatrains—as well as the rest of his rhymes—from Caz, but none of Caz's published lyrics are in this form.[13] Whatever the exact historical status of four-beat ballad quatrains in early rap, this form did not survive long beyond "Rapper's Delight" and, as we'll see, Kurtis Blow's "The Breaks."

The most poetically progressive, forward-looking lines in "Rapper's Delight" are embedded in Wonder Mike's signature hook:

I said a **hip**	**hop** || the **hippie**	the **hippie**	11
To the **hip hip** *hop* || a you **don't** *stop* the **rock** it	12
To the **bang** *bang* **boogie** || say **up** *jumped* the **boogie**		12
To the **rhy**thm of the **boo**gie || the **beat** [B]	10 + beat

What's different here is that the lines have longer syllable counts, as many as six stresses, fewer end stops, and a lot more rhyme. Right after he raps his two quatrains in verse 1, Wonder Mike returns to this semi-nonsensical, semi-scat performance mode ("But first I gotta bang bang \|\| the boogie to the boogie / Say up jump the boogie to the bang bang boogie / Let's rock \|\| you don't stop / Rock the rhythm that will make your body rock").[14]

As it turned out, the poetics expressed so briefly here were to become dominant a few years later—spurred also, as we shall see, by Melle Mel's innovations. But already in this signature chorus the rhymes are much denser and less predictable than in the song's verse quatrains or couplets, and they're spread throughout the lines, which have greater space to contain them. We can hear and feel a rhythmic lineage from this chorus's exuberant silliness to the entertaining boast in the first couplet of Nas's "N. Y. State of Mind," where the syllable count is even higher, where all stresses rhyme or, in one case, alliterate, and where extra pauses and overridden pauses create a truly *funky, kicking rhythm*:

Rappers, I **m**onkey **fl**ip 'em with the **f**unky **rhy**thm
I be **kickin'**, | mu**sic**ian, \|\| in**flic**tin' compo**si**tion

The key difference, of course, is that Nas's syllabic pyrotechnics are also meant to make sense, in contrast to Wonder Mike's nonsense poetry.[15] But both artists are about spitting syllables for the sake of spectacular flow and the rhythmic entertainment it can offer.[16]

What also persisted in "Rapper's Delight," were the couplet form and its end rhyme, the basic four-beat rhythm, and the strong expectation of caesural break and end stop. Meanwhile Mike's few uniquely frolicsome lines remained a dormant model of poetic potentiality until the rap line expanded, making space for more rhymes and for more varied and nuanced phrasal rhythms. In effect, the hook of "Rapper's Delight" evolved into the normative verse line of the nineties, while one of the two forms in its verses, the quatrain, morphed into the most common chorus stanza in later rap songs.

Kurtis Blow (1980)

It couldn't have happened without the breakout popularity of "Rapper's Delight." Kurtis Blow, a twenty-year-old DJ, MC, and breakdancer with persuasive confidence and a voice to die for, walked into Mercury Records and came out with an enviable contract: two singles which, if they hit the charts, would guarantee an album. They did. "Christmas Rappin'" topped 400,000, and "The Breaks" went to 500,000. Suddenly a major record company was sponsoring and profiting from rap music. This was a huge deal, and it also couldn't have happened without Kurt's vocal presence, his steady yet rhythmically varied flow and intonational versatility, and his ability to sound musically magnetic. Compared with the MCs in "Rapper's Delight," he was also an obviously denser and cleverer rhymer, as these lines from "Christmas Rappin'" show:

> Not a **preacher** or a **teacher** || or a elec**trician**
> A **fighter** or a **writer** || or a poli**tician**
> The **man** with the **key** to **your** ig**nition**—
> **Kur**tis **Blow** is compe**tition**

And he was more relatable and more real. Although his tracks had the trappings of the dancehall aesthetic of "Rapper's Delight," they differed in that their verses explicitly took on social issues. In "The Breaks," Kurtis Blow does MC a party, but he doesn't forget to remind his listeners that the dance-break is a break from the difficulties that they face in their ordinary lives. Capitalizing on the wordplay that conjoins dancing and ghetto living, he refers again and again—always comically—to common bad breaks, monetary and sexual:

> KB: *And* the **IRS** says || **they** *want* to **chat** |
> (A): *That's* the **breaks** || *that's* the **breaks** |
> KB: *And you* **can't** ex**plain** || why **you** *claim*ed your **cat** |
> (A): *That's* the **breaks** || *that's* the **breaks** |
>
> KB: If your *wo*man steps **out** || with an**oth**er **man** |
> (A): *That's* the **breaks** || *that's* the **breaks** |
> KB: And she **runs** off **with** him || to Ja**pan** |
> (A): *That's* the **breaks** || *that's* the **breaks** |

There are also the not-so-common, ever-to-be-hoped-for lucky breaks. The song's linguistic focus on its title idea is anything but boring or redundant because of the variety of human experience touched upon. Moreover, the linguistic *quality* of the rapping, its sustained wit, is memorable, and anticipates the normatively captivating surface intelligence of subsequent rap poetry at its best. Nothing like this wordplay occurs in "Rapper's Delight":

> *Breaks* on a **bus** || *brakes* on a *car* |
> *Breaks* to *make* || **you** a su*perstar* |
> *Breaks* to **win** | and *breaks* to *lose* |
> But *these* here *breaks* will **rock** your *shoes* |
> And *these* | **are** | the *breaks* |
> *Break* it *up*, *break* it *up*, *break* it *up*!

To understand what Kurtis Blow means, you have to dance. "The Breaks" demonstrates why a break that *rocks your shoes* is so important to take. To deal with the bad breaks in life like being cheated on, getting fired, and being so broke that you have to borrow money from the mob, it may help somewhat to be discerning and critical ("to the girl in green, don't be so mean"), but at the end of the day, the break you take to play his song "The Breaks" and get yourself moving is the best one. It lets you break up life's constant quarrel. It lets you stop the fighting and feel "up," not down. It doesn't let you forget the bad breaks, but it gets you up dancing even as it enumerates these bad breaks with inimitably funky styling.

"The Breaks" shares with "Rapper's Delight" and lesser hits like Lady B's "To the Beat Y'all," Sequence's "Funk You Up," and Treacherous Three's "The Body Rock," an emphasis on rhythm and having fun while dancing and partying, but it was more progressive in its thematic coherence, in its recognition of social realities, and in its relative brevity. The song lasts eight minutes, but the rapping time is just 5:15—quite close to the eventual temporal norm for vinyl.

Still, "The Breaks" remains decidedly Old School in its poetics. Because the song's primary function was to be danceable, not as in a lot of later rap to dazzle a listener with complex rhyme patterns and complicated wordplay, its individual lines usually contain around ten syllables, seldom featuring more than twelve. Short line length aside, its stress patterns behave fairly predictably. A listener can almost always expect a pause in the middle of the line, a pause at the end of the line, and minimal rhythmic variation in the phrasing.

Like all the rappers in "Rapper's Delight," Kurtis Blow, although much more expressively varied in his intonations, almost always stresses whatever syllables fall on the beat—including function words like *of*, *if*, or *up*. Such funky linguistic behavior, in which without exception stresses and pauses are

Line	Stress-Time Pattern	# Beats	# Stresses
Clap your **hands** ‖ everybody	/ x / ‖ / x / x ǀ	4	4
If you **got** ‖ **what** it **takes**	x / ǀ / ǀx / ǀ	4	3
Cause **I'm** Kurtis **Blow** ‖ and I **want** you to **know**	x / \ x / ‖ x x / x x / ǀ	4	4
That **these** ǀ **are** ǀ the **breaks**	x / ǀ / ǀ x/ ǀ	4	3

obedient to the norm of our sense of beat, would seem quaint after Rakim, but it made perfect sense in its disco setting.

While the verses of "Rapper's Delight" were predominantly in couplet form, with quatrains as the minority option, Kurtis Blow's two hits established couplets as the norm. "Christmas Rappin'" is entirely in couplets, and "The Breaks" contains just one quatrain—the song's hook, declaring who he was and calling for audience participation. Yes, this is the same stanza used throughout *Hustler's Convention* and inserted by Wonder Mike and Big Bank Hank into "Rapper's Delight," but Kurtis Blow spaces its syllables out by means of syncopating pauses so that every line occupies four beats in the bar

Compare Wonder Mike:

Line	Stress-Time Pattern	# Beats	# Stresses
Now **what** you **hear** ‖ is **not** a **test**	x / x / ‖ x / x / ǀ	4	4
I'm **rappin'** **to** the **beat**	x / x / x / ǀ	4	3
And **me**, the **groove** ‖ **and** my **friends**	x / x / ‖ x / x / ǀ	4	4
Are gonna **try** to **move** your **feet**	x x x / x / x / ǀ	4	3

Instead of taking up a first three beats of the bar and giving the floor to the bassist's fill as Wonder Mike does in lines 2 and 4, Kurtis Blow's second and fourth lines have virtual beats which shift emphasis to the rhyme filling the fourth beat—much like a jazz soloist might use rests to syncopate a phrase. For talented rappers like Kurtis Blow, this technique, which carries into his couplets, opens space for innovative rhymes.

In effect, this stanza announces the MC's poetic prowess, and that's it. We never hear it again in this song. Followed by a four-bar musical break and then by rapping in couplets, this stanza was, we now realize, the very first rap chorus. For what in essence is a chorus but a contrastingly song-like stanza offering a thematic summary and separated from the rapped verses by a musical break?

Some of Kurtis Blow's couplets, however, mimic *abab* quatrain rhyme effects even as they remain couplets-with-pauses. When the song alternates between call and response, the audience's response effectively suspends Kurtis Blow's end-rhyme for a full bar with the repetition of the same half line twice between each of the lines—

KB: You **say** last **week** || you met the **perfect guy**
(A): **That's** the **breaks**, that's the **breaks**
KB: And **he** promised you the **stars** || in the **sky**
(A): **That's** the **breaks**, that's the **breaks**
KB: **He said** his **Cadilac** was **gold**
(A): **That's** the **breaks**, that's the **breaks**
KB: But he **didn't say** || it was **ten** years **old**
(A): **That's** the **breaks**, that's the **breaks**

The effect is somewhat like that achieved by James Brown in "Say It Loud—I'm Black and I'm Proud," where he trades bars with his band and the live audience. Unlike James Brown, who keeps repeating the imperative to an audience who keeps repeating the slogan, Kurtis Blow, interacting with a similarly repetitive "audience," changes his rhymes and rhythms constantly, and one of lines even has an extra stress and lacks the expected medial pause.

As the "audience"—with greater regularity than the rapper—stresses a syllable on each of the four musical beats, they effectively realize the rap line's basic template, vocalizing the beat's pulse and setting the stage for the rapper's contrasting vocal variability. Meanwhile, they delay the rapper's rhyme, making each rhyme stand out more from the monotony of the audience chant. The listener hears two line groupings in tension with one another, a basic one and one full of variation. Paired together, the contrasting yet reinforcing rhythms sound good, as a good time should. Meanwhile, as the audience trades bars, the repetition of *breaks* gets semantically paired with pairings in tension with it, and *create* tension through semantic opposition: *guy* and *sky*, *gold* and *old*. Ultimately—in the song's final movement—the listener hears a sixteen-bar verse articulating continuous fun (and continuous acceptance of life's hard knocks) along with a varied and evolving story of male sexual hustling and female disillusion.

Call and response here also captures, on vinyl, a feature of live performance, conferring on "The Breaks" an "authentic" club feel. The live atmospherics are enhanced by sampled hand-clapping and other club noises, all contributing to the illusion that this record is transporting us right into a disco where we can freely dance. And indeed, "The Breaks" is not a song simply to be listened to. Verses 1, 2, 3, and 4 are each separated by eight-bar musical breaks, short teasers. Then a sixteen-break comes between verses 4 and 5, and then after verse 5 there are forty bars (1:18 minutes) of music followed by the "Just Do It" bridge; and then the call-and-response verse 6, just quoted in part, is itself followed by another forty bars and a long fade-out (1:45). That's a lot of space without poetry. The rapping is insistently social and, in turn, gives it up to music and dancing, for these ARE the BREAKS.

Afrika Bambaataa (1982)

Two years later, Afrika Bambaataa—a DJ often referred to as the "Godfather of Hip Hop"—put out two hits of his own: "Planet Rock" and "Looking for the Perfect Beat." Like Kurtis Blow, Bambaataa rejected the Black Power movement and the revolution it called for. But while Kurtis Blow could only be heard advocating partying as a viable escapism, Bambaataa took a different approach. His "Looking for the Perfect Beat" motivated the dance-break to accomplish a mood—a *feeling*—which he used to present, and represent, the Universal Zulu Nation, an Africanist yet inclusive organization aiming to attain social justice, an end to religious struggles, a rewriting of colonialist and racist history, and universal acceptance of peace and unity among human beings.[17]

The values had formal consequence. In espousing beliefs that focused on the pursuit of truth, Bambaataa and the Soulsonic Force were left with little room to develop worldly arguments. "Looking for the Perfect Beat" explicitly recognizes all the participants in the song as *universal people* with *mortal motivations* who are *looking for* (nothing other than) *the perfect beat*. To create an effect of community unity, neither a single musical component nor an individual person contributing sound or speech exercises privilege in either a formal or thematic way. In fact, the whole song is governed by this ideology: nobody raps solo, and the crew is synched with the recorded audience by means of frequent call and response. As the crew rhythmically varies the phrase "looking for the perfect beat," the "audience" repeats the crew's every variation. In this way, all are absorbed into one homogenous *feel*—the *feel* of the perfect beat.

As a further consequence of this homogeneity, the formal distinction between choruses and verses in "Looking for the Perfect Beat" is blurred. Unlike in "The Breaks," where the listener can readily identify a verse by its rhythmic variation, thematic development, and detailed particulars, a listener of Bambaataa's "Looking for the Perfect Beat" cannot. For one thing, Afrika Bambaataa and the Soulsonic force *choose* not to develop any theme—except that of the quest for the perfect beat. Moreover, the entire 6:51 minute song is saturated with repetition in both the music and the rapping. On top of that, Bambaataa never dominates the crew and the crew never assumes a position of privilege over the audience. Whatever specialized knowledge the crew may express is echoed by and incorporated into the recorded audience's response.[18]

The musical structure itself is unifying rather than differentiating. It does not set verse or chorus boundaries. Distributing privilege uniformly throughout the song, the sampled beat, a dense, bar-long, electro-funk loop, remains constant no matter what group is rapping. During musical breaks, the beat continues, modified only by additional samples layered over it. It's all about unity.

It follows that "Looking for the Perfect Beat" deploys call and response very differently from "The Breaks." As we've seen, the audience in "The Breaks" repeats the same words again and again between Kurtis Blow's everevolving, rhythmically differentiated rap lines. In "Looking for the Perfect Beat," the audience also repeats itself, but in doing so it echoes the crew's proximate rhythms, simulating rhythmically identical line pairs, each rhyming with the next while simultaneously varying its rhythm from that of the previous couplet.

```
 /  x   x   x   / x   x ||  /   x    x x   / x   x
```
Looking for the perfect beat (Searching for the perfect beat)
Looking for the perfect beat (Seeking for the perfect beat)

```
 x   /  x   /  || /   x   /
```
Say Hit that beat (Hit that beat)
```
 x   /  x   /  ||  x   /  x   /
```
That perfect beat (That perfect beat)
```
x  / x   x    /  || x  / x   x  /
```
I gotta get mine (I gotta get mine)
```
x  / x   x    /  || x / x   x    /
```
I gotta get mine (I gotta get mine)

This use of call and response arises from the song's homogeneity rather than from individual contributions to the collective party feel.

Ultimately lacking both a nuanced formal structure and any overt thematic statement (other than the actuality of the music and words themselves), "Looking for the Perfect Beat" is best described as a house-party song. It was for the experience itself—the *feel* of unity.

"The Message" (1982)

While Bambaataa's "Planet Rock" and "Looking for the Perfect Beat" were big hits, inspiring DJs to adopt similar electro-funk beats in later rap, their lyrical content left so little room for reflection or response to worldly concerns that later MCs almost inevitably, living as they did amidst the daily challenges of ghetto life, sought to give poetic expression to their experiences. They wanted to rock the party, for sure, but they wanted also to keep it real.

A glimmer of focused social commentary can be found in one (and only one) of Kurtis Blow's songs, "Hard Times," on the B-side of his album *Kurtis Blow* (1980):

Hard times spreading just like the flu
You know I caught it just like you
The prices going up, the dollars down
You got me fallin' to the ground
Turn around, get ready, check out the time
Get ready all people for the future shock
Hard times (Hard times)
Hard times (Hard times)
To the bridge

In the bridges between the four short raps, we hear "ho! . . . yep! . . . I get funky! . . . ha ho! . . . digga digga digga!" and some fantastically funky scatting. It's real and it's fun, but more fun than real, and the reality is somewhat abstract. Kurtis Blow's upbeat final rap, repeated after a very long dance break, proclaims that the way out of hard times is a function of attitude, hope, and individual effort: "Hard times is nothing new or mean / I'm gonna use my strong mentality / Like the cream of the crop and the crop of the cream / Beating hard times, that is my dream / Hard times in life, hard times in death / I'm gonna keep on fighting till my very last breath." This would become the credo, sometimes actualized, often more fantasy than real, of almost all subsequent MC rapping: the way out of the ghetto is *success*, the American dream, the African American dream.[19]

"Hard Times" was anything but a hit. But, "The Message," by Grandmaster Flash and the Furious Five, released the same year as Bambaataa's hits, was a huge success, a serious-yet-funny depiction of the harrowing life of the ghetto framed within a funky beat. It appealed to a new and somewhat different audience—an audience appreciative of Kurtis Blow's superfunky style yet looking for something more substantial. "The Message" boldly proclaimed through its title its role in communicating the truth. It didn't say that the party's over or that the party's bullshit, but it seemed to insist that the party be informed by consciousness: let's keep dancing, but let's also admit that we're in a bad situation and we need to wake up to some serious social discourse. Following "The Message," rap's next wave would be defined by witty social commentary, combining the serious lyrical content of Lightnin' Rod, Bambaataa's house party aesthetic, and Kurtis Blow's fly performance style.

Enter the co-authors of "The Message," Duke Bootee and Melle Mel, whose flow styles, respectively cool and "close to the edge," cohere in communicating what many listeners regard as rap's first and most influential masterpiece.[20] Within the packed 7:15 track is an intro hook, five increasingly long verses, and choruses between each verse. This is the first rap hit, then, in which choruses function like choruses, offering a repeated and indelibly memorable thematic summary of the song's increasingly tragic message. Here's Duke Bootee's hook:

It's **like** a **jung**le some**times** || it **makes** me **won**der
How I **keep** from **go**ing **un**der [beat, beat]
It's **like** a **jung**le some**times** || it **makes** me **won**der
How I **keep** from **go**ing **un**der [beat, beat]

Already, we're entering a new poetics. The chorus is a quatrain but not a normal one with four different lines. It repeats two couplets, avoiding elaboration, sustaining the focus. The meter is four-beat, but the long lines have five stresses, not four, and the short lines occupy only two beats yet contain three stresses, and the long lines flow (enjamb) right into the short lines. It's funky but very edgy, a new sound.

The repeated chorus expands on the hook by adding these lines at the outset:

Don't | **push** | **me** | 'cause || **I'm close** | to the | **edge**
I'm | **try-ing** || **not** to **lose** | **my head** (ah huh | huh | huh)

With this addition, the chorus becomes even edgier. Beyond just talking about going under, Mel *sounds* desperate, like he's about to blow his mental gasket. All the extra Kurtis Blow-like pauses, all the extra stresses, unevenly placed, seven per line, combine with the add-on paralinguistic grunts to create this effect.

The verses all contain couplets, but these couplets' components, rhythms, and formal status change effectively from verse to verse. In Mel's verse 1, all the lines fall into couplets, but we hear contrastingly uneven lines: six syllables, then thirteen, nine, thirteen. The stress and syllabic rhythms are also—as in the chorus—wildly varied. So is what we see. Couplet 1 describes the ghetto's material destruction ("broken glass everywhere"), the anti-social action pervading it ("people pissing on the stairs"), and the attitude of alienation sustaining it ("they just don't care"). In couplet 2, the speaker complains further about the smell and the noise of the neighborhood, but realizes that, lacking any money, he's lost all choice in the matter. The chain of physical, behavioral, and psychological degradation is profound—a kind of sociological poetry:

Broken **glass** || **everywhere**
People **pissing** on the **stairs** || you know they **just** don't **care**
I **can't** take the **smell** || **can't** take the **noise**
Got no **mo**ney to move **out** || I **guess** I **got no choice**

In verse 2, attention shifts from personal complaint to a witnessing of other struggling ghetto-dwellers. Now even the regularity of the couplet form breaks down. Mel's portrait of the crazy lady consists of a couplet, a one-liner off-rhyming on the couplet, an internally off-rhymed one-liner, and then an *abcb*-quatrain whose non-rhyming lines also work as internally rhyming one-liners:

Crazy lady livin' in a **bag**
Eatin' out of garbage pails, she used to be a **fag-hag**
Said she **danced** the **tango**, skipped the light **fandango**
The Zircon **Princess** seemed to lost her **senses**
Down at the **peep**show, watching all the **creeps**
So she can tell the stories to the girls back **home**

She went to the **city** and got Social **Security**
She had to get a pimp, she couldn't make it on her **own**

This is the poetics of alienation, desperation, ironic clash—not a special effect but stunningly pervasive in this song. Duke Bootee's verse 4 covers alienation from school, the appeal of gangs, and then random, horrific acts of violence as if they were cartoon rumors, surreally "healed." The "I" in the verse can't avoid the filtered fear such events inspire, so he holes up as if *he* is a criminal on the run. Mirroring this social confusion, the *heart/start* couplet's rhyme spills over into a one-liner—or does the *park/dark* line complete a triplet? The *gun/run* one-liner echoes with nothing, enjambing into an incoherent last couplet whose quick-punch *last/glass* rhyme adds extra surreality:

My son said, Daddy, I don't want to go to **school**
'Cause the teacher's a jerk, he must think I'm a **fool**
And all the kids smoke **reefer**, I think it'd be **cheaper**
If I just got a job, learned to be a **street sweeper**
Or dance to the **beat**, shuffle my **feet**
Wear a shirt and tie and run with the **creeps**
'Cause it's all about **money**, ain't a damn thing **funny**
You got to have a con in this land of milk and **honey**
They pushed that girl in front of the **train**
Took her to the doctor, sewed her arm on **again**
Stabbed that man right in his **heart**
Gave him a *transplant* for a *brand* new **start**
I *can't* walk through the **park**, 'cause it's crazy after **dark**
Keep my hand on my **gun**, 'cause they got me on the **run**
I feel like a **outlaw**, broke my *last glass* **jaw**[21]
Hear them say: "You want some more?" livin' on a **seesaw**

Mel delivers the final verse of "The Message," a stunning twenty-eight-line summary of ghetto life from birth to early death. He begins with an abstract, universal third-person narration ("A child is born with no state of mind, / Blind to the ways of mankind"), but then, situating the child in the ghetto, fuses the narrative mode with elegy and second-person prophesy, foreseeing a life with almost no possibility of a good future:

God is smiling on you but he's frowning too
Because only God knows what you'll go through
You'll grow in the ghetto, living second rate

And your eyes will sing a song of deep hate
The places you play and where you stay
Look like one great big alleyway

In the scenario Mel traces, "you" will drop out of school, emulate hustlers, become a stick-up kid, do time in prison, and end up as a sex slave before committing suicide. Almost every couplet is lucid, chilling, and closed—yet rhythmically clashing,[22] making the unfolding narrative seem both edgy[23] and inevitable. The sole exception occurs at the couplet enjambment of "undercover fag" into "being used and abused." Almost every end rhyme is brutally exact—except for the variant final off-rhymes of *lost* and *forth* and *song* and *young*:

Now your manhood is took and you're a Maytag
Spent the next two years as a undercover fag
Being used and abused to serve like hell
Till one day you was found hung dead in your cell
It was plain to see that your life was lost
You was cold and your body swung back and forth
But now your eyes sing the sad, sad song
Of how you lived so fast and died so young

The formal, rhythmic, and tonal range achieved through Melle Mel's and Duke Bootee's collaboration is impressive—amazing, really, in the context of their few rap forebears, and it is utterly effective in its application. Verses 1–4 reveal the experience of social dissolution as increasingly insane, chaotic, and desperate. Then verse 5 narrates that experience as a staged, inexorable tragedy.

In the short run, the poignant, heartbreaking political clarity of "The Message" did not emerge as a dominant force in hip hop culture, as it was displaced by the anger and defiance of "gangsta" rap and the happy bravado of "party and bullshit" rap. Nevertheless, its legacy is evident. "The Message" is now universally recognized as one of the greatest rap songs ever composed—and its final verse as Mel's signature achievement. Kool Moe Dee in *There's a God on the Mic: The True 50 Greatest MCs* (2003) ranks Melle Mel as #1. He comments:

Pound for pound, "A Child Is Born" is the greatest rhyme ever! When you talk about Melle Mel, you're talking about a plethora of superlatives, and a series of firsts. First of all, he's the first emcee to explode in a new rhyme cadence, and change the way every emcee rhymed forever. Rakim, Biggie, and Eminem have flipped the flow, but Melle Mel's downbeat on the two, four, kick to snare cadence is still the rhyme foundation all emcees are building on. . . . In 1982, Afrika Bambaataa shifted the planet with "Planet Rock" and Melle Mel shifted lyrical content with "The Message." [24]

Although somewhat muted in the 1980s, the persistent and growing influence of "The Message" on lyrical content can be heard in many "conscious" rap songs about social injustice, the tragedy of gun violence, the abuse of women, and, recently, even homophobia. Big Boi's verse in the Outkast song "Reset" creatively paraphrases Mel's classic "A Child is Born" verse, and there's even a rhythmic tribute in *Hamilton* to the "makes me wonder how I keep from going under" chorus lines. More broadly, the stylistic and formal daring of "The Message" proved a lasting legacy to rappers from coast to coast. We can hear it in the styles of Ice Cube, Snoop, Tupac, MC Lyte, Big L, The Notorious B. I. G., Lauryn Hill, Yasiin Bey (Mos Def), Talib Kweli, Common, Eve, Lil Wayne, André 3000, Lupe Fiasco, Kendrick Lamar, and countless others.

But however we evaluate the importance of "The Message" for the hip hop tradition as it would unfold in the following decades, its immediate impact was huge. It created, in effect, the role of the serious solo MC. The tight thematic coherence of its verses, its verse sequences, and the complementary give and take of its verses and choruses set the standard for the vinyl rap song, a song short enough for radio play, a song deep enough to warrant repeated listening, and a song with a message.[25]

Beat

Busta Rhymes emerges onto the stage. He curls the microphone to his lips. He breathes in, "When I step up in the place ay yo I step correct." The crowd's eyes converge on the MC. "I got that head nod shit that make you break your neck." The crowd's heads pulse in a unison nod. "And you know we come through to wreck the disco tech." With each "hit" in the beat, the crowd begins to flirt with dance styles—embodying the rhythm with a move of their own. "Throw your hands up in the air, don't ever disrespect." The hands obey, returning to the beat of the DJ. "Woo-hah Woo-hah, I got you all in check."

In hip hop, the beat is basic, but *beat* can mean several different, related things: (1) a musical collage of sampled recorded or digitally produced percussive and tonal sounds arranged in 4/4 time—the composition over which the rapper foregrounds his verses; (2) any single strong pulse (*ictus*) within that composition, on or near which the rapper may articulate a stressed, metrical syllable or, for variation, a pause; (3) the single beat considered as a durational (e.g., "quarter-note") unit, hence a measure of tempo, typically registered in beats per minute (bpm); (4) the position of any single beat within the bar—beat 1, beat 2, beat 3, beat 4; and, (5) the common experience of beat shared by the DJ, MC, and audience in response to the rhythmic pulse of any rap song.

Remembering Wonder Mike's quatrain in "Rapper's Delight," we can say that his foundational categorization of the art—"I'm rappin' to the beat"—refers to the first meaning of *beat*; the next three meanings relate to particular musical features at play in the beat itself; and the final meaning generalizes from Mike's characterization of rap's affective purpose, which depends on the shared human *sense of beat*: "And me, the groove, and my friends /

Are gonna try to move your feet." Much as we may admire the intricate, innovative beats produced by legends like DJ Premier and Kanye West, or the particular flows of Ice Cube, Tupac, Biggie, Nas, Guru, Lauryn Hill, Eminem, or André 3000, our listening response to their complex musical compositions and poetic verses is innate. Our sense of beat is grounded in a motor capacity shared by every member of the audience. Rappers can see it from stage, as can every attendee from looking around the audience at a rap concert. That familiar unison head nod and foot tap that falls on each and every beat throughout the song comes from our common sense of beat. These gestures mark the pulse of every DJ-looped or studio-produced beat, whose intricacies, in turn, sophisticate and structure the overlaid rap verse.

Let's use our epigraph couplet as an example. One Be Lo caps his verse in Binary Star's "Reality Check" with two claims that might be dismissed as bad-taste braggadocio: "You ain't never heard an emcee speak like this / And Rodney King ain't never felt a beat like this." So, not only is his flow unique, but the beat he's rapping to is more brutal than the LAPD nightsticks that pummeled Rodney King. Hyperbolic MC boasting is perfectly normal, but it's impossible to imagine One Be Lo and Senim Silla approving of this iconic act of racist cruelty. We can nevertheless take this line literally, in that the rap beat, like a physical beating, impacts the whole body with a feeling-response, but the musical beat is far more powerful in a good way. It's worth noting that the actual beat track of this ephemeral indie group's song is very catchy, but very modest garage-band in quality—not loud, not brash, not overwhelming, and not as "artistic" as the piano and voice sampling that interrupts it. One Be Lo's main idea here probably concerns the interplay of beat and voice. The repetition of "ain't never" introduces a parallelism most strongly expressed by the two-stress, multi-rhyming of "**speak** like **this**" and "**beat** like **this**." Otherwise the phrasal rhythms differ considerably, and—most effectively— considering the allusion to Rodney King—the second line sounds relatively soft and even compassionate, with a falling stress at the end.

The artistry of hip hop asks to be heard and felt in the body, then welcomed into the conscious mind, including the emotions. It does not ask to be understood analytically—even though MCs, producers, and hip hop heads *do* understand it analytically and regard their understanding as nothing more than basic rap literacy. Simply put, it depends on ongoing attention to the interplay of rhythmic patterns in the musical beat and rapped verse lines. The commentaries and statistics in this book are themselves grounded in just this attention to the interplay the beat and the poetry. We listened to, transcribed, scanned, and coded the syllable streams in rap lines in relation to their place in the ongoing beat. As we experienced and coded each line as a sequence of vocal events, each with its own pattern of different kinds of syllables and pauses, we merely confirmed and codified what all other listeners hear and feel in response to any rap track. With very few exceptions, each line has a beat-timed set of set of four stressed syllables, and one or more of these key stresses also rhymes. So we coded these two types of beated, stressed syllables **B** and **R**. Meanwhile each line has a highly variable pattern of unstressed syllables (unrhymed or rhymed), **U** and **V**, occurring before, between, or after the four beated and stresses syllables, as well as, possibly, extra stressed syllables (unrhymed or rhymed), **S** or **$**, as well as expected and unexpected pauses. The rhythmic possibilities within any individual line are huge, but all of them are anchored on the simple, required, predictable sequence of four metrical stresses in time with the four musical beats.

But if our engagement with rap's beat is as rudimentary as a head bob responding to a bass throb, or a quarter-note count synced with four stresses, the compositional beat itself is highly complex, like the poetry rapped to it. Among the beat's many compositional factors, those affecting flow include the length of its sample loop, its mix of percussive versus melodic components, its volume, its harmonics, its dissonance and, of course, its tempo.[1]

Considering tempo alone, we can observe that many rap beats fall within the range of 90 to 100 bpm, which conveniently corresponds to the usual speed of human speech. Since MCs need not only dazzle their listeners through rhythmic mastery, rhymes, and wordplay, but also need their message apprehended at first hearing, it makes sense that they would prefer this mid-tempo range—and that producers, in turn, would compose beats designed to optimize the expressive impact of rap verses. A mid-tempo 4/4 beat typically works in sixteenths, providing a template of sixteen quarter notes or quarter rests—temporal spaces realized by the MC in sixteen short syllables or pauses per bar. Actual rap lines, of course, rarely contain sixteen-syllable chains. Not only would such a rhythm sound monotonous, but language doesn't work that way. Our grammar requires phrases of varying length set apart by pauses. If this grammar is going to work within musical and metrical limits, its phrasal units need to fill similar intervals and its pauses need to recur in expected locations; but these linguistic features also need to vary in order to sound natural. The actual result of rapping at mid-tempo, in any case, is a line length ranging for the most part between eleven and fifteen syllables.

But as we all know, rap tempos vary widely. Love songs, sex and seduction songs, and buddah songs feature languid flows over slow-tempo beats. Congenial battles like Biggie's and Method Man's "The What" (1994) may also feature slow beats, while more truly combative battles seem to gain force from fast-tempo beats, allowing each antagonist to spit rhymes more menacingly. Genre, setting, personality, and artistic intent all affect tempo choice. Some rappers are comfortable and competent at any speed; others prefer mellow or rapid tempos; and still others, like Krayzie Bone and Twista, deploy fast rap as a signature style. Fast-tempo rappers may either increase the bpm of their 16ths or, within a slow or moderate tempo, "double-time" in 32ths (modeling their lines as thirty-two 8th notes).[2] At maximum speed, overt syllabic dexterity may compromise the message—or more accurately, it may itself comprise the message. And since communicating a mastery of flow is inevitably one of every MC's goals, the tendency to rap at a tempo teasingly two or three clicks above easy comprehension may prove irresistible. To quote E-40:

> Sometimes I rap fast, sometimes I rap slow, but the majority of the time, I'm not rapping too fast—a lot of cats is just listening too slow. I had to slow it down on my most recent album, just so that everybody else could catch up—I had to let them make like Heinz and catch up, that's why I did it. But I still turn it up a notch when I spit my fast rap—I do it every once in a while. I mix it up, I do it all, I still do my thing with the fast rap, but I also had to [slow] it down because everybody ain't got a lot of patience to figure out what I'm saying.[3]

The Basic Beat

Just as a pumping heart (*lub-dub, lub-dub*), a pumping lung (inhale, exhale), and motor activities like walking and running (left-right, left-right) have dichotomous parts, so does our fundamental sense of beat. We naturally group musical beats into complementary pairs. In any two-beat rhythmic phrase, one of the beats will be weak and the other will be strong, so if the audience bobs its head twice, one of the head bobs will concur with a stronger musical prominence than will the other head bob. Listeners may tap their feet on all four beats of the measure, but they may also clap their hands or snap their fingers only on the weaker beats. In fact, at the simplest level of phrase (two beats), the division between the stronger and weaker beat is often danced out within the corporeal vocabulary of dance moves: head bobs, hip sways, snaps, taps, and claps. The hip sways, snaps, and claps often only concur with the weaker beat, while the head bobs and taps often occur on both the strong and the weak beats. This two-beat phrase (*lub-dub*), with its relational sequence of strong and weak beats, provides the foundational symmetry from which music's more complex rhythms arise.

Very few musical or poetic forms actually follow this simple two-beat structure as the standard phrase, but many of them extend and stylize it across a four-beat span. Rap, blues, and most popular songs and ballads are grounded on a four-beat musical phrase. Not surprisingly, then, rap's ubiquitous time signature is 4/4. In this measure, each beat may be understood conceptually as a unit of time (analogous to a metrical foot), each taking the length of a single quarter note, with four such quarter-note beats in each bar. In actuality, however, both the performance and experience of the beat is more percussive and thus momentary, so that the quarter note in effect represents the beat and its aftermath until the next beat.

As in the simplest duple beat-phrase, beats within a 4/4 configuration have a hierarchical structure. However, in 4/4 the duple-duple grouping becomes more complexly hierarchical, not merely a succession of parallel phrases. Each beat in the bar has its complement, like the *lub* to the *dub*, but none of the beats is equal in weight. The strongest musical prominence falls on the first beat of the bar. It is complemented and followed by the weakest beat, the second. This pair forms the first half of the bar, occupying a segment of time that stretches from the first beat to, but not including, the third beat. Within the second sequence of two beats (which extends from the third beat to, but not including, the first beat of the following bar), the stronger beat is the third beat, paralleling the hierarchy in the first sequence. The fourth beat, while still a weak beat, holds more prominence than the second beat because of its terminal and transitional position, and here the drummer—and DJ, and rapper—will often improvise some ornamentation (a fill) to herald the prominence of the next first beat of a bar.

Restating this beat hierarchy according to common musical jargon, beat 1, the *downbeat*, is the inherently strongest of the four, followed by beat 3. The onsets of these strong beats are the likeliest for chord changes. They also mark the provisional boundaries for both the rapper's and the sampled beat's rhythmic phrases. We will call beats 1 and 3 *on-beats* (so that beat 1 is simultaneously an on-beat and the downbeat). Meanwhile beats 2 and 4 are commonly known as the *off-beats* or *weak beats*. These weak beats, again, are not equally weak but hierarchical: beat 4 is relatively stronger than beat 2, and because beat 4 typically occasions a flourish to anticipate the downbeat of the next bar, it is known as the *upbeat*. This is summarized in the following figure.

Position	One	Two	Three	Four
Emphasis	1	4	2	3
Name	*Downbeat*	*Weak Beat*	*On-Beat*	*Upbeat*

Fig. 1. Relative strength of the beats within the bar.

Modeling a single bar's pulses, or ictus beats,[4] helps us apprehend what underlies hip hop's creativity and innovation—the rhythmic dynamic between the poetry and its musical backdrop. Four-beat regularity fosters some degree of musical and poetic regularity, but the dynamic differences among the individual ictus beats accommodates irregular and even disobedient departures from the norm, each departure emerging from the already unique interplay between the beat's baseline and the rapper's flow. Musically, the stronger ictus beats are 1 and 3; poetically, the stronger beats are 2 and 4, where rhymes most consistently occur. Between beats 1 and 3, and then between beats 3 and 1 again, fall the twin spaces where the rapper can engage in a musical call and response with the beat—spaces of relative freedom within rap's rhythmic template. These zones of creative opportunity extend between the on-beats and across the weaker off-beats, inviting the rapper to fill them with rhymes, pauses, and other flow-nodes and flourishes.

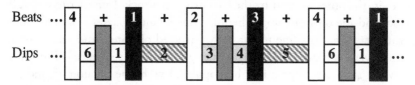

Fig. 2. Layering between the beats and dips.

Figure 2 shows the layering between the beats and dips. The tallest bars represent the four ictus beats, numbered in sequence, and the relative darkness of these bars indicates the beats' relative prominence. The set of three small gray bars meanwhile marks the normative poetic boundaries of rap lines, their onsets, midpoints, and endpoints—formal features realized in approximately ninety percent of the lines in our database, where pauses occur between (and thus create the boundaries between) dips 3 and 4 and dips 6 and 1. The gradation of tone in the dip boxes is meant to depict the relatively expansive, relatively less constrained musical spaces within which rappers normally exercise their freedom of flow.[5]

The Sampled Beat

Even though all hip hop beats manifest the same fundamental 4/4 structure of paired on- and off-beats, enabling the rap line's metrical requirements and liberties, each beat composition is, of course, unique. Each beat has its own tempo, timbre, and attitude; its own looped or digitally sampled notes, and perhaps vocals; its own drums, scratches, bass line, instrument blasts, harmonics, white noise, and other possible effects—gunshots, police sirens, broken glass, clinking glasses, laughter, shrieks, hoots, grunts, or a trumpeting elephant.

Unlike many traditional musical forms, each hip hop beat is compiled, not recorded. Rather than a sound track or mix of live musical instruments or live vocals, it is a musical collage of sampled, previously recorded sounds.[6] Sampling is basic to hip hop aesthetics, and accounts for much of the internal tension in the beat itself, its rhythmic lurches, its harmonic zigzags, its indecorous surprises. Especially in early rap, the beat's rhythmic, melodic, and harmonic components are often compressed into a single bar, which is repeated with various modulations throughout the song. Within this bar the downbeat might be filled by the floor tom of a jazz drummer recorded in 1965, the other on-beat by the bass drum of a rock drummer recorded in 1990, and the off-beats might be filled one or more snares from still other drummers. The bass line might be constructed of notes from one or more bass players, and these notes might or might not be re-sequenced. The spaces between the ictus beats might be populated with one or more quotations or snippets or unrecognizable fragments of song vocals, as well as various percussive and melodic instrumental sounds.

Some of the tracks on some early albums, such as Eric B. and Rakim's *Paid in Full* (1987), feature the DJ's solo work, and as such they exhibit virtuoso beat improvisation and variation; but most hip hop beats, from the wheels-of-steel days to today's digital studio productions, are composed so as to accommodate rap verses as well as, increasingly, choruses. Because the rapper's syllable stream needs to fill each line with recognizable words and phrases, the sampled beat has always contained sufficient space to support the poetry—space in the form of musical rests, perhaps, or space cleared by backgrounding some sample sounds. These are, in effect, shared spaces, where the DJ and MC play together. Percussion can elaborate these spaces as long as *some* constancy is retained on the bar's four beats, which might be done simply by looping the same chord changes or by adding a bass kick on every beat. Meanwhile, harmonic elements like pitches in a certain key and noises as familiar and small as a DJ's scratch encourage rappers to augment and fluctuate their voices so as to claim phrasal freedoms which might otherwise disturb the beat. In this way, the interplay between the rapper's verse lines and the beat resembles that between an improvising jazz horn soloist and his or her rhythmic and harmonic accompanists on drums, bass, and piano. By extension, the play of the chorus lines against the beat resembles that of a jazz singer or soloist reverting to the stricter, non-improvised melody of the song itself.

Thus the beat coincides with, complements, and frames the rapper's syllable stream, which in turn both reinforces and ranges freely between its ictus beats. A listener experiencing what Busta Rhymes calls "that head nod shit" and counting out beats 1 2 3 4 will simultaneously be enjoying the ongoing flow. We can illustrate this interplay of beat and rap by examining some musical snippets from songs by Rakim and Lil Wayne.

Sample Samples

Rakim earned his colossal reputation by revolutionizing hip hop. In hindsight, his DJ Eric B.'s beat from "I Know You Got Soul" seems quite modest, especially when contrasted with the rhythmic pyrotechnics of "Chinese Arithmetic," but its crisp and uncluttered samples opened up room for the MC's poetry to take the spotlight of the hip hop stage. Rejecting the loud, busy, hard funk sample sounds emerging from groups like N. W. A. and Public Enemy, Eric B.'s sampling not only grants his MC much more rhythmic freedom; it also marks a cornerstone moment in the evolution of hip hop's identity, which for the first time became distinct from the punk, jazz, and rock samples it used to motivate its music. At a time when rap was just emerging from its infancy, but when it was also becoming constrained by the politicized topics of groups like Grandmaster Flash and the Furious Five and Public Enemy, *Paid in Full* renovated the rap sound. It promoted a return to simple drum-kit and bass samples and a celebration of rhythmic wordplay, but this reversion enabled a forward leap for the function of rhyme and stress patterns. As the spaces in the musical bar became less crowded, the poetry could become more complex. In particular, the rapper could rhyme now in new places other than on beats 2 and 4 and could include extra, off-beat stresses and unexpected pauses in the line. Rakim's flow flourished within these freedoms.

Figure 3a shows the first set of bars.

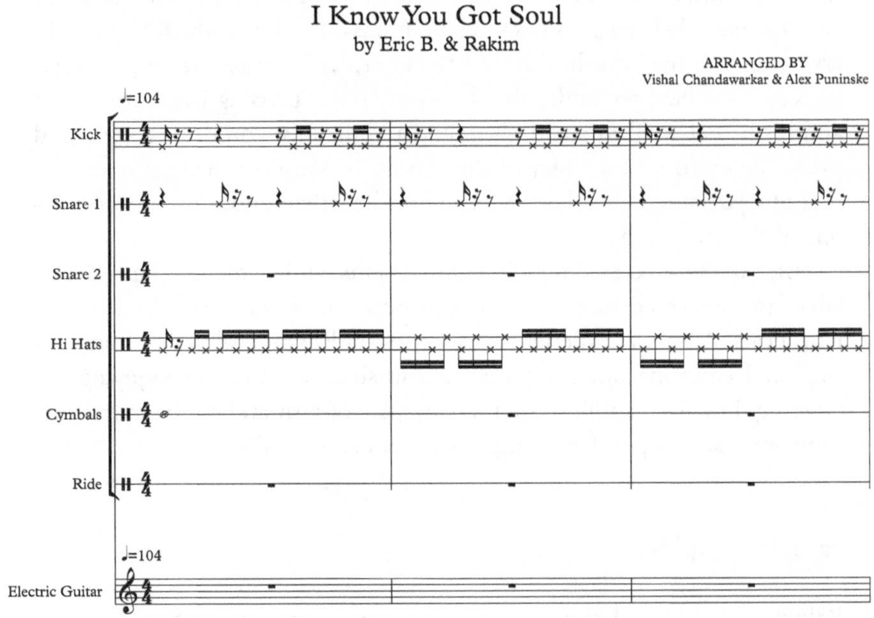

I Know You Got Soul
by Eric B. & Rakim

ARRANGED BY
Vishal Chandawarkar & Alex Puninske

Fig. 3a. Snare patterns in "I Know You Got Soul" by Rakim and Eric B. from *Paid in Full* (transcribed).

This is the beat skeleton, composed from three drum tracks in tension with one another. With the onset of Rakim's verse, another snare track further complicates and elaborates the *musical* tension while meanwhile enabling *poetic* clarity. Specifically, the kick drum has been fattening the hi-hat hits at the on-beat and surrounding the snare hit at the back half of each measure. When the rapping is introduced onto this platform, the second snare begins to guide its stress patterns, as we can see in the next two bars, illustrated in Figure 3b.

Rakim's first line picks up on the upbeat of the fourth measure and spans a bar and an eighth note. His style, unlike that of the MCs before him, does not confine the rap line to the space of a bar. His lines can span more than four beats, and they often have five stresses, one of them not coinciding

Fig. 3b. Rakim's flow and backloadedness over more than four beats in "I Know You Got Soul" by Rakim and Eric B. from *Paid in Full* (transcribed).

with the musical beat. A line might begin on the second beat of a measure, or perhaps on the upbeat, as it does above. This play with the rap's previous rhythmic expectations not only gives fresh variety to Rakim's flow; it also helps flesh out the original tensions of the break-beat (in place by the three drum tracks). The next three bars, seen in Figure 3c, return to more normal rhythms although they meanwhile, as in the previous bars, take advantage of pauses to splice the sense of metronomic time.

These two bars both innovate similarly: they backload all of the line's stresses and rhymes into the second halves of the half lines (within the second and fourth quarter-measures). This radical syncopation of time breaks one of the first traditions of early rap music, its one-bar-to-one-line ratio. Rakim's disobedience to this bar-to-line ratio pioneered further expansion of the line unit, and it opened doors for rap artists to veer from and return back to the beat in other more varied ways. It resulted in longer couplets, longer delays in line resolution, and more freedom with the expected medial pause in the line. Without Rakim's experimentation with line-unit shape and duration,

Fig. 3c. More backloadedness in "I Know You Got Soul" by Rakim and Eric B. from *Paid in Full* (transcribed).

the smooth, jazzy syncopation of his flow would not have been possible, and rap itself would never have become the multibillion-dollar industry it is today. As represented by "I Know You Got Soul," *Paid in Full* was the harbinger of changes that came to characterize all contemporary rapping.[7]

Granted, Eric B. and Rakim's avant garde style was not for every rap artist or consumer. Many rappers still adhere to the four-stress-four-beat norm—the familiar, original, and enduring rhythm of hip hop. And despite the continued relevance of *Paid in Full*, many listeners today, accustomed to songs like "Monster" by Kanye West, remain unfamiliar with naked beats made from short sample phrases. The length of the sample loop has become longer, extending commonly through two or four bars, even as the beat samples have gotten denser. Lil Wayne's "A Milli" from *Tha Carter III* exemplifies the multi-bar loop, in this case occupying eight bars, in which the beat and flow stand in tension to one another in much the same way as does early big band swing.

These eight bars repeat themselves throughout the song with only one sound being fattened by an additional sample. Structurally, however, the poetry differs drastically from what we saw in Rakim's lines. Weezy flows with a two-beated-stress-to-bar ratio, with many of his lines spanning two bars. From his first verse onward, the two-stress-per-bar ratio is interspersed and the placement of pauses becomes much more liberal, giving the contained space of a line variable durations of time. All the while, however, Weezy raps over this sample at tension and with the rhythms of the snare. While his stresses may not always coincide with the snare drums, his rhymes more often than not do. With that immediate tension in our ears, the 808 bass offsets his flow with a call-and-response, front-loaded tension. This represents a departure from those "rules" that even Rakim's sample adhered to, and it exemplifies rap's self-renewing nature. It constantly discards rules to gain more lyrical freedom, all the while finding order in simple, yet recognizable rhythms—like that of the snare drum, beating predictably at tension with the rap.

This eight-bar loop exemplifies the freedom that such beat units grant. An MC can choose to call and response with the bass-line rhythms, with those of the drum kit, or with those of other sounds. Since the musical phrases against which he or she is rapping now span well over the space of two half lines (which typically enclose two and only two grammatical phrases), the rapper is freed from repeatedly conforming with—or clashing with—the beat, and he or she can create more expansive and more flexible linguistic structures. Such flexibility, in turn, promotes the standard sixteen-bar verse format, which is easily subdivided into two eight-bar constituents. With the beat loop repeating itself only every eight bars, Weezy can in effect create eight-bar expressions sprinkled with variations that not only link smaller phrasal internally but which also reach forward—semantically, syntactically, and rhythmically—to those in the next eight bars. In sum, the phonic, rhythmic, narrative, and metaphorical relationship units are much longer, and they work within complementary symmetries.

Making Beats Today

The sampling and poetic innovations we've just reviewed are hardly unique. Rap continues to remake itself long after sample techniques have developed well beyond the nostalgically celebrated "digging in the crates." Longer and looser sample phrases have given rise to new syllabic, rhythmic, intona-

A Milli by Lil Wayne
Produced by Bangladesh

ARRANGED BY
VISHAL CHANDAWARKAR

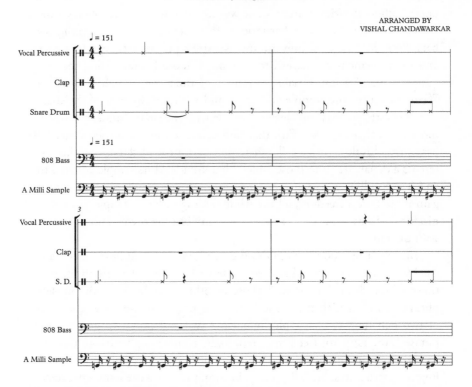

Fig. 4. "A Milli" by Lil Wayne from *Tha Carter III*.

tional, and rhyming freedoms, and these freedoms have in turn encouraged DJs and producers to steer hip hop sounds in new compositional and technological directions.

For example, rapping has recently been welcomed into the theater of jazz by modern jazz pianist Robert Glasper in *Black Radio*. This experimental album challenges sampling itself as a technique by using only live instrumentation to create the beat. In much the same way that the individual instrumentalists of a jazz trio solo over the live riffs, Lupe Fiasco, Talib Kweli, and Mic Check solo with their verses. Because the instruments are live, Glasper can experiment with less rigid backdrop beats, allowing them no repetition whatsoever for as many as sixteen bars. As Glasper's live musicians improvise, they perform a function similar to that of the sampled

beat, meanwhile occasionally stealing the spotlight from the rapper. Now the rapper can jam constantly in call-and-response mode rather than simply in response to a prescriptive beat. As the group interacts, the length of the solo space for the rapper may extend to varying lengths over a thirty-two-bar solo, as in "Always Shine (feat. Lupe Fiasco)" and "Black Radio (feat. Yasiin Bey and Talib Kweli)." This is hip hop with a different hat, because as any listener and many artists will tell you, the only thing that matters for being hip hop is *sounding like hip hop*.

To clarify, although Glasper's project would seem to abandon the skeleton rules that give hip-hop its regularity, it never abandons its adherence to and interplay with our sense of beat. Glasper's live band still obeys hip hop's play with our innate sense of beat, and for that reason it still sounds like hip hop even though it outsources the beat to live musicians.

Similar rule rejections occur in the beats of production mogul rapper and DJ Kanye West. Kanye's sample loops are long and complex, and they pay homage to an entirely different sound of rap than does "I Know You Got Soul." Kanye's beats demonstrate that Eric B.'s simple beat and its tight relationship with the basic beat's prescriptive structures is a relic of the past;

today, there's a whole lot more happening in the musical backdrop. Kanye's beats often have four- and eight-bar loops, as in "A Milli," and they employ a recorded sample sound as part of the sampling composition. Like Glasper, Kanye rejects two of the major sampling norms of Old School hip hop. For Kanye, the percussive and harmonic elements of a rap beat need retain only a minimum threshold constancy—as little as a bass kick on every downbeat of a bar, or as much as looping the exact same chord changes on both beats one and three. The liberty bequeathed by that spectrum of rigid-to-fluid backdrop accommodates the creativity in beat making that we see today, which in turn affects the rhythmic variety of what the rapper can overlay.

If Robert Glasper's and Kanye West's rule changes exemplify new and different theaters for rapping, Electronic Dance Music (EDM) creates new stages for DJing with a rapper. DJs like Pretty Lights, Major Lazer, and Flosstradamus (Trap) invite rap *into* their beats. Some DJs splice rap lines to make them behave like sample sounds, retaining hip hop structures and even beat-composition traditions while reversing the roles prominence of beat and words. In "Sunday School" by Pretty Lights, Biggie's rap lines are *sampled* responses to rhythmic phrases by the beat, and cordon the beat to its boundaries. In Flosstradamus's "Banned II," Kendrick Lamar's verse is overlaid upon a distinctively electronic Trap beat.[8] These movements, like Glasper's and Kanye's, are faithful to the tradition that is hip hop. While retaining the same feel, flexibility, and edgy sound, they pay homage to the tradition before them, even digging through a crate or two for samples. Even in Pretty Lights' latest album *A Color Map of the Sun,* he takes nineties recording equipment to create his own crate of records with live recordings. When put to a purist's skeptical test, such DJs respond to challenges to their approach as 9th Wonder did at the University of Michigan's Rackham Auditorium in 2012: sighing, running his fingers along his scalp, and remonstrating that "it just needs to sound like hip hop, man."[9]

Rhythm

Rappers, I monkey flip 'em with the funky rhythm
I be kickin', musician inflictin' composition
   —Nas, "N. Y. State of Mind"

Poetic *meter* is like time in music, experienced as a beat. Poetic *rhythm* is like the notes and rests—and how they are played. We are hardwired to produce and enjoy these rhythms, but we can't share them unless we're immersed in their rhythmic history. For any poetic tradition, this means learning and activating the rhythms inherent in its language, as embodied in its cultural expressions.

Once upon a time, rap rhythm could behave like an Old Folk ballad or hymn or jingle set to a disco beat:

Now **what** you **hear** is **not** a **test**
   I'm **rappin'** **to** the **beat** [B]
And **me**, the **groove**, **and** my **friends**
   Are gonna **try** to **move** your **feet** [B]

These again are Wonder Mike's first verse lines from "Rapper's Delight." They're grouped into a centuries-old *quatrain stanza* rhyming *abcb* with no fixed syllable count and only three stresses in the even lines. The fourth beats there are *virtual beats*: pauses in the poetry but heard in the music and felt in the body. Very few rappers ever used this form, but all rappers used its basic rhythmic components: four-beat lines with no fixed syllable count. Rather than following Wonder Mike, they worked in *rhymed couplets*, another form that's been around for hundreds of years:

> Now I'm feelin' the highs || and ya feelin' the **lows** |
> The beat starts gettin' || into your **toes** |
> Ya start poppin' ya fingers || and stompin' your **feet** |
> And movin' your body || while you're sittin' in your **seat** |

These lines by Master Gee all have four stresses on the beats, and they're grouped into couplets, each with its own end-rhyme echo. A medial pause divides them into two two-stress halves, and a terminal pause after the final-stress rhyme provides closure and integrity. This is the dominant form in hundreds of thousands of rap couplets, still heard in the work of artists like Jay-Z, André 3000, MC Lyte, Nas, Nicki Minaj, Lil Wayne, and Kendrick Lamar.

But rap has become a lot looser, funkier, longer-lined, and unrulier—that is, far more rhythmically complex—than what Master Gee could have ever imagined. We've already noted that Wonder Mike's playful, nonsensical riff ("I said a hip hop the hippie the hippie / To the hip hip hop, a you don't stop the rock it") anticipates Nas's monkey-flipping funky rhythms over a decade later, and that Melle Mel's handling of extra stresses and pauses prefigures many of the rhythmic innovations of Rakim, Ice Cube, and the major MC players of the 1990s (including Nas, The Notorious B. I. G., and Jay-Z), which still persist in the work of contemporary rappers.

We've just constructed a rudimentary rhythmic history starting with "Rapper's Delight," but rappers were flipping rhythms before then; and unlike the hastily assembled The Sugarhill Gang trio of Wonder Mike, Big Bank Hank, and Master Gee, these earlier poets rapped to beats sampled and looped by independent DJs, sound-system technicians unaffiliated with any radio station who worked as party facilitators. DJ Kool Herc was one of these hip hop originators, a fully acclimatized New Yorker with Jamaican roots. Notwithstanding the mostly accurate myth that rap music was born and bred in the United States, Herc's roots reveal another history, taking us back to Jamaican dancehall dub music, the rhythmic environment where hip hop rapping really—or also—started, back to the late 1960s and early 1970s, back to producers like Lee "Scratch" Perry," who figured out how to erase and remix the vocal tracks of hit songs and add samples to them, and to DJ's like Big Youth who could not only manipulate the "sound system" consoles but who would rap over their beats.

Big Youth had as many as seven singles on the Jamaican Top 20 chart at one time, with four remaining there for an entire year. His rapping style was a loud (yet, at times, smooth and pretty), semi-melodic, often-ad libbed chant featuring riffs like "as I would say, as I would tell you" and "doo wa shoo woo a shoo an shoo a day." His shortest line on the super-hit song "Screaming Target" (1972) consists of a single syllable on the downbeat, "AAAOW," a scream simulating the agony of being caned (and referencing a scene depicting corporeal punishment in Jimmy Cliff's "The Harder They Come"). This cry of pain and humiliation contextualizes the whole song, including its pervasive wit and fun. Big Youth's rapping is both danceable and political. He samples K. C. White's "No, No, No" in such a way as to represent the "no" of social oppression, elaborating this negativity into a series of conventional admonitions—

No no no you should never be a fool
No no no not at all
No no no you should go to school and learn the rules

—which culminate in class-conscious irony: "and so you can come to get, um civilized." Screaming, joking, riffing, swaying, and swinging are all present in Big Youth's styling and statements, which combine sharp politics, clipped phrases, and smooth partying.[1]

Jamaican dancehall/dub roots were very much at play in early hip hop rhythms, but the Jamaican fusion of politics and partying didn't mix so easily in the United States. Most early New York rap was disco-funk poetry, and even Afrika Bambaataa's Universal Zulu Nation movement (with its anti-gang focus on unity, peace, love, and fun) barely touched on the serious social issues articulated by Melle Mel in "The Message." Much of the West Coast "gangsta rap," on the other hand, either addressed these issues aggressively or celebrated hard partying, but rarely mingled these themes. Note, however, the smooth, artful, figurative conversion of hostility into humor in Ice Cube's rap in "Straight Outta Compton" (1987)—

*Nig*gaz start to **mumble**, they wanna **rumble**
Mix 'em and cook 'em in a pot like **gumbo**

—in seeming contrast to Ice-T's more "literalistic" fantasies in "Mic Contract" (1991):

Hit the trip**wire**, *duck* from the *gun***fire**
Broken glass, screech'n car **tires**,

> Bodies hit the **deck** as I commence to **wreck**
> E**ject** another *clip* and *drip* **sweat**

Also note that the menacing threats articulated by each of these gangsta personas are dressed in artful rhymes and entertaining phrasing. No one in the process of shooting automatic weapons from a speeding vehicle, after all, is going to use or think language like "I commence to wreck," and in point of fact Ice-T's entire song is an extended metaphor about battling for MC dominance. The point is not that gangsta rap can be reduced to mere entertainment, but rather that its political message is both outspoken and well-spoken.

Compare these even more clipped lines by Chuck D from Public Enemy's "Fight the Power" (1989):

> **Listen** if you're **missin'** y'all
> **Swingin'** while I'm **singin'**
> Givin' whatcha **gettin'**
> **Know**in' what I **know**
> While the **Black** bands **sweating**
> And the **rhythm rhymes rolling**
> *Got to give us* what we want
> *Gotta give us* what we **need**
> Our *freedom* of **speech** is *freedom* or death
> We got to fight the powers that **be**

There's alliteration and parallelism here, and the rhyme scheme shifts from two internal-rhyme singletons to successive *abab* and *abcb* ballad stanzas—*want* and *death* are starkly unrhymed. But all these lines have only two stressed syllables. Chuck D subordinates complex sound play to a rhythmic minimalism, which sets up the repeated call and response to follow: "Lemme hear you say . . . / Fight the power." While the poetics resemble those of a political rally more than previous rap, the beat in this song is classic hip hop, with jagged loops and dissonant chord mixes. And, as the video demonstrates, it's totally danceable: with rappers, dancing demonstrators, and marching Black Panthers all on the move together. The politics of "Fight the Power" were then, it could be said, entirely necessary, but thankfully for the art of hip hop as a genre, Rakim's contemporary rhythmic interventions, followed by the work of rappers like Big L and Guru, eventually led to a new fusion of politics and poetry such as those heard in Big Youth's records.

Not that this fusion ever dominated the American rap scene. Soon enough, a new kind of flamboyant, lavish, and effusive party style took over, more or less leaving politically consciousness rap to fend for itself as a minority voice. That's where the money was, and the party followed the money.[2] To quote from Biggie's "Party and Bullshit" (1993)[3]

> Hon*eys wanna* **chat** || but all *we wanna* know is where the party **at**

The Meter under the Rhythms

The three rap lines below all have identical metrical features: four stresses on the beat and two pauses, one at mid-line, another at the end. Queen Latifah's line from "U. N. I. T. Y." only has metrical stresses, which here are boldfaced and underscored. Mos Def's, from "The Rape Over," has an extra (non-metrical) stress before the medial pause, here only boldfaced, and an extra pause before the second beat. Common's line from "Chi City" has three off-beat stresses, for a total of seven. In other words, each of these metrical lines expresses its own particular rhythm:

```
     1                    2              3     4
You put your hands on me again || I'll put your ass in handcuffs | (Queen Latifah)
1         2              3        4
I leave the | knife and fist fight || filled with glamour | (Mos Def)
1                2        3     4
I'm back like a chiropract || wit b-boy survival rap | (Common)
```

Just as the hip hop beat dances around the rhythm of its four pulses with shifting syncopations of multiple drum, base, and melodic sampled tracks, so in hip hop poetry the one-track syllable stream not only hits the beats with stresses but weaves extra syllables between them. Having no fixed syllable count means that for rap—unlike hymns, ballads, sonnets, or Shakespeare's blank verse—there are *no prescribed rhythms* between the metrical beats and pauses. Theoretically, within rap's ordinary tempo range, 4/4 bars can house as many as thirty-two or as few as four syllables per bar. In our database of 4,115 verse lines, we find 3,770 different rhythmic forms, but this impressive diversity is nevertheless governed by metrical stresses and pauses.

We can describe rap's metrical model as a hierarchical rhythmic system. This is grounded on the musical beats, arranged in two on-beat/off-beat pairs. Over the beats fall two syllable-sequences, each of which normally contains two stresses timed to the paired beats.[4] Each of these syllable-sequences forms words grouped into half-line phrases, and the line then consists of two half-line phrases, as diagrammed in Figure 5. Note that rap's four-beat meter has three coordinated regularizing components, which, however, accommodate one or more deregularizing components. This makes the rhythm of the rap line at once predictable and infinitely variable: What regularizes the rap line are (1a) an expected *caesura* or medial pause [||], (1b) an expected *end stop* or terminal pause [|], and (1c) *four beated stresses* [/] spaced two-and-two across the caesural divide. What deregularizes the rap line is (2) that it has *no fixed syllable count* in the intervals [(x)] around and between these pauses and stresses.

Line unit	[......................................]
Half-line units: words and phrases	[....a-verse......||...b-verse.......]
Versification: syllables & pauses	(x) / (x) / (x) || (x) / (x) / (x)	
Meter: gestural/musical template	B B || B B

Fig. 5. Rap's metrical model.

In summary, the line's two metrical pauses and its four balanced stress prominences, or *lifts*, on or near the metrical beats [B][5] grant integrity, symmetry, and regularity both to the line unit and to its halves, the *a-verse* and the *b-verse*. Meanwhile the line's six intervening *dips* contain variable linguistic events. Even as regularity is sustained by the expected pauses and stresses, variety is ensured by uneven syllable counts and shifting contours (achieved through extra pauses and/or extra stresses) within lines, within half lines, and within the line's six dips, as well as by the occasional avoidance of the line's medial and terminal pauses.

We've observed that extra stresses and extra pauses do begin proliferating from the late 1980s and have since been prevalent in similar frequency.[6] Even with this evolution towards complexity, however, the basic metrical template has remained stable throughout the history of rap. An overwhelming majority of lines do have medial and terminal pauses, even though rappers feel free to glide through one or both of these pauses. Unlike the merely normative medial and terminal pauses, which aid in aligning the line to the musical beat, the four-stress pattern is a strict metrical requirement. A maximum of seven stresses may occur in rap lines, but the four-stress minimum is fixed.[7]

Fixed? Well, not quite. Anyone familiar with the work of The Notorious B. I. G. and Bone Thugs-N-Harmony knows that rap verses may occasionally contain "disobedient" three-stress lines. These non-metrical variants destabilize the beat in catchy or edgy ways. Such lines, deployed by a small minority of rappers over a fairly brief period, behave analogously to musical triplets except that their time span is the entire 4/4 bar rather than a quarter-bar.[8] They differ radically from those metrical rap lines which vary only by substituting a long-pause virtual beat for a quarter-beat phrase—such as we find in Wonder Mike's quatrains or in this line by Rakim:

<pre>
    1   2   3   4
  I es<u>cape</u> ~~~~~ || when I <u>fi</u>nish the <u>rhyme</u>
</pre>

Instead, a string of three off-beat stresses fills the same temporal space as would four metrical stresses, and this rhythmic shift is accentuated by the absence of a mid-line pause.[9] The fourth line in this extended rhyme sequence from Common's "Chi City" illustrates the phenomenon:

The **game** need a **make**over || My **man** retired | **I**'ma take **over**
Tell these **half**time **nig**gas || **break**'s **o**ver
I'm **raw** | **hust**las || getcha **ba**kin' **so**da
Too many **rape** the **cul**ture
Leave **rap**pers with ca**reers** || **and** their **faith** **o**ver
It's a **war** goin' **on** || you can't **fake** bein' a **sol**dier

Here the three-stress variant is powerfully mimetic, its missing component expressing, fleetingly, a sense of loss, even as it melds rhythmically within a series of normally variant lines, some of which contain three-stress half lines and unexpected pauses also generating three-part rhythms.

The fact that rare, non-metrical, three-stress lines do occur is suggestive of a more general truth about rap artistry: that MCs possess a vast repertoire of techniques for rhythmic variation even beyond syllable-count variation within dips, beyond the insertion of extra stresses and pauses, beyond the avoidance of expected pauses, beyond the use of long, beat-length pauses in lieu of metrical stresses. The phenomenon of three-stress triplets, although outside the hip hop mainstream, illustrates what's constantly exciting about rap as a poetic genre: the inventiveness of flow itself, which includes a seemingly infinite range of rhythmic nuance. No one else sounds like Guru. No one else sounds like Lil Wayne. Ditto Method Man, Tupac, Snoop Dogg, or Biggie. All of these rappers cultivate subtle individual habits of rhythmic flow which—along with their distinctive tones of voice—give them their idiolects.[10] Rakim's pauses are never exactly the same length. Rappers like Jay-Z and Missy Elliott use many varieties of stresses. The art of first-class MCing requires this level of virtuosity.

And then there is rhyme—the focus of our next chapter. Rhyme is rap's most prominent rhythmic variant. Since rhyme enhances syllables, it adds extra weight even to stressed syllables, so within any string of metrical stresses it can make some of them more prominent than others. Rhyme can also add weight to extra, non-beated stresses, and rhyme can even add a subtle potency to unstressed syllables. Such rhythmic nuance happens over and above the ways in which the beat track's sample hits—a bass note, a tight snare, a loose snare, a clap, an opening hi-hat—can fatten or thin down this or that syllable. And meanwhile, as we've already seen, rhyme may occur in as many as four *metrical positions*, as well as in *off-beat positions*, allowing countless permutations of *temporal rhyme structure* within the rap line.

Stress, Semantics, and Spacing

Rap, like all poetic arts, is based in its language of origin. It deploys English speech contours, including stresses and intonations, to express thoughts governed by common, habitual grammatical patterns. When people speak English, they typically break up their speech not only into formal units like phrases, clauses, and sentences, but into *tone units*. These tone units may correspond with grammatically logical phrases, but they may also express thoughts like "well, you know uh," or "hey, I'm thinking I might wanna maybe." Whatever the unit of speech, it's likely to end with a stress and some kind of pitch accent, followed by a pause. These normal speech contours help scaffold the flow of rap, which is also spoken (in a stylized way), and which, like other poetry, is structured into rhythmic units—half lines, lines, couplets—more regularly than those in normal speech.

And at the level of beat, rap in English is stress-timed, like English itself. In conversation, we differentiate stressed words from unstressed words in a semantic hierarchy. We stress our content words (nouns, verbs, adjectives, adverbs), but we don't stress our merely dutiful function words like prepositions, conjunctions, and pronouns. We modulate our stressed and unstressed syllables in this way without even thinking about it, and we do this rhythmically. We space out the stresses in our key words so that they fall at regular intervals. We may say "Cali**for**nia," for example, but then we will also say "**Cali**fornia **drea**ming"—so it sounds good. This is called *eurythmy*.[11] What we hear in rap—a rhythmic articulation of important stressed syllables—is what we already hear in English, the difference being is organized into regularly pulsing four-beat lines, not just speech that naturally pulses on continuously.[12] As a result, what we experience when we hear any competent rapper is an ever-unfolding thematic grid. If we mute his or her non-beated words, we still get the essential meanings:

Fuck	police	straight	underground	
young	nigga	bad	brown	
other	color	so	think	
have	authority	kill	minority	[Ice Cube]
used	be	Malcolm	X	
Now	planet	one	KRS	[KRS-One]
know	say	genu-	ine	
Don't	hardrock	really	gem	
Babygirl	respect	just	minimum	[Lauryn Hill]

The Syllable Stream

As we expand our attention from the line's regular repetition of metrical stresses to the entire complex of its rhythms, our focus shifts to the spaces between these stresses. Any of the line's six dips, three per half line, may potentially be filled with some combination of unstressed syllables, extra stresses, and pauses—or with nothing at all. It is these syllable-count and pause variations within the dips which determine a line's flow and feel. Here are four of Big Boi's lines from verse 1 of Outkast's "Reset," with the stress contours marked and the syllable counts of the dips and half lines tallied:

x / x x x / x x ‖ / x   x   x / x   1/2/2‖0/3/1   8‖6
From T&A to DNA, feelings turn to children

x x x / x   x x x x x x / x ‖ / x   x   x   /   3/7/1‖0/3/0   13‖5
Incarceration without rehabilitation really don't mean shit

       x x / x / ‖x x x x   x /x   x x   /   2/1/0‖5/3/0   5‖10

Little Ricky's home, he gotta serve probation for six months

       x x x   / x x \   x x / x ‖ / x x   /   3/5/1‖0/2/0 11‖4

But Uncle Donnel and Ol' Dirty Bastard still in the joint

Granted that all rappers (and regions, periods, song types) may have their own particular styles, whatever the stylistic influences on this song may be, Big Boi uses some unusually long dips and he *never* raps a line with syllables filling all six dips. Together, these techniques generate a feel of edginess. It's hard to spit seven straight syllables between beats, even at a modest tempo, and Big Boi therefore must accelerate in such spots; but then he goes to the other extreme and cuts syllables, denying whatever smoothness one or two syllables might have lent to an empty dip.

And each particular line has its own special rhythm. Following Melle Mel's lead in "The Message," Big Boi's verse characterizes human life from conception and birth through childhood, adolescence, and adulthood as a condition increasingly damaged by social adversity. In this context (but for the moment avoiding Mel's ominous tone), the line about conception sounds appropriately pleasant and fun, wittily rhyming the erotic play, molecular events, and emotions required to generate children. Its eight-six rhythm sounds lovely too: it copies the rhythm of a ballad stanza, whose asymmetrical pairing approaches the Golden Ratio. The only jarring thing about this line is that *children*, it turns out, rhymes with *existence*. This smart rhyme, echoing only the paired vowels and a nasal [n], sounds ugly, and it flips whatever warm feelings we might get from imagining children into their mere existence. In contrast, the "incarceration without rehabilitation" line is extremely harsh thematically and cacophonous rhythmically. Note the ugly polysyllabic words of the first half line (contrasting with second half line's blunt expression), the extraordinarily long seven-syllable dip, the empty dips before and after the third and fourth stresses, and the extreme syllabic asymmetry of the two half lines.

The next two lines form the verse's final couplet, with the teenager on parole and the two adults still incarcerated—a blood relative and a fellow rapper (the Wu-Tang Clan's Ol' Dirty Bastard, who would soon would die in prison at age thirty-five). Each line is imbalanced, but together they present a chiastic symmetry: their frame of short half lines ending on "home" and "the joint" hints at the dismal expectation of recidivism for young black males—home for now, but probably heading back inside. And the second line has an extra stress, complicating its awkward rhythm. Finally, where's the rhyme? If *children* and *existence* rhyme only through assonance and the nasal [n], *months* and *joint* have nothing in common except the [n]. Such dissonant rhymes support the rhythmic clash and cacophony produced by the extremely varied syllable counts in Big Boi's dips, half lines, and lines.

Line length in our database of verse lines ranges from five to twenty-two syllables.[13] This twenty-one-syllable line is rapped by Lupe Fiasco in "Dumb It Down":

Or **ly**ing in the **de**sert | I'm **fly**ing on **Pe**gasus || you're **fly**ing on the **phea**sant

Like Big Boi, Lupe works with longer dips, but not to create dissonance. Where Big Boi clips syllables from at least one dip per line, Lupe fills all six dips, meanwhile eurythmically spacing off-beat stresses within two of these dips—each in the a-verse. This half line, containing an astonishing fourteen syllables and four stresses, could stand alone as a complete line, but Lupe doubles time here to keep the beat. Its off-beat rhyming stresses give weight to the dips, not only allowing no more than three consecutive unstressed syllables, but making the upbeat feel like the downbeat and vice versa, backloading beats 1 and 2. Lupe demonstrates this rhythmic mastery just after comparing his rise in the hip hop community with Leon Spinks, the boxer who upset Muhammad Ali in the 1978 heavyweight championship, and now he flaunts the speed of his mythical steed, the airborne "Pegasus," compared with the fancy but clunky "pheasant" ridden by his contemporaries.[14] This boast is about syllabic speed, control, and versatility. Two pauses separate three seven-syllable phrases, and while the impressive rhythms are loaded into the front of the bar, the knock-out punch that finishes the bar is delayed till the final two syllables. Like a trumpet player improvising as he threads through a jazz lick, Lupe flirts with the rhythms, only to reclaim prosodic control in the more predictable, tighter b-verse.

In stark contrast, our shortest lines have medial dips of just one syllable, with empty initial and final dips in both half lines. Here is The Notorious B. I. G. rapping portly syllables in "Notorious Thugs," sounding like Sonny Rollins sometimes does on tenor sax. Note how Biggie adds one syllable and then another to the third and fourth lines, projecting confident ease:

```
 /   x   /   || /   x    /
Spit your game, talk your shit
```

```
  /    x    / ||  /    x    /
```
Grab your gat, call your clique
```
    /    x    / || /   x    /    \
```
Squeeze your clip, hit the right one
```
  /    x     /  ||x  /   x   \     /
```
Pass that weed, I got to light one

Over the history of rap, average rap line length, has been about thirteen syllables, with the great majority of lines falling in the twelve-to-fifteen syllable range, as the graph below indicates. Although the familiar rap lines of an "in" period, say 1982 to 1984 (think Kurtis Blow, Afrika Bambaataa) or 1994 to 1996 (think Big L, Biggie, Jay-Z, Mobb Deep) show relative constancy in meta-features like line length and dip behavior, emcee innovation from one period to the next has driven line expansion. Meanwhile line types from earlier periods often continue to resurface—in portions or as a whole—serving as tokens, allusions, or tributes to prior styles and emcees, meaning that overall growth can take longer to surface, despite longer lines being more frequent but often offset by shorter ones.

Taken together, Figures 6 and 7 reflect this innovation. The push to develop novel sound styles and flows can be seen in line length range expansion as time goes on, but these average and median line lengths fluctuate within a relatively narrow range, governed by principles of eurythmy and contained, in part, by a tradition of homage and conscious reference. Expansions skirt three boundaries: heightened variation, audience expectations of rhythmic forms (i.e., their manifest rhythmic template), and the rules of the game. We note that the somewhat slower oscillation between line lengths in the beginning of the graph is likely also influenced by distribution norms and music publication frequency, which affect how quickly artists react to trending line types.

As evidenced in these figures, this relatively restricted norm suggests that line length per se is not a major consideration for rappers trying to vary their flow. Extraordinarily long or short lines, however, often serve as special effects meant to color a particular theme, as well as, in some cases, opportunities to demonstrate poetic prowess. Here is Biggie again, mixing up his syllable counts in "Warning" from six to sixteen to twenty to eight. Both of his signature lines—short, compact, and supremely confident—have four balanced stresses, but, lacking the expected medial pauses, they sound at once tough and smooth. The longer lines each have extra stresses. Only the hyper-aggressive, twenty-syllable line has a caesura, and the absence of this

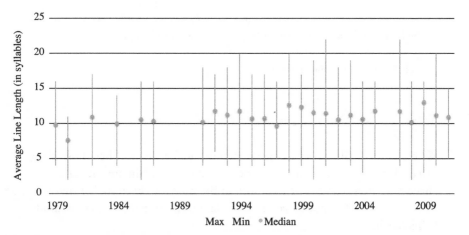

Fig. 6. The average length of rap lines from 1979 to 2009, showing maximum, minimum, and median lengths. Averaging about thirteen syllables, rap line length has remained roughly stable, ticking up slightly in recent years, but range has expanded, as has the variation within these lines. (Note: the graph includes non-syllabic vocal events.)

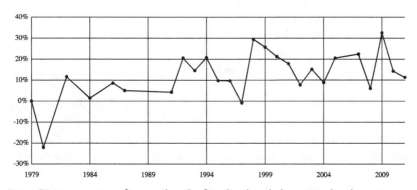

Fig. 7. Percent variation of average length of rap line length, by year, indexed to 1979.

pause in the previous longish line allows it to express the first line's cool, understated assurance while displaying its hot, flashy weaponry.

```
/    x  /  x   /    /
```
Betcha Biggie won't **slip**.
```
x  x  x   \ x /   x   x   \   / x   / x x x   /
```
I got the **calico** with the **black talons** loaded in the **clip**

x x x /   x   x / x x ‖ x x / x x x \ x / x x
So I can **rip** through the **ligaments**, put the fuckas in a bad pre**dicament**,
   x / x   /   / x   /
Where all the foul **niggas went.**

Extra Stresses, Extra Pauses, Unexpected Glides

When Lauryn Hill addresses the women in the first verse of her "Doo Wop (That Thing)," her rhythms of course vary, but they maintain the same balanced four-stress pattern we have seen in Big Boi's rap. Even so, her rhythms feel comparatively upbeat, genuine yet jazzy, emotionally earnest without being harsh:

  /   x   x / ‖ x   x   x x / x   /
Who you gon' tell when the repercussions spin
  / x   x   x   / ‖ x   x   / x x x   /
Showing off your ass 'cause you're thinking it's a trend
  /   / ‖ x x x x / x x x /
Girlfriend, let me break it down for you again
  x   / x xx / x ‖ x   x / x x x/
You know I only say it 'cause I'm truly genuine

The secret is in the dip lengths and in their quality. Like Big Boi's dips, they contain (here) exclusively unstressed syllables and no interruptive extra pauses. And they are shorter, with a maximum of four syllables. Now, one problem with scanning syllables as either stressed or unstressed is that we miss the subtle range between these two categories, and in fact the "re-" in *repercussions* and the "break" in *break it **down*** are each slightly more pronounced, giving these four-syllable dips a eurythmic feel. And the rest of the intervals are one, two, or three syllables long—intervals long known and felt as musically pretty.

When Lauryn turns to address the men in her second verse, she inserts extra stresses with rougher phrasing between them, extending her dip length to five and repeatedly clumping stresses together. In the middle line here, all six stresses fall on rhyme words, drawing attention to the triple-rhyming half lines. In this rhythmic context, the x x x dips in all three lines sound mocking, not genuine:

x   /   x / ‖ x   x   x   x   / x x   x   /   \
Let's stop pretend, the ones that pack pistols by they waist men
/ x x x   /   \ ‖ / x   x   x x   /   \
Cristal by the case men, still in they mother's basement
x   x x   /   / ‖ / x   x   x   \ x /   \
The pretty face men claiming that they did a bid men

We have seen that both Lauryn and Biggie add extra stress-complications to their lines, and that Biggie sugars the flow of one of his lines by gliding through the expected medial pause. In this next unusually long (seventeen-syllable) line, Lauryn also foregoes the caesura:

x x / x x   x   /   x x / x   \ x x   x x   /
Let it sit inside your head like a million women in Philly Penn

About ten percent of all rap lines glide through the medial pause even though in almost every one of them there is a medial syntax break where a pause *could* naturally occur. In Lauryn's line, for example, the a-verse consists of a main clause with an imperative verb, and the b-verse consists of a long phrase in the form of a simile. There's a grammatical juncture but no performance pause, suggesting that the main reason for avoiding the caesura is to vary the rhythm—and perhaps simply to make a very long line easier to get through. Obviously this factor doesn't influence these signature glide-through lines by Lil Wayne—

I'm a young money millionaire
Tougher than Nigerian hair

—which are short yet deliciously fluidly drawling. Note that all of the consonants in the first line are liquid ones, but Weezy can glide through sounds of any kind.

A similar stylistic effect on a larger scale occurs where rappers avoid end pauses, gliding from one line to the next. Talib Kweli's fluidity between lines and between half lines (as well as his surprise pauses, extra stresses, and extra rhymes) define his flow as demonstrably non-monotonous and metro-competent. His first verse in "Definition" opens with two enjambed lines, followed by a line without any medial pause but with pauses after beats 1 and 3:

> **Brook**lyn New York **Ci**ty || where they **paint** murals of **Big**gie[15]
> In **cash** we **trust** 'cause it's **ghet**to **fab**ulous, || **life** look **pret**ty
> What a **pi**ty | **blunts** is still **fif**ty **cents** | it's in**tense** |

In the "what a pity" line, neither the unexpected pauses nor the absence of the expected caesural pause are thematically necessary, for simply shifting the place of the initial exclamation would produce a rhythmically normal line. Talib Kweli's intent, clearly, is to create tonal surprise and instability. Meanwhile, the first pause highlights the rhythm-and-rhyme echo of "life look pretty" and "what a pity," making the sequence sound jarringly inane. The enjambments at the end of lines 1 and 2 are also features of style, not expressions of grammatical logic. Serious thematic ruptures occur between all three lines, but these remain unarticulated, as if we are experiencing blurred cultural clashes—which we are.

This is actually the norm for enjambment in rap. Although some MCs run lines together logically, when there is no syntactic juncture, as does Snoop Dogg in "Gin and Juice"—

> Later on that day || my homey Dr. Dré
> came through with a gang of Tanqueray |

—it's far more common for the glide to override an expected, logical pause for emotional effect. When Tupac Shakur does this, as in "Keep Ya Head Up," is tone is often one of earnest anger:

> I wonder why we take from our women
> Why we rape our women || do we hate our women? |

Conversely, end stops may also be used stylistically as a kind of tease, to call attention to line endings which *should* logically flow right on through, uninterrupted. Biggie does this in "Party and Bullshit" to create comic suspense:

> Bitches in the back looking right | eous |
> In a tight | dress || I think I might | just | ←
> Hit her with a little Biggie 101, how to tote a gun

So does KRS-One in "Hold." Because this entire composition uses just one homophonic rhyme (*hold/hole/whole*, etc.), end stops may actually underscore moments, as at the ends of the first and third lines, where there "should" be no pause:

> I make a mayonnaise sandwich || out of some whole- | ←
> Wheat| I'm feelin' weak, | I can't hold |
> I gotta rob somebody tonight || and take the whole | ←
> Bank roll || some cash I gotta hold |

By now it should be abundantly clear that rappers constantly vary their rhythms by changing their syllable counts within lines, half lines, and dips, and by inserting, removing, or shifting their pauses. But how free—or, statistically speaking, how random—is this variation? Let's look again at Lauryn Hill's long line:

> x x / x x   x   / . x   x / x   \   x   x   xx   /
> Let it sit inside your head like a million women in Philly Penn

Here we insert a dot [.] in our scansion to indicate the syntax break (between the main clause and simile) where Lauryn might have paused but didn't. The dot is a placeholder for the expected medial pause. It lets us visualize what we may not hear, that the line still has six metrical dips, but dip 3 is empty and dip 4 has two syllables. The whole line has this dip pattern: 2/3/0 2/6/0.[16] In both half lines, the medial dips are the longest and the final dips are empty. In the a-verse, the two-and three-syllable dips are utterly common, and its phrasing echoes that in many other lines of "Doo Wop (That Thing)." In the b-verse, the super-long medial dip, with its extra stress, and the triple rhyme of *million, women,* and *Penn,* along with the missing medial pause—make the flow feel powerfully unique.

What does it mean—or rather, how does it feel?—that Big Boi's medial dips are also longer than his other dips, and that Big Boi's final b-verse dips are also relatively short (one syllable or none)? How do KRS-One's, Biggie's, Talib's, Mos Def's, Common's, Jay-Z's, and Lil Wayne's lines relate to this pattern, or is there even any pattern? Are their flow habits and flow choices matters of individual style, or are they generic to rap itself? Both, it seems. As we look at some statistics on rap rhythms, we'll discover that although rappers may differ greatly in their particular rhythmic choices, they also conform, consciously or not, to rhythmic norms.

The Big Picture

From 1979 to the present, many MCs have strived to create and market their own differentiated voice and flow. No one else sounds quite like Mel, or Rakim, or Ice Cube, or KRS-One, or Guru, or Snoop, or Tupac, or Biggie, or Lauryn Hill, or Eminem—the list goes on and on. Meanwhile there are commonalities and influences. We can hear a little bit of Kurtis Blow in Mel, for example, or of Cold Crush in Public Enemy, or of André 3000 in Kendrick Lamar. And there are regional rapping styles which may both persist as such and influence individual MCs in other regions. In these ways, rap style can be said to be constantly evolving and shifting. Throughout its history, however, rap's rhythms have always adhered to the four-beat, four-stress metrical template. As we've seen, a few rappers have occasionally inserted three-stress lines into their verses, either with virtual beats expressed within pauses or, more radically, foregoing this temporal filler and taking up only three-quarters of a bar. But with these rare exceptions, rap lines have adhered to the rhythmical norm of four stresses on the beat, typically grouped in pairs.

Meanwhile the syllable rhythms have changed. The most common line length has grown from ten syllables to twelve to thirteen, and meanwhile, with the addition of extra stresses (beyond the four on the beat) and extra pauses (beyond the medial and end-line pauses), the line's rhythmic behavior has become less obviously restricted by the meter. In turn, the *range* of line lengths has expanded greatly—from between five and twelve syllables to between five to twenty-two syllables. As we've already noted, the number of uninterrupted unstressed syllables within dips is limited—both for reasons of eurythmy and because it difficult to spit such syllable-strings—so it makes performance sense that longer lines would produce extra stresses and pauses. In early rap, extra pauses occurred as infrequently as one out of every ten lines; today, a listener would not be surprised to hear extra pauses once every five or even fewer lines. In addition, the rap line's rhythm has changed as a result of an increasing deployment of imbalance, both between the a-verse and b-verse and among the line's successive dips in each half line.

So, when we listen to songs from the earliest rap era (1979–1982), we may hear plenty of rhythmic variety, which is the nature of hip hop, but we also keep hearing formulaic phrases, such as b-verses with rhythms of **/ x /** and **x x / x /**. And we keep hearing lines with no fewer than nine syllables and no more than twelve. Complementing this regularity of length, we keep hearing regular caesural and terminal pauses. We might hear an off-beat stress from time to time, but we're never expecting such a flourish. All in all, the rap line is quite predictable in a disco kind of style, characterized by metronomic on-beat stresses, short dips, and regular pauses. If rap had gone out of style in 1982, as some predicted, we might treat these rhythmic behaviors as features of the quaint genre known as disco rapping.

As noted in Hot Vinyl, Duke Bootee and Melle Mel's performance on "The Message" was rhythmically groundbreaking. Not only did they form couplets with lines of extraordinarily uneven syllable lengths, some of their lines linked long a-verses and short b-verses, among others with proportions more like Kurtis Blow's. This technique—which in effect destabilized a-verse expectations—was quickly adopted by the entire rap community, and it came to define the rhythmic behaviors of the genre altogether. As this happened, there were huge creative and commercial consequences for MCs. If rap was not going to sound monotonous and predictable, if the rap audience came to *expect* rap to sound rhythmically fresh and unpredictable, then MCs would be compelled to create their own individually identifiable flows. This is where Rakim came in and why he looms as one of rap's most important innovators. A New York MC whose main goal was to get played on the radio and who famously rapped that "it's not where you're from, it's where you're at," Rakim ushered in a new era.

Up to 1987, rhythmic stagnation threatened the genre. While a-verse rhythms had continuously become more complicated, the b-verse had remained relatively unchanged—until Rakim introduced a particular kind of rhythmic backloadedness. With *Paid in Full*, Rakim and Eric B. gave mainstream rap greater rhythmic and syntactical flexibility. Over the minimalist beat of Eric B., Rakim's flow made use of syncopation, frequent off-beat stresses, longer b-verses, and expected enjambment. In Rakim's 1987 hit "I Know You Got Soul," the very first line illustrates this new kind of stress density, which in effect adds weight to the dips while destabilizing a listener's expectation for a caesural pause. The italicized syllables are unbeated stresses:

It's **been** a *long* **time** || I **shouldn**'a *left* **you**
With**out** a **strong rhyme** to **step** *to*

In the very first line, Rakim packs in six stresses over four beats. The two extra stresses cluster at the back end of the a-verse and at the back end of the b-verse, so each half line ends with paired stresses. This backloaded rhythmic density shifts the sense of constant time that we came to expect after "The Message." With Rakim, rhythmic jolts occur between our head bobs and toe taps in the second half of the bar. It's jazzy, it's sexy, and it caught its listeners by surprise. This is syncopation in action, decorating the weaker of the on-beat dips with rhythmic frills.

Rakim's rhythmic backloadedness in turn changed the hierarchy of dip weights. The second dip would continue to be one of the longest, but now the fifth dip would become almost as long and of parallel importance. Even as the intricate rhythmic play of the rap line was concentrated especially in the medial dips between stresses 1 and 2 and between stresses 3 and 4; the lengths of the first, third, and sixth dips remained relatively predictable fixtures in the shape of the line. By way of compensation, almost all of the other dips, especially the fourth, expanded somewhat, while the first dip actually shrank. The main effects of these shifts were that the rap line become longer while its onset became much more coordinated with the musical downbeat.

Many hip hop fans, while acknowledging the importance of Rakim, assume that the stylistic evolution of the line was primarily a consequence of rapping faster over the same tempo. We believe instead that its secret lay both in the introduction of extra, optional stresses and in the concomitant use of the extra, optional pauses. For example:

```
x /   x \ x   / x
I do this for my culture
  x   x   x    / |  x x \ x x   / ‖  x x / xx x   /  x
To let 'em know what a nigga look like when a nigga in a Roadster
  /   x   x   x   /  ‖x x /   x   x / x
Show 'em how to move in a room full 'o vultures
  /  x x   / x‖x   /   x x x x  / x
Industry shady it need to be taken over (Jay-Z, "Izzo (H. O. V. A.)")



  \   x x    /     x  x x   /  x ‖   / x   \ x   x x   /
Be havin' dreams that I'ma gangster—drinkin' Moets, holdin' TECs
  / x   x   x   / . x     x / ‖ x x  /
Makin' sure the cash came correct then I stepped
  x /   x   x   /  ‖ / x x x    /
Investments in stocks, sewin' up the blocks
  x /  /  ‖ x x  / x    x  \ x  /
To sell rocks, winnin' gunfights with mega cops (Nas, "N. Y. State of Mind")
```

The expansion of the line continued through the 2000s, when MCs would introduce yet another lengthening innovation, which resulted in the twenty-plus-syllable line. Aesop Rock and Lupe (again) demonstrate their lyrical control over busy lines:

Fathom the **spli**cing of first generation **fuck** up or **trickle**-down anti-hero **smack**
(Aesop Rock, "Daylight" 2001)

Or **ly**ing in the **de**sert | I'm **fly**ing on **Pe**gasus ‖ you're **fly**ing on the **phea**sant
(Lupe Fiasco, "Dumb It Down" 2007)

With rhythms as dense and complex as these, creating surprise and variation had to rely on the use of a new type of line shaping. Instead of stabilizing line flow with medial caesuras, these lines merge the third and fourth dips, meanwhile segmenting the a- and b-verses into smaller parts. Mos Def demonstrates this structure as early as 1998, just before it becomes permanent in the genre:

```
/  x  x  x   / x ‖  /  \  x  \  x  /
No Batman and Robin, can't tell between the cops
 x  x  / x |  /  x . /  x | x  /  \  x
and the robbers, they both partners, they all heartless
```
(Mos Def in "Respiration")

It's hard to conceive how much more variation could occur in a single line without disrupting the criteria of the four-beat rhythmic template. Although rappers often value rhyme as their most important poetic contribution, they understand that it can only be audibly effective when set within an intelligible flow. Ultimately, rap depends on a clear conversation among the rhythms of rhyme, the rhythms of the syllable-stream, and of the beat itself. Over a busy rhythmic line, rhyme offers a kind of variation and stability, anchoring the end of rhythmic phrases with signaling rhymes.

Frontloaded Beat, Backloaded Rap

So far we've looked at rap rhythms mainly as temporal patterns laid over the ongoing musical beat, but it's important also to realize that the beat and the poetry interact in a dynamic of systemic rhythmic opposition. The musical beat is always frontloaded in that the downbeat and the next on-beat (in third position) feel stronger than the two off-beats (in second and fourth position), but the poetry is almost always is contrastingly backloaded.[17]

Most obviously, rhyme frequently marks the off-beat stresses 2 and 4, but only rarely marks the on-beats stresses 1 and 3:

> Been had a little **horsy** named Paul Re**vere**
> Just me and my **horsy** and a quart of **beer**
> Riding cross the **land**, kicking up **sand**
> Sheriff's posse on my tail 'cause I'm in de**mand** (Ad-Rock)

> I like 'em brown, yellow, Puerto Rican or **Hai***tian*
> Name is Phife Dawg from the Zulu **Na***tion* (Phife)

> Yo, from the first to the **last** *of it*, delivery is **pass***ionate*
> The whole and not the **half** *of it*, vocab and not the **math** *of it* (Mos Def)

In rap, stressed syllables on the beat are always louder and often longer and differently pitched than other syllables, and since rhymes not only typically fall on these strong syllables but add still more emphasis to them, rhyme patterns are an excellent indicator of linguistic prominence.[18] But citing rhyme positioning as evidence of rap's backloadedness doesn't address the question of *why* this backloadedness occurs. The best explanation is also the simplest: it's natural. In English, as already noted, there are two kinds of accents which give prominence to certain speech components: stresses and intonations. Stresses mark some classes of words as more important semantically than others, but intonations, also known as pitch accents, combine with stresses to give contextual information about whole strings of words. The main reason we can differentiate questions from statements is that they end with different pitch accents. Pitch accents can also communicate that information is old or new, that irony is intended, or that a speaker is done talking for the moment—among many other things. We use pitch accents (as well as stresses) unconsciously, but these tonal markers communicate a lot of what we mean and feel. A seemingly simple, clear sentence like "I love you" can sound—and be—affectionate, passionate, routine, false, whining, defensive, desperate, or even hostile, proving that meaning may reside not so much in the words as in how the words are manipulated. "I love **you**," with a down-gliding pitch accent on the stress, can translate as a defensive "I love you, not her." "I **love** you" with an up-gliding pitch accent on the stress, can communicate defensiveness *and* desperation.

Like anyone else expressing ideas and emotions, rappers use lots of different intonations, but they do this mostly within the metrical grid. Because pitch-accented stresses mark the end of phrases and clauses, followed by pauses, these prominences in rap tend to fall at the ends of a- and b-verses, line units, and couplets. The medial and terminal pauses prompt accented stresses, which are further formalized by rhyme. All of which is to say that even though the counterpoint between the beat's frontloadedness and the flow's backloadedness is musically exciting, it's also totally natural. We suspect that this rhythmic counterpoint, perpetually stimulating, subtle, and even magical, is one of the secret reasons for rap's popularity and endurance.

Two couplets from Tupac Shakur's "Keep Ya Head Up," each deploying triplet phrasing,[19] help to show how intonations support rap's backloadedness:

x   I   x   x x   2   x   3   4 x x
Last night my buddy lost his whole **family**

x   x x   I   x   **2**   x x x   3   x   x   x **4** x x
It's gonna take the **man in me** to conquer this in**sanity**

x   x   *I* x x   **2**   x   x x   **3**   x   **4**
And I *realize* momma *really* **paid the price**

x   x x   I   x   **2** x   3   x   **4**
She near*ly* **gave her life** to **raise me right**

Tupac's technique is similar in both couplets, but he shifts one-beat triplets to two-beat triplets, or in other words, from feminine rhymes and multi rhymes extending past the beat to two-stress multis hitting successive beats. Both couplets have strongly backloaded alpha lines, and both couplet units are strongly backloaded in that their beta lines contain more rhymes. We might imagine that the second couplet's backloadedness is mitigated by the secondary *realize/really* rhyme on beat 1 of the alpha line and by the fact that all four stresses rhyme in the beta line, but Tupac's actual *performance* of these rhymes, his intonations and degrees of stress on the various syllables, is completely backloaded. In these quotations, the underscores of the off-beats indicate what we hear: that *momma* takes a lot more stress than *realize*, and that the rhyme chain sounds like "**paid** the **PRICE** . . . **gave** her **life** . . . **raise** me **RIGHT**."

Fans of Tupac value the earnestness conveyed through this sort of predictable accenting of theme, but critics may find his flow somewhat too predictable.[20] In general, rappers need to keep mixing it up to earn our interest. Not all of Mos Def's lines rhyme on every off beat. Some of Phife's lines have internal rhyme. And more importantly, rappers have increasingly cultivated ways of mitigating the essential backloadedness of their poetics. Eliminating rhyme is not one of these ways. Eliminating end rhyme, in particular, is not one of these ways. Even though, as we have seen, Big Boi concludes his verse on "Reset" with a non-rhyming couplet; André 3000, also of Outkast, likewise at times experiments with non-end-rhyming lines; and a few indie rappers like Aesop Rock also (rarely) withhold end rhyme, this is always a special effect.[21] There is no free verse rap, and there is no blank verse rap. Rap rhymes. Within this constraint, however, rappers do a number of things to mix things up, to mitigate the predictability of their backloadedness.

One way, as we've seen, is to glide through the expected caesural and/or end pause, in effect denying the half line or the line its tonic structure—no pause, no pitch accent. Another is to alter the line's segments either by substituting alternative pauses or by inserting additional ones:

> What a **pity** | blunts is still *fifty* **cents** | it's in**tense** | (Talib Kweli)

> What is | paper to a **nigga** if the **nigga** don't **stack?** |
> Why do these | **girls** || look so **good** in the summer? | (Common)

> **Wheat** | I'm feelin' **weak**, | I can't **hold** | (KRS-One)

Talib's line mixes it up further by rhyming syllables in positions 3 and 4, and by rhyming the position 1 syllable with an unstressed word. Within an unbalanced 1–3 line, Common deploys 2- and 3-position rhymes (repetitions) in addition to the end rhyme in one question, then in the next question he uses a 1-1-2 line with alliterating words in parallel positions. In KRS's 1-2-1 line, the three-and-one rhyme structure is like that in Big Boi's "T&A to DNA" line, but KRS's combination of brevity and rhythmic clash enables a totally different emotional response.

One of the most effective ways of mitigating backloadedness is to create a weld rhyme linking words in positions 4 and 1 of successive lines. Rhyme marks the end of the line, as usual, but then suddenly recurs, violating expectation. Like Biggie before him, Jay-Z is a master of this technique, here displayed in "Izzo (H. O. V. A.)":

> To let 'em <u>know</u> what a nigga look like when a nigga in a <u>Roadster</u>
> <u>Show 'em</u> how to move in a room full 'o vultures
> Industry shady it need to be <u>taken over</u>
> <u>Label owners</u> hate me I'm raisin' the status <u>quo</u> up
> I'm <u>overchargin'</u> niggaz for what they did to the Cold Crush

Another way to mitigate backloadedness is to spread rhyme everywhere, packing it into all or most of the beated stress positions, as well as elsewhere.

Nas's familiar lead couplet in "N. Y. State of Mind" epitomizes the technique, as does this couplet by Inspectah Deck in "Protect Ya Neck":

> Rappers, I **monkey flip** 'em with the **funky rhythm**
> I be **kickin**', musi**cian** in**flictin**' composi**tion**
>
> **I smoke** on the **mic like smokin**' **Joe Frazier**
> The **hell raiser, raisin' hell** with the **flavor**

The flow in these couplets and in Jay-Z's lines demonstrates that rhyme can be just as much a time-changer as can packed syllables or extra pauses. If rap's requirement for rhyme is satisfied by end rhyme, complemented and enhanced by pre-caesural rhyme, these rhymes rhythmically reinforce the line's standard tone units at the level of line and half line; and meanwhile they link words thematically and offer evidence of the rapper's competence. But once rhyme frequency, density, and even multiplicity become the earmarks of a more advanced hip hop competence, the rhythmic norms undergo a metamorphosis. Since Nas, since Biggie, since Lauryn Hill, since Eminem, it becomes necessary not only to rhyme but to create new rhyme textures. Especially when rap's mode of personal expressiveness is deployed within a battle of wits, "rapping to the beat" becomes minimal, and rapping rhyme by rhyme emerges as the primary lyrical weapon.

Rhyme

Go with the flow, my rhymes grow like an afro
—Big Daddy Kane, "Set It Off"

Rhymes are the synapses of flow, hooks of theme, and flashes of swagger. So vital is rhyming to rapping that rap verses are called *rhymes*.[1] Enacting his stage name, Busta Rhymes claims MC mastery, for to *bust a rhyme* means to create an original, ill rhyme, a rhyme as dirty-clean as a knockout punch. Almost all MCs keep *books of rhyme*, guarding them as their most important professional possessions—notebooks packed with rhyming words and phrases, catchy couplets, drafts of verses, and rhyme chains that could become the rhythmic/thematic skeletons of future verses. Freestylers, meanwhile, maintain a huge mental bank of associated rhyme words, and they structure their improvisations by means of a formulaic grammar organized (in part) by spaced rhymes on the beat. There's no such thing as blank verse hip hop.[2] Rap must rhyme. Although there do exist a very few isolated rhyme-less lines,[3] these are special effects and, in fact, the majority of verse lines contain between three and four rhymes.[4] Although rhyme is nothing new, rappers have reworked its forms, recalibrated the timing of its echoes, and revitalized its rhetorical force.[5]

Most essentially, rap rhymes are lyrical impacts. The best ones shoot out from the MC's "I" and hit the audience's "you" with delightful or disturbing surprises—boasts, jokes, lessons, or hard truths. Pharoahe Monch bares his battle with depression in "Post Traumatic Stress Disorder," quoting a personal demon:

> He said, *Let go of the pain, you'll never rock the mic again.*
> *Your choice, slug to the brain or twenty Vicodin*

In a comic boast reinforced by extreme raunchiness and absurdist mind-body dualism, KRS-One asserts in "Build Ya Skillz":

> Check, I control your mind with one rhyme I speak
> And get you open like a prostitute's buttcheeks

Neither of these rhymes was ever heard before. It's not ideas, or themes, or stories, or voice, or personality, or stage presence (or decorum, or "good taste") that make or break a rapper's street reputation; it's great flow and amazing rhymes—original, jaw-snapping, unforgettable rhymes: "Woo, did he really say that?!"

Rhyme impacts can involve not just the originality and cleverness of the word links, but their density—quantity versus quality. Our epigraph line from Big Daddy Kane is packed with mostly simple, monosyllabic rhymes, one per beat stress, but the final, far superior, and syncopated rhyme kicks in with the "afro" simile—an image of density and complication, as well as iconic blackness. Big Daddy Kane was a flat-top guy, not an afro guy, so he's not calling attention to his image, but he's certainly calling attention to how his rhymes *grow*. "Set It Off" (1988) is fast-tempo full-density rhyming, unremitting and anything but subtle. Which is not to say artless: *afro* soon acquires a clever couplet rhyme in *have no*, which immediately flows right into *problem*—a deft comedic touch:

> **Go** with the **flow**, my rhymes **grow** like an **afro**
> I enter**tain** a**gain** and **Kane**'ll never **have no**
> Problem . . .

A potential problem with rhyme density per se, however, is that it may become a predictable flow component, losing its capacity to surprise. In the 1990s, a new generation of MCs, influenced mainly by Nas, upped the rap game by perfecting rhymes that were both original and dense—quality *and* quantity—but their success depended on a continuously varying flow style. This is from Del the Funky Homosapien's "Press Rewind" (2000):

> Check my comprehensive catalog of crafts,
> I'm daft, I battle all like I don't have it all—
> Avant-garde Battlestar Galactica, got rhymes per capita
> I'm shining through the aperture, but I'm not gonna bust no caps for ya (nah)

When Nas rebutted Jay-Z's "Takeover" diss in "Ether," he saved his most damaging punch for last. Nas didn't win this battle because he ridiculed Jay-Z's silly role in "Hawaiian Sophie," or because he exhibited greater emotional maturity, or even because he called out Jay-Z on his disrespect for women. Nas won by insulting Jay-Z's meager rhyme repertoire, out-rhyming him while accusing him of plagiarism (*biting*):[6]

> How much of Biggie's rhymes is gonna come out your **fat lips**?
> Wanted to be on every **last** one of my **classics**,
> You **pop shit**, apologize, nigga, just **ask 'Kiss**[7]

The end rhymes Nas deploys to make this charge, on top of the previous *you on Jaz dick* and *clapped quick*, artfully echo Jay-Z's original boast, "R. O. C., we runnin' this **rap shit**," which had been repeated as a tedious advertising list of in-house talents (Memphis Bleek, B. Mac, Freeway, O & Sparks, Chris, and Neef). For good measure, Nas kicks in the delayed internal rhyme of "**last . . . shit**," proclaiming his victory even as he reconstitutes Jay-Z's *rap shit* into *pop shit*, denigrating Jay's lyricism while dismantling his rhyme.[8]

Why Rhyme?

Mainly because rhyme sounds good and plays a word game. Even infants use and enjoy it, babbling syllable-rhymes before they learn to speak, and all children and adults in a rhyme-forming culture can recognize and make rhymes. But what makes rhyme appealing? First of all, the echo it produces; and then also, in songs and poems, the rhythmic spacing of this echo, the way it keeps time from line to line, its predictable musical chime. Beyond this, rhyme offers suspense and surprise. We hear a sound in what we know is a rhyme word, and then we wait for the echo; and unless we already know the song or poem, we don't know what the rhyming word will be—and then we hear it, right on cue. So, *cue* could turn into *you*, or *blue*, or *true*, or *screw*, or *overdo*. A *word* could turn into a *bird*, a *turd*, or something more ab*surd*. We expect this kind of transformation to happen, so what's surprising is not *that* words rhyme, but rather *how* they rhyme.

Whether a rhyme is canned or creative, trivial or evocative, it connects words illogically, not out of grammatical necessity. We rhyme because we can, because so many words rhyme with so many other words, and we rhyme in poetry because the form we're working in demands it. End rhyme keeps time, line by line, and end-rhyme patterns can shape of line groupings into couplets, quatrains, and other forms. In songs, limericks, sonnets, and rap, rhyme is functional, and the actual rhyme links make thematic sense, but meanwhile rhyme's root meaningfulness is nonsensical. It happens that *word* and *bird* and *turd* rhyme, but their common sound is arbitrary. In French it's *mot*, *oiseau*, and *merde*, where the first two words do rhyme—but again, arbitrarily. Sense and nonsense coexist in every single rhyme. There must be pleasure in this sonic illogic or we wouldn't do it.

Here's Lil Wayne in "She Will":

> What goes **around** comes a**round** like a **hula hoop**
> Karma is a **bitch**? Well just make sure that **bitch** is **beautiful**

Formally, the couplet contains one end rhyme, binding its lines together, and an internal rhyme in each line, linking their a- and b-verses. Sonically, the end rhyme is an assonantal multi and the internal rhymes are both repetitions. What's mainly of interest here, though, is less the technique than the ease with which these rhymes work together. The opening cliché refers conventionally to karma, but Weezy flips it into a simile, literalizing karma's mysterious cyclical energy into a familiar toy. Moral consequence suddenly looks like childlike, dance-like, sex-like movement. The couplet is only half done, and it's already twisted. Now we hear a second cliché of a more moral, personal, and complaining kind. Karma's going to cause pain, which is why it's a bitch, but if we follow Weezy's advice we can avoid this consequence by making sure that our karma is beautiful—or alternatively, we can simply translate one sense of *bitch* into another: just make sure your woman is beautiful. Is this a philosophical truth, an avoidance tactic, or a joke? It may not matter terribly much because the rhyme of *hula hoop* and *beautiful* is blue-chip.

Without its particular rhymes, what does Weezy's couplet have to offer in the way of meaning or entertainment? Very little. The art is in the rhymes, and the scaffolding of rhyme makes the art possible.

Rhyme before Rap

Rhyme has been historically embedded in our poetic discourse since the Middle Ages. Because stress is fundamental to English semantics and speech rhythms, and because the verse systems of any language depend on its salient linguistic features,[9] we might guess that English poetry has always rhymed. Not so. Rhyme is not the only way to link stress-associated sounds, and in fact rhyme played no major role in English poetry during the first seven centuries of our poetic archives. Here are two lines from the Old English epic *Beowulf*:

þa **com** of **mo**re || under **mist-hleo**þum
Grendel **gon**gan, || **G**odes yrre **bær**
(Then came from the moor, under mist-hills
Grendel going, God's ire he bore)

The end-words don't rhyme, and nothing else in this passage rhymes. Instead, the a- and b-verses of each line are linked by *alliteration*: *more* and *mist*; then *Grendel, gongan*, and *Godes*. The moor and the mist-hills (fog) epitomize the monster's bleak, wilderness domain, and he is then associated contrastingly—subserviently—with God.

Alliteration was the required sound device in our earliest English four-beat verse. Rhyme didn't take on any importance until the fourteenth century, when English poets like Chaucer (who was patronized by the French-speaking English nobility) began to imitate French models, in effect composing French poetry in English. Because Chaucer wrote in English, his poetry naturally contained stress patterns, but he was imitating verse in a language without stresses, only pitch accents. Unlike the native poetry, which (as in rap) measured lines by their stress contours but had no prescriptive length, this new poetry measured lines by their syllable count, using end-rhymes to mark their time. Bearing in mind that all poetry then was meant to be vocalized, rhyme worked like a special musical note. Hearing a rhyme word, you knew you were at the end of an eight- or ten-syllable line, and you experienced alternating feelings of anticipation and resolution. Reflecting their fundamental metrical difference, rhymed French and then English syllable-counting is termed *syllabic*, whereas our native unrhymed English poetry is termed *accentual*, or *strong-stress*.

Rhyme came into English verse when England was transitioning from a two-class (nobility, peasants), two-language (French, English) agrarian society into a modern bourgeois society. As the English-speaking urban middle class grew more powerful, the French-speaking nobility needed and wanted to learn to speak English in order to compete and even to survive, and along with speaking English came their desire for a kind of English poetry that seemed familiar, even if no longer in French. Today, six hundred years later, we still have just two kinds of meter in English, stress-based and syllable-counting. But why did rhyme replace alliteration, even in four-beat poetry like Old Folk, blues, and rap?[10] Many rhyming songs contain alliteration

("Amazing grace! How sweet the sound"), but unlike rhyme, alliteration is no longer required in any English poetry.

One reason for the shift to rhyme is that Chaucer and his colleagues won the culture wars. As the new Lancastrian dynasty in England, beginning with the reign of Henry IV in 1399, patronized and marketed the new style, the old four-beat alliterative style, epitomized in works like *Piers Plowman* and *Sir Gawain and the Green Knight*, lost favor. Regarded as less literary, more oral in its traditions, it came to be viewed as rural rather than urban, folksy rather than sophisticated. Even today, those prejudices persist. Many literary purists regard the iambic pentameter of Chaucer, Shakespeare, Milton, and Wordsworth as *the* dignified poetic medium—and not without some justification; but these same critics often don't consider rap to be poetry at all. Ironically, contemporary literary poetry is largely unread and irrelevant, whereas hip hop poetry—brazenly urban, nuanced yet rough, unapologetically successful—faces strong cultural resistance. When Common was invited to the Obama White House, the event was spun by Fox News and other such media as an endorsement of gangster values. But KRS-One got it right: rap artistry arose from the "reality of lack," and resentment towards its culture runs deep. In the college curriculum, hip hop studies is now becoming somewhat trendy, but those who teach rap as poetry are still academic outliers.

Another reason for rhyme's surge was linguistic. English has always been a stressed language, but before the infusion of thousands of new French and then Latin words into our lexicon, its words were more commonly front-loaded by stress. Native polysyllabic words like *finger*, *earfinger* (little finger), *kingdom*, *slingshot*, and *Winchester* illustrate the tendency for stress to fall on the first syllable. It makes sense that a poetic system based on first-syllable stress patterns would rely on a correlative type of sound-play to lend extra weight to its normal contours. But once our language was flooded with borrowings like *confer*, *cathedral*, *cuisine*, *authority*, and *domesticate*, we no longer used a vocabulary quite so packed with front-stressed words. Therefore, the power of alliteration as a rhythmic and semantic marker diminished, and its viability as adjunct of four-beat meter became more and more problematic.

Although *confer*, *cathedral*, and *cuisine* do alliterate, their alliteration sounds feeble because it's not yoked to stressed syllables. The structural advantage of rhyme is that it occurs (or begins) on *any* syllable, wherever the stress falls in a word, and can then continue on through one or more subsequent unstressed syllables. Thus *confer* rhymes with *sure*, *cathedral* with *dihedral* or *dodecahedral*, and *cuisine* (of course) with *lean*. And not only does *scare* rhyme with *mare*, but *scary* and *scarily* rhyme with *merry* and *merrily*. The best MCs, possessed of huge vocabularies and always on the lookout for new rhymes, thrive on multisyllabic words and phrases.[11] *Domesticate* rhymes easily with *investigate*, but an MC might wrench-rhyme it with *masticate* or multi-rhyme it with *mess with Kate* or *confess too late*. At the start of his verse in "Notorious Thugs," Notorious B. I. G. spits a rhyme chain of *dangerous, bang with us, angel dust, label us, Notorious, love to bust,* and *strange to us.*

Is rhyme better than alliteration, then? Yes. It's more flexible. It can accommodate itself to words and word chains of all kinds of sizes and shapes and many semantic registers. More basically, because rhyme involves more than one syllable component, it can link exponentially more sounds than can alliteration. There are only twenty-two initial consonants in English.[12] If we add the consonant clusters beginning with [b], [p], [f], [d], [t], [θ], [s], and [k] (e.g., [bl] and [br]; [sk], [skl], [skr], etc.), the total number of distinct initial consonant sounds comes to less than forty.[13] But there are thousands of rhyme sounds, often combined in multisyllabic groupings. Because rappers compete over who can rhyme best, their competition puts a premium on new sound combinations, and the number of potential rhyme sounds is so large, their verbal jousts reach the highest echelons of lyrical craftsmanship that aural poetry has ever heard.

Taking a long historical-linguistic view of rap, we can see it as a hybrid form, combining the native English meter (four-beat, no fixed syllable count) with the French end-rhyme. Many of the earliest MCs used end-rhyme almost exclusively to delineate their couplets, much like earlier generations of singers and literary poets. Only in the later 1980s did innovators like Big Daddy Kane, LL Cool J, Kool Moe Dee, Grandmaster Caz, Treach, KRS-One, and Kool G Rap up the lyrical ante by introducing complex internal rhymes and interlinear rhyme chains. In recent and contemporary rap, many of the rhymes are no longer mainly structural; they're optional, extra, and ornamental; they're weaponized witticisms fired in the name of the game.

What Rhymes with What?

Syllables rhyme with syllables to make words rhyme with words. But for a rhyme to register, it must be heard as a prominent sound event, and for this reason rhymes usually coincide with stressed syllables. We might theorize that the articles *the* and *a* rhyme, but we would never hear their echo as such. Rap rhymes typically link content words that fall on metrical stresses or extra stresses in the line, but even an unstressed rhyme, if it's thematically loaded, may be conspicuous enough to grab our attention. The early West Coast rappers were especially innovative at syllabic disruption, introducing delayed syncopation in rhyming stressed and non-stressed syllables—a technique almost certainly inspired by Melle Mel,[14] then soon re-appropriated by East Coast MCs:

```
   \   /    /  || x x   /    x    /
You too, boy, if ya fuck with me
   x   x /   x   x  x / x .   /    x   /   x
The police are gonna hafta come and get me (Ice Cube)
```

```
   x    x   /   x  x  x    / || x  x   / x   /
Now it's time for me to make my impression felt
   x   /   x  || x /  || x    /   x   x   /   x
So sit back, relax, and strap on your seatbelt (Dr. Dre)
```

```
   x   x    /   x x  / || x x   /   x   x    x   / x  x
To my man G.O.V., I remember how you used to be (Guru)
```

```
   x   \    /   \     / || x  x   /    x  x   x / x x
The new moon rode high in the crown of the metropolis
   / x ||  x    / . x   /   x   /
Shinin', like who on top of this? (Mos Def)
```

These four passages demonstrate clearly that rhyme links can and do occur even when they aren't supported by normal stress prominences. The essential feature of rhyme then is structural. As is the case with all other figures of sound, rhyme's basic structure repeats itself by means of a sound echo from one syllable to another. What makes words rhyme structurally is the echo of the middle and final parts, but not the first part, of their core syllables. Like most other figures of sound, rhyme depends on both the repetition and non-repetition of syllable segments. In this way, it can express both similarity and difference. All syllables have three potential parts, a consonantal *onset*, a vocalic *nucleus*, and a consonantal *coda*. In the following chart, a chain of paired monosyllabic words, along with a display of their syllable parts, illustrates which parts match [●] and which parts don't [○] to produce our figures of sound:

	Onset	Nucleus	Coda	
mist	[m]	[i]	[st]	
	●	●	●	⟩ *repetition* [*homophone*]
mist	[m]	[i]	[st]	
	●	●	●	⟩ *pun* [*homophone*]
missed	[m]	[i]	[st]	
	○	●	●	⟩ *full rhyme*
kissed	[k]	[i]	[st]	
	●	○	●	⟩ *pararhyme*
cussed	[k]	[u]	[st]	
	●	○	○	⟩ *alliteration*
Kim	[k]	[i]	[m]	
	○	○	●	⟩ *consonance*
damn	[d]	[æ]	[m]	
	○	●	○	⟩ *assonance*
bang	[b]	[æ]	[ŋ]	

Before considering these figures of sound in detail, we need to redefine *rhyme* in non-literary terms applicable to rap and other oral performance poetry. English literary rhyme since Chaucer has been pretty much restricted to full rhyme. Although Chaucer did on occasion rhyme punningly,[15] he and later literary poets relied almost exclusively on nucleus-coda echo with onset clash. Rhymes yoked similar-yet-different sounds, hence different words, so word repetition didn't qualify as rhyme. And rhymes had to be exact. And since rhymes were formally required, all other figures of sound were regarded as inferior or ornamental.

But in rap, as in some other song traditions like the blues, word repetition does count as rhyme.[16] So does that other kind of homophone, the pun. And so does lowly assonance. In fact, every figure in our chart counts as a rap rhyme if and only if its syllabic nucleus is marked with a ●. Echo of a syllable's core vowel is all we need for a rap rhyme, whether that echo occurs in a full rhyme, a repetition, a pun, or an assonance. These vowel echoes, be they be temporarily intertwined or sequential, form the evolving links in the chain of rap flow.

As professional wordsmiths, MCs deploy not just these varieties, but also alliteration, consonance and, occasionally, pararhyme. Rap abounds with textured sound echoes ranging from dominant to prominent to supportive to subtle. *Consonance* is unobtrusive by nature, due to the fact that it is formed from less prominent syllable parts (often coda sounds), whereas *alliteration* may range from subtle to supportive to, in rare cases, dominant—at the level of a stressed rhyme. Key to all of these figures' aural impact is their relationship to stress and beat. Any figure of sound on an unstressed syllable is less likely to be "heard" than one on a stressed syllable, and any figure on an extra stress will probably be less prominent than one on a beated stress. Stress aside, rhymes—full rhymes, homophonic rhymes, and assonantal rhymes—dominate the flow—not only because they often mark metrical stress, but due to their inherent sound quality, the power of their resonant vowels.

We can quickly review the varieties of rap rhyme. Full rhyme occurs monosyllabically in Guru's *V* and *be*, Mos Def's *new* and *who*, and Dr. Dre's *felt* and *seatbelt*, polysyllabically in Nas's *musician/composition* and Kanye's *money/funny*. Simple word repetition is evident in Weezy's *around/around*, but Kanye's repetition *major/majors* makes a grammatical shift and Weezy's repetition of *bitch/bitch* makes a semantic shift, as does the *all/all* within Del's multi: "I **battle all** like I don't **have it all**." Since most word-repetition rhymes in rap do entail some alteration of meaning, be it contextual, grammatical, or semantic,[17] we can think of puns as being closely related to repetitions, both functionally and formally. Jay-Z tosses puns into the sound mix in "Monster"—

All I *see* is *these* niggas I've made **million***aires*
Milling about, **spill**ing they *fee*lings in the *air*

—with *millionaires* splitting into two freaky rhymes, and KRS-One's "Hold" has an exclusively homophonic rhyme scheme based on the words *hold, hole,* and *whole*. The wordplay in B. o. B.'s "Do You Really Have The Stamina" is particularly thoughtful:

Well, **pos**ing for pictures, and living on a **pos**ter—
The hardest thing for me, is to keep my com**pos**ure

Last but definitely not least: assonance. Technically, KRS-One's *speak* and *buttcheeks*, because of the slight coda change from [k] to [ks], is an assonantal rhyme, but more obviously assonantal are the components Nas's multis: *clapped quick, Jaz dick, fat lips, classics, ask 'Kiss*. Assonantal rhyme is far more frequent in rap than full rhyme, and there are several good reasons for this. Pragmatically, if vowel echo is all that's needed for a rhyme, if it's no longer necessary also to match coda sounds, then the number of available rhymes swells exponentially. A rhyming dictionary might tell me that *wand* rhymes with *pond, frond, bond, blond, respond, vagabond, demi-monde*, and about twenty other words, but if I alter the final consonant cluster to just one of its components I can also get *lawn, prawn, withdrawn,* etc., and *cod, wad, goldenrod,* etc.; and if I shift to completely different consonants and consonant clusters I can get *pot, Scotch, wrong, paw, synagogue,* and hundreds of other rhymes, all with the same vowel core; and if I want to wrench a few vowels or crush some consonants I might even be able to get *Ann, woman,* or *Aladdin* to rhyme with *wand.*

Aesthetically, this vast expansion of available rhymes allows rap to merge the harmonic musical echoes of its vowels with dissonant consonant clashes, to stay on key without losing its rough edge. Too many full rhymes would make for too little sonic tension, producing a bland, predictable, poppy style. And, of course, a reliance on assonantal rhyme also allows individual MCs to make myriads of creative choices about sound quality. Should a rhyme sound rough or smooth? Does a theme suggest cacophony, euphony, or a little of both? In this couplet from "Izzo (H.O.V.A.)," Jay-Z merges the sounds of two rhymes into the final word:

> I was raised in the **pro**-jects, **roaches** and **rats**
> **Smokers** out **back**, sellin' they mama's **sofa**[18]

Such flexibility with rhyme further allows MCs to flaunt their skill at ranging from one sound to the next. Here, Lil Wayne in "A Milli" has just been bragging that he doesn't need to write his lyrics—in fact he doesn't even have the time for it:

> 'Cause my seconds, minutes, **hours** go to the all **mighty dollar**
> And the al**mighty power** of that ch, ch, ch, ch **chopper**
> Sister, **brother**, son, **daughter**, **father motha**fuck a **coppa**
> Got the **Maser**ati dancin' on the bridge pussy **poppin'**

Full rhymes morph into assonances morphing into full rhymes. Later in this song, Weezy forges a chain from *sour* to *flower* to *Carter* to Mr. Lawn *Mower* to Michael *Lowry* to *doubt me*; comically wrenching *mower* so it rhymes fully with *flower* and, as well, linking *call me* to Gwen *Stefani*. Such freedom flips necessity, right? And necessity encourages a *momentum* of freedom, which can be "resolved" even in a nonsense rhyme—but still a rhyme!—the correction of which can kick off a new rhyme chain. This from Khujo's verse on Outkast's "Reset":

> Good does not come without pain
> Meaning, before it gets better, it's goin' get **worse**
> Like my homies on the sick side still dyin' over **turf**

That don't belong to **urse**, I mean **us**,
Left in the **dust**, try to catch **up**

With its looser, more inclusive standards for rhyme, rap affiliates with other oral/aural, non-literary traditions.[19] In ballads and blues, assonance also suffices for rhyme.[20] Singers, like rappers, know that the melodic core of language runs through its vowels, and professional singers, especially opera singers, are meticulously trained in how to navigate over cacophonous or vocally challenging onset or coda sounds.[21] The best MCs possess similar skills and are able to suppress or accentuate particular consonants at will. But rapping is not like singing an aria. Although vowel rhyming remains a constant, the noise and percussiveness of rap consonants is just as indispensable, so these same MCs excel as well at articulating and even exaggerating them. Conscious of their mastery of vocal dexterity, rappers like to talk about "spitting" their rhymes.

This dexterity is especially evident in wrenched rhymes. These have to be heard to be appreciated, for they don't seem to rhyme at all on the page. The vowels must be twisted to produce assonance, and then their framing consonants may require some tweaking too. In his *60 Minutes* interview with Anderson Cooper, Eminem riffs on "orange," a word with no known literary rhyme in English, to show how it's done,[22] and Kanye West performs an admirably ill example of it in this boast in "Barry Bonds":

I don't need **wri-t(i)ers**, I might bounce **ideas**
But only I could come up with some **shit** like **this**

Non-rhyming Figures

From what we now understand about assonance, it makes sense that rappers would not normally substitute alliteration, consonance, or pararhyme for rhyme. None of these have vowel echo. Alliteration has a front-loaded consonant echo, consonance has, at least sometimes, a back-loaded consonant echo, and pararhyme has both. Pararhyme, the loudest non-rhyming figure, actually flips assonance: it does everything assonance doesn't do, and doesn't do what assonance does.

Unlike alliteration and consonance, pararhyme is rare in rap—despite the fact that *hip hop* is itself a pararhyme, probably dating back before Wonder Mike's first lines in "Rapper's Delight":[23]

I said a **hip hop**, the **hip**pie the **hip**pie
To the **hip** hip **hop**, a you **don't** *stop* the **rock** it

Here *hip* and *hop* are each rhyme words, and they play with each other, but they don't rhyme. In the first line, the dominant rhyme is on *hip* (three times), and the *hop* on beat 2 receives a soft stress; in the second, the stress on beat 1's *hip* is very much subdued, and there is a triplet rhyme on *hop*, *don't* (wrenched), and *rock*, with *drop* taking secondary stress. We hear these lines, then, as successive rhymes on *hip* and then *hop*. No other such pararhymes occur in this fourteen-minute song, so the *hip hop* echo is an anomaly. In most rap songs, it is impossible to find a single pararhyme.

Jay-Z uses it twice in "Monster." In the first line he names *King Kong*; near the end of his verse he derides other rappers as "**fake fucks** with no **f**angs." In both the pararhyming name and the pararhyming and alliterating phrase he pairs adjacent stresses, one on the beat and the other not, neither of which are rhyme words. The only rhyme in either phrase is the end word *fangs*, rhyming with *veins*. Jay-Z is a consummately clever manipulator of syllables, and it's tempting to imagine that this particular phrase, like others in his verse, is intended to epitomize grotesque sound play, but the main point here is that his pararhymes don't function as rhymes.

Cannibal Ox's Vast Aire seems to strive for Gothic effect in "Raspberry Fields":

Either you like reincarnation or the smell of carnations
The sample's the flesh and the beat's the *skeleton*
You got beef but there's worms in your *Wellington*
I'll put a hole in your **skull** and extract your ***skeleton***

However, his next line interrupts the conceptual and rhythmic flow by calling out *skeleton* as a mistake: "Oh my God, said a word twice." So the rhyme repetition (along with the pararhyme) either constitutes a performance gaffe, left unedited, or more likely a calculated dramatization of the verse's initial imperative: "If first you don't succeed try, try again / Step up to the mic and die again." Vast Aire starts over right in the middle of the verse, and in his next run through the offending line is corrected, or "corrected," to: "I'll put a hole in your skull and extract your gelatin"—which also makes much a lot more sense.

Granted that Vast Aire's pararhyme is a victim of collateral damage, what is it about this figure's peculiar mix of echoing consonants and clashing vowels that rappers resist? A good hint may be found in Wilfred Owen's "Strange Meeting," a literary poem composed on the battlefield in World War I. It begins with these couplets—

It seemed that out of the battle I escaped
Down some profound dull tunnel, long since scooped
Through granites which Titanic wars had groined.
Yet also there encumbered sleepers groaned

—and continues on with pararhymes like *bestirred/stared, eyes/bless, hall/ Hell, grained/ground, moan/mourn*, some of which have clashing consonants as well as vowels. Due to the dissonant vowels, these rhymes feel like out-of-key notes in a solo. They might make sense as a thematic chain, but they create a kind of tension that builds rather than resolves anticipation.[24] To put it simply, they don't sound right. They don't sound like rhymes. In hip hop aesthetics, the beat should include some rhythmic clash and harmonic dissonance, and the poetic rhythms likewise need always to be edgy and unpredictable, but the beat also needs to be steady, danceable, head-bobbing, and the rhyme needs to rhyme.

Alliteration and consonance are contrastingly common. Each can function subtly in the construction of sonic texture, and consonance, with its relatively unobtrusive reliance on coda sounds functions primarily in that manner. These lines from Rakim's "I Know You Got Soul" beautifully illustrate the hierarchical interconnectedness of sound play sometimes found in rap:

I start to **think**, and the<u>n</u> *I* **sink**
*In*to the p<u>a</u>per, *like I* was **ink**.
Whe<u>n</u> *I'm* **writ**ing *I'm* tra<u>pp</u>ed *in* betwee<u>n</u> the **lines**—
I esc<u>a</u>pe [beat] when *I fin*ish the **rhyme**.

The end rhymes binding the successive couplets are full (*sink/ink*), then assonantal (*lines/rhyme*), and in each of these couplets there's an equivalent rhyme (*think . . . writ*ing) on beat 2 of the alpha line. Each couplet is also linked to its neighbor through cross-rhyming, with *like* anticipating the end rhyme to follow—*ing*, and *fin*—echoing the previous end rhyme, and clusters of *I*, *I'm*, and *in* further reinforce the two dominant rhymes. But meanwhile these rhymes are themselves linked by consonance, through their **n**-sounds, which in turn are present in *whe<u>n</u>* and *the<u>n</u>* and *betwee<u>n</u>*, and consonance also connects p<u>a</u>per, tra<u>pp</u>ed, and esc<u>a</u>pe. Some of the sound textures here may be discerned by few or no listeners, but they all impact, overtly or subtly, the feel of the poetry, in much the same way that a hierarchy of sample sounds makes up the beat.

Alliteration is more prominent than consonance because it arises solely from onset consonant echoes. Because it typically doesn't fall on beated stresses, however, alliteration can't capture our auditory focus the way rhyme can, even though, as attentive listeners, we may be very aware of its presence. In this line from Lauryn Hill's "Doo Wop (That Thing)":

/ x x / ‖ x x / x x x /
Niggas *fucked up* and you still de*fen*ding *them*

—the alliterative pairing marks an important disconnect in the consciousness of the women Lauryn addresses. Given the relative semantic weakness of most of the beated stress-words (*up*, *still*, *them*), the **f**-pair's relative semantic strength, its symmetry, and the way each alliterating syllable rhymes with its subsequent stress—all of these factors compensate for its tonal subordination. Nevertheless, because the alliteration occurs on unstressed syllables, we don't "feel" it as rhyme-equivalent. In this couplet from Gang Starr's "Work," the alliteration seems far less "necessary," far more ornamental, amidst Guru's flurry of sound play:

x x x x x / x / ‖ x / x /
Now Imma' start co*llectin*' **props**, con*nectin*' **plots**
x / x x x / x ‖ x x / x x \ x /
*Net*wor*kin*' like a **con***ference*, 'cause the **non***sense* is yet to **stop**

Here the main rhyme array—terminal and internal, full and assonantal—spreads over five beated stresses. A secondary array (co*llectin*', con*nectin*', *Net*wor*kin*') covers or frame-syncopates the rest. This rhyme-packed couplet also has three competing alliterations: on **c**, linking similar prefixes,[25] on **n**, tying *now* to rhymes within each array, and on **st**, cleverly connecting *start* and *stop*. The alliterative artistry is impressive—as a harmonic adjunct to the rhyme.

Very different from both Lauryn's and Guru's usage is Kanye West's alliteration in this couplet from "All Falls Down" (*The College Dropout*):

That **m**ajor that she **m**ajor in don't **m**ake no *money*,
But she won't drop out, her parents'll look at her *funny*.

Rather than falling on unstressed syllables and playing off against rhyme, the alliteration here gloms onto all four of the first line's rhyming syllables. The line's four alliterating rhymes feel baroque, contrived, and mocking, their monotony suited to the simplistic vocabulary ironically associated with this college girl (presumably an English major) too stupid to drop out.[26]

The alliteration in Nas's classic "N. Y. State of Mind" couplet functions far more cleverly than what we've seen so far:

> **R**appers, I *monkey flip 'em* with the *funky rhythm*
> I be **k**ickin', **m**u*sic*ian in*fl*ictin' compo*sit*ion

Nas frames his double-multi-rhyming alpha line by alliterating the most important link in hip hop poetics, rappers <> rhythm; then follows in the beta line with four straight repetitive rhyme-jabs on the beat. The clashing line rhythms, each explicitly produced by Nas's "I"-subject, in effect demonstrate a rhythmic range beyond the capacity of the other, generalized "rappers," who are left behind on beat 1, unrhymed, merely alliterating, subsumed by sound play into *this* rapper's monkey-flippin' composition.

Verses Versus Choruses

Consumers of rap songs today might assume that there have always been choruses framing and interspersed between the verses, but hip hop historians know it's not so. The hip hop chorus may be conceptualized as the verbalization of the DJ's hooks and breaks, the flipping of samples into song stanzas. There are proto-choruses in "Rapper's Delight"—*a hip hop, the hippy the hippy,* etc.; and *hotel, motel, Holiday Inn,* etc.—which serve as signature hooks for the different rappers and blend into their verses, but most choruses behave like those in other song traditions: they often repeat the same lines internally, and they repeat themselves throughout the rap song. These qualities are evident in Guru's chorus in "A Long Way to Go":

```
x   x  /   x   x / ‖   x   x   /   x    x    x    / x
It's a long way to go, when you don't know where you're going
x    /   x    x   x   / x ‖  x    x    /  [ / ]
You don't know where you're going when you're lost (lost)
x   x /   x   x / ‖   x   x   /   x    x    x    / x
It's a long way to go, when you don't know where you're going
x    /   x    x   x   / x ‖  x    x    / [B]
You don't know where you're going when you're lost
```

This relatively early chorus is rapped, but it behaves formally like a song refrain. With its posse-delivered fourth stress in line 2 and its virtual beat in line 4, it even has the sort of 4/3/4/3 stress pattern found in traditional ballad stanzas. The phrasing differs from that in the rap verses in being highly repetitive, with duplicated lines and half lines.[27]

Although such repetition can be effective for thematic emphasis, it's also a hallmark of commercialization. Market success in the music business depends on a catchy tune and memorable lyrics, and repetition, for better or for worse, makes lyrics more memorable. Here are choruses from Khia's "My Neck, My Back" (2002) and from Macklemore's "Can't Hold Us" (2013), each extremely popular in its day:

My Neck, my back,
Lick my pussy and my crack
My Neck, my back,
Lick my pussy and my crack   [Khia]

Here we go back, this is the moment
Tonight is the night, we'll fight till it's over
So we put our hands up like the ceiling can't hold us,
Like the ceiling can't hold us (X2)   [Macklemore]

As rap has become more commercial, its choruses have tended to be *sung*, not rapped, so as to cross over into pop. They have also tended to dominate song time. Khia's quatrain is repeated fourteen times in all, including four times in an elaborated version,[28] yielding a total of seventy-two chorus lines, compared with just thirty verse lines. Macklemore's song includes thirty-two chorus lines, fourteen chanted bridge lines (*na-na-na-na-na na-na-na*, etc.), and thirty verse lines—a somewhat more balanced ratio but still weighted toward chorus sentiments and, if you will, broad appeal. This historical shift toward the chorus's dominance is a big deal commercially, culturally, and artistically. If rap verses express, imitate, behave like real-life experiences filtered through ever-changing thoughts and feelings, choruses often act more like ads or easy truths (like directives, slogans, or cheers).[29]

Multis, Grids, and Chains

Rap verses have themselves suffered reduction in length and number to accommodate the expansion of chorus time in mass-market productions.

Gone are the days when an MC might feel free, like Odysseus in the *Odyssey* or Satan in *Paradise Lost*, to go on as long as he or she felt like it. Today the standard maximum length of a verse is sixteen bars, and shorter verses of fourteen, twelve, or even eight bars are not uncommon. Nevertheless, the tradition of original, drop-dead rhyming lives on. Unexpected rhymes like Lil Wayne's *millionaire/Nigerian hair, come to you/comfortable, tattoo/shampoo, barbeque/starving dude,* and *bullshit/full split* continue to surprise and amuse his fans while also making thematic sense by linking ideas in new ways. Rappers such as Kendrick Lamar and J. Cole typify contemporary rappers' (and their producers') awareness of and assimilation of classical hip hop rhyming traditions, so that they are able to include in their repertoires early West Coast off-beat rhyme syncopation, Dirty South drawling, NYC density, indie vocab, maybe even a little Cleveland harmony.[30]

We've already noted the unprecedented freedom of expression within rap rhyming as a result of its inclusion of all possible forms of vowel echo—not just full rhyme, but word repetition (with semantic and grammatical variation), punning, and especially assonance, including wrenched rhyming. But beyond the continual production of fresh rhymes over the past several decades, fierce competition among MCs has prompted several *formal* innovations. Some of these relate to the size and complexity of the rhyme event itself, while others have to do with how rhymes are spaced within lines, in successive lines, and even over verses and entire songs. Each type of formal innovation has the potential to influence the other.

Multis, or multisyllabic rhymes, are so common today that they can feel unremarkable. We expect them. They're part of the game now, and no would-be MC would even think of grabbing a mic without a few pre-cooked multis ready to spit. So, the thrill is gone. About the only thing that this rhyme by Mac Miller has in its favor is, possibly, its earnestness:

> How to get by, that's how we living in this **day and age**
> I bring some color to a World that's filled with **shades of gray**

But when multis first appeared on the rap scene—introduced in the late 1980s and early 1990s by the likes of Big Daddy Kane, Kool G Rap, Del, and Nas—they made a huge impression. They had hardly ever been heard before in rap or in other four-beat traditions like folk and blues, and in literary poetry they'd been used only in light verse or for comic effect.[31]

It's likely that light verse poets like Ogden Nash had it right: there's something about drawing out a rhyme unexpectedly over several syllables or even several words which, in the context of "normal" rhyme, is intrinsically entertaining. Certainly, that's the impression given by some of Big Daddy Kane's multis in "Raw" (1988), whether his overt attitude is clowning or theatrical bravado:

> I **appear right here**, and <u>scare and dare</u>, a **mere musketeer**
> That would <u>dare to compare</u>, I <u>do declare</u> . . .

> I'm not **new to this**, I'm **true to this**, <u>nothing</u> you can **do to this**,
> <u>Fuck</u> around with Kane and <u>come</u> out black and **blue for this**

> I'll get **raw for you** just **like** a **warrior**
> Rapping <u>like a samurai</u> and <u>I'll</u> *be* <u>damned</u> **if I**
> Ever let a Fisher-<u>Price</u> M*C hang*
> Their **rhymes** are toy, nothing but yin-*yang*

The first two quotations here, from verse 1, are indeed light. They also illustrate two alternative impacts of dense rhyming. Packing the couplet with rhymes on *all* of the beated stresses—at a time when most rhymes are end rhymes, with a few falling on beat 2—can create a startling *boom boom boom boom* sequence, prompting awe. Packing the alpha line with rhymes, including three multis, then delaying the final multi till beat 4 of the beta line can create suspense, culminating in the comic punch. Meanwhile the rhymes in both couplets are formulated from a very simple vocabulary (with the exception of *musketeer*), giving an impression primarily of syllable-display, not of joined ideas.

But the third quotation, at the end of verse 4, displays impressive rhyme blitz of conceptual associations. Big Daddy Kane carefully wrenches *raw for you* and *warrior* into sonic harmony, shifting the import of the song's title word. He follows this with an expanded multi (now propelled by the *like*-rhyme) containing the even more ambitious linking of *samurai* and *damned if I*, the second component powerfully enjambed, right on the brink, as if to imitate the samurai warrior's legendary ability to delay action and then strike in an instant. By the end of "Raw," we know that multis are more than a rhythmic gimmick. We know they can communicate powerful, unprecedented, and, at this moment in hip hop history, astonishingly original messages. Three years later, when Nas rapped his legendary verse in Main Crew's "Live at the Barbeque," its multis, now mingling with numerous "normal" rhymes, were similarly powerful:

*Rap*ping <u>sni</u>per, **speaking real words**
<u>My</u> thoughts *react,* <u>like</u> **Steven Spielberg's**
Poetry *attacks, paragraphs* **punch hard**
<u>My</u> *brain* is *insane,* <u>I'</u>m out to **lunch, God**
<u>Sci</u>ence is dropped, <u>my</u> *raps* are **toxic**
<u>My</u> voice**box locks** and excels <u>like</u> a **rocket**

Here the echoes are even denser and their sonic connections are even more complex—as are their intellectual connections. And the flow is edgy, rough, clipped, intense. What may have begun as light verse entertainment has fully morphed into spectacular ninja-warrior skill.

The infusion of multis into the rap line had big rhythmic consequences, direct and indirect. Most obviously, lines packed with phrase-sized multis situated at several beat positions are going to require a lot more syllables than lines with monosyllabic or bisyllabic rhymes. In Big Daddy Kane's "I'm not <u>new</u> to this | I'm *true* to this || <u>no</u>thing *you* can <u>*do*</u> to this," for example, the trisyllabics at positions 1, 2, and 4 in effect add six syllables to the line, for a total of sixteen, whereas in Tupac's "She nearly <u>gave</u> her <u>life</u> || to <u>raise</u> me <u>right</u>" from "Hold Ya Head Up," where the trisyllabics each straddle two beats, the line takes up a relatively modest ten syllables. A second rhythmic consequence is the insertion of extra, off-beat stresses. Although a two-beat multi like Nas's *Steven Spielberg's* is rhythmically unremarkable, the one it echoes, *speaking real words*, contains three stresses packed into just four syllables. When the multis become grammatically weightier, they typically result in lines both longer and stress-heavier than the average. Thus, Big Daddy Kane's "I ap**pear** right **here** | and **scare** and **dare** || a **mere** mus-ke**teer**" has fourteen syllables with six stresses; Lauryn Hill's "Doo Wop" line, "**Cristal** by the **case men** || **still** in they mother's **basement**" has seven stresses in thirteen syllables.[32]

The point here is not that multis start to crowd out normal rhymes in rap, but that they create a new context for rhyme, upping the competitive ante. This can be seen in the rhyme density of *all* of Nas's lines just quoted. Nas, Canibus, Big L, Biggie, Method Man, and scores of other 1990s MCs pack more rhymes into their lines than do their predecessors, so their lines become either longer, with extra stresses, or simply more stress-dense. Comparing lines from 1979–1987 with those from 1987–2013, the lines increase in length by about two syllables, accommodating more rhymes and, in turn, extra stresses and pauses.

Now, stuffing more and more rhymes into lines isn't easy to do without compromising a verse's ongoing intelligibility, its competent poetic expression in sync with its rhythmic flow. To compete as rhymers, MCs need large vocabularies and a keen sense of what kinds of phrases and figures will fit within the constraints of the beat—when, for example, to insert a timely metaphor or simile in order to fetch an otherwise off-topic rhyme word. There may be a critical mass for rhyme frequency: we are aware of no rap line with more than seven rhymes. How can an MC up the ante further, then, once having attained competence in high rhyme frequency?

One tactic, mastered by few, has been to complicate and even extend two-beat multis beyond the half line, as Lauryn Hill does in verse 2 of "Doo Wop (That Thing)." This requires strategy. Lauryn first creates a scaffold of end and internal rhymes based on the final vowel and nasal resolution of *women*, *men*, and *again*, running from *friend* to *semen* and beyond.[33] Then in verse 2, she arrays sixteen key rhymes on *they* (men) to support and sustain the volatile multi cluster:[34]

> **Let's** stop **pretend**, || *the* <u>ones</u> that **pack pistols** by **they waist men**
> **Cristal** by the **case men**, || **still** in **they** <u>mother's</u> **basement**
> The **pretty face men** || **claiming** that **they did** a **bid men**
> *Need* to **take care** of || **their** *three* and *four* **kids men**
> **They** facing a *court* case || **when** the <u>child's</u> sup*port* **late**
> *Money*-**taking**, **hea**<u>r</u>**t**-**breaking** || now you <u>*wonder*</u> <u>why</u> **women hate men**[35]

Starting with the b-verse of the first line here, Lauryn spits four half lines filled with three- or four-word multis, doubling the middle vowel in the b-verses by repeating *they*. In the third line's b-verse, she again includes *they* but shifts the vowel sequences. In line four, as her focus turns from the blunt irony of the men's swagger (claiming jail time yet living in their mothers' basements) to the painful truth of their social and familial irresponsibility, she inserts new rhymes to morph her multis into semantic flips. Those *Cristal-by-the-case men? The pretty-face men, claiming-that-they-did-a-bid men?* Mix in a new rhyme on *court* and *support*, and their boasting turns into a pathetic reality: "They facing a court case." As Lauryn expands the reach of her multis, she hardens her consonants, adding cacophonous monosyllabic punches to the flow. In lieu of light rhymes like *pretty* and *did a bid*, we hear *take, court, late, heart, break, hate*. The unique rap line without an -en end rhyme ends on *late*, which crashes right into *Money-taking, heart-breaking*, heading towards the end rhyme on *hate*—which is not an end rhyme at all. We hear why women hate men. Hate is flanked by, and divides, women and men. The missing men "rhyme" on disunity. After all the heartache, they are gone, but their rhymes still infect the home, distilled in the women's hardship and residual hatred. "Let's stop pretend" then, but then let's realize that the pain is shared—and why—and that we can move on from it and be "right within."[36]

Contrasting with this fluid manipulation of rhyme sounds is Eminem's grid rhyming in The Game's "We Ain't." Here the multi, if you will, occupies an entire line, and its sequence of four key sounds is pre-determined by the beat, producing a vertical rhyme scheme:

	1	2	3	4
Looking for answers, rap	sensation Eminem	battles to ward off	accu	sations
That he had	somebody	blasted. The	Mask of	Jason
Was found at the	scene of the	task with	masking	tape
And the victim's	penis up his	ass, a	basket	case
And they ask him to	clean up his	act, you	bastards	wasting
Too much time—	me no kiss	ass, and if	that's the	case

Eminem's actual *performance* of these lines is far less rigid than its grid pattern might suggest. It's backloaded, with stronger stresses on the off beats, so that emphasis is syncopated to weaker parts of speech—a verb rather than a subject, an object rather than a verb. The syntax varies from line to line, and the lines' rhythm varies too. Some lines enjamb, some glide through the caesura, but none of these shifts arise from grammatical necessity. Eminem is rapping here in his habitual manic style, but meanwhile there's this amazingly difficult rhyme pattern at play.[37] Not surprisingly, the full-line multi combos work better as a rhetorical tour de force than as a coherent statement.

This kind of extreme rhyme can't usually be sustained for more than a few lines, and multis have continued to be used most commonly as single-stress markers, only occasionally as two-stress markers spanning two beats. The main way MCs have upped the competitive ante with multis, then, is to space them more moderately but at immodest length. The Michigan indie MC One Be Lo in "enecS eht no kcaB" (2005) stretches this chain across a twenty-line verse, the rhymes always at position 4 and, a few times, at position 2: *say to you, they would do, paying dues, staying true, making moves, made it through, came to do, to name a few, say to you, stay with you, crazy glue, not afraid of you, maybe true, favorite crew, came with you, vapors too, David do, Pay-Per-View, cable crew, way to school, play with you, raise a fool, can't be cool, and Déjà Vu.* Compared with Nas's or Del's or Lauryn's multis, these feel relatively easy-going due to their triplet structure, which lends a degree of rhythmic predictability,[38] but the payoff for this more modest rhyming technique is that it can sustain thematic coherence at some length.

Of course, ease and difficulty are always relative when it comes to rap rhyming, and it can take as much talent to perform well in what jazz musicians would call a "cool" style as in a "hot" style. One Be Lo's counterpart in Binary Star, Senim Silla, raps with more pyrotechnics, but their two styles complement each other. In "Reality Check" (1999), it is One Be Lo who spits the more memorable couplets:

> Binary **Star**, super**star** it's no co**incidence**
> Every **verse is intricate**, this ain't a **circus in a tent**
>
> I bomb your **set** that's not a **threat** it's a **promise**,
> Got everybody **ridin'** on my **wagon** like the **Amish**,
>
> You ain't never heard an emcee **speak like this**,
> And Rodney King ain't never felt a **beat like this**.

Senim Silla, on the other hand, fashions a thirty-one-line chain end-rhyming on the first-person singular pronoun, which contains no less than eighty **I**-hits in full, assonantal, and multi format, with other interwoven rhymes in dense profusion and plenty of consonance and alliteration to boot. To accommodate all this sound play, not a few liberties are taken with grammar and thematic coherence, yet within its particular phrases and clauses the ideas are cuttingly, wittily sharp:

> Get a *grip* on yourself cuz you ain't *grip*pin' **mines**
> **Life** and **times**, *outta* **lies** rap **guys** *outta* **line** careers I **finalize**,
> **Collide** with this serenade **cyanide** you've **applied** for *Silla*-**cide**,
> The thing that makes *killas* **hide**
> Hang 'em **high** by they gold link **necktie**
> And *drain* 'em **dry** into tempest **eye**
> Now you *ain't* **Ki** so you *ain't* that **high**,
> Wanna be aero*nautic* and get *swatted* for *actin'* **fly**,
> *Master***mind's** *crafty* **rhymes**, **I'll** rip from *drafty* **lines**
> That chill **spines like** the **Alpines**, runnin' up on Senim *tur***bines**,
> A close encounter of the *worst* **kind**—
> Go *ask* the *cats* that *heard* I'm lyrical *turpen***tine**,
> Who wanna *taste* **mine I** gotta carry hell on the *waist***line**,

God gift to *bass***line** so let the *phlegm* **fly**,
I *semi 7–5* through the *M*-**I**, when **I** forcefully **Jedi**
In a *bulls***eye** *red*-**eye**, *heads* **fly** *bet* **I**, sharp*shoot dead*-**eye**
Snooze crews bed **bye**, Mary <u>Lou</u> *flippin'* **I** pistol pump *grippin'* **I**
Stompin', **I** *semper-fi* repre*sent*, *temper* **high**, signi**fy**—
Walkin' **rhyme** ain't nothin' *similar* or *Gemin***i**
In this *perimeter* 'cept *him and* **I**
Cats be cut **dry**, **I'm** a **wild** *wet* **guy**,
I be rainin' precipitation 'til it's one inch from *neck* **high**,
Arrest **fly** *kids mid*-**sky**, without an *a*libi
Who said you *rap* **tight**? *You* come un*rav*eled **by**
Slice of this *rap scalpel*, **guys** *quick* as *apple* **pie**
I'm learned in all schools of thought and *shit* you *baffled* **by**
Con*ceptual* intel*lectual fox* **sly**,
Silla *ox***ide rhymes** flow like a *rock***slide**,
You musta for*got* **I**, have your ass *knock*-kneed and *cock***eyed**
<u>B</u>ruised, <u>b</u>attered, <u>b</u>*roken up, open cut*, <u>d</u>ipped in <u>per*ox*</u>**ide**,
<u>D</u>eath to the <u>*P*</u>*op* **Fly**.

Homophonics

Such lengthy, dense rhyme chains are hard acts to follow. One rare alternative, however, is to play off against rap's dominant formal structure, the end-rhyming couplet. We expect paired rhymes to be successive, each pair having a new sound, with the key rhyme words normatively spaced ten or twelve syllables apart. That temporal gap allows for suspense and, more important, for intervening words, syntax, ideas, and emotions. The cognitive experience of this delayed-resolved and inclusive duality couldn't be more familiar. It works perfectly. But what happens if this experience is compacted into adjacent or nearly adjacent syllables?

The Chicago rappers Capital D and Iomas of All Natural do just that in "Double Speak" (2005), a song containing not just normally spaced end rhymes but back-to-back homophones:

We come to **rock**   **Rock** with me as we **roll**
Roll your windows down & let the people hear some **soul**
I **Sold** a couple **copies**   **Copy**cats they *bite* the **style**

My **style** is *really* **minor**   **Minors** *really* ain't **allowed**
Loud *music's therapeutic* to a brother's inner **state**
State your peace & keep it *moving,* time'll never **wait**
Weight is much too *heavy* for these *feather***weights** to **hold**
Hold comments til the **commentary** comes to a **close**
Close-caption   Cap is **rapping   Rapping** knuckles with the **mic**
Mike Jackson, Jackson Browne
Brown people all *unite*   to *fight* the **power**
Powerful forces   Force feed us false**hoods**
Hoods erupt, *disrupt* & *buck* the *struc*ture up for **good**
Good against the evil? Bush's *bat*tle lines are **trite**
Trying to *rat*ionalize his *greed*   He *needs* to get some **insight**
I **cite** the *whole* chapter & **verse   Well-versed** *virtuoso*
So if you want to hear from I-*O* y'all just **say so**

The two MCs trade lines, half lines, and even quarter lines in call-and-response mode, switching off between adjacent homophones. Completely dominating the end rhymes, these exuberant rhymes weld beats 4 and 1 or, sometimes also, beats 2 and 3, *conceptually overriding* the terminal and caesural pauses. Rhythmically, this rocks, as the first half line promises. What's new is not the homophonic rhyming itself, but its non-stop bap-bap styling.[39]

KRS-One's puns offer less fun but more profundity. He uses just three rhyme words in "Hold" (1995), a first-person ghetto narrative about lack, desperation, petty crime, manslaughter, incarceration, desperation, and partial acceptance. Cooperating perfectly in their semantic opposition and shared contexts, these words are *hold* (possess, grab, encompass, keep, persevere, solitary-confinement cell), *whole* (complete, all), and *hole* (debt, defective gap, puncture wound), with the compound variants *uphold* and *asshole*. The lines in "Hold" are short and lexically spare, the beat a noir slo-mo, but there are moments of delicious enjambment and sharp word play—

I make a mayonnaise sandwich out of some <u>whole-</u>
<u>Wheat</u>, I'm feeling <u>weak</u>, I can't <u>hold</u>

—where the meager nourishment is anything but wholesome and *hold* suggests both "hold myself together" and "keep the food down." Soon the narrator decides he needs to rob a neighborhood bodega and get some cash, but he can't hold his concentration to carry it off:

Half of me is sayin' maintain and **uphold**
Suddenly I bump into some **asshole**
He's cursin' me out, but this pistol that I **hold**
Took control, and in his head I put a **hole**
Ahhh man, now I'm lookin' around the **whole**
Area, the gun is still hot that I **hold**
I'm buggin' out and I don't know how much longer I can **hold**
I feel myself sinkin' deeper in the **hole**
So in my victim's pants I rip a little **hole**
And felt for the wallet, and took the **whole**
Bill-**fold**, forty bucks is what I **hold**
Suddenly I hear, Freeze! Police! **Hold!**

That's the second verse in its entirety. Soon the speaker is in the penitentiary, fights again, and ends up in the hole, where he strives desperately to maintain his sanity. Throughout "Hold," anger and isolation hold the mood, which is predominantly numb, hopeless, and chilling, even when it combusts into violence. It's the anger of the forced march, the anger of the refugee camp, against social forces too huge to grasp or grapple with. In the end, the only moral left is a spiritual one. At the end of the third verse, non-rhyming:

My needs and wants messed up my life on a whole
Damn. Just wasn't satisfied with life

And then, in rhyming prose: "The moral to the story is your addiction to your needs and your wants is what causes problems in your life. Make sure you got whatcha need. Put at a safe distance all the things that you want. It's wants that get you into trouble. This is the balance of life, the balance to life on a *whole*."

This sad morality tale could perhaps have been told in normal rhymed couplets or even in prose. Granted that all MCs—including professed spiritual teachers like KRS-One—try to rhyme well, what motivated him to create his unique homophonic rhyme scheme? Probably an inspired awareness of the power inherent in its three key words.[40] Each word is slippery, and each word counters its cousins. You can't hold on to what you're holding. No sooner are you holding money, having failed to hold your cool, then the police are yelling "Hold!" Nothing "whole" has unity, completeness, or permanence—neither wheat bread, a bank roll, a billfold, or a life.

Every "hole" is an irritant, gap, or wound. Nothing whole can hold and every attempt to hold what's whole has a hole. These rhymes enact continual social and psychological tension. Their amorphous unity of sound expresses a cruel paradox. With or without its moral, "Hold" is one of the saddest songs in hip hop. Its sustained, minimal rhymes may not wow us, jab us, or get us up dancing, but they do something else and something more, advancing the art.

Modes and Genres

They say you can rap about anything except for Jesus
That means guns, sex, lies, videotape
   —Kanye West, "Jesus Walks"

As a pulsing yet spectacularly complicated vocal art, rap is not so much an art of speaking as an art of being heard: an art of public lyricism. Self-expression (lyric) is rap's basic mode. But *rap songs*, although they seldom feature just one MC rapping a single verse, typically contain alternating verses and choruses, and not uncommonly they feature more than one MC; so they are normatively collaborative, not just lyric. The verses may be arranged so as to tell stories or even to represent interactive vocal parts; therefore, rap songs can also be narrative or dramatic works. This chapter will consider the four modes of rap—lyric, collaborative, narrative, and dramatic—and how these modes relate to issues of style, voice, and thematic coherence.

Good rap music needs to be rhythmically infectious, poetically effective, and fun to hear. It also needs to speak to common audience interests and experiences (such as love, sex, money, and personal aspirations) and social issues like poverty and oppression, gun violence, and drugs. Some of these topics aren't at all fun, but they're real, and if artfully expressed, they can be enjoyable to hear. In dealing with certain harsh or dangerous realities, some MCs adopt a teaching mode, rapping against social injustice generally, against drugs, gang warfare, police brutality, or unprotected sex specifically, or advocating some moral or spiritual solution; but most MCs rely on lyric or narrative modes to describe, through boasts and autobiographical stories, how they have overcome the adversities of ghetto life. These poetic modes often enhance truth with fiction. They depend on their audience's need for fantasy.

Given that rap's modes are predominantly lyric and narrative, Kanye's provocative complaint that Jesus has been excluded in favor of "guns, sex, lies, videotape" deserves our attention. Lyric psalms and narrative histories from Genesis to the Gospels figure importantly in the Bible, along with prophesies, letters, and books of wisdom. But in most African American church traditions, the dominant lyric forms—hymn singing, gospel singing, call and response—are all collaborative and congregational, whereas in rap music, the lyric voice, since the mid-1980s, has been almost exclusively solo. There are a lot of guns and sex in rap lyrics, and it's fair to say that much that's said by MCs about themselves amounts to hyperbole, a kind of lie. Of course, rap can and does accommodate spirituality, and quite a few "conscious" rappers honor Allah (if not Jesus) and may even adopt a quasi-preaching mode to advocate love, respect, and social justice. But the key components of rap poetics—the long, unruly line, crowded with rhymes, the complicated interplay of beat and voice, the pervasive tonal dissonance—are not particularly suited to religious expression. Nor are the components of rap poetics well suited to many of the traditional lyric genres or—partly due to the shortness of rap verses—to narrative genres that require complex character development. It follows that the dramatic mode is relatively rare in rap. Drama fares much better in theatrical plays or in films like *Sex, Lies, and Videotapes*.

Poets and Personas

Certainly many MCs do rap from life experience—the experience of lack, struggle, hustling, even crime. KRS-One was homeless when he began his career. Biggie, Nas, and Jay-Z each spent some time selling crack. Snoop Dogg, Ice Cube, Ice-T, and Eazy-E were Crips. Tupac Shakur was probably neither a Crip nor a Blood, but did prison time, and his parents were Black Panthers. Such experiences inform their verses, but their verses often inflate these experiences, filtering them through larger-than-life personas. Biggie, for example, was well past his period of street crime when he began rapping, yet in some of his verses, he acts as if he's still dealing drugs. Some rappers of modest means with no experience at all selling drugs or packing guns pretend that they are super-rich crime personalities who never pay taxes, sexually irresistible and tireless lovers, and perpetually high (yet hyper-alert or even spiritually realized) ninja street thugs fearless of death. They also commonly claim to be uniquely gifted rhymers who can and will battle and beat anyone who dares to challenge them. Since hundreds of competent MCs have made such claims, many of whom have dedicated lots of time and energy towards improving their art, there's obviously some ego and posturing at play. But as everyone realizes, it's mostly all in fun and an act: earnest fun, and a very profitable act. When The Notorious B. I. G. and Method Man engage in freestyle battling in "The What" (1994), they mock each other's sexuality, claim to be armed with multiple Glocks and TECs, and threaten each other with imminent death or time in the I. C. U., after which they duet a chorus, laughing, whooping, rocking the party. Whoever wins the battle, they'll be splitting the cash. Like a staged swordfight or a capoeira demo, it's skilled entertainment.

Performing Lyricism

The tradition of MCing dates back well before hip hop. Performance arts as diverse as the minstrel show, circus, vaudeville, and variety show often charged a master of ceremonies with the responsibility of warming up the audience and sustaining the buzz for the next number, act, or performer. When the featured artists were changing sets or instruments, the MC would keep the party going with wit and hype. His modes included storytelling, joke-cracking, mime, tap-dancing, and even lecturing or preaching. Whatever the activity between the acts, the MC would invariably draw the audience's attention to himself.

When hip hop was in its infancy and the main entertainment was in the dancing, the records being spun, and the DJ's production of looped beats, the MC's craft was subservient, consisting largely of jokes and jingles. But as the jingles evolved into more extended raps, the MC's work became the audience's focus, and the DJ's beat-making could seem subsidiary. The two roles flipped, artistically and formally. In many ways, however, the MC's verses between the choruses resembled the jokes and stories told between acts. To keep the hustle-bustle going, he or she would comment wittily about news and issues that the audience could relate to.

But these issues were intensifying. Before the record labels horizontalized hip hop's commercial reception, the audience's public life had long been confronted with the kinds of realities detailed in "The Message." By 1985, the "normal" hardships such as poverty, high unemployment, crime, and a disproportionately high (racist, classist) rate of incarceration were intensified by the crack epidemic. Rap topics came to include cautionary tales and portrayals of the crack hustlers on the street corner—a scene rife with Glocks, TEC-9s, sirens, and the overgrown fingernails of addicts, including prostitutes. Well before the life of the hustler and pimp began to be glorified as *the* gateway out of the ghetto—a cultural shift facilitated in part by rap's broader audience of suburban white youth, who could safely and voyeuristically romanticize the black urban experience—some rappers queried the possibly racist causation of the crack epidemic itself and highlighted the moral dilemmas confronting the street-corner hustlers. Rap's political voice could and did compete with rap's party voice. Getting high didn't preclude rebellious anger or social consciousness. The political voice, despite rap's increasingly elite poetic status under the stewardship of corporate record executives, screamed "fuck the institution that put us here."[1]

Rap's birth was not in any studio. "Rapper's Delight" was not its original anthem. Rap happened on the streets, in small clubs, in neighborhood homes. It could feel spontaneous, like the start of a local park's pick-up basketball game. Local poets with some skills were meeting up with their friends, or rather, posse, wherever there was a record or tape player, and after seeing an all-star DJ like Kool Herc slam-dunk a party with a few lines of rhyming wit, they'd practice doing the same. They'd practice shooting lyrical lay-ups, jump-shots, and dunks, so that when they could step up to the mic, they too could slam-dunk. They'd play the tape, then rap over it. After hearing a DJ hyping up a party using a call and response with the crowd—maybe at Sal's famous Disco Fever—they'd practice doing that too. As Cappadonna of the legendary Wu-Tang Clan recounts, "everyone was doin' it, *you know what I'm sayin'*."

Remember that Wu-Tang wasn't the first group of adolescent friends who started out by passing around the mic. The threesome in "Rapper's Delight" rapped in 1-2-3 sequence three times. Cold Crush followed the same model, with four MCs. Although Kurtis Blow rapped solo, he would always engage his studio audience in call and response. Posse rap predominated through the mid-1980s. Its tradition continued though Main Source's *Breaking Atoms*, where Nas's astonishing verse on "Live at the Barbeque" proved his breakout into street fame, leading to the eventual recording of *Illmatic*. Although this or that MC might leave the tight poetic community behind, making it to solo stardom, the sense of community persisted—and persists today, especially in cyphers. For each member, the mic offers a chance to grab everyone's ear, step into the spotlight for a minute or two, and say what you want to say about whatever you wanted to say about your hood, party, posse, skills, or self.

This short history illustrates how and why the MC's highly individualized voice has remained communal, how and why rap is modally both lyric and collaborative. Rappers may boast about their original rhymes and flow, or may narrate their own experiences, but they also often rap in sequence or battle each other in staged skill competitions. They may also bond in groups with names like "Binary Star." There's a continuum from posse rap and cyphers and battles to the rap game at large. Hip hop culture is formulated in part on continuous competition and tribute. It's as if everyone knows everyone, knows their latest mixtapes, knows their illest rhymes, and knows what and how everyone is rapping to what beats.

Lyric Personas

MC stage names reveal a lot about their social position and positioning— and about their performance modes. Many such names utilize a first name or initial or nickname or tag, any of which claims neighborhood familiarity. They say: "You already know me, and here I am again." Wonder Mike was a Michael, Big Bank Hank a Henry, Master Gee a Guy, Big L a Lamont, and so on. The nickname or simple initial loses the uncool formality of the given name, and then it's further enhanced by hyperbole, a falsification which may carry some truth. Sure, Big L was 5' 8", but he was big in the game until his untimely death. Was Wonder Mike a wonder? Did Big Bank Hank have a fat wallet? Was Master Gee a major talent or (just) a master of ceremonies? These are claims we can evaluate, then verify or reject, but meanwhile they drew a crowd. The Bronx's DJ Kool Herc was Jamaican-born Clive Campbell whose pseudonym was short for Hercules, son of Zeus and a renowned hero, but everyone loved and paid to hear his sound system and no one bothered to parse his name.[2] Grandmaster Flash also epitomized the hyperbolic boast, but no one who witnessed his performances doubted his name's accuracy. In truth, we *want* to make our favorite performers stars, so if they already have starry names it's okay.

Tagging is a way of inscribing the self in the city, which is just what Lawrence Parker did as KRS-One. He had already adopted as his middle name the name of Lord Krishna,[3] represented in Sanskrit by the letters K, R, and S. Adding "One," he proclaimed himself unique, the first, the best, asserting too that his tag was an acronym for "Knowledge Reigns Supreme Over Nearly Everyone." More modest tags include 2Pac, a cooler spelling of Tupac, Eminem (for **M**arshall + **M**athers), N. W. A. (Niggaz Wit Attitudes), and Nas. When Nasir Jones raps as Nas on *Illmatic*, he is Nasty Nas, representing the Queensbridge projects.

The style of urban tagging is lexical minimalism, but this is compensated by large, flashy graphics in graffiti and by bundled semantics in hip hop naming. The names put a high premium on uniqueness, in conformity with rap's main trope, the original ill rhyme; on familiarity, in conformity with rap's tough urban slang; and on hyperbole, in conformity with rap's dominant lyrical mode, the boast, with its dominant narrative mode, the autobiography of the self-made man. The boast's continuous trajectories can be easily traced from Kurtis Blow and Grandmaster Caz; to The Notorious B. I. G. and Nas; and to Jay-Z, Lil Wayne, and Kendrick Lamar. There are several kinds of boasts and success stories, but those with the most appeal within the economic constraints of the ghetto involve extraordinary skills, power, wealth, or sexual conquests. Many MC names advertise skills, of course, with Busta Rhymes owning one of the best names possible. With respect to power and wealth—or at least a style that simulates those things—the names can themselves embody bling, as in the case of Ice-T or Ice Cube, or they can simply sound cool, like Kool cigarettes. Quite often, during the 1980s and 1990s, they evoke the mack persona, or the thug or pusher persona, or, merging both, the mafia don persona. Grandmaster Caz's name claims not only supreme poetic mastery but Casanova's seductive sexual prowess. Big Daddy Kane, whose first album cover depicted him in regal attire surrounded by several adoring fly ladies, also epitomizes the pimp-in-his-Cadillac ideal (or cliché). Worthy female counterparts would include Foxy Brown, Salt-N-Pepa, Eve (the original woman!), and anyone named Roxanne. The thug persona is expressed relatively rarely in names like Killa, Kurrupt, Ghostface Killah, Gangsta D, and Bone Thugs-N-Harmony, and here it is important to bear in mind that irony figures in some such names. Public Enemy, for example, responds to a term particularly rampant in J. Edgar Hoover's FBI, and might (and did) refer to persons and groups opposed to the system; in other words, the name is provocative and proud. The Notorious in Notorious B. I. G. has a similar flavor, especially considering that the great rapper, with his alarmingly fat frame, was also Biggie Smalls. Within hip hop culture, these are fun names.

But scores of hip hop names reject hyperbole. A few rappers actually go by their real names. Eve really is Eve. Lauryn Hill is Lauryn Hill. Will Smith is Will Smith. Their names express unmediated self-confidence. It is interesting that Master Gee calls himself nothing more than what he is, just a master (of ceremonies), not a grandmaster. In "Rapper's Delight" he plays with the fact that he is third in line, that he has a cute little face with big brown eyes, and that the ladies like him for that. He uses modesty to successful ends. Not surprisingly, then, understatement commonly figures in hip hop naming. Think of Pee Wee, Shorty, Special Ed, Unknown DJ, Little Brother, or Lil Wayne. Or think of Lil' Kim, in fact petite and a Kimberly, but when she rhymes she's anything but little, she's formidable. Same with MC Lyte—nothing light or lite about her, she's a great poet with fantastic flow. This kind of modesty is in effect a hustle. Its paradox enhances the entertainment and is more interesting if less innocent that the grandiose claims made by early DJs and MCs.

Finally, hip hop names may proclaim specialized knowledge, traditional wisdom, or spiritual truth: Common Sense, Black Thought, The Roots, Guru, Black Star, Mos Def, Talib Kweli (Seeker, Truth). Or more than anything else they may express quirky playfulness, as with YoYo, Del the Funky Homosapien, Large Professor, Big Pun, or Snoop Doggy Dogg.

All these names, seen as a large array, describe the range of themes and attitudes that we find in rap music. A lot of it is boasting about success against adversity, with storytelling to back this up, which involves the representation of shared urban and African American hopes, fears, desires, and fantasies. A lot of it is the display of musical and poetic skill. A lot of it is wit, play, and nuanced understatement. A lot of it is teaching and, first and foremost, entertainment.

Shifting Messages, Shifting Modes

Although the different modes and genres of rap really do adhere to different formats, as we shall see, it's also true that the aesthetic goal of all rap music is to flip the beat with a perfect flow and rhymes that dazzle the mind. If these are delightful, most listeners are happy even if the message veers here and there, shifting cognitive designs like a kaleidoscope. We expect far stricter thematic coherence and generic clarity in literary forms like sonnets and odes. We allow, and maybe even prefer, rap performances to behave more like stand-up comedy, braggadocio, or secular sermonizing. In other words, the coherence and unity of a rap verse or song will often be only loosely topical, expressed in a mutable chain of ideas, couplet by couplet, articulated more through the sustained presence of the rapper's persona—killer, clown, party animal, prophet—than though sustained themes. What's tight in good rap is its unremitting linguistic focus on thematically sharp rhymes, apt phrases, and witty couplet shifts—in other words, on the aesthetic control of linked units whose very linkage depends on freedom from higher-level coherence. Each new rhyme, phrase, or couplet offers a new angle of perspective.

That said, many MCs can and do sustain thematic coherence, and their motivation to do so often reflects an awareness of mode and genre. Exposition and teaching, such as we hear in "The Message," Common's "I Used To Love H. E. R.," and Lauryn Hill's "Doo Wop (That Thing)," require the expression of coherent ideas. Narrative, if only due to its need to make chronological and causative sense within a discernible plot, needs to cohere more tightly than other, more pervasive lyric genres (such as the complaint, boast, taunt, or out-and-out battle attack), all of which will sound inauthentic if they exhibit anything like methodical logic—the more insane the better! On the other hand, good love lyrics should come off as coherently attentive to the Queen's glitter or the Bitch's pheromonic body, dripping with party sexuality. Good buddah songs don't need to sound intelligent, but they need to make coherently smoky, smooth, easy sense.

Lyric, Collaborative, Narrative, and Dramatic Modes

These can be defined as distinct foundational categories of poetic expression, whereas genres denote the particular kinds of works within these modes. A lyric poem might be a love song, war chant, hymn, psalm, lullaby, ode, elegy, complaint, or any other personal or communal expression. A collaborative poem might be a call-and-response work song, a litany, an operatic duet, or a staged poetry contest. Narrative might take form as an epic, ballad, romance, or autobiography. Drama might, generically speaking, occur as a theatrical play, which might be a tragedy, comedy, history, or melodrama; or might morph into an opera, musical, skit, mime, movie, puppet show, or even a dramatic monologue. Obviously, these modal and generic categories aren't fixed in stone. Couldn't a dramatic monologue also be lyric, narrative, or both? Isn't an autobiography narrative lyric?

Aristotle, the first ancient Athenian taxonomist of poetry, defined mode in terms of how the poet related to his or her production. In *On Tragedy*, Aristotle claimed that all poetry belonged to one of three basic modes. *Dramatic* poetry is *never* in the voice of the poet; all of its lines are created to be spoken by actors personifying characters. *Narrative* poetry *may* be told in the poet's voice but may also contain dialogue spoken by characters. *Lyric* poetry—supposedly—is *always* in the poet's voice. These categories are relevant to rap. The three verses rapped by Eminem but spoken by the character Stan in "Stan" are dramatic; much of Slick Rick's work, the Beastie Boys' "Paul Revere," Lupe Fiasco's "Little Weapon," and Immortal Technique's "Dance With The Devil" are narrative; and the vast majority of other rap songs are lyric. Most rap claims lyric authenticity, purporting to express the actual thoughts, feelings, and attitudes of the rapper.

Although foundational and still a useful starting point, Aristotle's tripartite modal scheme today feels dated. For one thing, it strongly favors representation over expression. Drama to Aristotle is the superior mode because it represents objective reality, not the poet's subjective reality; lyric is the inferior mode because if its utter subjectivity; and narrative falls between the two in that it alternates between representing characters' speech and expressing the poet's descriptions of their actions, settings, and so forth. Today we are much more willing to value subjective truth and lyric expression than in Aristotle's time. We may appreciate Shakespeare's sonnets as much as Shakespeare's plays, even though the sonnets lack the plays' monumentality, and if we enjoy hearing what MCs say about their own selves and situations, we don't necessarily feel that we are experiencing inferior art.

Additionally, Aristotle's notion of lyric is naïve: some literary lyric genres (like sonnets) and rap lyric genres (like boasting) *seem* to be in the poet's voice, and are performed by the poet, but they're often composed and performed in the voice of a dramatic persona. This is explicit when Eminem raps as Stan or Slim Shady, but it may implicitly so in rap songs with mack personas, gangsta personas, fly girl personas, or drawling Dirty South personas. Then too, a lot of poetry including rap is modally mixed. *The Canterbury Tales* is a collection of tales with interspersed dramatic interludes. Verse 1 of Nas's "N. Y. State of Mind" begins as lyric and shifts into narrative. And finally, Aristotle either didn't know or didn't care about the fourth mode: *collaborative*. This mode may be entirely cooperative and seamless, as in the Japanese *renga* tradition of linked verse or, if you will, in the can't-stop rapping of the Wu-Tang Clan; but it also shows itself in combative verse like the medieval *flyting*, Brazilian *desafia* music, and rap battles. Collaborations may take place within one song ("The What") or between songs (Tupac versus Biggie, Nas versus Jay-Z, Lil' Kim versus Nicki Minaj). In some rap battles, the emotions expressed are truly vituperative, yet the poetic output falls clearly within the ancient and global tradition of the poetry contest.

Before examining the lyric, collaborative, narrative, and dramatic modes of rap, we need to say a word about choruses. Early hip hop mostly consisted of verses interspersed with break beats, sometimes introduced with tags (like

Kurtis Blow's "and *these* ARE the breaks") or with very brief rapped choruses (as in "The Message"); but since then sung choruses have increasingly filled the structural spaces before, between, and after rapped verses. Increasingly, these choruses have also become longer even as the verses have shrunk to conform to the standard sixteen-bar norm, or even to twelve or fewer bars. Hip hop, it seems, has become more and more hip pop, and as this has happened, one of the quintessential features of rap, its verbal freedom, its structural volatility, has been somewhat tamed. Although artistically brilliant, Lil Wayne's "She Will" (2011) has two sixteen-bar verses by Weezy and three sixteen-bar choruses by Drake. Since Lil Wayne actively participates in the third chorus, one could say that the two artists share the stage almost equally, but the chorus lines outnumber the verse lines 48 to 32. In an earlier love/sex song, Khia's "My Neck, My Back" (2002), the ratio is 58 to 26. Both of these songs have an unusual degree of unity and coherence, hers even more than his. In Khia's song the verse and chorus lines all deal (simply) with sex; whereas in Lil Wayne's, the sexuality, while just as pervasive, is tempered by a complex web of philosophical, spiritual, social, and comical concerns. Other rap songs, many of them exhibiting far less thematic coherence verse to verse, rely heavily on summarizing choruses to articulate—and simplify—their "messages."[4]

Lyric Rap

This is rap's dominant mode, that of personal expression. We experience lyric mostly through the I-voice, as in these lines by Snoop Dogg, Lil' Kim, and Biggie:

> With so much drama in the L. B. C.
> It's kinda hard bein' Snoop D-O-double-G
> But I, somehow, some way
> Keep comin' up with funky ass shit like every single day.   [Snoop Dogg]

> All around the world I ball like a ball team.
> I stack chips, call me Mrs. Rothstein.
> Trix is for kids, silly rabbit, you're my offspring.
> Kim more anticipated than a LeBron ring.   [Lil' Kim]

> To all the ladies in the place with style and grace,
> Allow me to lace these lyrical douches in your bushes. [Biggie]

Note, though, that Snoop's individuality in "Gin and Juice" is contextualized by the Long Beach Crips—or alternatively, the Long Beach/Compton area—which he's differentiating himself from, or maybe also representing. Lil' Kim's individuality in "Black Friday" is constructed as a collage of adult sports and film references, so as to contrast with Nicki Minaj's childish gimmicks. Biggie's macho individuality in "Big Poppa" relies on flirtatious, comical obscenity addressed to the ladies. Rap's lyric voices, then, although to some degree personal, pretty much always bounce off of other individuals or groups, meanwhile representing a place, race, or gender. At times the personal I-voice morphs right into a we-voice, that of the crew . . . or even that of God's Chosen People:

> Straight outta Compton, crazy motherfucker named Ice Cube
> From the gang called Niggaz Wit Attitudes.   [N. W. A.]

> So here I go kickin' science in ninety-five
> I be illin', parental discretion is advised
> Still, don't call me nigga, this MC goes for his
> Call me God, 'cause that's what the black man is
> Roamin' through the forest as the hardest lyrical artist
> Black women you are not a bitch you're a Goddess
> Let it be known, you can lean on KRS-One
> Like a wall 'cause I'm hard, I represent GOD   [KRS-One]

Love/sex lyrics necessarily require the I-voice because most potential partners prefer intimacy. Romancing brings out the candlelight mood, courteous speech, and slow-tempo beats with sampled soul music and strings; or it brings out sexual posturing and humor. It helps to have a smoothly rough voice to pull this off, a voice like Snoop Dogg's or, as in "Ratha Be Ya Nigga" (1996), complementary voices like Tupac's *and* Richie Rich's.[5] Demonstrating that hip hop love need not be earnestly heart-felt, this duo shares the verses addressed to the lady. Their sentiments follow the venerable tradition of the blues singer's backdoor man, where the ambition is not to be her soulmate or friend, but to make her happy in bed:

> Look, now you was sprung from the introduction
> My conversation's full of game yet laced with seductions
> I see ya blushing like ya want somethin'
> Come get a taste of America's Most Wanted
> And let's get into some touching, erotic fucking   [Tupac]

I'll be your nigga, as long as we can understand
That I's the nigga and Sport Coat can be the man
He wine and dine, but me and you we whine and grind
And when I'm on the field keep him on the sidelines   [Richie Rich]

It's fun, it's an act, and its sex appeal is palpable. Snoop and Tupac always enjoyed strong female fan followings, and the producers of gangsta rap records in the 1990s were well aware of this market, so many an album contained the obligatory love song, an incongruously mellow interlude amid the flying bullets, police sirens, threats, and counter-threats. Like rap lyrics generally, the love/sex song typically includes some boasting, but its generic rules conform to the rhythm and flavor of seduction.[6]

Drinking lyrics, like love lyrics, date back thousands of years. There's of course a fair amount of Cristal and Hennessey in rap songs celebrating the high life of success, but more pervasive than alcohol are endo and blunts, signaling both a party mood and a commitment to the thug life. In fact, marijuana can almost claim its own lyric genre. Here the tempo is as slow as it can get, the voice is the collective we-voice, and since not much happens except sharing weed and staying high, the verses rarely show any thematic progression. The functional differentiation between verse and chorus tends to break down, as in an Afrika Bambaataa song where, similarly, the experience of unity controls the party mood. The classic is Bone Thugs-N-Harmony's "Buddah Lovaz," released on *Eternal 1999* (1995). Its minimal beat is comprised of sampled synth piano and bass notes, with an extraordinarily slow record skip. The four syllables in "Buddah Lovaz" fill one four-beat line. There are no verses, just slow lines traded in the inimitable Bone Thugs melodic style:

Keep hittin' that reefer, sendin' me straight to heaven (x4)   [Krayzie]

Keep rollin', smokin', and chokin'

Buddah lovaz
                                                                      [All]
Gotta learn to smoke the Buddah

I'm so glad you showed me, Krayzie, Layzie, Wish, Flesh   [Bizzy]

Reefer really makes me happy   [Krayzie]

Hydro, me just can't let a me high go   [Krayzie, Layzie]
Me smokin' upon that hydro
Me just can't let a me high go

Within the album, this song represents an island of tranquility. However, its opening words, "Nigga, it's the niggas night out tonight, nigga," are followed by howling. A snippet of dialogue near the end, claiming a shared ability to remain alert although high—

It's a Bone thang how a nigga like me smoke and maintain   [Layzie]

Maintain, maintain   [Krayzie]

—takes on an ominous meaning as "Buddah Lovaz" segues right into the ambush attempt in "Die Die Die." The proximity and indeed interconnectedness of drug-high spirituality and death also informs the Bone Thugs number one elegy, "Tha Crossroads," Biggie's *Ready to Die* (1994), his posthumous *Life after Death* (1997), and Tupac's *All Eyez on Me* (1995).

Stoner rap has become increasingly prevalent in the new millennium. Lil Wayne, Kid Cudi, Wiz Khalifa, Chief Keef, and others feature weed-smoking as a core lifestyle necessity. In some cases, smoking serves group unity, as between with Wiz Khalifa or Chief Keef and their respective posses; but the I-voice tends to displace the we-voice, for example in the chorus from Wiz Khalifa's "In The Cut" (2010):

We never low (low)
Away we go (go)
Like we supposed to go (go)
I always keep one rolled
I keep one rolled (x4)
In the cut, in the cut, rollin' doobies up (x4)

As in "Buddah Lovaz," there's some sampled stoned giggling, but it no longer sounds happy; it sounds gloating. So does this line from the intro, "And I prolly fucked your bitch nigga," and added boasts about wealth and sexual conquest: "Rolling all this weed I am holding . . . Come to my crib see money so big you can't fold it . . . Show money / Leaving show car low full of hoes for me / *hahaha* / It's so funny," etc. Mainly what we hear is Wiz's ego.

In Kid Cudi's "Just What I Am" (2012), the ego is no less prominent in both hook ("I need smokes / I need to smoke / Who gon' hold me down now? / I wanna get higher") and verse:

> Let me tell you 'bout my month y'all
> Endless shopping I had a ball,
> I had to ball for therapy, my shrink don't think that helps at all, whatever
> That man ain't wearing these leather pants
> I diagnose my damn self, these damn pills ain't working fam'
> In my spare time, punching walls fucking up my hand
> I know that shit sound super cray, but if you had my life you'd understand

In Lil Wayne's "Kush" (2007), the traditional association of weed and sex feels more like a party attitude in the chorus because it's we-voiced and because the wordplay evokes both sex and a basketball game—

> Yeah, and we smoke that kush
> Yeah, that kush
> Yeah, and we ball like swoosh
> Yeah, like swoosh

—but once Weezy starts rapping his verses the attention shifts from whatever "new shit" everyone's smoking and the "purple" (cough medicine with codeine) he's sipping to his own sexual activities, grille, diamond ring, and luxury coupes. As in other recent stoner rap, the I-voice takes over. Weed is featured less as an aid to group unity and more as an item (like pricy champagne) in the MC's personal inventory of success. To Lil Wayne's credit, he manages to rhyme on all these things with crisp humor and even some self-directed irony:

> I'm on that screw juice but I keep my shit together, not a screw loose
> Yeeaahh, word to my Gucc boots, I'm higher than a new suit

Seven years later, however, he's still using hard. In "Moment" (2014), his voice in the intro, as he repeats "Never question greatness," is so weak and slurred that it seems he could pass out any moment, but as if to dramatize his continued competence, he recovers his vocal volume and poise, offering— paradoxically—a stunning characterization of addictive thinking:

> Have my cake and eat it too, I want a bakery
> And see lately

All I've been doin' is celebratin'
Don't even know what I'm celebratin'
I know why you ain't celebratin', 'cause you ain't sellin' nathin[7]

As we contemplate the relatively long run of the buddah rap genre as compared with, say, the let's-cruise-and-see-what-trouble-we-can-get-into genre of gangsta rap—each of which changed year by year and artist by artist—it pays to reflect on the fundamental volatility of the lyric mode generally. Yes, there has been poetry about love, about mind-altering substances, and about social enmity and violence as long as there have been humans speaking languages, but all the lyric genres are susceptible to frequent shifts in social mood or Zeitgeist. There was a time before the emergence of N. W. A. when one of rap music's main lyric themes was, as with Afrika Bambaataa and the Zulu Nation, the diffusion of gang violence and the channeling of its social energy into constructive neighborhood-building. And there was a time, pre-Bone Thugs, pre-Tupac, pre-Biggie, when smoking blunts was not regarded as a key bonding experience; when even Biggie, in "The Ten Crack Commandments," could urge, "Never get high on your own supply"; when crack-heads and other addicts were regarded with disdain even by rappers who celebrated their actual or fictional drug-hustling; when the crack epidemic itself was viewed as a collaborative plot by the CIA and municipal police departments; and when some "conscious" rappers, inspired by Islam or other spiritual traditions, condemned all intoxicants.

The current surge in stoner rap may be attributable in part to demographics, to the particular appeal of weed among junior high and high school and college students, as well as to the music media's dominance by MP3 downloads easily marketable to this population, as well as to the lingering sense—soon to be trumped by marijuana legalization—that getting high is socially transgressive. This too will pass. We may expect new lyric genres to emerge and current ones to morph or dwindle. Rap music constantly remakes itself, shifting with the times. It's quite possible that some new movement of social consciousness, creating new genres with new voices, will come out of the currently predominant theme of self-absorbed hedonism. Hints of such a shift may be audible in the hip hop underground, where free downloads vie against the ninety-nine-cent iTunes dominance, and where a professed prophet like Jay Electronica is introducing new themes and perhaps new genres to the rap game.

It's fair to say that most of the cultural battling over the soul of hip hop— materialist versus spiritual, commercial versus indie, violent versus brotherly, misogynist versus feminist, stoned versus sober, partying versus political, capitalist versus working-class—has been waged within lyric. Let's close this section by quoting an early professed prophet and political ideologue whose hard, frank lyric styling never became dominant but has continually inspired past and emerging MCs. KRS-One's "Ah Yeah" was released the same year (1995) as "Buddah Lovaz." Its title phrase, as KRS's hook explains, is "whatcha say when you see a devil down" and "whatcha say when you take the devil's crown." As we've seen, KRS claims to represent God because "that's what the Black man is."[8] Here he enacts that role lyrically, taking divine vengeance against the forces of slavery and oppression[9]:

> While other MCs are talkin' 'bout up with hope down with dope
> I'll have a devil in my infrared scope,
> WOY! That's for calling my father a boy
> KLAK KLAK KLAK! That's for putting scars on my mother's back,
> BO! That's for calling my sister a hoe,
> And for you, BUCK BUCK BUCK, 'cause I don't give a motherfuck
> Remember the whip, remember the chant, remember the rope end
> You black people still thinkin' about vot-ing?
> Every president we ever had lied
> You know I'm kinda glad Nixon died!

Collaborative Rap

Already in this chapter we cited many instances of MC/posse collaboration, including "Rapper's Delight" and the Wu-Tang Clan, and we witnessed Tupac and Richie Rich collaborating in the verses of "Ratha Be Ya Nigga" and all of the Bone Thugs contributing solo and unison lines to the slow flow of "Buddah Lovas." The album *Eternal 1999* required close production collaboration between Bone Thugs-N-Harmony and Eazy-E, which resulted in the rare musical collaboration of their unique melodic styling and G-Funk beats. At its origin, rap music was defined by its fusion of sampled beats and four-beat poetry, by the collaboration of DJ and MC. Within songs, choruses collaborate with verses. MCs and producers collaborate in the creation of albums. In brilliant, game-changing albums—such as Kendrick Lamar's *DAMN.* (2017)—all the songs collaborate in saying something bigger than their sum.

Behind all such collaborations is a culture of incessant competition, tribute, and allusion. Beat-biters are derided, yet beats are emulated and occasionally sampled. Rhyme-biters are shunned, yet particular phrases and even vocal timbres may be appropriated as respectful allusions. KRS-One's vegetarian slogan, "suicide, it's a suicide" (1987), referring to the lives of pigs destined for the meat market, has become a rap meme, used by Ice-T and many others up through Pusha T. It sounds good, it resonates in many situations (including police chases), and it obliquely honors KRS-One. Lupe Fiasco, in the chorus of "Little Weapon," alters his voice with an audio processor to sound like Biggie, the point being to allude ironically and poignantly both to Biggie's assault lexicon (TECs, clips, etc.) and to the gunshots that killed him. Jay-Z begins his hit song "Izzo (H. O. V. A.)" (2001) by calling himself God (Jehovah) or, alternatively Hustler Of VA, meanwhile covering these claims in a pop veneer by quoting Snoop Dogg's *fo shizzle my nizzle* lingo:

> H to the izz-O, V to the izz-A
> Fo' shizzle my nizzle used to dribble down in VA

Musically and commercially, this allusive boast played well. Lil Wayne, in turn, slyly references the same allusion in "This Is The Carter" (2004), poking at Jay-Z's grandiosity by using their shared nickname in a song and album (*Tha Carter*):

> Who am I, young Wizzle fa shizzle
> Flow sicker than a third floor in hospitals[10]

Rap's ongoing collaborative-competitive banter is formalized in battles, be they in earnest or in game. A fine example of playful freestyle battling is the unreleased version of "The What," pitting Method Man against Biggie, a revision of which appears on *Ready to Die* (1994). Because many of Biggie's original lines are revised and spliced into the album version, while Method's lines remain intact, much of their fresh repartee goes missing in the album—even though Biggie's flow and rhymes may have been "improved" (and made more relevant to the album's dominant themes). Biggie's original opening lines go like this:

> All it's **takin'** | is some **m**arijuana and I'm **makin'**
> MC's **break fast** | like **flapjacks** and **bacon**
> **Back spins** to **windmills**. | Who's **still** the **gin drinker**?
> **Ill thinker** | explodin' when the **paper hits** the **ink**

The chain of ideas here may not seem particularly coherent, but the sound density is amazing. Even as the second couplet veers away from the first in its imagery, it preserves the dominant–*ack* rhyme of the first, also transmuting the unstressed–*in* sound into a stressed rhyme syllable, also expanding the–*i*-assonance into the–*ill* rhyme, also combining the previous–*k* and–*in* sounds into a new–*ink* rhyme. Given the density of these rhymes, there seems little doubt about who's going to win this battle, right?

But Method's response is inspired in its specificity. We must assume that Biggie had his opening couplets prepared in advance because they're just too carefully interwoven and too witty to be plausible as spur-of-the-moment freestyle. All he needs to rhyme, he claims, is a couple of tokes, unlike other MCs, who require normal food; by extension, other MCs' rhymes are as ordinary as flapjacks and bacon, standard menu items; and meanwhile, there's the fat man joke (he's had *plenty* of flapjacks and bacon, and maybe would do well to diet only on dope!); and moreover (the pun comes from the performance pause), his rhymes are making the other MCs break . . . fast. We could elaborate further on Biggie's *back spins, windmills, gin drinker*, and his linking of *thinker* and *ink* to the theme of *writing*, but here is Method's series of counter-jabs to Biggie's breakfast metaphor and ink—and to his sounds:

> Here I **am**, | I'll be **damned** if this ain't some **shit**
> Come to **spread** the butter **lyrics** over hominy **grit**
> It's the low killer **death trap**, | yes I'm a **jet black ninja**
> Comin' where you **rest at**, | **surrender**

Method uses understatement in the first couplet to launch his counterattack, but the wit is fierce. "Here I am"—just me, I don't need anything but myself to battle you, not even dope!—which is pure jive in that Method is certainly as heavily into his drug of choice as Biggie. Meanwhile, countering Biggie's food metaphor, Method observes that what he has just heard amounts to *digestive waste* . . . which also means, of course, "excellent product." This paradox nicely expresses that what's going on is a battle of wits between two mutually respectful foes. Now Method adds a standard side to Biggie's derogatory breakfast menu, but whereas grits might normally epitomize (white) blandness, his pronunciation of "hominy" puns on *harmony*, and the grits turn into singular *grit*—tough determination. Biggie's *ink* in turn is transmuted to the *jet black* African American core color, also the hue of the ninja's robe. Meanwhile Biggie's rhyme chain of *spin/wind/ink/gin/drink/ think/ink* is capped by Method's *ninja*-chain, asserting that Biggie is just a *contender* who must *surrender*, that he's looking "cold-booty like your pussy in *December*." Method's ability to flip rhymes and figures is present as well in in his counter to another of Biggie's couplets:

> Mothafuckers thought I **slip** | bust my **lip**, right?
> You didn't know the extra **clip's** on my **hip**
>
> Nigga stop **bitchin'**, | button up ya **lip and**
> From Method all you **gettin'** is a can of ass-**whippin'**

Method's direct quotation of "lip" is underscored by the echo of *bust* and *button*. Biggie's posture meanwhile is reversed and humiliated as his armed *hip* is flipped into an *ass-whippin'* (picking up the *booty* and *pussy* from two lines prior).

Now who's winning this war of words? Method's flow may be rougher and his rhymes may be more modest than Biggie's, but Method's freestyle ability to counterpunch and jab thematically is impressive in its own right. Although he can never compete with Biggie's supreme rhythmic flexibility, at once quick and smooth, Method's own pugilistic style of heavy drawl and pause serves him excellently. It lets him rhyme, memorably, "Shaolin || Island." In the line, "Hey, I'll be kickin' || you son, you doin' all the yappin'," it adds a performative direct address to "you son," otherwise simply the direct object of "kickin'." In the line, "I'm not a gentle || man, I'm a Method || Man," it flips "gentleman" into his own name, now presented as a system name and an exclamation. For many listeners, these *moments* prove more memorable than Biggie's superlatively smooth flow.

This kind of styling contest depends on equivalently excellent skills, hard-earned and hard-fought, on a respected, legendary tradition of collaborative battling, and on a culture attuned to the tracking and evaluating of particular performances in fine detail. These MCs collaborated not only directly with each other but implicitly with those like Mel, Kool Moe Dee, and LL Cool J who preceded them, just as they no doubt hoped to inspire later great battlers. And all such poetry contenders collaborate with their avid, highly informed fans, knowing that whoever seems to be winning or seems to have won during and after their exchange, the verdict will come down from the street in the days and weeks to come.

Each production faces evaluation, in effect fighting to be heard and fending off the competition. In this regard, collaboration is closely allied with rap's predominantly lyric mode. No one struck back against "Stan" precisely because, as drama, it was self-contained. No one struck back against Mel's birth-to-death narrative in "The Message" or against the narrative works—instructive, silly, moral, or horrifying—of Slick Rick, the Beastie Boys, Lupe, or Tech because, again, none of the rapping in this mode was perceived as personal boast, threat, or challenge.

The same can even be said of All Natural's "Double Speak." Its continually collaborative back-and-forth pun-styling sounds thematically combative—

> **Loud** *music's therapeutic* to a brother's inner **state**
> **State** your peace & keep it *moving*, time'll never **wait**
> **Weight** is much *too heavy* for these *feather***weights** *to* **hold**
> **Hold comments** til the **commentary** comes to a **close**
> **Close-caption Cap** is **rapping. Rapping** knuckles with the **mic**
> **Mike Jackson, Jackson B**rowne
> **Brown** people all *unite* to *fight* the **power**

—but its poetics are totally non-threatening. The song competes with none other. It's formally unique. It represents an idea, style, and mode, but it behaves like an installation.

More typical, traditional, and ordinary are the non-stop sparring and swagger pervading mainstream rap's lyric mode, full of aggressive boasts, jabs, snide asides, and brutal humor. These are exemplified extraordinarily by Kendrick Lamar's verse on Big Sean's "Control," featuring both Kendrick on verse 2 and Jay Electronica on verse 3. In a gesture that would be astonishing in any other kind of music or poetry, Kendrick disses both of his collaborators.[11] He proclaims, "I'm the King of New York / King of the Coast, one hand, I juggle them both," and he reports that he's heard that the big debate in the barbershops on who are the best MCs has reached a kind of consensus in the triumvirate of "Kendrick, Jigga [Jay-Z], and Nas," along with Eminem and André 3000. He then goes on to call out J. Cole, Big K. R. I. T., Wale, Pusha T, Meek Mill, A$AP Rocky, Drake, Big Sean, Jay Electronica, Tyler the Creator, and Mac Miller for their mediocre output, adding—

> I got love for you all but I'm tryna murder you niggas
> Trying to make sure your core fans never heard of you niggas
> They don't wanna hear not one more noun or verb from you niggas

Now, the strongest responses to this scathing attack came from those who were unnamed in Kendrick's verse, hence excluded from the who's who of those who somehow matter: among others, Hopsin, Cassidy, Papoose, Joell Ortiz, Joe Budden, Stro, Kevin Hart, King Los, Claude Kelly, A$AP Ferg, and Lupe Fiasco. Their biggest beef is with Compton-born Kendrick's claim to be King of New York, crossing regional boundaries and constituting a kind of hip hop blasphemy, especially in the face of Sean's respect for Tupac and Biggie in the first verse. But Eminem, who responded with his own diss of Kendrick, said in a media interview that he admired "Control," thought it was good for hip hop and claimed a place in the honorable tradition of rap battling.[12] Or as one on-line commentator put it, "Kendrick killed everybody!"

Narrative Rap

A fairly extensive catalog of rap stories could be amassed, and it would include the Beastie Boys' "Paul Revere" (1986), N. W. A.'s "Boyz-N-The-Hood" (1987), Slick Rick's "Children's Story" (1988), Common's "I Used To Love H. E. R." (1994), KRS-One's "Hold" (1995), The Notorious B. I. G.'s "I Got a Story to Tell" (1997), Nas's "Rewind" (2001), Immortal Technique's "Dance With The Devil" (2001), André 3000's "A Life in the Day of Benjamin André (Incomplete)" (2003), Lupe Fiasco's "Little Weapon" (2007), and Kendrick Lamar's "The Art of Peer Pressure" (2012). Memorable narrative also occurs in songs not mainly cast in this mode. Coming right on the heels of his MC shout, "Everybody just rock and dance to the beat," Wonder Mike's anecdote in "Rapper's Delight" about being a captive dinner guest when "the food just ain't no good" has no purpose other than to make us laugh. On the other hand, Mel's grim fable of the anonymous lost life in the last verse of "The Message" caps that song's sketches of urban despair. As this list suggests, rap narratives include tall tales, teacher tales, morality tales, anecdotes, allegories, autobiographies, and social histories.

Although rap storytelling is much more common than rap drama, it's far less common than rap lyric, the mode that informs such first-person expressions as boasting, loving, partying, teaching, protesting, or beefing. A sustained, song-length narrative requires comparatively more detachment, more distance from the spontaneous or spontaneous-seeming performance self. Minimally, it requires a plot, which necessitates that lines, couplets, even verses follow a coherent sequence, usually chronological. It requires a believable setting, believable actions with believable motives and consequences, and (be they autobiographical, historical, or fictional) believable characters who may have lines of their own.[13] In other words, narrative requires skills over and above those needed to rap. So not all rappers can do narrative, and not all rappers want to do narrative. Contemporary cypher freestylers, for example, don't want to do narrative.

Paradoxically, because narrative requires extra attention to things like plot coherence and time management, the qualities of rhyme complexity and flow that we might expect, say, in a battle rap or boast may suffer. We've already observed that Mel modifies his edgy poetics in "The Message" when he shifts into narrative mode at the end. Although his rhythms remain wrenched and his rhymes remain memorable, suddenly Mel's couplets become closed, clear, progressive units. In the narrative traditions that follow from Mel's example, the couplet form continues to be clearer and less cluttered than what we find in more common rap expressions. At times, this clarity even feels poetically weak, as in Slick Rick's "Children's Story":

> Once upon a time not long ago,
> When people wore pajamas and lived life slow,
> When laws were stern and justice stood,
> And people were behavin' like they ought ta: good,
> There lived a Lil boy who was misled
> By anotha Lil boy, and this is what he said:
> "Me, Ya, Ty, we gonna make sum cash,
> Robbin' old folks and makin' tha dash,"
> They did the job, money came with ease,
> But one couldn't stop, it's like he had a disease

There's an unusual degree of parallelism here ("When . . . When . . . and . . . and . . . Lil boy . . . Lil boy"), and the rhyming is pretty much restricted to end-rhymes,[14] but if the syntax were less predictable or if the lines were jammed with rhymes, the increased poetic opacity might make Rick's story harder to follow. In Slick Rick's case, we might think that his poetic simplicity is due to his evocation of bedtime storybook style or due to him being Old School, but it may also be a useful stylistic adjunct of narrative itself.

Immortal Technique's "Dance With The Devil" is certainly one of the most horrifying rap narratives ever, detailing a gang initiation involving assault, rape, and murder, the victim of which is ultimately revealed to be the assailant's mother. Tech's lines are long but leisurely, and although two of the three couplets below contain rhymes of a more contemporary nature, end rhymes still predominate. Note that the middle couplet, describing the victim, contains only end rhymes and is comparatively bleak. In the first couplet, the internal rhymes intimate the disturbing dramatic irony of the situation, and the final couplet's rhythmically halting multi is tonally anything but clever—it's ominous:

> They **drove** around the projects **slow** while it was **raining**
> **Smoking** blunts, drinking and **joking** for enter**tainment**
> Until they saw a woman on the street walking a**lone**
> Three in the morning, coming back from work, on her way **home**
> And so they quietly got out the **car** and **followed her**
> Walking through the projects, the **dark**ness **swallowed her**

Finally, there is only end-rhyming at the narrative climax, subtly enhanced by alliteration.[15] The relatively matter-of-fact language only heightens the pathos:

> Right before he pulled the trigger, and ended her **life**
> He thought about the cocaine with the platinum and **ice**
> And he felt strong standing along with his new **brothers**
> Cocked the gat to her head, and pulled back the shirt **cover**
> But what he saw made him start to cringe and **stutter**
> 'Cause he was staring into the eyes of his own **mother**

Lupe Fiasco's handling of narrative in "Little Weapon" contrasts in its relative stylistic flamboyance:

> I killed another **man today**,
> Shot him in his back as he **ran away**,
> Then I blew up his hut with a **hand grenade**,
> Cut his wife's throat as *she* put her **hands to pray**,
> Just five more **dogs** then *we* can get a **soccer ball**,
> That's what my commander **say**. How **Old**?
> Well **I'm like** ten, **eleven**,
> Been **figh**ting since **I** was **like** six or **seven**,
> Now *I don't know* much about **where I'm from**
> *But I know* I strike **fear everywhere I come**,
> **Gov**ernment *want* me dead so I **wear** my **gun**,
> I really *want* the rocket launcher but I'm still too **young**,
> This candy give me courage not to **fear no one**,

> To **fear no pain**, and **hear no tongue**,
> So *I* **hear no screams** and *I* **shed no tear**,
> If I'm in *your* **dreams** then *your* **end is near**.

Rather than using an "objective" third-person voice, Lupe develops the child soldier as a subjective, dramatic first person character. The soldier is regularly drugged with "candy" by his commander, and he's a traumatized child doing things no child should ever have to do, so it's not surprising that his narrative feels incoherent and directionless. He's killed at least two people today (maybe also children in the hut), neither in a valorous manner. His verbs express sheer violence, paired with cruelly complicating multis. His victims aren't really human, they're *dogs*, rhyming with the *soccer ball* he and his comrades will get if they kill five more. The lines never settle into charity. Who knows if they'll get their soccer ball, it's just a promise. And: "I don't know . . . / But I know. . . ." "Government want . . . / I want . . ." As with normative lyric rap, there's a lot going on here and it's creatively unstable, edgy, and terrifying. The six concluding multis, five of them triplet epistrophes hinging on "no," leave no doubt about the soldier's dulled mental condition. He's become a phantom killer, a sociopathic "I" versus "you," completely out of touch with external and internal emotions.

At this point, it's worth remembering the role that narrative usually serves in rap: not to enable the construction of thematically coherent story-songs, but to lend authenticity to lyric verses. The logic, style, flow, and rhyming of this sort of supporting narrative has a lot more in common with Lupe's "Little Weapon" than with Tech's "Dance with the Devil," and it blends nicely into its lyric context. Verse 1 of Nas's "One Mic" contains a subsidiary narrative passage of five lines:

> Yo, all I need is one mic, one beat, one stage
> One nigga front, my face on the front page
> Only if I had one gun, one girl and one crib
> One God to show me how to do things his son did
> Pure, like a cup of virgin blood; mixed with
> 151, one sip'll make a nigga flip
> Writin' names on my hollow tips, plottin' shit
> Mad violence who I'm gon' body, this hood politics
> Acknowledge it, leave bodies chopped in garbages
> Seeds watch us, grow up and try to follow us
> Police watch us [siren] roll up and try knockin' us

One knee I ducked, <u>could it be my time is up</u>
<u>But my luck</u>, I got up, the cop shot again
Bus stop glass bursts, a fiend drops his Heineken
Richochetin between the spots that I'm hidin' in
Blackin' out as I shoot back, <u>fuck gettin' hit</u>!
This is my hood I'ma rep, to the death of it
'Til everybody come home, little niggaz is grown
Hoodrats, don't abortion your womb, we need more warriors soon
Sip from the star sun and the moon
In this life of police chases street sweepers and coppers
Stick-up kids with no conscience, leavin' victims with doctors
IF YOU REALLY THINK YOU READY TO DIE, WITH NINES OUT
THIS IS WHAT NAS IS 'BOUT, NIGGA THE TIME IS NOW!

Nas's lyric begins with expressions of his shifting aspirations for single-minded focus, as poet-performer, as man (with "one gun, one girl, one crib'), and as disciple to one God. The lyric voice demonstrates Nas's inability to attain such focus. The Eucharistic cup of "virgin blood" can be understood as more ordinary bloodshed, but whatever it's made of is soon mixed with 151 rum, which segues into criminality—which is being observed both by our children and by the police. Just as the lyric passage keeps flipping erratically, the narrative insert (authenticating the violence stemming from the police's role) shifts from past tense to present tense, follows a confusing series of flash events, and even shifts back into lyric mode within the narrative segment. The point is not that Nas has lost his poetic control; it's that his control consists in expressing an authentically unstable lyric and narrative subjectivity. Nas's moral clarity emerges in his final message, that killing and being killed is not the answer, but as his lyric demonstration argues, this resolution can only have arisen out of the actual experience of social conflict and psychological confusion.

Dramatic Rap

As influential as Lightnin' Rod's *Hustler's Convention* was in modeling a spectrum of MC personas, its purely dramatic mode has been largely ignored by MCs themselves, who prefer to rap in lyric genres like boasting, seducing, protesting, or teaching, in the collaborative genre of battling, or occasionally in the narrative genres of storytelling or history-telling. As we have seen,

Lightnin' Rod, working exclusively within an unpromisingly rigid 4/3/4/3 quatrain form, managed to create unique, differentiated voices for the characters of Sport, Spoon, Hominy Grit, extra hustlers, black cops, and even a white cop. To do this, he relied somewhat on appropriate vocabulary, but his main devices were vocal: each character had his own voice quality (gravelly, smooth, etc.) and speech mannerisms, expressed through intonations. Lightnin' Rod's vocal legacy lives on, not just in the decades-long and ongoing "conversation" among MC personas, but in the artistry of concept albums like Outkast's *Speakerboxxx/Love Below* set, or Kendrick Lamar's *DAMN.*, in which multiple voices compete in social and psychological continuums. Meanwhile, hip hop's cultural traction as a poetic, musical, and artistic phenomenon has resulted in the assimilation of MCing, DJing, break-dancing, and other dance skills like popping and locking into a variety of dramatic performance spaces and media,[16] eventually to include film,[17] TV,[18] and Broadway musicals, most notably Lin-Manuel Miranda's *In the Heights* and *Hamilton.*

Our focus here, however, is on drama in rap songs, where MCs play different dramatic rolls. On a very modest scale, Eminem adopts Lightnin' Rod's sort of vocal clowning in "The Real Slim Shady" (2000) to impersonate feminist critics who sound as monotonous as a turntable, who protest his sexist attitudes yet, against their better judgment, are sexually hooked:

> *Chigga chigga chigga*—Slim Shady, I'm sick of him
> Look at him, walking around grabbing his you-know-what
> Flipping the you-know-who. Yeah, but he's so cute though!

Lil Wayne in "A Milli" (2008) similarly provokes, then impersonates, the derision of white racists:

> I open the Lamborghini hopin' them crackers see me—
> Like look at that bastard Weezy
> He's a beast, he's a dog, he's a motherfucking problem

But such dramatic gestures are fleeting diversions within ongoing boasts. Is the rarity of sustained dramatic characterization in rap due to a scarcity of precedent, or is MCing itself a stubbornly lyric enterprise? Old-time MCs, like comedians, may have been master entertainers and impressionists, but they may never have staged the sort of mini-dramas found in literary dramatic monologues or in radio plays.[19] To rap lyrically in a particular persona, sharing this or that anecdote, opinion, personal claim, gripe, or tidbit of gossip requires less compositional forethought than rapping dramatically in the voice of a different person altogether. And when the MC's reputation comes to rely increasingly on writing original rhymes for his or her own flow—as well as, optimally, being able to improvise such rhymes—the attraction of dramatic rapping may be almost nil.

A dramatic rap song requires unusually tight thematic and structural control, whether or not its particular components express what might seems like casual, spontaneous thinking. The Notorious B. I. G.'s "Warning" (1994) exemplifies such control. It's a hip hop mini-play in two scenes with two contrasting formats, rap and skit. Scene I consists primarily of a soliloquy spanning two verses, in the rapper's familiar thug persona, who refers to himself alternatively as Biggie and Big Poppa. Awakened by his pager (the sampled sounds of its beep and ringtone), he shows himself both groggy and acutely aware of details. Several of these lines are rhythmically awkward, with just three stresses or with off-center pauses, but the speaker is very clear about the time of day and who's paging him and why. He's also criminally circumspect enough not to name the gambling spot:

> **Who** the **fuck** is **this?**
> **Pagin'** me at **5:46** | in the **mornin'**
> **Crack** a **dawn** || and **now** I'm **yawnin'**
> **Wipe** the **cold** out my **eye**
> **See** who's **this** || p̲agin' **me** | and **why**
> **It's** my nigga **Pop** || from the **bar**bershop
> Told me **he** was in the **gamblin' spot** || and heard the **intricate plot**
> Some **nig**gas wanna **stick** you || like **fly paper neigh**bor
> **Slow down love** | **please chill** || **drop** the caper

Biggie's speech winds down with the indirection quotation of Pop's message, as if Biggie is registering it carefully, attempting to calm down his informer. This reveals among other things that, even in the face of what is looming as an immediate threat to his life, Biggie can remain cool—which he does for the remainder of the song. At this point, Pop's voice comes in through Biggie's pager, enhanced by an audio processer, and dialogue ensues:

> *Remember them **niggas** from the **hill** up in **Browns-ville***
> *That you **rolled dice wit** || **smoked** the **blunts** and got **nice wit?***
> **Yeah** my nigga **Fame** || **up** in **Pro-spect**

Nah | dem my **nig**gas | **nah || love** wouldn't disre**spect**
*I **didn't** say **dem,** || they **schooled** me to some **nig**gas*
*That you **knew** from back **when,** || when **you** was **clockin' minor figures***

Over the next nine and a half lines, which (extraordinarily) span the two
verses, Pop's speech elaborates on Biggie's foes' murderous intentions and
on what information they have on him. The verses are separated formally
by a "chorus" of sorts, consisting of Biggie's fourfold repetition of "**Damn |
nig**gas **wan**na **stick** me for my **pa**pers," but Biggie's lines in no way respond
to Pop's reminder of the chain of loyalty, his implicit offer to use his Mac-10
machine pistol on Biggie's behalf, or his question about Biggie's plan:

So thank **Fame** for warnin' **me || now** I'm **warnin' you**
I **got** the **Mac,** nigga || **tell** me what you **wan**na **do**?

Biggie, in other words, is all about self-reliance. One of the song's great
moments is when Pop's half line is completed by Biggie's, in a radical and
comical shift of tone:

And they heard you got || half of Virginia locked down
They even heard about the crib you bought your moms out in Florida
The fifth corridor . . . || Call the coroner
There's gonna be || a lot of slow singin'
And flower-bringin' || if my burglar alarm starts ringin'

And for the next thirty lines, Biggie rhymes *all purpose war* and *Rottweilers
by the door, clip* and *bad predicament, reload* and *explode, Beretta buck* and
betta duck, and so on. The encapsulating statement is this six-syllable line:
"Betcha Biggie won't slip."

So we are expecting a shootout. There's silence, broken by some sampled
dog barking, then more silence. And then this multivoiced, mostly sotto
voce skit, constituting scene 2:

"Shh . . ."
"Come on mothafucka!"
"I'm comin' as fast as I can"
"Just bring yo mothafuckin' ass on come on!"
"Are we gettin' close? Huh?"
"It's right over here"
"Man, are you sure it's Biggie Smalls crib man?"

"Yeah I'm sure mothafucka come on"
"Oh fuck, it better be his mothafuckin' house"
"Fuck?"
"It better be this mothafucka's house"
"Oh shit!"
"What? What's wrong man?"
"What's that red dot on your head man?"
"What red dot?"

"Oh shit, you got a red dot on your head too!"
"OH SHIT!"

Then two gun shots. Then silence. That's it. The impact of this cartoon rap drama depends on our realization that Biggie's battle boast is a soliloquy grounded in fantasy. There are no actual Rottweilers at the door, since the only barking dogs are outside, and Biggie's arsenal is probably more modest than claimed. Biggie represents invincibility. His would-be assassins turn out to be incompetent fools, but until we hear their all-too-human voices in the skit the dramatic suspense is powerful. And the end surprises: it's not fire-power that wins, but intelligence, technology, and marksmanship. Weapons with night-vision scopes.

Another coherently dramatic rap hit is Eminem's "Stan" (2000), composed primarily of four dramatic monologues which, as a set, delineate a tragic failure of dialogue between Stan, an increasingly obsessive and deranged fan, and his hip hop idol Slim Shady. Eminem raps verses 1–3 as Stan and verse 4 as Slim. The chronology is painful, ironic, and powerfully moral in its impact. The first two verses are fan letters addressed to Slim; the third, also addressed to Slim, is a tape recording made by Stan as he drives toward a bridge intent on killing himself, his girlfriend, and his unborn child; and the fourth is Slim's delayed response to the two fan letters. The sequence is rapped over a base sample from Dido's "Thank You," and her opening lines form the chorus. Dido's repeated lyric expressions of lonely love evoke, in the song's dramatic context, the silent sentiments of Stan's victimized girlfriend:[20]

My tea's gone cold I'm wondering why I
    Got out of bed at all,
The morning rain clouds up my window
    And I can't see at all,

> And even if I could it'll all be gray,
>> But your picture on my wall
> It reminds me, that it's not so bad,
>> It's not so bad.

Throughout "Stan," the verse lines brilliantly express dramatic meanings. As said, three of the four verses are ostensibly letters, which would neither rhyme nor obey metrical rules in real life; but *these* letters nevertheless work as dramatically significant discourses displaying character change, tension, and ironic timing. Their poetic features signal psychological and thematic nuances which would be lost in flat, epistolary prose.

In verse 1, Stan seems like a fairly "normal" fan even though the first words out of his pen/mouth are abnormally whiny. It's the stress patterns and tones which betray how weird he really is:

> **Dear Slim**, ‖ I **wrote** you but you *still* ain't **cal**lin'
> I left my **cell**, | my **pag**er, ‖ **and** my home phone at the **bot**tom

Not only is Stan someone who expects a phone call in response to a letter, but he's impatient, as communicated by the secondary stress on "still." He's a bit obsessive, like any fan, leaving three numbers at the bottom of the letter, but his unusual stress on "and" suggests that he feels he deserves credit for such thoroughness. Which is weird. His two-stress "Dear Slim," taking up a full half line, is inordinately ponderous, as is his hero fixation, expressed later in this verse by the obsessive and also fawning allusions to Bonnie, Ronnie, Skam, and Rawkus.[21] Here the word "cell" may well connote—to us, if not to Stan—more than just a mobile phone, while "at the bottom" certainly forecasts, with dramatic irony, both Stan's addictive bottoming out and his vehicle's plunge to the bottom of the river after verse 3.[22]

Composing normally silent letters as performed rap verses also introduces rhyme as a powerful dramatic tool. After immediately blaming Slim for not calling him, Stan makes a deferential and probably disingenuous tactical retreat: "There **prob**ably was a **prob**lem at the **post** office or **some**thin'." This would be a relatively sane statement if its insincerity weren't communicated by Stan's sullen intonations; and, again, there is a subtle irony here. The rhyme of *probably* and *problem* reveals a symptom of Stan's craziness. As is shown in verse 4, Slim has always planned to write Stan and has been tracking the details of his letters, but he's been too busy to write, and Slim did not intentionally snub Stan at the Denver concert, etc., so Stan's version of probable reality is always his main problem. Almost every couplet in this song has equivalently resonant rhymes. Those in this passage from verse 2, highlight the extreme codependency of fan to idol:

> I can re**late** to what you're **say**ing in your **songs**
> So when I have a shitty **day**, I drift away and put 'em **on**
> 'Cause I don't really **got** shit else so that shit **helps** when I'm de**pressed**
> I even got a tat**too** of **your** name across the **chest**
> **Some**times I even **cut** myself to **see** how much it **bleeds**
> It's like adrenaline, the **pain** is **such** a sudden **rush** for me

Or consider this multi end-rhyme chain concluding verse 1, which pretty much says it all: *didn't want him, biggest fan, did with Skam, pictures, man, shit was phat, hit me back, biggest fan, this is Stan.*

As already noted, stresses in these vocally rendered letters do a lot to cue themes and also attitudes. In normal English—including normal rapping—stresses usually mark content words (nouns, verbs, adjectives, adverbs), which label objective realities. Stan's abnormal stress on *and* in "my cell, my pager, and my home phone," turns a neutral conjunction into a resentful whine. Of course the nouns themselves are also revealing in that they refer to communication—which is what Stan desperately wants. Much quieter is his sequence of "my . . . my . . . my." Those redundant little possessive pronouns don't seem to mean much, but they're suggestive of Stan's neediness. He is someone who wants to own or be close to everything he admires, and this drive causes him to cross the line in his P. S. to Slim: "We should be together too."

So the tragic plot and themes are clear enough. The title character's issues are clear enough. We're shocked but not surprised when we hear Stan addressing Slim in verse 3—

> Dear Mister-I'm-Too-Good-To-Call-Or-Write-My-Fans,
> This'll be the last package I ever send your ass

—or when we realize he's not writing at all but literally ranting, drunk and drugged up, or when we know he's going to kill both himself and the one person he can and should be closest to. We're not surprised when Stan screams and curses Slim. Nor are we surprised to learn—and hear—that Slim's letter in verse 4 is contrastingly thoughtful, calm, caring, and clear about the normal fan-performer boundaries. The dramatic plot works well.

But what makes this a great song is the meticulousness of Eminem's writing, which impacts the skill of his rapped acting.

It turns out that Stan and Slim speak in contrasting line rhythms and rhyme patterns.[23] But to keep things relatively simple for the moment, let's return to those personal pronouns. Everyone uses them from time to time, as need arises, and Slim uses them normally, usually as unstressed words but stressed for special emphasis. In Slim's letter, such stressed pronouns are clustered mostly in this passage:

> And **what's** *this* **shit** about **us** *meant* to **be** together?
> **That** type of *shit*'ll make **me** not want **us** to **meet** each other
> I **rea**lly think **you** and your **girl**friend **need** each other
> or **may**be **you** just **need** to **treat** her better

Slim's extra stressed syllables and his chain of "us . . . me . . . us . . . meet" seem to point to a not inappropriately visceral response to Stan's P. S., but it's clear that Slim has let go of whatever unease he feels almost immediately, because otherwise he would stress the "I" at the start of the third line. The tone of Slim's two uses of "you" is not accusatory at all, but one of well-meaning counsel. And the stressed "you" in Slim's last line is one of song's saddest moments:

> Some dude was drunk and drove his car over a bridge
> And had his girlfriend in the trunk, and she was pregnant with his kid
> And in the car they found a tape, but they didn't say who it was to
> Come to think about it, his name was . . . it was you, damn!

Contrastingly, Stan stresses first and second person pronouns inordinately in his letters, nine times in verse 1 and, as his obsession heats up, twenty-two times in verse 2. In the tape-recorded verse 3, the number shrinks to thirteen, but he uses the name Slim. These lines are indicative: "**Hey Slim**, that's **my** girlfriend **scream**in' in the **trunk** / But **I** didn't slit her **throat**, **I** just tied her **up**, / See **I** ain't like **you**."

At the song's climax, we do hear sampled screams, but it's Stan who's mainly screaming. At other times in verse 3, Stan's voice actually sounds quite similar to that of Slim Shady in other songs: high pitched, manic, vituperative, very unlike the Slim in this song, whose voice is probably much closer to that of the "real" Eminem or even the "real" Marshall Mathers.

However we parse Eminem's voices and personas, it is clear in "Stan" that his performance of the four verses is as carefully realized as his writing of the dramatic parts. Complementing the increasingly loud sampled thunder in the background, Eminem amps up Stan's volume and raises his pitch verse by verse, meanwhile making his pauses and intonations more and more erratic. In verse 3, Eminem slurs words and roughens syllables while increasing their pace to demonstrate Stan's intoxication and crazed state—a performance demanding unusual artistic control. In verse 4, Eminem lowers both pitch and volume in order to highlight Slim's seriousness and, at least on this one occasion, sober compassion.

This is a rare dramatic moment within Eminem's predominantly lyric repertoire. Slim Shady's usual role as a "dramatic" persona is to distill and articulate punk attitudes of angry, apolitical alienation, to give voice— comically, alarmingly, violently—to transgressive, offensive thoughts often beyond even rap culture's standards of decency. Here, Eminem flips Slim into a decent, fallible, emotionally engaged, consummate professional MC with an imagined fan he understands but can't help. Is this the "real Eminem"? Maybe, but it would be hard to prove that from the work. Whoever Slim represents in "Stan," Eminem elsewhere almost always raps lyrically, boasting, quarreling, complaining, teaching, and even dissing Donald Trump, but above all else demonstrating his intense flow and superlative rhyming.

It takes rare detachment and compositional skill to compose rap drama in a short rap song, to create thinking, acting characters like Stan who are neither MCs nor representations of a subset of MC attitudes. Admittedly, Stan is just an ardent rap fan, not a king, pirate, professor, auto worker, or boutique owner. Since there's probably an ardent rap fan inside every MC, maybe it's not so great an imaginative leap. But by *differentiating* Stan so clearly from Slim and by subsuming their verses—and Dido's choruses— within a dramatic plot, and by giving each character his own voice, Eminem has created a rare product, a truly dramatic rap song.

Hamilton

Although hardly the first theatrical production inspired by hip hop or relying strongly on rap dialogue, *Hamilton* has unquestionably been the most critically acclaimed, most successful (weekly gross topping $3,000,000), most expensive (tickets maxing at $998), and most hyped. Here's an Expedia ad:

Think the Founding Fathers were all britches and powdered wigs, constitutions and declarations? Think again! This rap-filled romp through revolutionary times offers a totally new—and totally entertaining—take on the early days of America, as seen through the eyes of rowdy republican Alexander Hamilton.

Marrying rap, R&B, and traditional musical theater melodies, *Hamilton* is the Public Theater sensation making its long-awaited debut on the Broadway stage. History buffs and hip hop fans alike are sure to be captivated by the stories of Alexander Hamilton, George Washington, Thomas Jefferson—portrayed by black and Hispanic actors—as scrappy, striving immigrants in a new land.

Lin-Manuel Miranda, who wrote the lyrics, music, and book, comments on the musical's portrayal of our white Founding Fathers by black and Hispanic actors: "Our cast looks like America looks now, and that's certainly intentional. It's a way of pulling you into the story and allowing you to leave whatever cultural baggage you have about the founding fathers at the door."[24] The historical fact that Hamilton was not only a scrappy intellectual prodigy but an immigrant (from the Caribbean island of Nevis) born out of wedlock flips what might otherwise have been a modish casting gimmick into a relevant contemporary message. As is boasted during the staged Battle of Yorktown, "Immigrants, we get the job done."

Thus the deployment of rapping is pointedly progressive, and this deployment is also artistically crucial, as signaled by the fact that every character who solos in the opening song raps his or her lines—whether not they ever rap again. Although *Hamilton* is often cited as a hip hop musical, in actuality it's a hip musical which aligns the messages of multiple musical styles against each other and, especially with its hip hop discourse, in a dynamic of internal conflict. All of the American revolutionaries rap, but their particular styles correlate with their particular personalities and ideologies. George Washington, the commander in chief, speaks rather than sings his words, like his fellow revolutionaries, but as the primary, lone, and at times isolated voice of practical wisdom—as distinct from ideological zeal—Washington may be characterized as a master of spare prose, not so much a rapper as a revolutionary *above* the hip hop fray. But all the other revolutionaries—Hamilton, Jefferson, Madison, Burr, Lafayette, Laurens, Mulligan—are enthusiastic rhymers, each with his own singular style and particular skill set. They are rappers whose commonalities support each other in political collaboration, but whose political beefs come out in rap battles, a. k. a. cabinet meetings, supervised by Washington.

Meanwhile many other musical styles play off against each other, from jazz to soul to funk, all fluidly mingled with a variety of traditional Broadway lyric styles. King George always sings his soliloquies in a biting, witty British Invasion manner, but most of the other characters, including the (male) revolutionaries share space with a whole range of American styling. In effect, all of the rapping in *Hamilton*, is performed to beats infused with non-rap sampling.

Rapping in *Hamilton* is almost exclusively male—which some audience members, expecting not just an affirmation of diversity but some consciousness of gender equality, have no doubt found irksome. During "Say No To This," which narrates and dramatizes Hamilton's affair with Maria Reynolds (the first major sex scandal in American history), Hamilton raps his own part in the story, but the song itself is for the most part a slow jam, with Maria vamping her poor-me blues to seduce her man; but when her pimping husband recites his letter of extortion, he raps! It's a male thing, then.

The sole exception comes from within Angelica Schuyler, Hamilton's soulmate and intellectual equal. Angelica raps powerfully and with considerable skill during "Satisfied," in which her role is that of bridesmaid at the wedding of Hamilton and her sister Eliza. Angelica's rhymes here rival those of Hamilton elsewhere, but her rapping is never public, never open, and decidedly *not* articulated during the nuptial ceremony. Angelica raps during an extended "rewind" aside, the spotlight on her private reminiscence, and when she raps she expresses her inner desires, her genuine wit and libido, her sense of what-might-have-been had there been any possibility of gender equality. As she notes,[25]

I'm a girl in a world in which
My only job is to marry rich
My father has no sons so I'm the one
Who has to social climb for one
So I'm the oldest and the wittiest and the gossip in
New York City is insidious
And Alexander is penniless
Ha! That doesn't mean I want him any less

This is the first of three recognitions she remembers having had soon after she first met Hamilton, immediately after falling hard for him. Not only could she never marry for love, but Eliza was helpless and needed her, and Eliza would be—possibly in contrast to Angelica—dutiful and good, a proper married woman and mother.

Angelica's *narration* of her rewind experience is in Broadway recitative style: "I remember that night, I might / Regret that night for the rest of my life / . . . I remember that dreamlike candlelight / Like a dream you can't quite place / But Alexander, I'll never forget the first / Time I saw your face / I have never been the same / Intelligent eyes in a hunger-pang frame / And when you said "Hi," I forgot my dang name / Set my heart aflame, ever'y part aflame." There ensues a hushed dramatic reenactment of their first awkward, clipped, passionately charged conversation, but the song blasts wide open with Angelica's remembered *lyric experience* of her subjective reaction:

> So so so—
> So this is what it **feels** like to **match wits**
> With someone at your **level!** What the **hell** is the **catch? It's**
> The **feeling** of **freedom**, of **seein' the light**
> It's Ben Franklin with a **key and a kite!** You **see it, right?**
> The conversation lasted two **minutes**, maybe **three minutes**
> Ev'rything we said in total **agreement, it's**
> A **dream** and it's a **bit of a dance**
> **A bit of a** posture, it's a **bit of a stance.** He's a
> **Bit of a** *flirt*, but I'm 'a **give it a chance**
> I **asked** about his *fam'ly*, did you **see** his **answer?**
> His **hands** started *fidgeting*, he looked **askance?**
> He's penniless, he's *flying* by the **seat of his pants**

Angelica in this rap spits syllables as fast and as fluidly as Alexander ever does, and she has a mastery of multi rhyming, alliteration, anaphora, and many other rhetorical devices—which soon fades, however, as she retreats to her normative mode of dutiful, nurturing, sisterly womanhood. Her sentiments shift toward girly romantic, and her rhymes turn simple:

> Handsome, boy, does he know it!
> Peach fuzz, and he can't even grow it!
> I wanna take him far away from this place
> Then I turn and see my sister's face and she is

Well, so much for gender equality in *Hamilton*. But after all, it's a man's world, then and now, isn't it? And after all, this musical historically concerns our Founding Fathers, with a secondary role assigned to Eliza, the excellent wife of one of them, and arguably the musical's moral hero; but we can't imagine Eliza ever rapping. Then too, *Hamilton*, being very much a musical—however hip, however infused with hip-hop—is inevitably constrained by the traditional romantic tropes of Broadway. And we must admit that insofar as rap is itself dominated by the performance of masculinity, the use of rap as an almost exclusively male discourse style in *Hamilton* benefits from a kind of cultural verisimilitude.

In any case, *Hamilton* succeeds excellently in connecting rap style with character. As already observed, Washington's style is stolid. Aaron Burr, who is functions as Hamilton's foil throughout the musical, advises the young vocal enthusiast, "Talk less. Smile more. Don't let them know what you're against or for," so not surprisingly Burr raps in a circumspect, short-lined, and minimally rhyming style—and he often keeps his remarks to a minimum. During the musical's second song, "Aaron Burr, Sir," many of the revolutionaries-to-be gather at a Manhattan tavern, where we are quickly introduced to Laurens, Lafayette, and Mulligan, who boast respectively about their drinking, Frenchness, and sexual prowess—all with some rhyming competence, but none of them of MC quality. Laurens and Lafayette rely only on end rhymes till line 4, then spice up these exit lines with internal rhyme; Mulligan adds an internal rhyme to line 3 and further complicates line 4 with a terminal multi, capping a rhyme by Lafayette. Clearly they're collaboratively freestyling, as Lafayette and Mulligan each rhyme their initial syllables on their predecessors' final syllables:

> I'm John Laurens in the place to **be**!
> Two pints o' Sam Adams, but I'm workin' on **three**, uh!
> Those redcoats don't want it with **me**!
> Cuz I will **pop** chick-a **pop** these **cops** till I'm **free**!
>
> **Oui oui**, mon a**mi**, je m'appelle Lafa**yette**!
> The Lancelot of the revolutionary **set**!
> I came from afar just to say "Bon**soir!**"
> Tell the King "Casse **toi!**" Who's the **best**? C'est **moi**!
>
> **Brrrah brraaah**! I am Hercules Mulli**gan**
> Up in it, lovin' it, yes I heard ya mother said "Come **again?**"
> Lock up ya daughters and **horses**, of **course**
> It's hard to have **intercourse** over four **sets of corsets**

Burr is invited into the cypher, but he respectfully-disdainfully declines:

> LAURENS: Well, if it ain't the prodigy of Princeton college!
> Give us a verse, drop some knowledge!

> BURR: Good luck with that: you're takin' a stand
> You spit. I'm 'a sit. We'll see where we land

Needless to say, the best rapper is our title character, the scrappy, ambitious immigrant genius who, like Burr, passed through college in record time but who, very much unlike Burr, became Washington's aide-de-camp in his early twenties. Hamilton raps like Big Pun, or Nas, or any number of other super-competent NYC rappers of the mid-1990s, using multiple internal rhymes, plenty of multis, wordplay, dense phrasing, and highly variable rhythms. When he goes up against Jefferson in "Cabinet Battle #1," Hamilton's argument, wit, energy, and craft are far superior. As Lin-Manuel Miranda has commented, just as when Nas famously counterattacked Jay-Z's diss, this battle—for the future of the American economy—leaves no doubt about who won. Like Jay-Z, Jefferson may have written the book (*Decoded*; The Declaration of Independence), but he is totally etherized by his upstart rival.[26]

Washington speaks both as president and as the battle moderator: "Ladies and gentlemen, you coulda been anywhere in the world tonight, but you're here with us in New York City. Are you ready for a cabinet meeting??? The issue on the table: Secretary Hamilton's plan to assume state debt and establish a national bank. Secretary Jefferson, you have the floor, sir."

> 'Life, liberty and the pursuit of **happiness**.'   (Jefferson)
> We fought for these ideals; we shouldn't settle for **less**
> These are wise words, **enterprising** men **quote** 'em
> Don't act **surprised**, you guys, cuz I **wrote** 'em

> Oww!!!   (Jefferson/Madison)

> But Hamilton **forgets**   (Jefferson)
> His plan would have the government assume state's **debts**
> Now, place your **bets** as to who that **benefits**:
> The very seat of government where Hamilton **sits**

> Not true!   (Hamilton)

Ooh, if the shoe fits, **wear it**   (Jefferson)
If New York's in debt—why should Virginia **bear it?**
Uh! Our debts are **paid**, I'm **afraid**
Don't tax the South cuz we got it **made** in the **shade**
In Virginia, we plant seeds in the **ground**
We **create.** You just wanna move our money **around**
This financial plan is an outrageous **demand**
And it's too many **damn** pages for any **man** to **understand**
Stand with me in the **land** of the **free**
And pray to God we never see Hamilton's **candidacy**
Look, when Britain taxed our **tea**, we got **frisky**
Imagine what gon' happen when you try to tax our **whiskey**

At this point the crowd reacts, "That's my alcohol!" while Washington intercedes formally: "Thank you, Secretary Jefferson. Secretary Hamilton, your response." This contrast underscores the potential conflict between government and popular opinion which would eventually explode during the Whiskey Rebellion. But meanwhile, Jefferson has made his eloquent enough, states' rights argument, invoking the agrarian slave economy and deploying mainly end rhymes, a smattering of internal rhymes and a duly boastful, sarcastic, smug, and flaccid delivery.

Hamilton matches Jefferson's sarcasm while offering a more sophisticated economic vision, further poking a hole in Jefferson's enlightenment philosophy by taking a moral dig at the slave economy. At the end, he belittles Jefferson by crudely flipping his "if the shoe fits" dig, bringing in a standard "assume the position" battle trope from The Notorious B. I. G. and others— ironically commanding the slave-owner to suffer the kind of corporal punishment his henchmen may have inflicted on his laborers. And how has Hamilton earned this claim to power? Well, because he's right, of course, and also because his verse is jammed with multi rhymes, proving his superior intelligence.[27]

Thomas. That was a **real nice declaration**
Welcome to the present, we're running a **real nation**
Would you like to join us, or stay **mellow**
Doin' whatever the hell it is you **do in Monticello?**
If we **assume the debts**, the **union gets**
A **new line of credit, a financial diuretic**
How do **you not get it?** If we're **aggressive** and **competitive**
The **union** gets a **boost.** You'd rather give it a **sedative?**

A civics **lesson from a slaver**. Hey **neighbor**
Your **debts are paid** cuz you don't **pay for labor**
"We plant seeds in the South. We **create**." Yeah, **keep ranting**.
We know who's **really** doing the **planting**
And another thing, Mr. Age of **Enlightenment**
Don't lecture me about the war, you didn't **fight in it**
You think I'm **frightened** of you, man? We almost **died in the trench**
While you were off getting **high with the French**
Thomas **Jefferson**, always **hesitant** with the **President**
Reticent—there isn't a plan he doesn't **jettison**
Madison, you're **mad** as a **hatter, son**, take your **medicine**
Damn, you're in worse shape than **the national debt is in**
Sittin' there **use**less as **two shits**
Hey, turn around, bend **over**, I'll **show you** where my **shoe fits**

A New Lyricism

As argued earlier, the lyric mode dominates rap, often enriched through collaboration—whether in the form of a battle, through posse rap, or simply by more than one MC contributing verses in a rap song. Narrative is relatively uncommon.[28] Where it does occur, narrative is generally restricted to two genres, the exemplary tale (c.f., Aesop, sermon stories) and the tall tale (c.f., the traditional African American toast), each of which are compatible to lyric insofar as the lyricist anoints him- or herself the teacher or entertainer. Compared to the number of rapped exemplary tales, such as Tech's "Dance with the Devil" or Guru's "Just to Get a Rep," first-person toasts in the manner of Blowfly's "Rapp Dirty" (1980) are, we found, relatively rare. André 3000's autobiography in one verse, "A Life in the Day of Benjamin André (Incomplete)," is motivated by the lyric impulse, and even Kendrick Lamar's "DUCKWORTH." in *DAMN.*, although mostly a biography of his father, serves mainly as a revelation and karmic window into the life of the rapper himself. Indeed, narrative more commonly exists as an adjunct to lyric *within* songs (c.f., Nas in "One Mic"). Escaping an ambush might require a first-person toast to reinforce a boast, and the import of the boast might range from "I'm the toughest" to "I'm a real product of the hood." We consider "The Message" a paradigm for the merging of narrative and lyric: expression of the lyric self is subsumed in historical/cultural/institutional narrative, and the other way around. The song contains brief narrative sketches and one longer exemplary birth-to-death tale, with lyric choruses blending objective teaching ("it's like a jungle sometimes") and subjective expression ("sometimes I wonder how I keep from going under").

Even rarer modally is rap drama, such as Eminem's "Stan." The proto-rap *Hustler's Convention* remains little known except to serious hip hop heads, and although it certainly influenced the early construction of various rap personas, it was never a model emulated by would-be dramatist MCs. Today, the most salient and renowned dramatic rapping is that which has been adapted to *Hamilton*, but this Broadway musical lacks the traditional ethos of hip hop in its subject matter and stylistic purposes. *Hamilton's* blockbuster status contrasts ironically with that of *The Hamilton Mixtape*, which sold only 187,000 album-equivalent copies despite its star-studded cast, featuring both rappers (e.g., The Roots, Busta Rhymes, Usher, Nas, Queen Latifah, Wiz Khalifa, and Chance the Rapper) and non-rappers (e.g., Alicia Keys, Sia, and John Legend) alike.

The lyric mode dominates the game, predominantly in the genre of the personal boast. Public boasts by their very nature, be they in ancient ("heroic") tribal cultures or in contemporary close-knit urban communities, tend to invite competitive counter-boasts, rebuttals, or—if the original boasts seem unmerited—open ridicule. Thus the personal boast can slip easily into collaborative mode. Collaborative skill-trading genres like the formal debate and the poetry contest have been around for thousands of years. Today we have more or less staged, more or less cooperative battle rapping, which can "degenerate" into insult-swapping in the tradition of medieval flyting and the dozens.

Other lyric rap genres do exist, of course, including the love/sex/seduction song, buddah song (in the tradition of the more boisterous drinking song), protest chant, teaching essay in verse, elegy, eulogy, and others. But a many lyric genres simply don't exist in rap music. No haiku: After two or three lines, MCs are just warming up. No nature poem: the hip hop world is urban, not rural, and never pastoral. No lullaby: MCs may have babies to care for, but they craft verses to enliven rather than calm their audiences.

Indeed, if we consider the rap lyric from the perspective of world poetry, either musically or formally, it's a nearly unique phenomenon. Lyric poetry was originally sung, not chanted, but rap is non-melodic chanting. Lyric poetry mostly exists in stanzas, but rap works line by line, couplet by couplet. Extraordinarily, the rap lyric is not only stichic in form, but its essential poetics—rhythmically complicated, grandiose in its rhyming, altogether opaque and noisy—share almost nothing with the poetics of literary stars like William Wordsworth, who defined lyric poetry as "the spontaneous overflow of powerful feelings: it takes its origin from emotion recollected in tranquility." Maybe rap lyrics do behave a little bit like William Blake's seldom read, prophetic books (*The Four Zoas, Milton, Jerusalem*), with their long lines and heavy rhythms. Do they behave like Walt Whitman's "Song of Myself"? Well no, at least not until recently, and if so, not with Whitman's optimistic, transcendental, American enthusiasm.

In contrast to rap boasting, which puts forth a narrow and often comically grandiose persona of the self, Kendrick Lamar's *DAMN.* (2017), as well as Pharoahe Monch's *PTSD* (2014), and J. Cole's *4 Your Eyez Only* (2016), offer listeners a far more complex identity—one that's culturally determined, inherited, and traumatized. Throughout his album, J. Cole articulates a kind of despair directed by his socio-economic inheritance. In "Immortal" he asks:

> Have you ever seen a fiend cook crack on the spoon?
> Have you ever seen a nigga that was black on the moon?
> Have you ever seen your brother go to prison as you cry?
> Have you ever seen a motherfuckin' ribbon in the sky?

Pharoahe Monch, in *PTSD*'s title song, "Post-Traumatic Stress Disorder," laments:

> When your cerebral ceases to administer solace
> And the only Faith you have left is a CD
> From a singer who had a son with Christopher Wallace
> Tomorrow is never, hope is abolished
> Mind and soul have little to no unity
> Life threw a brick through my window of opportunity
> My immune system lacked diplomatic immunity
> When asthma attacks the black community
> Where do you go from there?

And Kendrick Lamar's *DAMN.*, where the dominant syntactic devices are anaphora and end-line repetition, emphasizes the sense of being stuck in a cycle, both macroscropic and microscopic.

The entire album rewinds to the beginning after "DUCKWORTH.," the final, anecdotal narrative of his father's criminality and miraculous survival, on which hangs the conception and subsequent (nurtured, damned) life

of the rapper himself. Meanwhile each song's title concept—LOYALTY.,
PRIDE., HUMBLE., LUST., LOVE., XXX., FEAR., GOD.—is driven by
a different repetition. "DNA." poignantly exemplifies this:

> I got power, poison, pain and joy inside my DNA
> I got hustle though, ambition, flow, inside my DNA
> This that put-the-kids-to-bed
> This that I got, I got, I got, I got
> Realness, I just kill shit 'cause it's in my DNA
> I got millions, I got riches buildin' in my DNA
> I got dark, I got evil, that rot inside my DNA
> I got off, I got troublesome heart inside my DNA

So does "FEEL.":

> I feel like I'm losin' my patience
> I feel like my thoughts in the basement
> Feel like, I feel like you're miseducated
> Feel like I don't wanna be bothered
> I feel like you may be the problem
> I feel like it ain't no tomorrow, fuck the world

The exhausting repetition, full of oxymoron, reflects Kung Fu Kenny's experiential damnation. At the prosodic level, the feeling is both ugly ("LOY-
al-ty LOY-al-ty LOY-al-ty") and monomaniacal within each song.

Each of these complex forays into the psyche comments on current
African American issues, and indeed, on American culture generally. Each
proclaims, artfully, that black lives matter. Had these albums appeared ten
or fifteen years earlier, they probably would have been received as fringe
projects, possibly retaining cult status. Today, they are commercially viable.

Verses, Songs, and Albums

KOD, album of the year, undebatably
My cadence be the greatest we've seen since the late MC
Whose name was The Notorious—Dreamville stacked like the Warriors
—J. Cole, "Album of the Year"

So far we've focused mainly on the formal surfaces of lines and couplets, but MCs constructing verses, songs, and even albums are doing more than just flow and rhyme. Songs, as planned artistic endeavors, offer a chance to translate ephemeral wit into familiar, coherent, and even memorable structures.

Songs require artists and producers to control multiple rhythmic dimensions. The beat and flow must somehow suit the song's mood and message, and the rhyme patterns, which frame ever-expanding meanings, must somehow support the song's tone and themes. In other words, our experience of rap songs will have been produced by a complex, perception-organizing process. As we listen, we can already sense what the song might be about after just a few bars, whether it's a story, boast, or sermon or whether it's meant to be funny, scary, or serious.

Our quick comprehension of all this information—content, tone, genre—is simultaneous yet differentiated. We experience musical time on two temporal planes, that of the *rhythm* and that of the *rhyme*. Each plane is involved in the other, with the rhythm of the ongoing syllables, words, and phrases arriving at and passing through the bars' and couplets' rhyme grids, and with the spacing of the rhymes depending, in turn, on beated syllables and syntactic pauses. We experience each plane phonically, corporally, and cerebrally, and from their interplay we rapidly pick up multiple emotions and meanings. Within this complex temporal medium, rappers can weave locally meaningful statements and word links which anticipate additional structures of meaning, eventually forming meaningful verses.[1]

This sense of time, striated over the syllabic rhythms, is rap's fundamental expectation-organizing axis. To make linguistic sense and meet rhythmic expectations, half lines, lines, and couplets have prolonged linear forms, as do the phrases and sentences they contain, as well as rap's larger units—its verses and choruses, songs, and even albums. In truth, a lot of rapping isn't required to make much logical, coherent, or thematic sense as long as it makes surprising sense as it goes, as long as the vocab and flow and rhymes are *nice*. Even so, the poetry often does make sustained sense.[2]

That it *can* make sustained sense makes sense, formally, at least post-vinyl. The pre-vinyl rap styling captured on "Rapper's Delight" was about catchy rhymes and continuous, danceable flow, not about thematic coherence. In the immortal words of Master Gee:

> All I'm here to do ladies is hypnotize
> Singin' on n on on n on on n on
> The beat don't stop until the break of dawn
> Singin' on n n on n on on n on
> Like a hot buttered a pop da pop da pop
> Dibbie dibbie pop da pop pop ya don't dare stop

And in fact this can't-stop-won't-stop aesthetic never really disappears from rap. It's part and parcel of every verse that sounds natural and spontaneous (even if recorded in multiple studio takes, even if spliced), and it persists with a vengeance in contemporary freestyle,[3] where thematic volatility and brilliant rhyming go hand in hand. Nevertheless, post-vinyl rap, even as it continues to value a high degree of couplet-to-couplet freedom and fluidity, is constrained by commercial necessity to package memorable, marketable "statements" within time frames fixed by radio-play norms.[4] This requirement typically translates into time-determined *sequences* of verses, with choruses added to underscore particular themes. Lines are still grouped into couplets, which are bundled into verses, but these verses are (more often than not) governed by musical norms—as with the sixteen-bar verse—than by the kind of poetic stamina displayed in the fourteen-minute "Rapper's Delight." Typically, sets of two or three verses are bundled into songs, and these verses tend to follow some sort of logical order. As often as not, too, the verses are introduced, separated, and concluded by sung choruses which, beyond the present-moment spontaneity of rap styling, combine to create a relatively sophisticated, quasi-literary form, one also conforming to song structures generally. In sum, the post-vinyl rap song typically contains multiple building blocks arranged to produce thematic focus and progression. It usually will have a title expressing some summary focus. It will have one dominant beat, one tempo, one musical mood coloring the meaning of the verses and choruses collectively. It's not just rap, it's a *rap song*. [5]

To take an example from the classic era, the title of Gang Starr's "In Memory Of" (1998) promises an elegy, and this promise is delivered immediately in the hook, which, by naming the dead and by interspersing their names with memorializing phrases, defines it as a communal, not individual, elegy: "Mami Mary, Mary Coleman that is / I love you, rest in peace. You still here though / Word up, this goes out to you / Mary Parker, Loretta Randall / Grandfather Bill / Ron Emanuel, Robert N'Blangio, Uncle C, Alicia Elon / Giovanni." The beat is slow. The mood is solemn. The names of the dead are accented by reverb (echoed: remembered). Verse 1 eulogizes Giovanni in particular, but subsequent choral litanies continue to list the deceased, with "rest in peace" now incorporated as a sample from Biggie's "You're Nobody (Til Somebody Kills You)." In the penultimate chorus, hip hop celebrities, lesser lights, and unknown soldiers are honored: "Keith "Cowboy," Scott LaRock / Prince Messiah (rest in peace) / Buffy the Human Beatbox y'know / Tupac Shakur (rest in peace) / Pinkhouse, SubRoc / OG Boo Bang, salute! (rest in peace) / Seagram's, Killa Black from Mobb Deep / Biggie Smalls, yeah (rest in peace) / Lance Owens y'all."[6]

"In Memory Of," then, although issued soon after the murders of Tupac and Biggie, is *not* primarily about hip hop heroes; it's about the black community.[7] Among the honored dead are close male friends (including DJs, MCs, pimps, and gangsters) and beloved—and strong—women. In significant contrast to hip hop performance demographics, women and men are equally represented. In the final chorus, community representation becomes even more inclusive, with Princess Di joining Betty Shabazz. The choruses trace a trajectory of fame, for the Mary Coleman named first of all remains obscure but most listeners will recognize Princess Di and Betty Shabazz; and Tupac and Biggie are indeed named in the penultimate chorus. Yet the song confers memorial, not fame. It respects and represents the unknown deceased along with the known.

Guru's verse sequence emphasizes this thematic point. Verse 1's Giovanni was an otherwise unknown, but seemingly superlative thug whose main importance lay in his having inspired and encouraged the MC to pursue his art:

> To my man G. O. V., I remember how you used to be
> You were the illest man alive now I'm reading your eulogy

Eyes so serious, you told me hold my head
Pursue this rap shit and go forward never backwards
While you gripped TECs tight, and ran niggaz out of town
I ripped up mics, showin' wack niggaz how to sound[8]

Verse 2 honors Brian B, an analogously unknown but flamboyant pimp ("So many hookers on your schedule / Slammin Cadillac doors and mackin' whores on the regular"). Here it is worth noting that both Giovanni and Brian B met violent, occupationally hazarded deaths according to Guru's narrations, Giovanni from two gunshots from an unknown assassin, Brian B knifed in bed by his premier whore, an addict.[9]

The choral litany of dead DJs and MCs, obscure as well as famous, works as a musical bridge to verse 3. Here, death gets a lot deeper, not by shifting the focus, as might be expected, to Tupac and Biggie, but by continuing to honor unknown heroes and unknown victims. Gang Starr's message is that the assassination of great rappers willing themselves to threaten and defy gun violence isn't the headline story: Killa Black, for example, died of depression-induced suicide. Neither theirs nor others' deaths, however, should be treated as ghetto business as usual. Instead, hip hop can (and should) embody a new, necessary spirituality. Guru's third rap treats death no longer as a random, intra-community event, but rather as the ultimate expression of racial and class oppression:

To all my brothers doin' time, whether or not you did the crime
You know the system is devised to keep you deaf, dumb, and blind

True enough, but our awareness of injustice needs to transcend victim-consciousness: "It's easy for us to blame society / But now it's way too late, and we must take responsibility." Offering a moral and spiritual solution to those still living on the streets, Guru expands memorialization to a world-historical scale.[10] His eulogy advocates love, not violence, as the only way to forestall and maybe even alter the systematic oppression dating from the Slave Trade[11]:

To all my brothers in the streets
I know you feel you gotta hustle 'cause your peeps gotta eat
Makin' moves right and exact; don't wanna see you layin' flat
Don't wanna see ya catch a bullet black.
If we don't build we'll be destroyed
That's the challenge we face in this race of poor and unemployed

Freud, a philosopher—but I'm a realist
So philosophize this, without love we won't exist
To those who passed out there, in the deserts and the jungles
With pain on their shoulders, and heavy bundles
I pray each one will ascend to new heights and new enlightenment
And this is why I'm writin' it, yeah, this is in memory of

The final chorus tolls yet more names of the known and unknown dead—all of them now known by name,[12] a few also by small details (e.g. *Sam-O, 183rd*; *Killa Black from Mobb Deep*), even fewer by anecdotal histories. Set within the four shout-out choruses are three progressive rap verses, all under the aegis of one operative title, all set to one elegiac beat, all culminating in prayer and celebration. It's still hip hop, where "philosophy" is suspect. It's not all Biggie and Tupac either, it's also Buffy, the Human Beatbox. It still has fun with indecorous rhymes like *Cadillac doors / mackin' whores* and *unemployed / Freud*. It's good rapping in an artful, memorable rap song.

What Makes Verses?

Formally, rap verses almost always consist of a series of rhymed couplets, which may occasionally be interrupted by one-liners, expanded into triplets, paired up to form quatrains, or extended into even longer rhyme chains. But couplets are the norm, providing a steady rhythm of incremental repetition. Although each couplet is fixed by its end rhyme, it may also exhibit internal rhymes in various numbers and positions as well as an enormous variety of rhythmic patterns, depending on its dip lengths and pauses. A couplet's rhymes may be self-contained or may spill over into adjacent couplets, breaching its formal boundaries. Grammatically too, a couplet may be *closed*, or self-contained, or *open*, either completing the syntax of a previous couplet or spilling over into the next couplet, or both. Whether couplets are closed or open, each will have its own internal rhythm, rhyme pattern, and grammatical logic.

Groups of lines enable poetic strategies. We've already seen how Duke Bootee and Melle Mel deploy one-liners, triplets, and even some open-couplet spillage in the first four verses of "The Message," in order to capture the chaos of ghetto life. Mel's very first image is "broken glass everywhere," and that's how his couplets usually feel—until he shifts into the inexorable series of closed couplets in his final verse. Chaos and then gravitas, consciously achieved: this was the formal achievement which inspired so many future MCs. The couplet norm, in other words, allows formal predictability and unpredictability.

This is true even in sets of closed couplets, which would seem on the face of it to be highly restrictive. Each loops through its own discreet end rhymes, finding closure in a pitch drop and pause at the final stress of line 2.[13] Exactly the same loop closure occurs in eighteenth-century literary poetry. These couplets in Jonathan Swift's "Description of a City Shower" wittily describe, in exactly twenty syllables apiece, the individual or collective measures that city people take when it starts to rain. A shower may even unite sworn enemies:

> The tucked-up sempstress walks with hasty strides,
> While seams run down her oiled umbrella's sides.
> Here various kinds, by various fortunes led,
> Commence acquaintance underneath a shed.
> Triumphant Tories and desponding Whigs
> Forget their feuds, and join to save their wigs.

Because these couplets are closed they are extractable, quotable, memorable. The same is true at the start of verse 2 of Snoop Dogg's "Gin and Juice" (1993):

> Now that I got me some Seagram's gin, [1]
> Everybody got they cups, but they ain't chipped in.
> Now this type of shit happens all the time— [2]
> You got to get yours, but fool I gotta get mine.[14]

But just because couplets are grammatically self-contained doesn't mean that they can't also comprise thematically progressive sequences. Swift's set of three shifts from individual to collective responses to the rain shower, then shifts from the general to the specific. Among the "various kinds" of people assembling under the shed and forced to get acquainted may be the politicians; alternatively, these Tories and Whigs may be too aloof to share a shed with those they supposedly represent—they may be gathered at a more refined location, but wherever they are they're united by their class interests, "to save their wigs." Snoop Dogg's two couplets display their own coherence. In the first, he has the gin bottle and others are predictably eager to mooch. In the second, line 1 generalizes that this kind of thing happens all the time, but line 2 flips the parallel, with Snoop in effect making sure he gets what *he* needs. In subsequent couplets, Snoop is in charge, dispensing captivating music and attracting an eager female by drinking in the street and flirting with her, then rejecting her advances so he can hang with his posse. It's all party time. Snoop's thematic flip is to turn what might have been a cynical list of other folks' opportunistic greed into common fun.

And just because closed couplets have tight unity doesn't mean that they all share the same structure. To work well in sequence, they need to vary grammatically. Swift's first couplet about the seamstress has a front-loaded shape, with a main clause (subject in a-verse; verb and adverbial phrase in b-verse) occupying the first line and a subordinate clause (flowing through the caesura) occupying the second line. His third couplet consists of just one main clause, with its dual subjects (Tories in a-verse; Whigs in b-verse) taking up the first line and its dual verbs similarly positioned in the second line. At first listen, Snoop's two couplets might seem to share exactly the same structure, each propelled by a "now," each having a full clause in the first line, and each with "but" after the caesural pause of the second line. And it's true that these two couplets work in parallel, but their initial clauses are subordinate and main, respectively. Syntactic variety aids logical flexibility, adding an element of surprise to a relatively fixed form.

Aside from grammatical variation, rappers can free things up by tweaking how particular couplets interconnect, either through grammar or through rhyme. By creating grammatical patterns that go beyond the couplet boundaries, that is, by using *open couplets*, they push their phrasal flow against their rhyme loops; by extending their rhymes beyond the couplet boundaries, they push their rhyme flow against their phrasal loops. Or they can push both sense and sound in tandem. Or they can push neither, relaxing the flow into its normative couplet-by-couplet rhythm. In the space of a single sixteen-bar verse, they may do all of these things at various points.

An extra tactic is to break up the couplet sequence with alternative forms: one-liners, triplets, quatrains, and longer chains. After his two closed couplets starting verse 2 of "Gin and Juice," Snoop Dogg shifts to open couplets, with the phrase "he / Who listens" straddling the third and fourth couplets. Also, although couplets 3 and 5 have their own full rhymes, the entire chain maintains the same assonantal rhyme, and the verse ends with a full-rhyming tercet, whose integrity is reinforced by internal rhymes:

Everything is fine when you listenin' to the D-O-**G**   [3]
I got the cultivating music that be captivating **he**

Who listens, to the words that I **speak**   [4]
As I take me a drink to the middle of the **street**
And get to mackin' to this bitch named **Sadie**   [5]
She used to be the homeboys **lady**
Eighty **degrees**, when I tell that bitch **please**   [6]
Raise up off **these** N-U-T's, 'cause you gets none of **these**
At **ease**, as I mob with the Dogg Pound, feel the **breeze**

With thematic appropriateness, these couplets and triplet all merge in
a happy blur. In verse 3, the flow chokes and sputters through two one-
liners between the first and second couplets, but the first of these one-liners
coheres to the preceding couplet by means of internal rhyme, and the second
couplet contains, beyond its own new rhymes, repeats the rhyme-names of
the gin and weed just prior:

Later on that **day**, my homey Dr. **Dre**
Came through with a gang of **Tanqueray**
And a fat ass **J** of some bubonic chronic
That made me choke, shit, this ain't no joke
I had to back up off of it and sit my cup **down**
Tanqueray and chronic, yeah, I'm fucked up **now**

Snoop's interruptive one-liners proved trendsetting. KRS-One clusters
no less than four of these in a row in "Ah Yeah" (1995) using them quite literally for a series of righteously vengeful verbal assaults, fired off like bullets:

WOY! That's for calling my father a boy
KLAK KLAK KLAK! That's for putting scars on my mother's back,
BO! That's for calling my sister a hoe,
And for you, BUCK BUCK BUCK, 'cause I don't give a motherfuck

Biggie's use of this technique, as we would expect, is contrastingly cool in
style, and is formally more complex. In these lines from "Warning" (1994),
his couplet (in the voice of Pop) splits grammatically into two sentences, but
then his two subsequent one-liner's enjamb one into the next. The secondary
assonantal rhyme of the couplet becomes the sole, thrice-heard rhyme of the
first one-liner and the second component of the second one-liner's multi.
The tonal effect of these divisions and combinations is one of steady shifting,
appropriate to the situational suspense:

Some <u>niggas</u> wanna <u>stick</u> you like fly **paper neighbor.**
Slow <u>down</u> love please <u>chill</u> drop the **caper.**
Remember them <u>niggas</u> from the <u>hill</u> up in <u>Brownsville</u>
That you *rolled* **dice <u>wit</u>,** *smoked* the blunts and got **nice <u>wit</u>**

Mos Def's multis in "Respiration" (1998) leak and mutate similarly through couplets and one-liners, mingling as well with numerous secondary rhymes:

the Shiny Apple
Is **bruised but swee**t and if you **choose to eat**
You could **lose your teeth,** many **crews retreat**
*Nigh*tly **news repeat** who got <u>shot down</u> and <u>locked down</u>
Spot*light* to **savages,** *NASDAQ* **averages**
My narrative rose to **explain** this <u>existence</u>
<u>Amidst</u> the harbor *lights* <u>which</u> **remain** in the <u>distance</u>

The formal boundaries are somewhat firmer in Common's "Heat" (2000), but the rhyme within the first one-liner bleeds subtly into the next one, which in turn carries into the secondary rhyme of the subsequent couplet:

Got a **clip** for these **niggaz** on the net, sellin' my **shit**
Let's just say you Ramone and I'm **Spit**
In a <u>habitat</u> of <u>Cadillacs</u> and <u>battle raps</u>
And *peop<u>le</u>* that trav<u>el</u> at the *speed* of *need*
Never *agree* with the <u>ways</u> of the **world**
Cats <u>say</u> anything—like they <u>say</u> to they **girl**

These examples typify the couplet-based, yet also couplet-smashing style of some of the more ambitious and creative MCs from the 1990s and early 2000s. The couplet remains the formal norm, but its boundaries continually expand and contract, break and reform under the influence of grammatical variation and rhyme manipulation. In the very earliest rap, couplet expectation was almost always neatly fulfilled, but not long into the game, with Duke Bootee and Mel, came complication and surprise. Now one-liners or tercets may not feel so new, but they can continue to surprise us, and their odd line count always creates rhythmic syncopation against the evenness of couplets.

With four-line bundles, or quatrains, the rhythmic impact is very different. Quatrains predominate in choruses, as well as in songs generally, but they're rare in rap verses.[15] This may be due to the fact that rapping is basically a line-after-line (or *stichic*) process. Since lines are formed of two distinct half lines, bundling lines into couplets allows rappers to superimpose a higher level of duality, most obviously expressed in the couplets' paired rhyming end-words. Rappers move through these hierarchical rhythmic, syntactic, and semantic dyads without losing any line-by-line fluidity. Quatrains, by contrast, are obviously stanzas in a way that couplets are not,[16] and some of their rhyme schemes (*abcb, abab, abba*) group lines into bulky units whose coherence is likely to challenge line-by-line flow. [17] Probably for this reason, almost all rap quatrains avoid these multiple-rhyming forms, relying instead on an *aaaa* grouping. They are doubled-up couplets.

In "U. N. I. T. Y." (1993), Queen Latifah opens all three of her verses with *aaaa* quatrains. In each case the effect is to introduce a problem (1. men calling women *bitches* and *hos*; 2. domestic violence against women; 3. women dressing like sluts to attract men).[18] Each generic sexist problem is then addressed with a feminist response broken down into successive, relatively closed couplets—which work well for moralizing:

> Instinct leads me to another flow: [Q]
> Every time I hear a brother call a girl a bitch or a ho
> Trying to make a sister feel low,
> You know all of that gots to go.
> Now everybody knows there's exceptions to this rule.   [C]
> Now don't be getting mad, when we playing, it's cool,
> But don't you be calling me out my name—   [C]
> I bring wrath to those who disrespect me like a dame.

In "Love Is Blind" (1999), Eve deploys *aaaa* quatrains more pervasively, making them her primary form, only occasionally interspersing them with couplets. The impact of Eve's quatrains is one of unmitigated wrath, as if she's taking what she might have said in a couplet and piling on. She makes no attempt in this song to offer any solution—other than one that might result from shaming. Note how effectively Eve packs her quatrains with semantically powerful rhyme sequences and with internally coherent anaphora:

> Ayo, I don't even know you and I hate you
> See all I know is that my girlfriend used to date you
> How would you feel if she held you down and raped you?
> Tried and tried, but she never could escape you
> She was in love and I'd ask her how? I mean why?
> What kind of love from a nigga would black your eye?

What kind of love from a nigga every night make you cry?
What kind of love from a nigga make you wish he would die?

It goes without saying that most rappers are unlikely to adopt this level of earnestness. Perhaps flipping—or flipping off—Queen Latifah's positive message, Lil Wayne opens the first two verses of "A Milli" with short quatrains rhyming on *air*. After the relatively polite opening one—

(*A milli, a milli*) A millionaire,
I'm a young money millionaire
Tougher than Nigerian hair
My criteria compared to your career this isn't fair

—he likens himself to a "venereal disease" and his composition to a "menstrual bleed / Through the pencil," and goes on to brag about how he doesn't have time to write his lyrics, he's too busy pursuing the almighty dollar. After the relatively raunchy quatrain in verse 2, he continues to flaunt and bask in his I-could-care-less persona:

A million here, a million there
Sicilian bitch with long hair
With coke in the derriere
Like smoking the thinnest air
I open the Lamborghini hopin' them crackers see me
Like look at that bastard Weezy
He's a beast, he's a dog, he's a motherfucking problem
OK, you're a goon but what's a goon to a goblin?
Nothing, nothing—you ain't scarin' nothing
On some faggot bullshit call him Dennis Rodman

And elsewhere in "A Milli," Weezy extends his rhyme chains well beyond quatrain boundaries (e.g., *private, sly bitch, sly bitch, sly bitch, my bitch, my bitch, surprised bitch*). In this context, his quatrains, both thematically and formally, seem more offhanded than those of Queen Latifah and Eve. We can view them simply as couplet pairs or as generic rhyme chains, but whatever we call them, they demonstrate formal flexibility, or rather rhyme for the fun of it.

André 3000's embedded quatrains (and other forms) in "A Life in the Day of Benjamin André" (2003) show a seemingly unique poetic prowess, impressive in its formal range and thematic felicity. Lines 1–8 consist of back-to-back ballad-stanza *abcb* rhymes, so that the autobiographical narrative begins pointedly with *non-rhymes* on two defining words, *Georgia* and *music*, on *oranges*, the oft-cited word which supposedly can't rhyme with anything, and on "yeah nigga, right," expressing sarcastic rejection.[19] It's as if André is cueing vulnerability at the onset of his career and love life. Other stanza configurations include a brilliant triplet multi-rhyming "same age, but I / same page, but in / I paged you when" (10–12); a thematically tight *ababaa* quatrain-plus-couplet (13–18); a short-line *abba* envelope (20–23); successive *aaaa*, *aaaa*, and *abba* quatrains (24–35), followed immediately by an *aababb* sestet (36–41); and then an *aababb* sestet (44–49). Aside from an isolated *abab* quatrain at lines (78–81), the rest of the verse is entirely in couplets and a few one-liners—until the last twelve lines, organized into an *aaaa* quatrain and two *abab* quatrains. Any and all of these departures from the couplet norm are worthy of commentary, all are timely and intelligent, and it's especially impressive that the verse is framed by clusters of larger forms which organize ideas more complexly than couplets can.[20] No wonder Weezy wants to associate himself with André and other greats, and to rise above them:

> They say I'm rapping like B. I. G., Jay and Tupac,
> André 3000, where is Erykah Badu at?
> Who that?
> Who that say they're gonna beat Lil Wayne
> My name ain't BIC, but I keep that flame man

Song Structures

In many jazz compositions, after the melody, tempo, and key are established by the ensemble, several instrumental soloists (trumpet, sax, piano, maybe bass and drums) improvise in sequence, often in thirty-two-bar units, ultimately returning to the original melodic line. To some extent, the solos are individualistic and competitive, but they also offer collaborative statements about the song's harmonics, mood, and themes.

Once in a while a rap song will display an eerily similar structure, for example Big Sean's "Control," with successive solos by Big Sean, Kendrick Lamar, and Jay Electronica. "Control" is most definitely an exemplar of collaborative, competitive rap soloing, but it has no chorus—rap's analog to the jazz tune's melody. Nor do its verses conform to a standard musical duration. Big Sean takes forty-eight bars, Kendrick takes sixty-two, and Jay takes twenty-five. This virally famous song didn't make Big Sean's *Hall of Fame* because of sample copyright issues, but it did function as a kind of ad for the album even as it stood apart as an internet release. It made its own rules: no standard sixteen-bar verses, no choruses, just "straight rap shit," as Big Sean posted pre-release.

Why does a baseball inning have three outs? Why does every boring high school five-paragraph essay have three and only three evidence paragraphs, framed by an intro and a conclusion? Why do we speak of this, that, and the other thing? Why do blessings and curses repeat the same words thrice? Apparently there is some human consensus that triads are useful, powerful, handsome rhythmic structures. As a rule, musical and poetic forms express what we want to hear, and rap is no exception—just a little more unruly than some other art forms. So yes, the mainstream rap song has three verses, and they are usually quite well behaved musically, fitting into sixteen-bar units (or today, often twelve-bar units), and they have repeated choruses recurring between each verse, often serving as both an intro and conclusion. Although all three verses are typically rapped by the same MC, they are also expected to differ one from the next, perhaps by focusing on related but different themes. Meanwhile, they are also expected to contribute the song's particular "message" or mood.

We just saw that André 3000 uses just one 120-bar verse (and no chorus) for his autobiographical recollections and ruminations. Lil' Kim uses just one longish verse to blast Nicki Minaj in battle. KRS-One's "Rap History" uses just one succinct verse. Canibus's seven-minute "Poet Laureate II" also has no chorus, and Eminem's equally long "Rap God," despite its repetition of "I'm beginning to feel like a rap god," is essentially non-stop. Clearly rap songs like these mean to go up against the mainstream grain, and they evoke, some of them, an earlier hip hop ethos from a somewhat less commercial time, when rappers felt they had the license to rap as long as they wished (like Coltrane on *A Love Supreme*). Or alternatively, these songs evoke the indie ethos. Formally speaking, a one verse song implies something about the self-sufficiency of the artist, so it works perfectly for autobiography and battling. It also implies an attitude about how ideas work. If three-verse songs remotely resemble the evidence paragraphs of high school essays, then single-verse songs resemble dramatic monologues, political speeches, or impromptu story-telling.

A different structural principle motivates posse rap. "Rapper's Delight," with its nine on-and-on verses by three rotating MCs, and Cold Crush

Brothers' "Fresh Wild Fly and Bold," can be viewed as early examples, but posse rap was epitomized and popularized by the Wu-Tang Clan, followed by Bone Thugs-N-Harmony. Big Sean's "Control" alludes back to this tradition and its ethos, as does A$AP Mob in much of their work. In a song like Wu-Tang's "Protect Ya Neck," there is perhaps—perhaps—some controlling theme at play (some believe it to be a sustained attack against the record industry), but most listeners experience it more in terms of its performance energy, with multiple rappers all styling with enthusiasm, displaying their varied flow skills, eagerly passing the mic one to the next. If narcissistic ostentation and commercial stardom stand as MC norms, posse rap blasts that ethos by replacing or at least mitigating it with a kind of gang solidarity.

Two-verse rap songs manifest still another formal alternative. They may be viewed as macro versions of rhyming's echo-essence, which is duality. Dualities can express an impressive variety of relationships, to include identity (twins), contrast (red, blue), opposition (good, evil), hierarchy (good, better), unexpected coincidence ("What are you doing here?"), and many more. Surely the best, most memorable rap rhymes have resulted from an inspired awareness of the magical coincidence of arbitrary word sounds. As a structural principle of song organization, however, coincidence may work perfectly well for the ongoing mic exchanges of posse rap, but most songs require a more substantial thematic organization. Hence our three-verse and two-verse songs. Aesthetic norms and cultural expectations no doubt play a large part in sustaining these forms, but the underlying mechanics of time are probably key to their success. Why do soccer and basketball games have two halves? To give the players a chance to rest? Well sure, but also to present to the spectators—and to formalize in the players' own consciousness—an awareness of the drama of combat. As the game moves toward its conclusion, one side is going to win and every moment of play potentially counts; but the time perspective shifts from a now-and-later view to a then-and-now view. Although sages through the ages remind us that we are happier if we can be here now, most humans are preoccupied with the temporal dualities of past-present and present-future. We can't help it. Our big brains make us think that way. It's hard to think just of this; we seem to need to think about this and that.[21]

Two-verse rap song may simply showcase two rappers, each making his or her stylistic statement while expressing different takes on the song's topic. Binary Star's "Reality Check" (One Be Lo, Senim Silla), Nas's "Life's a Bitch" (AZ the Visualiza, Nas), and Drake's "HYFR" (Drake, Lil Wayne) all do this. So, in a sense, do songs like Jay-Z and Biggie's "Brooklyn's Finest," with multiple short verses traded back and forth, and Queen Latifah and Monie Love's "Ladies First," with longer alternating verses; but in songs like these, the mode of dual expression is more like call-and-response battling or like a mutual empowerment session than a deliberate positioning of contrasting statements.[22]

Lil Wayne's (and Drake's) "She Will" is a particularly ambitious example of structural dualism. Formally, it consists of two verses by Wayne and three verse-like choruses by Drake, arranged verse 1, chorus 1, verse 2, chorus 2, chorus 3. Extraordinarily, Drake's choruses are slightly longer than Wayne's sixteen-bar verses.[23] All five units are rapped, and indeed Drake's verse-like choruses contain some lines longer than any of Wayne's. Although the setting of this song is never explicitly established, it's likely from the diction shared by both rappers—especially "pop" and "pop that pussy"[24]—that it's a strip club,[25] and the song makes it obvious that the two rappers, even though their thoughts about their respective situations differ greatly, are each focusing on the same dancer with similarly generic desires. It makes sense, then, that the song's verses and choruses share formal features as well as observations, vocabulary, rhetorical devices like repetition, and, to a degree, tone. These convergences are enabled by the emo beat itself, minimalist, minor-key, somewhat ominous, anything but joyous. The track even contains moments of near silence, such as between the second and third choruses, where the beat stops altogether, leaving only a tonal chord. As chorus 3 starts, sampled club-crowd sounds are suddenly introduced, signaling, it seems, a shift from private lyrical space to social space, but even these sounds, like Drake's rapping and like the beat itself, are subdued.[26]

Let's first consider Drake's persona's interests and preoccupations. In all three of his slightly varied choruses, he observes that the dancer has just started to "pop it for a nigga" (Weezy? Anyone? Everyone? No one, since it's all an act?), then he sees (or imagines) that she looks back at him and tells him "it's for real." One thing clear from this narrative is that she has not popped her pussy for him; otherwise she would be facing him alluringly, not looking back. So how much of this is for real? Possibly not much at all, possibly a lot of it. Strip club rules forbid the dancers from hooking up with patrons, but as a matter of social fact there are VIP rooms where, for a certain amount of money, these rules are routinely overruled. Hence:

> Do it for the realest niggas in the fuckin' game right now
> She will, she will, she will
> Maybe for the money and the power and the fame right now
> She will, she will, she will

Drake's attitude, however, is more romantic, as he imagines that the two of them might escape the club and hook up elsewhere. That's his interest, or rather his obsession; but careful attention to Drake's *she will* phrasings in all three choruses reveals a nuanced vacillation of outlook and attitude, from predictive to doubtful, from cynical to hopeful to anxious to sad.

And it's not at all clear whether he is concerned only with his own particular "future" with the stripper or he is thinking about Weezy as well—perhaps as a rival to be envied but more likely, as it seems, as a collaborator in sharing the evening's spoils. Drake's plural surely is intended to include himself as one of "the realest niggas in the fuckin' game right now," and the double meanings present in "the fuckin' game" support this as well—notwithstanding the hints of delusion or at least irony present in "realest" and "right now." If only.

Meanwhile Weezy is having his own ideas, also to some extent repetitive. Each of his verses opens with the tag, "I tell her." This may seem at first like a command, but if it is one it works only at the level of wish, not direct address, and this wish soon gives way, in each verse, to ruminations more like soliloquys and less like ogling fantasies. Each verse opens and closes almost identically:

> I tell her "now gon' pop that pussy for a real nigga"
>
> . . .
>
> But I'm Ray Charles to the bullshit
> Now jump up on that dick and do a full split!
>
> I tell her "now gon' pop that pussy for me"
>
> . . .
>
> But I'm Ray Charles to the bullshit
> Now hop up on my dick and do a full split!

These erotically charged lines paradoxically frame Wayne's musings. At the conclusion of each verse, the word *split* denotes both a rare kama sutra position and absence or separation. Weezy's reflections focus less on the woman's physicality than on his reputational position in relationship to her. He raps about his astrological sign, his ethical balance sheet, his courage and creativity, and his ability to satisfy women. As he does this, he employs formal devices that imply a conscious detachment, for example: purely metaphorical action ("Life on the edge, I'm dangling my feet"); chiastic exchange ("I tried to pay attention but attention paid me"); shifts in point of view contrary to fact ("Haters can't see me, nosebleed seats"); awareness of historical precedent ("I'm Ray Charles to the bullshit"); philosophical awareness ("Karma is a bitch? Well just make sure that bitch is beautiful"); acceptance of death ("Looked in the face of death and took its mask off"); formal reification ("I'm all about 'I,' give the rest of the vowels back").

What this song presents is two contrasting personal attitudes supported by structural dualities: Drake is relatively engaged, preoccupied, and horny; Wayne is relatively detached, narcissistic, and happy.

Albums

As producers think about producing not just singles but albums, their focus shifts from how a song's verses (and choruses) can play optimally against its beat to how a particular set of songs can work optimally together. For pre-digital, vinyl albums, song sequence was crucial. What song should begin the album, or should it instead begin with an intro, a track containing no rapping but a mix of beats, samples, and skits? How should the album end, with a final song or an outro? Should the songs alternate between this and that mood, or between faster and slower tempos, or between lyric and narrative? Or should there be some larger trajectory? Should the album's songs be grouped thematically and, if so, should these such groups be organized by skits[27]? More generally, what topics, tonalities, genres, and flavors will give the album its special appeal? If hit singles—or singles to be hyped as hits—are to be included, where in the song sequence where should they fall? And for every one song, this question: what thematic or musical bridges or chasms can optimally connect it to and distinguish it from the songs before and after it? The most successful producers are creative controllers with an expansive vision and an eye for minutia.

Consider the inclusion of "The What" in *Ready to Die*. As the album's unique freestyle battle, this song is an anomaly; but being both combative and highly entertaining, it fits perfectly within the album's array of moods. The overall trajectory of *Ready to Die* moves from derivative gangsta themes ("Gimme the Loot," "Warning," "Ready to Die") through mack junior mafia ostentation, to darker and more personal explorations of murder and mortality ("Suicidal Thoughts"). Within the middle area of this trajectory, Sean Combs sandwiched "The What" right between "One Last Chance," a raunchy sex-boast, and "Juicy," the upbeat, soul-sampled, success-celebration which became Biggie's biggest hit, still remembered and memorialized on "It Was All A Dream" tee-shirts. "The What" adds gritty fun to a miniseries of fun, gritty songs.

"One More Chance" opens with a skit composed of a series of hang-up voice messages from variously flirty, frustrated, disillusioned, and mightily pissed off women of romantic interest. Biggie's verses begin—

> When it comes to sex, I'm similar to the Thrilla in Manilla
> Honeys call me Bigga the Condom Filla

—and end with these lines:

> Backshots is my position, I got you wishin'
> For an intermission, fuck the kissin'
> Lick you down to your belly button, I ain't frontin'
> They don't call me big for nuttin'. All of a sudden   [into hook]

Now, if we recall Biggie's first verse in the unreleased version of "The What," we'll remember that his initial blast of rhymes is impressively tight, teasing, light-hearted, hilarious, but not at all aggressive or tough (the initial topics are weed and food). All he needs to battle Method Man is a little marijuana, not flapjacks and bacon, etc. This kind of playfulness also shows itself in their chorus duet, in their super-witty retorts, and in their simultaneous speaking as they transition from verse to verse—a rare and apparently last-minute performance choice cooked up right before their first studio take. While preserving these components of hip hop play in the album version, Puffy (and, legend has it, with the full consent of Biggie, who thought he had lost the battle) had many of Biggie's lines rewritten. Suddenly Biggie is talking not to Method Man but to no one in particular about himself and his sexual practices:[28]

> I used to get feels on a bitch
> Now I throw shields on the dick, to stop me from that HIV shit

Although this brand of self-absorbed misogyny would seem irrelevant to rap battling, which forefronts rhyming skills, it offers clear thematic continuity— rather than utter discontinuity—with the album's preceding song.

The relationship of "The What" to the album's following song, "Juicy," is somewhat less obvious although they share a common mood, which is quite simply the satisfaction from *rapping*—an enjoyment overriding thematic *claims* about the enjoyment of power and sex. "The What" is a poetry contest and a poetry collaboration. Biggie and Method Man are each having fun as they battle, and their choral duet mixing self-reliance, sex, and guns (and death)—

> Fuck the world, don't ask me for shit
> And everything you get ya gotta work hard for it
> Honies shake your hips, ya don't stop
> And niggaz pack the clips, keep on

—reads like the ultimate hip hop cliché but *sounds* like the happiest party in town. The chorus, not incidentally, could stand as the juxtapositional thematic motto for *Ready to Die* in its entirety. But meanwhile a single line added to the album version in Biggie's last verse creates a clear pathway into "Juicy": "Excuse me, flows just grow through me." This is supplemented by Biggie's assertion that he's "a motherfucking rap phenomenon." "Juicy" then substantiates these claims with a long series of before-and-after contrasts, many of these detailing his wealth and comfort, realized through commercial success:

> Birthdays was the worst days
> Now we sip champagne when we thirsté

But many also deal with the evolution of rap itself and with Biggie's part in this:

> Remember Rappin' Duke, duh-ha, duh-ha
> You never thought that hip hop would take it this far
> Now I'm in the limelight 'cause I rhyme tight[29]

Beyond the links between "The What" and its neighbor songs, continuity with the *album* as a whole is achieved by quoting other songs ("Biggie Smalls is the illest," in chorus third-person), a technique pervasive in *Ready to Die*. In his second revised verse, Biggie plugs the album directly, linking it with his own commercial success ("guaranteed another video"), but he also uses the title as a descriptor of his volatile personality. The realness of this attitude he authenticates by citing his father's abandonment of his mother, characterizing him as cowardly and a homosexual—

> Ready to die, why I act that way?
> Pop Duke left Mom Duke, the faggot took the back way
> So instead of makin' hoes suck my dick up
> I used to do stick-up, 'cause hoes is irritating like the hiccups

—in turn using this childhood trauma to explain the selfsame misogyny he has been flaunting up to this point. It's ambivalent moments like this which lift *Ready to Die* up from clichéd mack thematics into *real* realness—which is always complex.

It seems as if Biggie has to contemplate his mortality at regular junctures in the album. Biggie's momentary doubt in "Unbelievable" leads him to revisit his views from "Ready to Die" and thoughtfully probe whether he really *is* ready to die in "Suicidal Thoughts." As he contemplates the meaning of his mortality over a one-sided phone call to Puffy, he seems to have asked (and answered for) himself whether he had lived with the right values, and what God would do to him for his sins—

> When I die, fuck it, I wanna go to hell
> 'Cause I'm a piece of shit, it ain't hard to fucking tell
> It don't make sense, going to heaven with the goodie-goodies
> Dressed in white, I like black Timbs and black hoodies
> God'll prolly have me on some real strict shit
> No sleeping all day, no getting my dick licked
> Fuck that shit, I wanna tote guns and shoot dice

In Biggie's worldview, hell would, of course, be far worse than life on earth, where he can at least enjoy a don's power and sexual freedom. But it's all ephemeral, and death and judgment could come at any moment. Biggie names some of his sins, which range from drug-dealing and petty theft to extortion, and decides that he has alienated both his mother ("I know my mother wished she got a fucking abortion") and the pair of sisters ("baby mamas") with whom he has been involved in a complicated reproductive relationship. Seeing himself as an inveterate perpetrator of evil, he turns on himself, attempting suicide. Puffy, clearly disturbed by the news, hurries over in true superhero style to save Biggie's life just in time to produce *Born Again.*

But Biggie the don is back in this next album, even more *real* and further entrenched in his gangster ways, perhaps because he believes, like Dr. Faustus, that personal redemption is unattainable, or perhaps because he is addicted to his gangster lifestyle. Either way, he seems to accept and even glory in his habitual "fuck it" attitude, continuing to flaunt his bravado in "Who Shot Ya?"

> Clip to TEC, respect I demand it
> Slip and break the 11th Commandment
> Thou shalt not fuck with nor see Poppa
> Feel a thousand deaths when I drop ya
> I feel for you, like Chaka Khan I'm the don
> Pussy when I want, Rolex on the arm
> You'll die slow but calm
> Recognize my face, so there won't be no mistake

What's *right* for Biggie is what Biggie wants to do, and this choice is manifested in his stylistic consistency.

This sort of character return and stylistic stability are hardly unique. Through each of the Carter albums, Lil Wayne reliably displays his wry, flamboyant personality, expressed though his uniquely relaxed yet precise flow and trademark (yet widely copied) techniques, such elaborate off-rhyme chains. Part of the reason we may find such consistency alluring, even in response to circumstantial changes of theme from album to album, is that reflects a kind of integrity—not just a hustler's integrity but an artist's integrity. In contrast, we experience something more like personal transformation in Nas's and Eminem's albums. Nas grows up from an edgy, brilliant Queensbridge storyteller in *Illmatic* to a sensitive, amend-making musician in *Street's Disciple*; Eminem changes from a ruthless, raunchy MC to a philanthropist between *The Real Slim Shady* and *Recovery*. But what's consistent either way is that these MCs' serial albums—presuming continuous commercial success—solidify their reputations as *rap stars*. Whether or not their themes change, they either keep being great, or they get better and better, or they return to their original greatness after a lapse or two.

More collaborative groups are perhaps freer to devote themselves to narrative and lyric structures serving some larger purpose. For example, The Roots concern themselves with conscious rap, favoring satire and morality plays often dealing with complex issues like God, modern American culture, and African revisionist history in albums like *Phrenology, Organix, Rising Down, Undun, Game Theory, How I Got Over,* and *. . . And Then You Shoot Your Cousin*. None of the archetypes define the group. Similarly, in a much more immediately audible way, Outkast shows two sides of themselves—and two ways of looking at the world—in their simultaneous release of *Speakerboxxx* and *The Love Below* produced, respectively, by Big Boi and André 3000. The double album speaks back and forth, disc to disc, engaging its respective characters, themes, and styles in a sustained dialectic.

The MP3 revolution has probably helped encourage rappers not to align themselves strictly to fixed album personas. Take, for example, Kendrick Lamar, who explores "new" sides of himself through *Section.80* and *good kid, m.A.A.d city* while also remaining consistent with much of his original persona's Compton-fixed features. His choice allows him to be flexible enough to rap in conscious songs outside of his album as well as party songs inside it, meanwhile maintaining his fan-given right to instructional narrative within his albums.

Kendrick's early choice reflects—but is hardly determined by—the heavy influence of contemporary marketing of single songs, sold at ninety-nine cents apiece. Quite a few albums today sound less like a live performance, or less like a complexly integrated thematic and musical statement, and more a collection of singles, some of which need to be suited to radio play, some of which need to be suited to iPods and gyms, and some of which need to be suited to party environments. And quite a few shorter albums have been produced in response to the ubiquity and portability of digital music. In the summer of 2018, a series of commercially successful releases, including *DAYTONA* (Pusha T), *NASIR* (Nas), *EVERYTHING IS LOVE* (The Carters, a. k. a. Jay-Z and Beyoncé), *Streams of Thought, Vol 1* (Black Thought), *Ye* (Kanye West), and *KIDS SEE GHOSTS* (Kid Cudi and Kanye West), together averaging seven songs, suggest a significant shift. Some of these albums come at the expense of thematic complexity and unity, evidenced by these rappers' prior work.

Where does this leave us today? Let's first summarize the digital-directed trajectory we've just been considering. At least in the mainstream, we're seeing shorter lines, more chorus-laden songs and shorter albums. We're also seeing more collaboration across EPs, albums, and singles. A decentralized distribution channel system, such as social media, has increasingly shifted the commercial pressure to the artists. Staying relevant today has also meant consistently producing non-album products in between albums, going on tour more often in order to defend their original fan base, and becoming a public persona. This is not necessarily a bad thing when framed in the context of rap's early non-solo acts. Today's smaller sets of songs can function as stand-alone projects apart from the artist's main corpus yet linked to a network of other songs, collaborations, record labels, and ideologies, increasing intertextuality and juxtaposing contrasting stylistic variants.

It might be imagined that these continuing trends would diminish the capacity of rap to present big albums to the listening public, albums that make a difference by introducing new attitudes, new themes, and new flows—albums like N. W. A.'s *Straight Outta Compton*, or Nas's *Illmatic*, or Lauryn Hill's *The Miseducation of Lauryn Hill*, or Eminem's *The Marshall Mathers LP*. But the classical big album is anything but dead; instead, its resurgence articulates a kind of counter to the digitalization of rap. Note the almost retro tone of this chapter's epigraph, articulated by J. Cole in "Album of the Year (Freestyle)":

> *KOD*, album of the year, undebatably
> My cadence be the greatest we've seen since the late MC
> Whose name was The Notorious—Dreamville stacked like the Warriors

Needless to see, this is self-promotion, *KOD* being the name of his most recent album and Dreamville Records being the label he himself founded. J. Cole dropped "Album of the Year" three and a half months after the release of *KOD*, April 18, 2018, so the song doubles as celebration of the album's success and as a kind of ad for his post-release concert tour. Just before these lines we hear: "Don't want to fuck up my vibe / Let's end it on a positive note, come see me live." This couplet pivots from the "body" of the freestyle to the explicit self-promotion—the "positive note." It follows a very loose sequence moving from boasts and witticisms to serious social problems like the opioid crisis and racist incarceration policies. In this context, the "positive note" becomes—arguably truthfully—J. Cole's performances, both live and within the album, for both of these take on tough, socially important themes and present the rapper himself as a complex human being, and exhibit an impressively nuanced and variable flow. Also noteworthy are the sentiments embedded here in this passage. The accuracy of the adverb "undebatably" is of course debatable, like the assertion that Dreamville is as stacked with talent as the Golden State Warriors; but "undebatably" rhymes with "the late MC," whose appellation "Notorious" handily rhymes in turn with "Warriors," and the point of it all is J. Cole's cadence. It's the best cadence since Biggie's. It emulates a great classic and is produced by a company whose emcees collectively emulate a great contemporary sports team. This is J. Cole's claim, and many of his listeners agree.

What's also true, then, about the present status of the rap album is that we are seeing, from 2015 to the present, an astonishing collection of important art. In the case of Eminem's contribution, the point is in the craft itself, its breathtaking rhyme-and-flow complexity. In all the other albums listed here, we discover an unprecedented complexity of psychologically and socially important themes, multilingual expressions, flipped or unusually nuanced gender attitudes, new beat structures and vocal mixes, and a deeper awareness of hip hop traditions. Listening to these albums as a representative collection should leave any listener receptive to the art of rapping grateful and amazed at the progress that's been achieved forty decades out.

- Kendrick Lamar, *To Pimp a Butterfly* (2015)
- J. Cole, *4 Your Eyez Only* (2016)
- Beyoncé, *Lemonade* (2016)
- Jay-Z, *4:44* (2017)
- Rapsody, *Laila's Wisdom* (2017)
- Kendrick Lamar, *DAMN.* (2017)
- Pusha T, *DAYTONA* (2018)
- J. Cole, *KOD* (2018)
- Eminem, *Kamikaze* (2018)
- Jay Rock, *Redemption* (2018)
- Lil Wayne, *Carter V* (2018)
- Cardi B, *Invasion of Privacy* (2018)
- The Carters, *EVERYTHING IS LOVE* (2018)
- Lupe Fiasco, *Drogas Wave* (2018)

Style

The universe expands length
The body of my text possesses extra strength
—Mos Def, "Mathematics"

Style in art is what's optional. A particular bowl of fruit, painted in oils, could be rendered realistically, looking more or less like what the eye might see, or it could be distorted in an impressionist, cubist, or expressionist style. One painter might turn the pear into a mango, another might add a banana. The painted fruit looks like fruit—kind of—but its colors, shapes, textures, and composition may vary. In a sense, style is what's personal. Or more accurately, style is cultural but also personal.

In this example, the still life genre, with its traditional bowl-of-fruit subject, is a cultural fact, but a painter could choose never to paint it or, if painting it, could choose among a variety of mediums, and then the style of representation could vary. At the same time, there are cultural constraints. Maybe the painter is in an art class and is told to do a still-life in watercolors. Refusal is possible but unlikely. Maybe the painter has a patron who commissions it. If the painter were an up-and-coming, late nineteenth-century Parisian, chances are that he or she would belong to and self-identify with impressionism. Working within the constraints of that particular style, the painter might be limited to particular color palettes, canvas sizes, brush-stroke techniques, and so on—but would still make choices, developing an individual style.

All metrical poetry (including rap) is stylized in the sense that even though its language needs to be intelligible, with recognizable words and functional grammar, it also must fit into rhythmic lines of one kind of another. Four-beat poetry in English—whether it was composed a thousand years ago in an Anglo-Saxon court or today in a Def Jam studio—has a different style from poetry composed in syllable-counting meters. In all four-beat poetry, the pattern of stresses is much more emphatic and regular (1 2 ‖ 3 4) while the rhythms of the phrases are much more varied. Sharing this metrical style, however, the Old English poets sound quite different from the Middle English long-line poets, who sound quite different from contemporary rap poets, and these differences relate to changes in the English language itself, to cultural shifts, performance spaces, and other factors. Within each historical four-beat style are regional styles and personal styles. Caedmon and the *Beowulf* poet sound unmistakably distinct, as do Langland and the *Gawain* poet, as do Kurtis Blow and Melle Mel, Lauryn Hill and Biggie Smalls, Ice Cube and Tupac, and André 3000 and Lil Wayne.

There's plenty of evidence to suggest that rap poetry is not unique within the English four-beat tradition in being accompanied by a percussive beat. One key difference, though, is that in all earlier manifestations, up to and including Delta Blues, the poet/performer plays his or her own instrument (harp, guitar), so that the tempo may vary slightly in response to shifts in mood, theme, or to linguistic events like pauses, whereas in rap the DJ or producer's beat is constant throughout, forcing the poet to keep time with it. The rap beat also inhabits more musical space more loudly and more demonstratively.[1] Having no control over the beat's behavior during a performance, the rapper has to sustain a flow which keeps strict metrical time while respecting its mood and conversing poetically with its musical features. The nature of this conversation has huge implications for rap style. Among other things, it means that each *song*, each with its own beat, will have its own particular style. For a blatant example of this individuation, compare Biggie's "Juicy" and "Who Shot Ya?"

Songs in other traditions may have similarly strict stylistic constraints, especially once they become popular as folk or copyrighted commercial standards. The meter, melody, key, harmonic structure, words, and phrasal rhythms (locked to the melody) of most songs are fixed, susceptible only to minimal alteration. Nevertheless, performance style can vary. The singer's tempo, volume, pause lengths, melodic flourishes, special inflections and stress variations; the instrumentation itself and how the particular instruments are played—all of these are optional, resulting in a vast range of possible styles. "Amazing Grace" can be sung solo or in unison or even as a call and response; inspirationally or ploddingly, mournfully or rejoicing, Lutheran or Baptist, Southern Baptist or Abyssinian Baptist; a cappella or accompanied by an organ, a piano, a jazz trio, a Dixieland band, an orchestra, a choir. Chances are that if "Amazing Grace" is sung in a church, it will be performed in a straightforward manner so that everyone can sing along comfortably—unless that church is one founded in Gospel worship.[2]

Which brings us back to hip hop styles. The hip hop beat is an amalgam of disparate and often discordant sampled sounds. Its foundational rhythms are disco and funk, often mixed with jazz, soul, Jamaican house party, kitschy orchestral components, and samples from almost anywhere. In other words, it's *all* optional. Similarly, the words and phrases are anything but fixed. The only non-optional components are the four-beat meter and the presence of rhyme. Couplets are conventional, but their expected occurrence may be disrupted by one-liners, triplets, and the like, or smeared over by enjambments and rhyme chains. There may be choruses with repeated phrases set into rhythmically predictable stanzas, but these too are optional. Since every song's beat is distinct, every song's verses, although constrained by the beat's tempo and influenced by its dominant musical style, will be invited to take off in pretty much any direction the rapper sets for them. In fact, the main constraints on rap styling are culturally imposed, arising from its limited thematic range and its limited rhetorical goals, typically centered on ostentatious self-representation. Rappers often flaunt huge vocabularies and are capable of rhyming on almost anything, but this component of style is restricted by their need to "keep it real."[3] You'll rarely find a bowl of fruit in a rap song, which will never resemble a still life. The whole Euro-elitist idea of depicting food (its beauty, its ripeness, its decay) as an aesthetic object of contemplation would feel effete in rap music. If there's any food in rap, it's going to be eaten, and rap's fetishized objects are all usable or else consumable commodities: TEC-9s, Glocks, clips, blunts, indo, Cristal, Tanqueray, Timbs, Rolexes, Lexuses, Benzes and, of course, sex.[4]

If we listen to Mos Def's "Mathematics," we experience one of many, many rap styles. Here's a segment:

> It's five dimensions, six senses, seven firmaments of heaven and hell
> Eight million stories to tell
> Nine planets faithfully keepin' orbit, with the probable tenth
> The universe expands length
> The body of my text possesses extra strength
> Power-lift the powerless up out of this towering inferno
> My ink so hot it burn through the journal

Eighteen syllables in one line, eight in the next . . . two couplets blanketing a tercet. Blunt rhymes, then a wildly original rhyme (*inferno*/*journal*). Rhythmic bursts and brakes, plenty of cacophonous consonants. There's humor mixed with seriousness. The numerology and the mathematics include arcane allusions, sociological stats, and Quranic facts. The voice is anything but smooth, it's the voice of an agitator-revolutionary, a truth-teller, a prophet. His flow is edgy, fiery. His mode is prophetic. His name is actually Yasiin Bey.

And there's a general take-away here about rap style. Like the universe, it "expands length," and at the same time, with its variable density, variable pauses, and repeated rhyming stress-bursts, it "possesses extra strength." This chapter attempts the difficult task of describing the range of historical, regional, and personal rap styles and making sense of their constrained and optional features.

Changing Rap Styles

The MC's most important object is the mic. Amplifying the rapper's voice in a public space, it epitomizes his solo art, makes possible his or her individual styling to and against the hip hop beat, and symbolizes the entire tradition of rapping. Think of Wonder Mike's punning, metonymic name. Think of Nas's claims in "One Mic": "Yo, all I need is one mic, one beat, one stage . . . All I need is one mic, that's all a nigga need to do his thing y'know . . . All I need is one mic to spread my voice to the whole world."

That's the performance message. Although the social manifesto of "The Message" remains paramount, rap's quintessential message is ultimately the amplified (empowered) voice itself. For better or for worse, that voice is now laid onto the third verse of countless pop songs, and the importance of that voice in that context is not so much what is being said, but the rhetorical authentication of earnestness or emotional depth which it supposedly confers. Rap counterpoint signifies that Shakira, or Rihanna, or Katy Perry, or Beyoncé really *means* it. In such instances, rap styling is an accessory, but in rap songs themselves, it is always a dominant and often predominant feature. If we imagine the rap game as one big virtual battle, then every MC is engaged willy nilly in a solo quest to be the best. [5]

Yet the criteria for "best" remain disputed, ranging from mass appeal to artistic innovation. It is commonly held that the main way to achieve that status is to become the most popular artist with the best sales—even if that means simplifying one's flow. As Jay-Z puts it in "Moment of Clarity" from *The Black Album*:

> I dumbed down for my audience to double my dollars
> They criticized me for it, yet they all yell "holla"

But if popularity or monetary success were a reliable measure of poetic excellence, YG, Future, and Sage the Gemini would be today's finest rap talents.[6] However, within its culture of competing artistic interests, rap music simply cannot be evaluated with success as the sole criterion.[7] Here the intersection of talent and timeliness becomes merit, as exemplified by the thematic relevance of N. W. A.'s *Straight Outta Compton*, Nas's *Illmatic*, Lauryn Hill's *The Miseducation of Lauryn Hill*, and Biggie's *Ready to Die*. Finally, some have won acclaim by being preeminent rhymers with unique flow, such as Mel, Rakim, Ice Cube, Nas, Snoop, Tupac, Biggie, André 3000, Lil Wayne, and Eminem. Here, style becomes the main criterion. What does Eminem actually *say* in his highly touted "Rap God"? It's hard to say, given that his verses assume the several discrete points of view, expressing a range of sometimes contradictory human and virtual attitudes and emotions and ideas; but no one but Eminem could have packed six thousand plus syllables into such variously rhyming and variously rhythmic lines.

It does, of course, matter what rappers rap about, and there is no doubt that major shifts in rap styles over the years have been correlated with thematic and functional shifts. When once upon a time the amplified voice of the MC served primarily to support the DJ in keeping the party moving, the main theme was, quite simply, keeping the party moving (on and on, till the break of dawn), which was facilitated by funny anecdotes, claims of poetic and sexual prowess, spontaneous situational commentaries, counting-out rhymes, and so on. No sober truths, no political agenda, no emotional trauma, and no poetic depth or complexity had a place in this. Meanwhile, the lines were short, rhymes were deployed in predictable metrical slots, and phrasal rhythms were typically simple and even formulaic.[8]

The style of this early period, sometimes known as Old School, has been labeled the "sung rhythmic style" by the musicologist Adam Krims in his *Rap Music and the Poetics of Identity* (2000). Krims does not mean that Wonder Mike, Kurtis Blow, Grandmaster Caz, or Ad Rock actually sang their lines, but rather that their style of rapping is fundamentally musical. As with most melodic singing, stressed syllables fall right on the beat, and phrasal units conform to the structure of the musical bars. Stylistic variation may be achieved by overt and often exaggerated intonations, but the syllable rhythms are quite predictably sing-songy, with short dips, and lines are quite predictably end-stopped with medial pauses. This style makes sense for party rap, for an audience mainly interested in casually dancing to the beat would either ignore or be annoyed by artistic variation such as unexpected pauses or rapid-fire syllable-bursts.

The stats from our database from 1979 through 1987—not including Rakim or West Coast gangsta—reveal that the rhythms of the typical line diversified little over those nine years. Between the release of "Rapper's Delight" and Rakim's *Paid in Full*, lines rarely exhibited any secondary stresses, rhymed or unrhymed; that is, the 1, 2, 3, 4 pattern of stresses on the beat was exceedingly predictable.[9] Dip lengths before, between, and following these stresses in the two half lines also remained quite predictable. Only the second dip changed its average length during this period, expanding ever so slightly, but the other dip lengths stayed constant. The initial dips in each half line commonly had just one syllable, uncommonly three, while two-syllable initial dips were generally avoided. Although the reason for this avoidance of two-syllable initial dips remains mysterious, its net impact was to restrict rhythmic variation there to just two options—"short" and "long."[10]

Just as predictable as the early rap line's phrasal rhythms were its rhyme patterns, which we might label minimal and maximal. In the minimal type, rhyme is restricted to the fourth stress (BBBR; "The beat don't stop || until the break of **dawn**"), fulfilling the couplet's end-rhyme requirement. In the maximal type, rhyme occurs on all four beated stresses (RRRR; "Singin' **on** n n **on** || n on **on** n **on**") or else on all but the third stress (RRBR; "**Hotel, motel** || Holiday **Inn**"). Other than these main patterns, there was little structural variation. Rhyme, in short, was not initially conceived as an ongoing option for stresses in the syllable stream. Nor was it used to mark (rare) secondary stresses or unstressed syllables.[11] Like rhythm, early rhyme was fundamentally structural, aligned with the musical beat and, in turn, the listener's expectation. It behaved like any other restricted musical element in a composite musical piece, rather than an MC's relatively optional element of style.

Which brings us again to Rakim, who was less a party rapper than a studio and stage MC who *wanted* people to hear new rhythms and who created an audience interested in listening, not just dancing. With the release of *Paid in Full*, the sing-song predictability of earlier rap suddenly became passé. Rakim's style has often been compared to that of a jazz soloist, to the improvisational work of Miles, Bird, or Coltrane, and we suspect that Adam Krims's terms for the two alternative styles which supplanted the earlier "sung rhythmic style" are both derived, consciously or unconsciously, from the history of jazz. These rather awkward but nevertheless relevant terms are "percussive-effusive" and "speech-effusive." Neither Rakim nor his great West Coast counterpart Ice Cube rapped in such a way as to merely support the ongoing hip hop beat; instead, these artists soloed in much the same way as hard bop instrumentalists would solo. Backed by a steady drum beat and within a particular harmonic structure, the bebop soloist would pointedly improvise *around* (not *to*) the beat, freely introducing complex rhythmic phrases and breaking through the rhythmic boundaries of the bar. This is what Krims means by "percussive-effusive"—a style of flow exemplified not just by Rakim but also by Ice Cube, Chuck D, KRS-One, Biggie, Jay-Z,[12] and Busta Rhymes. To rap this way does not mean to disregard the beat; on the contrary, it means to sustain the beat while also introducing rhythmic departures from it. These include new patterns of rhyme, secondary stresses, rhyme on some of these secondary stresses, additional pauses in the line, and the avoidance of expected end stop and caesural pauses by means of enjambment and the introduction of lines with no medial pause (BBBB, B|BB|B, B|BBB, etc.). This new flow is still danceable but, like bebop, it's hipper and soon became more hip-hop than what had come before. This new flow in effect made the MC more than an MC—a poet and a personality with an edge, enabling rap music to become more than party music. The rapper's voice could be earnest, instructive, cynical, angry, threatening, outrageous, narcissistic, or ridiculous. It could be a vehicle for political oratory, gangsta dramatics, or suave mack posturing.[13]

This range of moods did not all revolve around the MC's ego or persona. The new flow models made room for a kind of intellectual dialogue between rappers and the rap community, ultimately giving rise to the genre of *knowledge* rap, characterized by earnest, wise, spiritual, self-aware rapping. Committed to this style have been rappers like MC Lyte, Queen Latifah, Guru, Common, Nas, Yasiin Bey (Mos Def), Talib Kweli, Hopsin, Immortal Technique, Ab Soul, Lupe Fiasco, Kendrick Lamar, and many others, even Kanye West. Generally speaking, their styles deepen the rhetoric and relevance on topics like black identity, sexual identity and relationships, family ties, regional pride, existential crises, education, inaccurate history, and appropriate ethics. In this style, *how* the content is rapped is nearly as important *what* is being rapped about. To deal fully with these weighty, complex topics, a new style needed to emerge, one promoting still more variety of expressiveness. Krims calls this style "speech-effusive" rapping.

Of course, some artistic moods remained focused on flaunting a rapper's inalienable *right to egocentricity*, but even these moods could benefit from a quantum leap in rhythmic complexity. Battle rapping[14] may seem superficially like a chain of boasts and attacks, but its success depends entirely on stylistic control. A successful battle rap establishes street credibility through creative syllabic control while maintaining a highly self-styled discordant edginess.[15] The newer style proved ideal for battling.

To resume the jazz analogy, "speech-effusive" flow is a little less like classic fifties and sixties bebop soloing and more like that of such innovators as Eric Dolphy, Ornette Coleman, Anthony Braxton, and the late Coltrane, present still in contemporary artists like Brad Mehldau and Michael Brecker. As Krims's term implies, the rapper's voice (which, of course, has always been declaimed, shouted, or radio-voiced, has always been spoken rather than sung)[16] now claims even more grammatical and rhythmic freedom from musical conventions. This flow is preeminently speech as *contrasted* to music. Like natural speech, it follows its own shifting rhythms which, as in English generally, are stress-timed but, in the context of the hip hop beat, may sound especially unruly. More stresses may pack the line, and these stresses may be more likely to occur close together; creating clashing rhythms, or inordinately long strings of unstressed syllables that may challenge the predictably eurythmic contexts of the beated stresses. In the same way that Ornette or Dolphy might abandon normal harmonic obedience, shifting keys mid-solo, at times abandon the ongoing beat of the drum and bass (which might alter their own rhythms), taking off on wild, playful rhythmic tangents, so the so-called "speech-effusive" rappers often seem intent on controlling the higher-order rhythms of the rap song itself. Think of Big Pun, Method Man, Prodigy, Nas, Bone Thugs (especially Krayzie Bone), Twista, Yasiin Bey (Mos Def), Black Thought, Lupe Fiasco, Kendrick Lamar, and Eminem. A number of these MCs routinely shift cultural and emotional registers as they rap, and they can shift from one voice to another. Not surprisingly, they display a mastery of mixed diction, grammatical range, and rhetorical nuance. They also excel at intonation, deploying unexpected pitch accents, vocal effects, and pauses in order to underscore a particular point or to inject irony or humor. Such intonations and pauses reach outside of regular musical and linguistic vocabularies to create something like the rhythmic noise-enhancements peculiar to hip hop beats themselves. Some sound effects may be comically imitative, as in Method Man's cough in Wu-Tang's "Protect Ya Neck" (1993)—

> Niggas off because I'm hot like sauce
> The smoke from the lyrical blunt makes me **eughck**

—or Biggie's hiccupping "hiccups" in "The What" (1994):

> Ready to die, why I act that way?
> Pop Duke left Mom Duke, the faggot took the back way
> So instead of makin' hoes suck my dick up
> I used to do stick-up, 'cause hoes is irritatin' like the **hiccups**[17]

Other sound effects may simply project surprise and weirdness for its own stake, much like Dolphy's reed squeals and squeaks, the frog-sounds emerging from Braxton's contra-bass saxophone and clarinet, or the trumpet half-valves and croaks heard in contemporary jazz. Little quirks, odd musical speech-effusions. It is probably no accident that the beats behind such contemporary songs as Kendrick's "Control" and Eminem's "Rap God" are so complexly textured and dissonant as to flirt with chaos. This is rap music which not only asks to be listened to, it's rap music which can *only* be listened to.[18] Finally, it's all about the MC. The party's over; or rather, the party has moved to a different venue—with the old electronica of disco reincarnated in the new electronica of house.

What both kinds of "effusiveness" have in common is their commitment to variation and polyrhythmy. To some degree, these styles are successive historically, with bebop-like flow concentrated especially in the late 1980s and 1990s and with postmodern flow displacing it more recently. But the two "effusive" styles are anything but mutually exclusive. Tupac, Biggie, Wu-Tang, Treach, Lauryn Hill, and others incorporate features of both in some of their songs or can rap in either style of flow. Perhaps what lends André 3000 and Lil Wayne their own unique styles is that they can fluidly navigate among all three historical flows, retaining the smooth danceability of Old School while complicating it with more recent rhythmic ideas. Finally, it is the business of each and every MC to cultivate his or her own personal flow while also being inevitably influenced by rap's history and by rap's regional cultures.

The first commercially successful instances of bebop-like "percussive-effusive" rapping came out in the late 1980s. In New York, Rakim was introducing songs like "I Ain't No Joke," "My Melody," "As The Rhyme Goes On," and "I Know You Got Soul," stylizing his delivery by means of irregular pauses, syncopation, thicker and more varied rhyme textures, and varying syllabic speeds.[19] Each of these techniques offered liberation for MCs willing to emulate them, for each opened up an opportunity to escape expected rhythmic nexuses to new syntax patterns with new meaning-structures. That, in turn, allowed more rhymes grouped within a more complex rhyme nexus which rhymed *around* the rhythm nexuses.

Rakim's innovations caught everyone's attention, likely including the rappers in N. W. A. Just a year later, they released their 1988 hit album *Straight Outta Compton*. "Fuck Tha Police," "Gangsta Gangsta," and "Something Like That," while differing drastically in thematic focus and diction, presented another canonical example of the "percussive-effusive" style.[20] N. W. A.'s new use of six-stress-six-rhyme lines made them an instant hit among hip hop heads and rappers alike.[21] In much the same way as Rakim destabilized norms of flow, Ice Cube makes use of extra pauses, six-stress lines, and caesural elisions in "Fuck Tha Police."

> **You'd** rather **see** || **me** in the **pen**
> **Than me** and Lorenzo **rollin'** in the **Ben-zo**
> **Beat** a **po**lice || **outta shape**
> And **when** I'm **fin-ished** || **bring** the **yel**low **tape**
> To **tape** | **off** || the **scene** of the **slaugh**ter
> **Still** gettin' **swoll** of || **bread** and **wat**er

This is in sharp contrast with Rakim's spiritual rapping, and the function of extra stresses is to give a sense of edginess appropriate to the violent themes—a critique of the judicial system's treatment of black people. In the aftermath, *Straight Outta Compton*, the dominant thematic "gangsta" focus lessened previous emphases on regional style, and the West Coast G-Funk beats became the national norm, consolidated by albums like Ice Cube's *AmeriKKKA's Most Wanted/Kill At Will*.

However, none of these rappers made use of extra stresses and rhymes with the same frequency as the next generation, heralded by Nas. His 1991 debut verse on Main Source's "Live at the Barbeque" expanded upon the techniques of Rakim and N. W. A. in lines like these:

> **Poet**ry at**tacks** || **par**agraphs **punch hard**
> My **brain** is in**sane** || I'm **out** to **lunch, God**

Science is **dropped** ‖ my **raps** are **tox**ic
My **voice-box locks** and ex**cels** like a **rock**et

Though clunky in comparison to Nas's work in *Illmatic* (1994), this had a huge impact in the rap community. Nas packs mono- and multisyllabic words together in tight strings, supported by a variety of sound effects like assonantal rhyme and alliteration. While most of his lines still have a "percussive-effusive" feel, his innovative technique and its subsequent usage would allow for rappers to develop the "speech-effusive" sound.

From then on, rappers would expand the line to compete with Nas's multisyllabic rhyme patterns, allowing them to incorporate extra stresses into dips 1 and 3. By 1995, many rappers, even Biggie, who stuck with shorter lines, would exploit these rhythmic opportunities.[22] Big L, in *Livestylez ov da Poor & Dangerous* (1995) effortlessly weaves in and out of five, six, and seven stress lines, for example in "Put It On":

And **it's** a **fact** I keep a **gat** in my **arm reach**
I **charm freaks** and **bomb geeks** from here to **Palm Beach**

For Big L, the main casualty of packing multiple extra stresses into the line was the caesural pause, the fixture of the line most often used to stabilize flow and create rhythmic contrast. Additionally, Big L's long, dense lines are seldom, if ever, contrasted with short, simple lines. This might explain Big L's (and Nas's) relatively low commercial reward for his poetic skill, and also explain why rappers like Biggie and Jay-Z were hits in both the mainstream and underground.

By 1995, many rappers were packing seven stresses into a line (most of which were rhyming).[23] The line had gotten longer, but it grew in proportional fashion: the relationship between the dips would expand in a nearly uniform ratio. Because of the constituent relationships between the dips, the line is regulated by sequential dip-grouping. In terms of the musical beat, dips 6 and 1 and 3 and 4 are merged, and dip 2 and dip 5 each last for a whole beat. These groupings are symmetrical in musical time, and correspondingly, though roughly, in syllabic length. However, the relative syllabic density of the individual dips within these groupings is incongruous. We mentioned earlier that dip 6 would typically be shorter than dip 1, and dip 3 typically longer than dip 4. Each of these dips became longer in the nineties, but the summed length of dip 3 and dip 4 would, on average, sum to the average of dip 2 or dip 5. This grouping mechanism, in conjunction with rhyme patterning, holds together the integrity of the line while allowing the rapper considerable rhythmic liberties. [24]

But not everybody wanted to exploit these new choices—particularly not mainstream rappers. More rhythmically predictable groups like A Tribe Called Quest garnered much more popular attention than did Nas. In some ways, this resistance can be justified by practical and even philosophical differences in what listeners, artists, and hip hop purists think the music is for.[25] While Tribe's party-going target audience might suffice to explain their more monotonous styling, Atmosphere's commitment to messaging an indie audience might better explain theirs. Slug seems to approach Rakim-like rhythmic variation with skepticism, instead varying the Old School patterns by reweighting the dips, grouping them in new combinations. His work can be seen as a pushback against the mainstream, privileging Old School rhythms and linguistic clarity.[26]

Regional Styles

Rhythmic differentiation and convergence are a reflection of rappers' needs for both individuation and regional representation. Contemporary Detroit sound is vastly different from the New York sound, which differs from the Los Angeles sound, which differs from the Chicago sound,[27] all of which differ from the Dirty South (best captured by Atlanta). Within the New York sound alone, Brooklyn, the Bronx, and Queensbridge each have a different sound. These groups can be roughly categorized in terms of the major sectors of the country: East Coast, West Coast, the Midwest, and the South. Figure 8 shows that the syllabic density of the constituent dips of a dip group varies.

These statistics reflect that there truly *is* some line-based correlation between region and style; however, whatever claims we and others investigating average regional style may make can offer only limited insights subject to rebuttal.[28] First of all, given the competitiveness between MCs, intra-regional variation is high. Everybody knows that Nas, Biggie, Jay-Z, and Guru sound nothing alike, yet they are all New York MCs. A similar grouping problem is evident in this small subset of West Coast rappers, analyzed in Figure 9.

Still more problematically, battles, like the one between Biggie and Tupac, make it difficult to distinguish between which stylistic components belong to the rapper's syllabic control, which belong to battle-related performance choices, and which belong to regional norms. Figure 10 shows a dip length

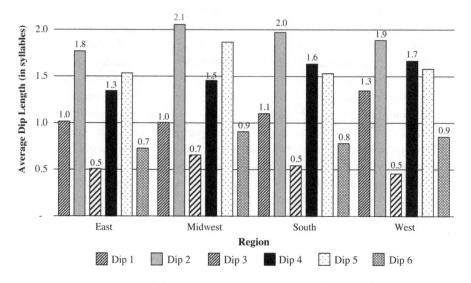

Fig. 8. Average dip lengths by region (East Coast, Midwest, South, and West Coast).

comparison between New York and Los Angeles. As we can see in Figure 10, when considering all cases, the average dip lengths are fairly similar, excepting that Los Angeles rappers tend to have *marginally* longer first, fourth, and sixth dips than New York rappers. Now we compare Biggie with other New York rappers. Figure 11 suggests that he seems somewhat stylistically typical of New York rappers.

However, we note a schism from the general regional style when analyzing "Who Shot Ya?" by Biggie. As a battle song, it functions as both a representation of his hood, Brooklyn, and his poetic prowess. Figures 12 and 13 are composite graphs, one superimposing Biggie in "Who Shot Ya?" over Biggie generally and New York generally, and one superimposing Tupac's "Hit 'Em Up" over Tupac generally and the West Coast generally.

And finally, Figure 14 compares "Who Shot Ya?" with "Hit 'Em Up."

As a listener can readily hear (and now see), Biggie's and Tupac's styles differ markedly both in their respective battle raps and overall. Even on "Deadly Combination" with Big L, Biggie, and Tupac, they sound distinctly different. On their solo work, it's easy to tell that the styles of "Ambitionz Az A Ridah" sound nothing like those of "Rap Phenomenon," and the same

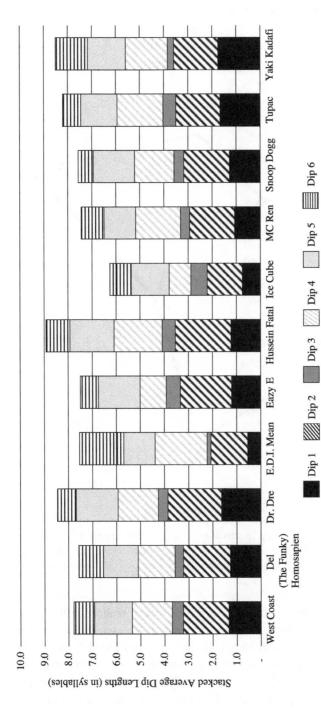

Fig. 9. Comparing dip lengths of ten West Coast rappers. The bar at the left shows the averages of all ten. Shaded regions represent average dip lengths; they are stacked here but do not sum to represent lines as a whole.

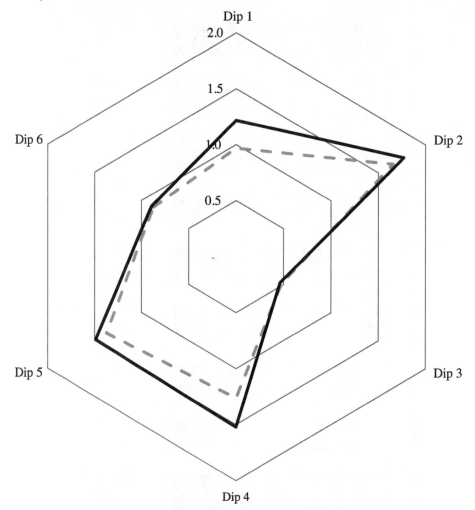

Fig. 10. Comparing average dip lengths of Los Angeles-based rappers (solid line) with New York City-based rappers (dotted line), with range of average dip length from .5 to 2.0 syllables. Length from the center signifies the number of syllabic events within the dip > 0.

can be said of "Secretz of War" and "Everyday Struggle." Obviously, the immediate differences are topical. Life in Los Angeles, put flatfootedly, is just not the same as life in New York. But over and above denotative qualities in these particular songs, further differences are manifested in the rhythmic preferences particular to each coast. By 1999, West Coast rapping styles had, on average, longer dips than East Coast styles, particularly with respect

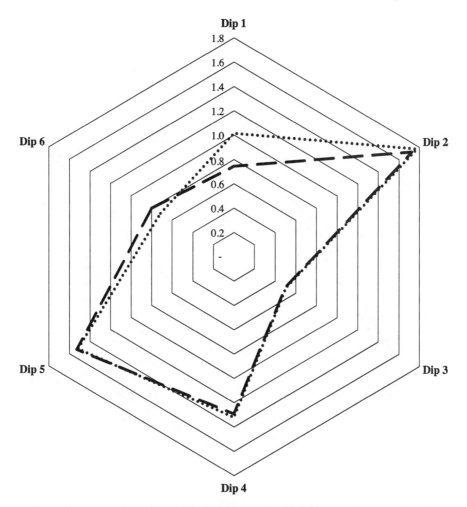

Fig. 11. Comparing Biggie (dashed line) with other New York City-based rappers (dotted line), with range of dip length from .2 to 1.5 syllables. Length from the center signifies the number of syllabic events within the dip > 0.

to dips four and six. Additionally, West Coast rapping was characterized by a smooth, laid-back feel, not only because Snoop and Tupac deployed more of a crooning style, but also due to its characteristic flow: there were fewer extra stresses, and rhythmic variation was achieved largely by means of varied phrase length, both within the dips and through the use of caesural elision and enjambment. The contrastingly edgy sound of East Coast rapping was produced through less frequent rhyme on the beat, dip-disrupting

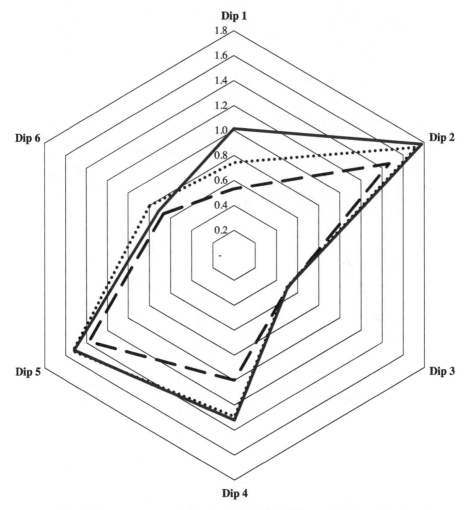

Fig. 12. Biggie: A closer look at "Who Shot Ya" (solid line) through the lens of average dip length. Biggie is represented by the dotted line; New York City-based rappers by dashed line. Range of dip length from .2 to 1.8 syllables. Length from the center signifies the number of syllabic events within the dip > 0.

pauses, and multiple extra stresses in conjunction with caesural elision and enjambment.

However, regional style becomes trickier once rap quarrelling begins between the coasts, as when the two rappers square off in "Who Shot Ya?" and "Hit 'Em Up." While both Biggie and Tupac conform more regularly to their individual coastal style in their respective songs, it is within a dif-

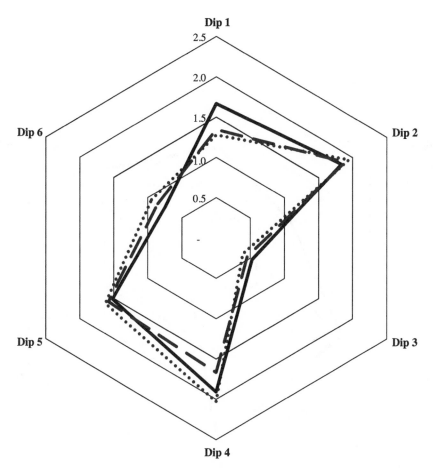

Fig. 13. Tupac: A closer look at "Hit 'Em Up" (dotted line) through the lens of average dip length. Tupac's overall style is represented by the contiguous black line; Los Angeles-based rappers by the dashed line. Range of dip length from .5 to 2.5 syllables. Length from the center signifies the number of syllabic events within the dip > 0.

ferent poetic setting. In the previous graph, we can see that both Biggie and Tupac's dip lengths, generally speaking, contract in the context of this battle. And this phenomenon can be explained by referencing the required musical edginess required of a diss track.[29] But there's definitely more at play here. It's likely that the sequence of the battle mattered—Biggie responds to Tupac and his crew, which could explain his higher frequency of punctuated rhythms relative to Tupac: he's eager to *get his own* with a blistering response. Not all of his dips contract uniformly—and he may have maintained a lon-

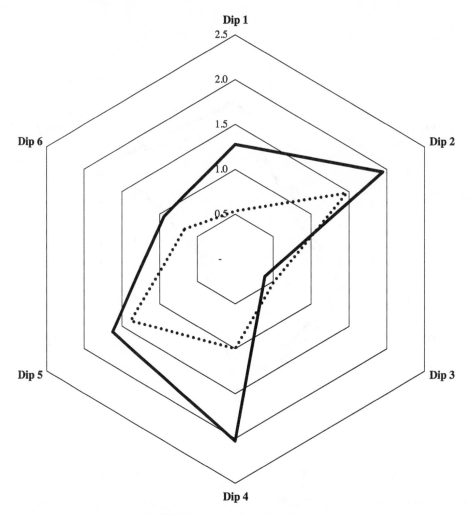

Fig. 14. Average dip length of "Who Shot Ya" (solid line) versus "Hit 'Em Up" (dotted line). Range of dip lengths from .5 to 2.5 syllables. Length from the center signifies the number of syllabic events within the dip > 0.

ger second dip in many cases in order to flip some of Tupac's rhythms. It would help if we could ask Biggie (RIP) and Tupac (RIP) whether they embodied their coastal style, or their coastal style was embedded in their personal style, or they made their individual coastal styles what they were, but even then, we couldn't be sure they would give us a straight answer—or even know.[30]

Outside of the Biggie vs. Tupac battle, the contemporary Kendrick vs. "low-bar jumpers" battle further illustrates the difficulties that come with comparing regional styles. In Big Sean's "Control," Kendrick claims to represent *both* coasts—

I'm Makaveli's offspring[31], I'm the King of New York[32]
King of the Coast, one hand, I juggle them both

—presumably because, although identifying with Compton on his album *good kid, m.A.A.d city*, he self-consciously shares rhythmic similarities with rappers like Eminem, André 3000, and Rakim. His style(s) beg(s) the question: is regional style relevant anymore?

The relevance of regional style depends on the pre-existence of regional dialects and cultural customs, which in turn depend upon regional stability (e.g., limited population flow) and regional consciousness. As rap's proliferation into the mainstream became less radio-driven, that is, less dependent on local media outlets, and more driven by national media to include syndicated radio, TV, large record corporations, and eventually iTunes, regional style has come to function increasingly less as a common mode of speaking and more and a sign of a rapper's particular authenticity. For this reason, we consider it appropriate to view rapping styles in the context of individual style.

One of the clearest examples of importing from regional tendencies is manifest in Lil Wayne's style, which incorporates elements of East Coast, West Coast, Midwest and Dirty South rapping to make a distinctive sound, which is further individuated by his voice. Wayne impressively blends all of the major regional styles musically and poetically in such a way that a listener can identify his flow almost instantly. We witness this integrated stylistic variety in "This Is The Carter," from *Tha Carter* (2004), a song whose overt purpose is to introduce this MC's work. The rhythmic diversity is broad, exhibiting both "speech-effusive" and "percussive-effusive" components in such a way as to emphasize these features' musicality.

Beginning with line 1, Weezy uses extra pauses in the b-verse:

Who am I ‖ **young wiz**zle | **fa shiz**zle
Flow sicker than a ‖ **third floor** in **hos**pitals

This already varied rhythm serves as a flow template for more complex variations all the way through the first verse. No a-verse is disrupted by an irregu-

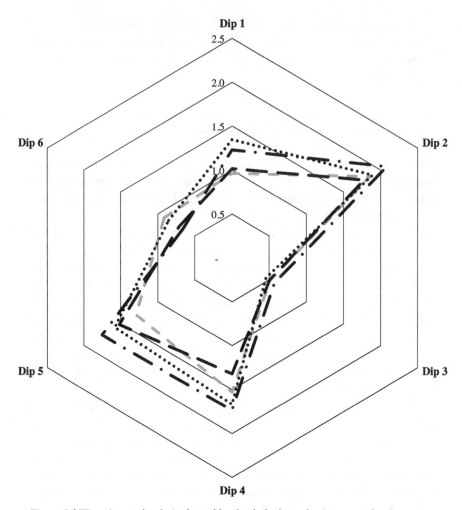

Fig. 15. Lil Wayne's varied style (indicated by the dashed gray line) compared to Los Angeles-based rappers (dotted line), New York City-based rappers (dashed line) and Atlanta-based rappers (hybrid dashed and dotted line). Range of dip length from .5 to 2.5 syllables. Length from the center signifies the number of syllabic events within the dip > 0.

lar pause. This rhythmic template shares some characteristics with lines from Rakim's "I Know You Got Soul" and "I Ain't No Joke," taking what we had noted to be Rakim's exemplary innovations and using them as regularities.

Wayne's first a-verse disruption in verse 2 is balanced by more or less fixed rhythms in the b-verse, but he only needs to maintain rhythmic congruency for about four lines before renovating that rhythm in turn:

> **Young | Moll || picture** the **broad lick**
> **All** the way **down** to the **balls ||** then she **wipe** it **off**
> If **getting mon**ey is **wrong ||** I ain't **right** at **all**
> I **young mon**ey a **car ||** I just **write** it **off**

Near the end of the second verse, he introduces a line with nine stresses. This mimetically repetitive line embodies in its series of demonstratives the song's musical essence by treating words as if they were purely percussive notes. It even has a b-verse pause:

> **This, this, this, this || this, this, this, this | this**

Having toyed with the rules of the a- and the b-verse individually, Wayne begins to play with the flow of both simultaneously in verse 3. "Speech-effusive," in its most basic sense, is the style of this verse and incorporates elements of both New York MCs like Yasiin Bey and Jay-Z, and Southern MCs like Big Boi and Khujo Goodie. Wayne opens his verse with a half line maintained *against* the beat, and a pair of nearly mirrored six-syllable dips:

> And **y'all** better blame **Baby**
> Cuz **he** the muthufucka that **made** me **||** and **I'm cra**zy And **y'all** ask **why ||** I
>   never **left** the **na**vy
> Cuz **he** the muthufucka that **pay** me **||** is **you cra**zy
> **Young, young, young ||** wiz**zle ba**by
> **Give** you yo **iss**ue, **|| me** don't wanna **kiss** you

Just after having resolved the rhythmic tension from the hanging half bar rhythm, he disrupts the a-verse with a pause, matching an a-verse rhythm from earlier in the verse—

> **No | no || no me** no want no **bull**shit
> So **|** so **stop** baller **blockin' ||** cuz a **nig**ga **hood rich**

—and, further destabilizing rhythmic norms, he skips pauses altogether in the very next line (which he had not done since the end of the first verse)—

And I **floss** every**day** be**cause** I **could** bitch
So **hol**la at ya **boy** || cuz I'm **still** on some **hood shit**

—only to mirror it rhythmically two lines later, and in the interim, rhythmically link "**No** | **no**" and "**Like** | **like**"—

Like | **like** || like what's **really good** wit
Ya **mom** or your Lil **boy** and your **sis**ter lookin' **good** shit

Wayne ties up the verse by denying a normative resolution till the very end. A 1|3 line is followed by rhythmic variations on earlier rhythmic variations, and the final line consists of yet another abnormal stress riff leading into a perfectly normal b-verse, a demonstrative sequence linking the rapper to his people. This is style with affect and impact:

Shit | **I'm** still **Ap**ple **Eag**le **wea**sel,
1–7 **Hollygrove** || **never** ever **leave you**
I **got y'all** || **wait**in' on my **sequel**
This, this, this, this, this || this is the **Car**ter **peo**ple

Weezy's versatility and commercial success were unmatched. From *Tha Carter* to *Tha Carter III*, rap fans and artists alike usually agree that he dominated the game, and many would put Weezy in their personal list of top five MCs. Popularly played in parties, cars, and radio, Weezy's "speech-effusive" music was received by both mainstream and intellectual audiences, in contrast to that of his jazz counterparts, who seem to appeal to primarily to highly intellectual, experimental-music listeners. Weezy, like Brecker and Mehldau, uses eight and sixteen bar rhythmic phrases, and it's difficult to imagine that there are larger structures that we, mere humans (not aliens), can make sense of. So, had Wayne reached the apex? Would rapping become chaotic and nonsensical if it were to exhibit greater variation?

"Is Hip Hop Dead?"

Many of Wayne's once-loyal listeners believe that he had indeed reached his apex, and that the beginning of what we now call contemporary rap spelled the end of hip hop's renaissance, which they believe began in the 1990s and ended in the early 2000s. This may well be true, formalistically, for not only is it difficult to make sustained sense within the larger, denser verse structures developed by the more "effusive" rappers, but it seems unlikely that these structures can tolerate any further expansion or density. Yet avant-garde rapping has continued nonetheless. Rap artists have taken rap in multiple diverging musical directions, even changing the poetic environment of the art. Black Thought's dizzying ten-plus minute verse on Hot 97 (2017; see https://genius.com/13280521) issues a call-out to the industry, effectively rapping that the rap game ought to remain the socially conscious voice of the disenfranchised:

Yo, I'm K-Dot Lamar meets 2Pac Shakur
Got profiled by a few cops, too hot to charge
Listen, somebody said a price tag was on a rapper's head
So we gon' see a nice bag when the rapper dead
The mask black, the flag green, black, and red
They'll probably wave a white flag after plasma shed
No doubt, yo, the game went they own route
I can't explain what these lame kids is talkin' 'bout

The game has indeed taken its own route(s), and many rappers will and have stayed their course in the face of these kinds of call-outs. For example, ScHoolboy Q follows an approach which broadly abandons ornamentation and rhythmic play as a prerequisite for good rapping—returning to the recurrently popular function of rap as party music. After two homogenous rap albums (*Setbacks* and *Habits & Contradictions*), Q shifted directions in *Oxymoron*. In the first ten songs, he pays homage to the tradition, consciously varying his style. For the last two, however, he consciously becomes repetitive, using the same rhythmic phrase over and over again. In "Break the Bank," verse one and verse three are analogous—neither has intra-linear variation.

GetMine my **nick**name || **O**-X and **co**caine
Nina my **new** thing || **blew** up be**fo'** fame
Heart filled with **oct**ane || **fi**-re in my **soul**
Burn through my shoe**string** || **came** up from boos**ting**

In at least one way, ScHoolboy Q is a hustler. *Oxymoron* sold 236,000 copies within a couple of months, toted as a rap album despite the assertions in "Break the Bank," in which he specifically says:

> Fuck rap, I've been rich, crack by my stick shift
> Oxy like concerts, always my bread first

And with just one verse in between:

> Fuck rap, my shit real, came up off them pills
> Hustle for my meal, grinding for my deal

One way of spinning it is to say that ScHoolboy Q's "Break the Bank" is a sophisticated commentary on—and cynical manipulation of—the uncritical rap listening audience. ScHoolboy Q didn't need rap to get rich, but his story sells in itself, and contemporary rap listeners are an easy target for profits. He says as much in the hook, which goes so far as to replaces rhythms with any-old-word-will-do-da-di-do:

> So now we 'bout to break the bank
> Money be on my mind
> Niggas talkin' 'bout, soundin' like
> La-da-di-do, la-di-da-di-da-di-do

He repeats the last line a few more times to drive home the message. All along, the beat keeps our attention, and Q has got us listeners so addicted to his "product" that he will get rich whether or not he varies his flow and whether he speaks sense or nonsense. It's all hustling.

Moreover, ScHoolboy Q seems to be saying something about the concept of *realness* in the rap game, suggesting that he didn't need to rap to authenticate his story, and style didn't need to affirm that either—his gangbanging past should suffice. The philosophical takeaway is something along the lines of: if you don't live it, don't rap about it, and if you do live it, don't stylize it. This move may, in part, be due to the new distribution norms of the genre. Thanks to the Internet, there's so much rap coming out at one time (in so many places) that it's more difficult than ever to stay on top of the game. It's a huge free-for-all, and blogs and forums adjudicate the status of best MC nearly as much as sales and free downloads do. Perhaps ScHoolboy Q is arguing that it's not flow, but rather *realness* that drives sales.

The popular YG and Sage the Gemini seem to aim for a similar rhythmic aesthetic, yet with a different purpose: to return rap to its party-going mainstream. To some extent, their poetic minimalism could be seen as an attempt to compete for airplay with the incumbent EDM music that currently dominates the college music scene. In sharp contrast to Weezy, Nas, and other technically proficient rappers, YG and Sage the Gemini use predictable rhythms solely geared towards keeping a party moving and rap almost exclusively about party-related topics, not unlike the MCs of "Rapper's Delight," albeit in raunchier fashion. They differ from Q in that their boasts are not about their gangster exploits or hustling capability: rather, they're about their women-wooing skills and partying. It might be said that they believe that what rap needs right now is a reversion to its original (eighties) practice. A$AP Rocky and his crew have similarly shifted towards this trend, and Jay-Z's *Magna Carta . . . Holy Grail* seems to have conformed to this trend in songs like "Tom Ford."

All these rappers capture impetuses and some of the major lyrical approaches to the game, but other schools of thought choose to experiment with the musical context of the poetry instead. Among others, chipmunk soul artist Kanye West, trap-rap artist Danny Brown, The Roots, and jazz-pianist Robert Glasper have sought to renovate the shape of the basic rap sound, with meaningful implications for lyrical style. Kanye's emphasis on the often hyperbolic texture of his beats in his latest two albums, *Yeezus* and *The Life of Pablo*, vastly reduces the importance of traditional rap flow, privileging instead the semantic focus of particular phrases, lines, and couplets. Rapping as we used to know it is replaced by mimetic punch lines, cultural slogans, and memes, such as his feud with Taylor Swift or the "slavery" of commerce. This shift, enabled by Kanye's radically layered and overtly "dramatic" beat productions, supplements the increasing dominance of rap choruses over rap verses.

On the other hand, Danny Brown has appropriated the trap and funk sounds of EDM artists and adapted his rap to their base rhythms and tempos (as has J. I. D.). Often, it means that he has to sacrifice caesuras much more often than is normative. For example, in "Toxic (feat. Danny Brown)" by Childish Gambino, the tempo is faster than usual for a hip hop beat, and the rhythms are driven by a loose snare and 808s. Arguably, his style itself favors caesural elisions (e.g., "Grown Up"), but the musical environment—the trap beat—seems to set this poetic expectation. Here is a couplet from Danny Brown's verse demonstrating this preference:

I'm a pill poppin' ET, Givenchy on a ten-speed
Hot like Britney in '03, ya know me

While some rappers lurch towards faster and faster tempos, other musicians and rappers are interested in softening the rigidity of the musical backdrop. The well-known group, The Roots, is, and has been, particularly successful at this, using live instrumentation to fatten the samples in their performances and albums alike. In doing so, The Roots have stayed close to traditional rap's musical aesthetic, with Black Thought and QuestLove rapping about socially conscious subjects in albums like . . . *And Then You Shoot Your Cousin*.

Another such effort, though less closely tied to hip hop tradition, is Robert Glasper's *Black Radio*, which has rap tracks featuring Lupe Fiasco, Bilal, and Yasiin Bey. With the intention of capturing a black sound, Glasper merges practices of live jazz with traditional rap while simultaneously addressing social consciousness and promoting self-awareness. Yasiin Bey's verse in "Black Radio" is an introduction, without the traditional support of a layered beat, and the result is a substantial difference manifest in phrasal length and pause frequency:

> Radio | sucka' never play me | Triple shade of black that my bleach should never fade me | they say he crazy | New York raised him in the 80s | Kill the Koch administration | Gangster renovation | Born in isolation-ation | I'll communication-ation | Ma Bell fiber optic | Presidential microscopic | Soul sonic remedy | Clinic right in the street | Operating in the dark | Surgery your wounded heart | Come together peel apart | Peel apart come together | Smoking on something good | Praying for something better | From out of better | Never rocking for forever ever | Ever ever ever ever | Forever ever ever ever | It's still a secret even when you tell 'em dumb dummies | Hush money, rent receipt and drug money |They cold gutter, want gun money | The chief rocker, fuel-injected Zulu horse proper, love boogie

As is readily heard, this sound is different than Mos Def's traditional sound, which is conditioned by a looser structure in the musical environment of the verse. Yasiin Bey and the drummer who set the basic rhythms, accompanied by bass riffs; this flips our normal expectations, in which the background beat sets the rhythmic template for the song.

Lupe's verse on "Always Shine" is further varied as it converses with more instruments in a subsequently looser instrumental arrangement. The variations can be sensed in the song, as the background beat is not fixed.[33] As we can see, the limitations of the rhythm become even fewer, and the stress patterns become even more "speech-effusive," incorporating frequent clipped three stress lines as well—

You **ever** see the inner **depths** of a **man's soul?**
Or **nin**ja **turt**les **pour**ing out of **man-holes?**
This is balance
Be**tween** a **com**ic and a **cons**cious, **that's** the **chall**enge
Be**tween** the **solitary** and the **conf**erence that I ex**amines**
That **I imag**ine was a **figu**re
Would **be** the **start** of **world peace** and the **trans**for**mation** of **nig**gas

Q, Kanye, Danny Brown, YG, Sage the Gemini, and Glasper represent the array of contemporary styles in hip hop. And even within stylistically mainstream hip hop there have been some thematic shifts simultaneous with these stylistic shifts: conscious rapping like that of Lupe Fiasco (e.g., *Food & Liquor II*) and Yasiin Bey (Mos Def) (e.g., *Black on Both Sides*) is also done by artists like Ab-Soul (e.g., *Control System*) and Kendrick Lamar (e.g., *Section80, good kid, m.A.A.d city, To Pimp a Butterfly,* and *DAMN.*), whose aims are to preserve and revisit some of the genre's darker thematic traditions. Kendrick's attitudes are captured on his hugely successful album, *good kid, m.A.A.d city.*[34] Kendrick's album revitalizes nineties aesthetics like coming-of-age storytelling, skits, and chorus-less songs. His work on Big Sean's "Control" also renews to traditions of nineties rap—the public boast.[35] But if Kendrick's verse on "Control" weren't enough to catalyze a renewed focus on poetry, Eminem's "Rap God" did the rest. Adapted to a disco-like beat, "Rap God" does *everything* we previously mentioned with the exception of the infusion of jazz background beats, and consciously explores an entirely foreign poetic ambiance.

There is much to be excited about in the new generation of rap music. Following the rap purist path, Brooklyn-raised Joey Bada$$, CJ Fly, and Stro come up alongside tradition-conscious contemporaries like J. Cole, Logic, Tyler the Creator, A$AP, Remy Ma, Jalen Santoy, Chance the Rapper, Cardi B, Isaiah Rashad, Vince Staples, Jay Electronica, Rapsody, Oun-P, Locksmith, King Los, Papoose, Danny Brown, Ab-Soul, Pusha T, Action Bronson, Dyme-a-duzin, Joyner Lucas, and Kaj Kadence. In his BET Backroom freestyle, Stro nails it:

So stop with yo fakin'
Before I have to turn rude boy like a Jamaican
Yes I'm part Jamaican if you're curious
With flows like iPhones, yo it's Siri-ous

So get wit, or get hit, lip split
I'm stacking up my chips, food like the truthful snit[ch]
I'm telling y'all watch out for this young generation
Write mentally, I'm a problem, especially when I start pacing
I keep the game on lock whatever the case is
From A-Z you gotta rate me whatever the Jay is [36]

And rap styling continues to pervade and invade, devolve and evolve. Pop singers like Justin Bieber now sound like desultory, semi-melodic, minimalist emo rappers, and some rappers like Drake and Nicki Minaj have flipped this style of pop lyricism into their own songs. Meanwhile Eminem has upped his own tour de force "Rap God" rapidity by spitting an average of 10.3 syllables per second on Nicki Minaj's "Majesty" (*Queen*, 2018). New flows and rhymes are emerging and being merged in new contexts and configurations, and some of this is genius work.

In *DAMN.*, Kendrick Lamar combines lyric, narrative, and dramatic modes, expressing these through multiple personal, collaborating, and sampled voices as well as clashing beats. The album overlays structures of chiasmus, reverse, and interlace onto that of a traditional song sequence. And Kendrick's techniques are unique. At the close of the album's last song, "DUCKWORTH.," his themes are simultaneously psychological, social, personal, metaphysical. The "chicken incident" line, wherein Kendrick's father and his eventual producer come within a split second of being, respectively, killed and serving life in prison, has only three stresses—open-ended and fragile. Until the last couplet, we hear no medial pauses and no final pauses, so the speaker sounds at once manically possessed and/or divinely controlling. And during this stretch the couplet rhymes themselves rely more on their unvarying / **x x** rhythm than on their crackling sound echoes. Finally, the single double-duty *life* rhymes hard twice, on *die* and *gunfight*. Boom:

You take two strangers and put 'em in random predicaments
Give 'em a soul so they can make their own choices and live with it
Twenty years later, them same strangers, you make 'em meet again
Inside recording studios where they reapin' their benefits
Then you start remindin' them about that chicken incident
Whoever thought the greatest rapper would be from coincidence?
Because if Anthony killed Ducky, Top Dawg could be servin' life
While I grew up without a father and die in a gunfight

Appendix 1
Flow Variants

The following chart shows some of our data. When we scanned and coded rap lines for our original database, we recorded all varieties of pause as well as all syllables coded with respect to their stress, rhyme, and position relative to the beats. Here we consolidate the coding strings to include only the prominent medial and final pauses and the more prominent syllables, those which are stressed, rhyming, or on the beat. In the language of our coding, we extracted elements C, D, B, R, $, E, and F from all of the lines. Take, for example, the second line from Lil' Kim's diss track "Black Friday,"

Fedex beef || straight to your door

—transcribed in our database as BURCBUU$RE but here consolidated as 'BRCB$RE'

We then grouped all lines with identical prominence patterns. In the process, we discovered some interesting features in the clustered stresses in the dips, some of which are correlated to variation in line length. The Lil' Kim line above is thus stored as:

Type 'BRCBR$RE', 8

While the letter string delineates prosodic prominences, the numeral 8 refers to the line's actual syllable count. Both C and D and E and F, which mark respectively the presence or absence of medial and final pauses, are included in the letter string, whereas Lil' Kim's single unstressed, unbeated, and unrhyming syllable is included in the 8 tally.

Figure 16 shows the average length of the ten most common types of lines, when types are defined by strong-syllablic events. The longest average line type is $BBDB$BE, which has twenty-two syllables. Logically, the gen-

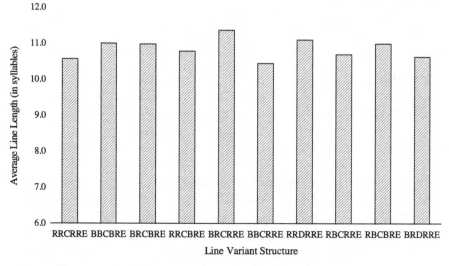

Fig. 16. The ten most common variants (in rank order reading from left to right, including all line types) and their average line length.

eral correlation here (and throughout) between stress density and line length would be expected according to the norms of English eurythmy. Most of these lines have medial caesuras as well as pauses at the end of the line, and many have additional pauses between beats 1 and 2.

Though the line types we've captured take a lower resolution snapshot of rhyme/stress combinations, we found that as early as 1984 there were at least 131 verse line types in existence; by 2011, there were more than 600. The shortest verse lines have have as few as five syllables (e.g., Biggie's "Notorious Thugs"). While lines lengthened more generally, certain years show inflection points in line length trends. Prior to Rakim and 1986, line lengths increase slowly and line lengths vary less often—ten syllable verse lines are ubiquitous during this period. Post 1987, the verses line approach twelve syllables on average, and meanwhile the spread between the minimum length and maximum length in the period could be as high within the same song.

Chorus lines also became longer and more varied, particularly after 1995. Post 1995 lines show considerably more variation (generally six to ten syllables versus six to seven) than do those in the early rap chorus lines of the 1980s, culminating today in, for example, Drake's long chorus lines in mixtapes like *Views*.

Appendix 2

Variants by the Years

We can take a closer look at the constituents represented by the average and most common lines. In their aggregate, the rap lines in our database fall under a normal bell curve. However, this aggregation is not particularly informative except in the abstract, as rap styling tends to move in relationship to previous styles. In order to learn more about what rhythmic styling dominated musico-poetic paradigms, we segmented our database's lines into historical year groupings often referred to by rap academicians.

The figures that follow show the percentage of lines (y-axis) of a given length of the line (x-axis) in the relevant year-groupings.

Figure 17 shows that the nine to twelve syllable line was the predominant rap line of the 1979–1982 bunch (e.g., The Sugarhill Gang, Melle Mel.) The range here was twelve syllables, but that variation was hardly a stylistic feature, for the outliers account for less than half a percent in this sample. Conversely, a high percentage of lines fall within a narrow range.

Figure 18 covers the period from 1983 to 1986 (e.g., Kurtis Blow, Cold Crush Brothers).

We've grouped this set separately to look at the time during which rap seemed ready to die for want of innovation, and in many ways the rap line reflected this sense of stickiness to the norm. 1983–1986 saw a higher relative frequency of eight- and thirteen-syllable lines, but a lower relative frequency of ultra-short line. This proclivity reflects a retrenchment in conservative style. The range of line length is the same, but the maximum length is shorter, and the outliers are fewer (note: lines below do not exclude lines with nonsyllabic events).

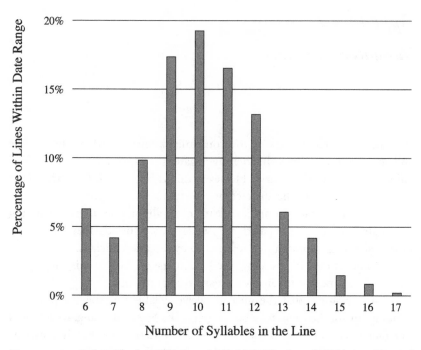

Fig. 17. 1979–1982 (e.g. The Sugarhill Gang, Melle Mel). Number of syllables per line, and percentages of each, during this period.

1987–2000 (e.g., Rakim, Nas)

This large grouping is often touted as the "Golden Age of Rap," and indeed Figure 19 shows significant change from the previous grouping. There's an interesting downward pressure on the relative frequency of the standard line; for example, the number of ten-syllable lines fell from nearly 20 percent to about 12.5 percent and this is reflected in a widening bell curve. Additionally, we see the maximum length rise, accompanied by an expansion in the range (now fifteen). Although this graph seems slightly skewed to the left, that may be accounted for by the musical preference for shorter lines by rappers and is reflected in the average line length being higher than the median line length. So, we see that the majority of lines will tend towards the shorter end—but they're going up in length: they're now between ten to fourteen syllables.

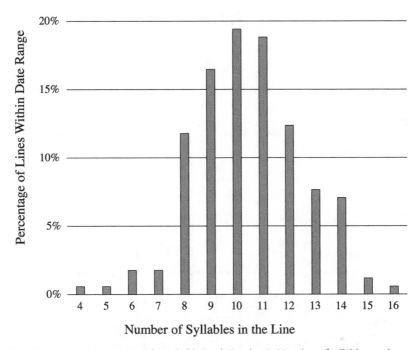

Fig. 18. 1983–1986 (e.g. Kurtis Blow, Cold Crush Brothers). Number of syllables per line, and percentage of each, during this period.

2001–2014

We seem to be in the middle of a paradigm shift in this line-length snapshot. Interestingly, there is some downward pressure in the center of the bell curve, which could mean that we will see more lines falling in the extremes of line length, and by contrast, fewer in the ordinary/standard line. One musical factor to be cognizant of when viewing this snapshot is that the tempo of songs, i.e., the musical template is beginning to become faster— some rappers even rap at 150 bpm, and that may require shorter lines to balance longer ones.

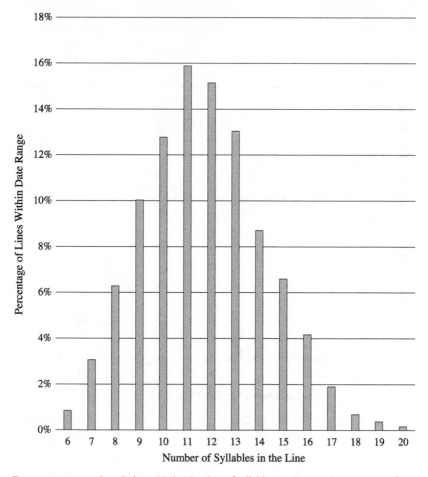

Fig. 19. 1987–2000 (e.g. Rakim, Nas). Number of syllables per line, and percentage of each, during this period.

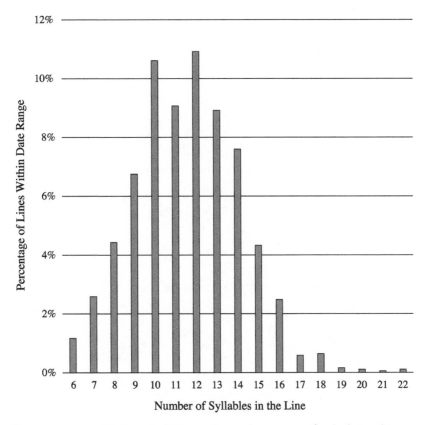

Fig. 20. 2001–2014. Number of syllables per line, and percentage of each, during this period.

Root Terminology for Rap Poetics

Poetry = language set into rhythmic lines: the ABC song, "Amazing Grace," Homer's epics, Nyabinghi rasta chanting, any sonnet, any limerick, Hamlet's soliloquy, a poem by Emily Dickinson, W. B. Yeats or Langston Hughes, any rap verse, any rap chorus, The Notorious B. I. G.'s "Juicy."

Poetics = the study of what poetry is and does, in particular, how poetry works: not so much what it means as how it feels, the structures and dynamics of its sounds and rhythms, their norms and rules, and creative licenses.

Oral poetry = all poetry primarily meant to be heard, not read on the page. This includes all early epics, like Homer or *Beowulf*; songs, even "literary" verse like that in Chaucer's *Canterbury Tales*, which the author originally recited; or like that in Shakespeare's plays, which were originally guarded from publication and meant to be acted only; and it includes all rap—whether originally written down and memorized, read in the studio, or freestyled.

Oral formulaic poetry = oral poetry composed on the spot by often illiterate professional bards. The craft, typically passed down through rigorous apprenticeship, requires not just the memorization of stories and standard narrative sequences, but the ability to master innumerable linguistic formulas so that phrases will always fit into metrical patterns. In Homer, for example, whenever anyone speaks to anyone else, the formula is TON [or TAYN]-da-MAY-bet-ta-PAY-ta ("To him [or her] then spoke . . ."), and if the speaker is Athena the formula is thay-A-glau-CO-pis-a-THAY-ney ("the goddess, gray-eyed Athena"). It's a lovely line, but Athena is also always gray-eyed so that she'll fit into the rhythm of dactylic hexameter. Due to global cultural hegemony and the spread of literacy and digital technology, oral formulaic poetry is pretty much a lost art, most recently practiced by Serbo-Croatian, West African, and Kyrgyz bards, but proficient rap freestylers may justly claim a place in this venerable tradition.

Chant = line-by-line poetry, also known as *stichic* poetry (from Greek "row, line"). Chant is one of humanity's two main verse modes, with performance styles ranging from declamatory to tonal. Each line follows the same meter but may have varied phrasal rhythms, and the poetry can continue on with no rules for closure. Chant may be performed a cappella (Torah chanting), or with a harmonic drone (Vedic chant), or may be accompanied by percussive instruments like drums or strummed harps (Homer's epics, West African griot chants). In the case of rap verses, the background beat is both percussive and harmonic.

Song = stanza-by-stanza, or *strophic*, poetry. This is the other main verse mode, with a melodic performance style backed by instruments such as a lyre, flute, or oud. Here the individual lines may vary in meter but are grouped into formal stanzas, each requiring closure. Examples include Sappho's poetry, carols, hymns, ballads, sonnets, and rap choruses.

Rapping = a style of chanted poetry assimilating features of oratory, preaching, variety show MCing, jive radio DJing, and African and Caribbean chant traditions. Rapping is emphatically rhythmical and loud enough to grab your attention—as in the talking blues by Woody Guthrie or Bob Dylan, The Last Poets, Gil Scott-Heron, Lightnin' Rod, and all the hip hop MCs from "Rapper's Delight" to the present.

Rap = hip hop rapping, that is, rapping to a sampled beat; by extension, the musical genre featuring this kind of rapping. Performance styles may vary from declamatory shouting to a smooth flow, including some semi-melodic pitch variation, but all rap verses conform to the same four-beat meter.

DJ = creator/composer of rap beats, mixer of samples, maker of loops, gradually with the advent of digital sampling displaced by or evolved into the producer.

MC = the hip hop poet.

Sampling = the appropriation of part of one sound recording for use in another; by extension, the creation of an entirely new musical composition out of such parts—a musical collage. Rap sampling draws from a wide variety of sources, often manipulating and blending them so as to produce subtle or blatant tonal clashes. For example, one might juxtapose a melodic snippet from a popular theme song, like that in the

Bugs Bunny cartoons, with drum beats from a James Brown song, and then add a bass line from yet another source. Allowing such samples to contextualize each other, the DJ or producer in effect claims originality and creative ownership, and for that reason sampling is *not* regarded as plagiarism in the rap community. On the contrary, sampling is a precondition for originality—the bricks in the architecture of any effective beat. As an instrumentalist's notes are to a classical musician, so sampled recordings are to a hip hop DJ.

Beat (1) = a song track composed of mixed, sampled sounds, 99.99 percent in 4/4 time. The collage of samples is emphatically percussive and looped so as to provide a four-beat metrical scaffold for the rapper's stressed syllables and rhymes, with a tempo and a textured tonality suitable for the song's themes and the rapper's particular flow.

Beat (2) = an *ictus* beat: any single strong pulse within the composition, on or near which the rapper articulates a stressed, metrical syllable or else, for variation, a pause.

Beat (3) = the single beat considered as a durational (e.g., "quarter-note") unit, hence a measure of tempo, typically registered in beats per minute (bpm).

Beat (4) = the position of any single beat within the bar: beat 1, beat 2, beat 3, beat 4—alternatively, *downbeat, weak beat, on-beat, upbeat.*

Bar = a musical measure in any time signature; in rap, a measure of 4/4 time, and by extension, the line of rap poetry laid over it.

Line = the basic incremental unit of rhythm and sense in poetry. Musical in origin and in essence, the line is what distinguishes all poetry formally from prose or normal speech. In rap, the line and its meter are directly governed by the 4/4 bar.

Meter = an underlying template or basic rhythmic structure constraining the behavior of poetic lines. Meter in poetry is analogous to time in music, and rap meter follows the hip hop beat: just as each bar has four pulses arranged in paired on-beat/off-beat units, each normative metrical line has four stress prominences and a phrasal division into half-line units.

Rhythm = any discernible temporal or spatial pattern, such as the repetitive rhythm(s) of surf or the fractal rhythms of a fern or a coastline. In language, there are the rhythms of successive syllables, the rhythms of and within words and phrases and sentences, and the rhythm of a speech or a conversation. In poetic language, there are metrical and non-metrical rhythms; the rhythms of stressed versus unstressed syllables, rhymes, half lines, lines, and couplets; and larger forms, like choruses and verses and songs. When poetic language is subject to a meter that imposes a common regularity on each line, as in rap, the rhythm of a line—as distinct from its meter—is its actual linguistic behavior, its actual sequence of particular sounds, syllables, stresses, and pauses.

Flow = rap rhythm, how any MC spits syllables in the here and now; also the generalized quality of a particular rapper's rhythm, or the generalized rhythmic quality of a song or a verse; how he or she varies, mixes, spaces, bends, and syncopates vocal sounds over this or that beat. Even more generally, flow may be identified with groups (Bone Thugs-N-Harmony) or genres (battling, buddah), locales and regions (Compton, Cali, Dirty South) or periods (Old School).

Syllable = the basic rhythmic unit of speech. Words can have one (*speech*), two (*rhyth-mic*), three (*syl-la-ble*), or more syllables. In English, syllables can be stressed or unstressed and may also be pronounced with pitch accents.

Stress = an emphatic marker of content words like ***rapper*** or ***syllable*** or *notorious*. In English speech, stresses tend to occur at regular intervals, so ours is categorized as a stress-timed language. Although they are fixed features of word pronunciation, in ongoing speech they may in effect migrate or disappear. There are stresses in *Michigan* and in *University*, but one of these stresses may disappear in the longer noun phrase *University of **Michigan***.

Eurythmy = "pleasant rhythm." To satisfy the rhythmic expectations of English, stresses may change positions so that they won't occur too close together. Thus, we have *California* and ***dreaming***, but we also have the song phrase *California **Dreaming***. In a sense, meter imposes eurythmy on poetic language. The hip hop beat gets us up dancing or bobbing our heads, and the MC's flow, which includes metrical stresses "rapped to the beat," makes it all sound good. That obviously doesn't mean that rap always sounds pleasant; it can also—and at the same time—sound nasty, harsh, tough, or hostile, and one of the best methods for making rap sound not so pleasant is to violate eurythmy by clustering stresses together. The general tendency in all oral traditions (ballads, nursery rhymes, blues, pop songs), however, is to build eurythmy into its poetics. A traditional practice enabling this is to assign eurhythmic stress to normally unstressed syllables or "little words." Thus, we would ordinarily speak of an ***English**man*, but: "**Fee! Fie! Foe! Fum!** / **I** smell the **blood** of an **Eng**lish**man**." This practice is relatively common in early rap, as in Wonder Mike's "I'm **rap**ping **to** the **beat**."

Rest = a measured musical interruption in the flow of notes or percussive sounds.

Pause = a linguistic interruption of the flow of syllables, often a "natural" break between phrases or longer units of speech. In rap, some such pauses may be metrically motivated and therefore normative, like those at the line's midpoint and end. Other pauses, relatively brief or relatively long, may occur optionally at other places in the line.

Caesura = medial pause: the expected vocal pause in the middle of the poetic line, a metrical feature of four-beat verse and of verse in many other systems. For example, "I smoke on the mic ‖ like smokin' Joe Frazier." Although most rap lines contain a caesural pause, this is an expectation, not a requirement. Rappers often vary their flow by avoiding caesura in particular lines. But why does this pause even exist as a metrical expectation? Why does it occur in other four-beat meters and in world poetry generally? Why we want to hear lines divided into two parts? Like most traditional poetic features, it seems to correspond with our basic physiological rhythms, such as breathing and walking. And it helps enable poetry to satisfy the human sense of beat, repeated as twin on-beat/off-beat sequences.

End stop = the expected vocal pause at the end of the line. As with caesura, it's an expectation, not a requirement. Here too, rappers may vary their flow by avoiding the end stop, allowing one line to flow right into the next. As a normative feature, the end stop reinforces a line's formal unity and integrity, may lend extra weight to a final prominence like a rhyme, and confers on the line a sense of resolution corresponding to that at the end of a musical bar.

Virtual beat = a beat that is not realized in any stress prominence; rather, it is felt during a pause in the poetic line. In Wonder Mike's ballad quatrains in "Rapper's Delight," the even lines have three beated stresses followed by a virtual beat: "I'm **rap**ping **to** the **beat** [B] // . . . Are gonna **try** to **move** your **feet** [B]." Rakim inserts a beated pause on beat 2: "I es**cape** [B] ‖ when I **fin**ish the **rhyme**."

Rhyme (1) = a sound echo typically linking two stressed syllables or longer chains of syllable starting with stresses: *rhyme* and *time*, *rhythm* and *flip 'em*, *cable crew* and *pay-for-view*. Normally, rhyme links stressed syllables by repeating their *nucleus* (internal vowel) and *coda* (terminal consonant or consonant cluster), plus any additional unstressed syllables in the rhyming word or phrase. Although most rhymes do involve natural stresses in content words, serving both as musical chimes and thematic

links, many rappers manipulate their flow by "demoting" normally
stressed syllables and "promoting" normally unstressed syllables—a
license which may also expand the number of potential rhyme words.

Rhyme (2) = a rap verse, a rap song, or the act of rapping itself.

End rhyme = a rhyme giving extra prominence to the end of the poetic
line, coinciding with beat 4. End rhyme is abundant in rap not only
because it accentuates the upbeat and gives closure to the line, but
because it serves as the primary means of formalizing couplets.

Internal rhyme = loosely speaking, any rhyme positioned otherwise than
an end rhyme. Rhymes between syllables on beats 2 and 4 are especially
common, but internal rhymes less commonly mark beats 1 and 3, and
they may often connect with rhymes in previous or successive lines.

Multi = a polysyllabic rhyme composed of syllables from more than one
word. Such rhymes are sometimes called *mosaic rhymes* where they
occur in literary poetry. Traditionally, they have been used mostly for
comic effect, as in the work of Chaucer, Marlowe, Byron, Ogden Nash,
and others, but rap MCs deploy them for that and many other effects,
meanwhile demonstrating mastery of the craft through original rhyming.

Rhyme chain = any rhyme sequence that involves three or more rhymes.
Such sequences often extend through multiple lines and, in doing so,
may be useful in mitigating the potential monotony of discreet, successful couplet rhymes. At the extreme, rhyme chains may continue
through and entire verse, as witnessed in Senim Silla's usage in "Reality Check." And even beyond this, Lauryn Hill's "Doo Wop (That
Thing)" rhymes almost entirely on the syllable–*en* (rhyming *men* and
women), and KRS-One's "Hold" throughout rhymes homophonically
on its title.

Assonance = echo of prominent vowels; a variety of rhyme. In songs (but
not hymns) and in many other oral poetic traditions including rap,
assonance alone suffices to constitute a rhyme. This makes sonic sense
because the vowel is indeed the necessary nucleus and most dominant
sound in any syllable. Lil Wayne, for example, rhymes *vowels* not just
with *bowels* but with *hours*, and rhymes *sidekick* with *sly bitch*.

Consonance = echo of consonant sounds—a relatively minor, ornamental
sound device.

Alliteration = echo of initial consonant sounds. This too is an ornamental
figure, but due to the frequency of front-stressed words in English it is
far more prominent than mere consonance. In earlier centuries, before

the use of rhyme in English verse, alliteration was a structural requirement in the poetic line, marking most of the stressed syllables in four-beat verse: from the pre-Conquest *Beowulf*, "**G**rendel **g**ongan || **G**odes yrre bær"; from the fourteenth-century *Piers Plowman*, "In a **s**omer **s**eason, whan **s**ofte was the **s**onne."

Pararhyme = echo of framed consonant sounds, the syllable *onset* and *coda*, as in **hip hop**. Notwithstanding the name of our genre, pararhyme is a very rare figure of sound in rap.

Scansion = marking out the rhythmic patterns of poetry, translating its temporal flow into a spatial representation. As poetics is to poetry, scansion is to meter. *Poetry is never meant to be scanned*, so the only reason to scan lines is utilitarian: to be able to contemplate or communicate what is going on with the rhythm. Conventional scansion marks are:

/ = stressed syllable	x = unstressed syllable	\ = secondary stress
|| = caesural pause		= end-line pause or other pause	B = beat

For example:

```
x  /   x   xx    /   ||x x    /    x  \   / |
I got so many rhymes I don't think I'm too sane (Nas)
   B         B           B          B
```

```
 /    \    /  ||x  /  x   x ||  \ x x    x / xx |
Straight up weed, no angel dust, label us Notorious (The Notorious B. I. G.)
 B         B            B             B
```

```
 / x  x   x   /   \  ||  x  x  x    / x    /   \  |
Cristal by the case men, still in they mother's basement (Lauryn Hill)
 B         B      B              B
```

Couplet = a two-line formal unit bonded by end-rhyme, the expected and dominant rhyme pattern in rap verses.

Quatrain = a four-line unit, also shaped by rhyme: the most common song stanza and a frequent in rap choruses but rare in rap verses. When the first hip hop records were being produced, some MCs like Wonder Mike and Grandmaster Caz used quatrains in some of their verses, but this practice soon faded out, yielding almost completely to couplets. Still, some MCs, such as André 3000, deploy quatrains in their verses for special effect and to bundle expansive associations. Black Thought's ten-minute Hot 97 freestyle consists mostly of *aaaa*-rhyming quatrains.

Rap verse = one continuous stichic rap characterized by continuous ongoing variation of theme and rhythm; often shaped musically into sixteen bars but in theory and in practice also able to be stretched out as long as the MC wants.

Rap chorus = a strophic, song-like form characterized stylistically by verbal, thematic, and rhythmic repetition; occasionally rapped by the MC but more frequently performed by another artist or artists.

Rap song = a collaborative DJ-and-MC performance, a musical and poetic composition merging rap with the hip hop beat, optionally also including choruses which serve as musical interludes between the rap verses and which headline the song's common theme.

Mixtape = generally, a free compilation of rap songs. Whether distributed on cassette tapes or digitally, these often display samples much more recent than those found in albums. Because they are not for sale, mixtapes thus more readily evade copyright issues. Ephemeral by design, they also tend to be less formally constrained than albums which, in contrast, are marketed for success and longevity.

Album = a compilation of songs marketed in a medium suitable for an extensive playlist—vinyl LP, cassette tape, CD, or digital download. Albums are typically organized by one or several principles, such as a thematic focus or trajectory, a musical idea, or a particular generic range.

Notes

1. The art of flipping is basic to hip hop poetics. Semantically and culturally, rap flips negatives into positives: *bad* means strong, *shit* means good stuff, and *ill* means incredibly talented or full of mojo. The rap beat itself is constructed by flipping separate sounds from other sources—sampling—and when MCs rap they continuously flip words from remote cultural contexts and memory nodes into their verses which, in turn, flip rhymes onto stress contours.

2. See verse 3 of "What They Gonna Do," featuring Sean Paul (*The Blueprint 2: The Gift & the Curse*, 2002). All of its lines, with possible exception (according to Genius) of the "Rilke" line, rhyme by repeating "flow" at the end of a phrasal multi: e.g., "God with the flow . . . involved with the flow . . . y'all with the flow . . . Mar with the flow . . . evolve with the flow . . . Rucker Park with the flow." (Jay-Z evokes Rembrandt along with Rilke, but readers of literary poetry won't miss his channeling of Walt Whitman in this verse.)

3. We treat "Rapper's Delight" extensively in the chapter on Hot Vinyl. Here it should be noted that both of our initial examples of rap poetry differ from the normative couplet form. Wonder Mike's ballad stanza, rhyming *abcb*, with alternating four- and three-stress lines, appears only rarely in early rap verses even though it will become a standard form in choruses later on. Couplets always link two successive lines with rhyming end-words, and this couplet rhyme typically achieves its integrity by contrasting with adjacent rhyme sounds. Jay-Z's rhymes in verse 3 of "What They Gonna Do" are multis (or polysyllabic sequences), which are normal in hip hop after 1990, but Jay-Z deploys these multis to enhance end-word repetition of "flow," denying the couplet form its integrity. These redundant rhymes extend a practice initiated by Lauryn Hill in "Doo Wop (That Thing)," where rhymes on and between "men" and "women" dominate the thematics (cf. Senim Silla's verse in Binary Star's "Reality Check"). Such

222 · Notes to Page 3

departures from the norm are considered in the chapter on Rhyme. Although the couplet is unquestionably rap's primary, quintessential form, it is also true that during the past two decades a number of MCs have deployed extended rhyme chains as well as rhythmic modifications to loosen up the couplet's predictable sequencing.

4. The mythic Homer is always blind, which means, if nothing else, that he couldn't read or write. He was an illiterate poet able, after a long apprenticeship, to freestyle his way through an epic thousands of lines long. Until about 2,700 years ago, all poetry everywhere was composed during performance, by ear and by memory. Until very recently, even literary poetry was written to be performed, as well as to be studied by silent readers. Even today, most literary poets think of their poems as having voices, meant to be heard. In other words, poetry is normatively an oral art. We reject the viewpoint among some rap scholars (cf. Paul Edwards, *How to Rap 2*, pp. 191–94) that rap is music, not poetry. We would urge instead that rap, while indeed unique in being tightly constrained by a musical beat, behaves in many ways like traditional world poetry, chanted by oral poets like Homer, the West African griots, and countless others.

5. Thousands of lines of Old English verse were preserved in writing by monks before the Norman Conquest of 1066. Although they exhibit some bookish features, the poems (heroic narratives like *Beowulf*, histories, saint's lives, riddles, charms, even a couple of love poems) all are set in a four-beat meter following strict rules of alliterative structure. They display the normal earmarks of oral-formulaic composition, such as repetition and stylized diction. In Homer, the dawn is always rosy-fingered, Athena is grey-eyed, women are neat-ankled, and blood is black—so that the formulaic noun-adjective combinations will fit rhythmically into the line, and the poet doesn't have to think about such details as he improvises. In Old English verse, for similar reasons, kings are ring-givers, the sea is the whale-road, and poets unlock their word-hoards.

6. Cheryl L. Keyes, in *Rap Music and Street Consciousness* (2002, pp. 17–38), offers an excellent overview of the stylistic roots of rap music as transmitted from West African oral poetry through slave culture in the United States, the emergence of jive talk in jazz and in radio DJ jingles, and Black Arts Movement (BAM) poetry. Keyes also documents the importance of Alex Haley's *Roots: The Saga of an American Family* (1976) in popularizing our appreciation of cultural indebtedness to West Africa. The prevalence in rap of toasting, indirection (signifying), word play, rhyme, the couplet form itself, call and response, and effusive performance styles integrated with dancing and musical accompaniment all find analogues in West African poetry performances. See Isidore Okpewho, *The Epic in Africa: Toward a Poetics of the Oral Performance* (1975) and *African Oral Literature: Backgrounds, Character, and Continuity* (1992).

7. We discuss the Jamaican influence and that of The Last Poets and Gil Scott-Heron in the chapter on Hot Vinyl. The four-beat meter of rap, as indicated below,

is essentially the same as that in blues stanzas and in the non-literary traditions of older English verse generally. The Harlem Renaissance poet Langston Hughes, among others, explicitly incorporated blues rhythms and themes into his literary poetry, and later Black Arts Movement poets like Amiri Baraka (previously LeRoi Jones), Nikki Giovanni, and Sonia Sanchez, allied with the Black Power Movement, developed new rhythmic models for African American literature—including the inclusion of collo-quial speech.

Although often unacknowledged, the influence of the dozens, a persistent African American tradition of collaborative insult, has figured importantly in the formation of rap MC personas and especially in the subgenre of battle rapping. See Elijah Wald, *Talking 'Bout Your Mama: The Dozens, Snaps, and the Deep Roots of Rap* (Oxford UP, 2014), a thorough and appreciative history of collaborative insult games in America, touching on their African Roots and their broad influence on African American cul-ture dating from the nineteenth century. Wald's final chapter (pp. 183–200) details the impact on hip hop battling, noting as well that while the dozens may no longer be heard on street corners, bars, or in schoolyards, it currently is manifest in a "flood of commercial and electronic dozens spin-offs" (192), including MTV's *Yo Mamma* and innumerable YouTube amateur performances.

8. In hip hop culture, hustling is often touted as the main—or only—path to success, given the systemic poverty of ghetto existence, with gun violence seen both as an adjunct to hustling and as a necessary defense against police oppression. The pimp in his Cadillac is given due respect. Jay-Z, The Notorious B. I. G., and many others rap boastfully, sometimes with a measure of remorse, about selling crack cocaine back in the day. Jay-Z in *Decoded* details the continuity of talent between hustling and rhyming as his primary story, and the ethos in Biggie's classic "Ten Crack Command-ments," with its strictures against snitching and its commonsense practical wisdom ("Don't get high on your own supply") carries far beyond drug-dealing. Cash money, it goes without saying, is a good thing, fetishized in G's and Benjamins and reified in Lil Wayne's record label, and Jay-Z caps this trend when he boasts of his spectacular success as a capitalist entrepreneur. But see also the anti-hustling countercurrent in the proto-rap album *Hustler's Convention*, in Melle Mel's "The Message," and in a great deal of "conscious rap" from the 1990s to the present day. Given the grave, systemic income inequality in America today, the very notion of the self-made man may strike some as a fantasy, similar to the fantasy of making it as a professional football or bas-ketball player. Still, the phenomenal economic success of the very best rappers—and of producers like Dr. Dre and Sean Combs—is undeniable and, for some, inspiring.

The American myth of the self-made man dates at least as far back as Benjamin Franklin's *Autobiography*, which traces his rise from poverty, extolling the virtues of frugality, temperance, and persistence—as well as the public display of industriousness. When Franklin needed to buy more paper for his fledgling printing business, he made of a show of transporting it himself by wheelbarrow: "Thus being esteem'd an industrious thriving young man, the Merchants who imported Stationery solicited my Custom, others propos'd supplying me with Books, and I went on swimmingly." Henry Clay is said to have coined the term while arguing in the Senate for a tariff which would benefit "enterprising self-made men, who have whatever wealth they possess by patient and diligent labor." Important source texts for the bootstrap myth include William M. Thayer's *Poor Boy and Merchant Prince, Or Elements of Success Drawn from the Life and Character of the Late Amos Lawrence* (1857), Charles C. B. Seymour's *Self-Made Men* (1858), and Horatio Alger's young adult fictions, including *Ragged Dick* (1868). Today, despite increasing income inequality and social stratification, the myth of the self-made man continues to appeal to many Americans, inspired by Ayn Rand and others, and is actively pushed by libertarians and by the Republican Party establishment. Historically allied with religious moral instruction and then with social Darwinism, the myth of the self-made man has functioned both to inspire hope among the socially disadvantaged and to serve as justification for class divisions: those who don't "make it" lack moral fiber or haven't tried hard enough. Most recently, the construction of Donald Trump's political brand relied crucially on his fake (and ghostwritten) self-made-man autobiography, *The Art of the Deal*, as well as on incessant self-promotion, culminating in his crusade advancing the racist, anti-Obama, "Birther" conspiracy.

Persistent racism in policing, criminal sentencing, educational opportunity, employment, and housing makes the ideal of the self-made man (or woman) less credible for African Americans than for other predominantly working-class groups. For an excellent history of the constraints on black freedom after the Civil War, see Elizabeth Anderson, "The Quest for Free Labor: Pragmatism and Experiments in Emancipation," *The Amherst Lecture in Philosophy* 9 (2014): 1–44. Anderson writes: "To the freed people in all post-emancipation regimes, freedom entailed not being under the subjection of a boss. For the vast majority, this required a realistic prospect of landownership, so that, with a few years of labor at good wages, any black family would be able to save enough to purchase a plot and become a yeoman farmer, or at least a peasant proprietor. For the planters and most government policymakers, freedom meant minimal abolition. They hoped that the plantation system would survive intact, with gangs of workers driven to grueling, relentless labor under the discipline of an overseer" (p. 21). In the United States, the eventual compromise precluded widespread independent land ownership by "yeoman farmers," resulting instead in sharecropping. Meanwhile, white settlers in the West were granted free homesteads. And the rest is history—as expressed in divergent employment opportunities, school segregation, and red-lining (all of which continue de facto today), resulting in the formation and preservation of the urban ghetto itself.

9. It is axiomatic that metrical verse in any language will deploy that language's salient vocal prominences, regularizing them artfully. Since English is a stress-timed language, English meters have always been grounded in regular stress patterns. Before the Norman Conquest, English stresses typically fell on the first syllables of words, so Old English meter was both four-stressed and alliterative. After the Conquest, the influx of French words into English resulted in less predictable stress positioning, so alliteration became less viable and was eventually replaced by rhyme. In French, by contrast, there are no stresses; instead, French vocal prominences involve pitch intonations—in particular, pitch lifts prior to pauses. French meters rely on syllable-timing rather than stress-timing structures, and they mark regular mid-line and end-line junctures by pitch lifts.

So what happens when French MCs, influenced by American or British MCs, rap in French? The results can vary, and some of the variation is naturally due to individual flow. If we consider the contrast in articulation between the bap-bap stresses of, say, Ice Cube and the smooth, almost level stresses of Guru, the self-proclaimed "king of monotone," we won't be surprised to detect similar stylistic ranges in non-English rap. Nevertheless, every language will impose its own limits on a rapper's flow. Simply put, stress is alien to French speech, and pitch lifts don't occur often enough in French to work as replacements for stresses in a four-beat rap line. In French rap, off-beat pitch lifts can work perfectly well to mark the mid-line pause and the end-line pause, much as these junctures are marked by stress and rhyme in English rap. Beyond this, French rappers don't sound much like they are rapping in French, and some French rappers even avoid using pitch lifts before the expected half-line pauses. In Explicit Samouri's "Le Roseau" (2005), for example, Leeroy spits syllables with neither stresses nor pitch lifts nor expected pauses, whereas Specta shapes phrasal units in his lines by means of stresses and pauses.

Not surprisingly, the bilingual Haitian MC Izolan deploys a credibly contemporary New York flow when he raps in English, but when he raps in (French) Creole—the national language of Haiti—his rap phrasing never compromises Creole intonations. These differences are evident on *Femen Bouch Nou* (2011) and *K-TAFAL* (2013).

To our English ears, all Japanese rappers may sound as though they stress syllables on the beat and work in rather effusive post-1990 American flow styles. But Japanese rap is of course informed by the salient features of the language, to include the absence of stress per se and the differentiation of syllables into "short" (one mora) and "long" (two morae) types. Per several informants (especially MC M. T. Z.), we understand that Japanese rappers often import English-like stresses accents while varying considerably in their readiness to alter standard Japanese pitches, intonations, and even grammatically functional syllables. Of the two MCs in Rappagariya, Q sticks relatively closely to standard Japanese intonations although he paces himself in a unique way, but Yamada Man shifts accents frequently (Rappagariya, "Do the Gariya Thing," 2000; https://www.youtube.com/watch?v=AHXFiFGZ4dg). Somewhat more radically, Hunger, the solo MC of the group Gagle, is happy to rearrange accents, intonations, and normative pacing in order to achieve his flow ("Rap Wonder DX," 2004; https://www.youtube.com/watch?v=qM-CbIo8h38). Utamaru and Mummy-D, the MCs of the widely acclaimed group Rhymester, each commonly alter not just accents but even word pronunciations. In the following lines (Rhymester, ft. F. O. H., "Uwasa no shinsō," *The Truth behind the Rumor*, 2001, 1:17; https://www.youtube.com/watch?v=Gi3cShjXQJE), the two syllables in brackets are dropped by Mummy-D:

/ xx / x x \ x / / xxx /
shittaka butta busu to kasudomo ga
x / x xx / x x   / x x / x
[a]rigata*garu* misu*ta* [a]bu*sutorakuto*

("Mr. Abstract, whom only ugly women and trashy folks who pretend to know stuff appreciate") In this couplet, we hear a catchy interweaving of assonantal rhyming on **o-u, a-o**, and **a**, contrasting with clear multi rhymes ("Lor**d have mercy/damashi**a; **wa kami ni natta/wa shitabi ni natta**") in the couplets surrounding it. The dropped syllables tighten Mummy-D's flow, maximizing the impact of his sonic mosaic.

Based on these examples, it seems that the requisites of rhyming and the prosodic demands of four-beat meter are chief motivators of linguistic adaptations in non-English rap.

10. This occurs often in battle rapping, where the standard sixteen- or thirty-two-bar verse structure is disregarded. See, for example, Lil' Kim's "Black Friday" (2011).

11. Some examples of contemporary griot performance:

https://www.youtube.com/watch?v=zQMFN-whbEU
https://www.youtube.com/watch?v=QdrPmZwsXiM
https://www.youtube.com/watch?v=u6MY3v-WA94
https://www.youtube.com/watch?v=hxezzVNbQFI
https://www.youtube.com/watch?v=ISg3MTog9MA
https://www.youtube.com/watch?v=LC71Ne5MwB0

12. For early colonial recognition of these traditions, see Richard Ligon, *A True and Exact History of the Island of Barbados* (1657), and Robert Renny, *An history of Jamaica* (1807). More recent examinations include: Orlando Patterson, *Sociology of Slavery* (1969); D. A. Bisnauth, *History of Religions in the Caribbean* (1970); Ivy

Baxter, *The Arts of an Island* (1970); Joyce Lalor, *Traditional Songs of the Caribbean* (1979); Wendell Logan and Marjorie Whylie, *Some Aspects of Religious Cult Music in Jamaica* (1982); Daryl Cumber Dance, *Folklore from Contemporary Jamaicans* (1985); Richard Rath, "African Music in Seventeenth-Century Jamaica: Cultural Transit and Transmission," in *The William and Mary Quarterly* 50 (1993): 700–726; Olive Lewin, *Rock It Come Over* (2000); Edward Seaga, *Folk Music of Jamaica* (2000); and Malena Kuss, *Music In Latin America And the Caribbean* (2004). Artistry in Motion performs Kumina in a 2013 recording which can be viewed at http://www.youtube.com/watch?v=Elwz5MGSXfs. In Modes and Genres, we speculate further on Kumina's influence on the contemporary trope of the rapper's prophetic or divine status.

13. Although most rap lines presented on web sites like Genius and A-Z Lyrics are metrically correct, conforming to the four-beat, couplet-with-end-rhyme norm, errors of lineation occasionally occur, especially where the syntax clashes with the meter, or where the normative rhyme structures are avoided, or more generally, in verses of unusual rhythmic effusiveness by rappers like Prodigy, Talib Kweli, Eminem, Lupe Fiasco, and Lil Wayne. Relying on the evidence of our ears, we have corrected such lines in our scansions and hence our database coding. To cite just one example of internet scribal error, Tupac's five lines from "Ratha Be Ya Nigga," which we quote in Modes and Genres, is misrepresented by Genius and other sites, obscuring the meter and losing the rhyme chain. Whether the site in question is a wiki or merely a textual resource, practically no attention is paid to poetics, and when one site launches new song lyrics, the others duplicate these uncritically.

No doubt because rapping is so essentially an oral/aural experience, there exists within hip hop culture a relatively blasé attitude about textual format. Traditionally, lyrics belong exclusively to the rapper and have no presence in the public domain. They may be guarded in his book of rhymes as closely as any Elizabethan play script, and, unlike other song lyrics, they are never meant to be copyrighted or covered. So what difference does it make how they are arranged? After all, the rapper—who may write them out in half lines, full lines, or in a prose format cut by slashes—has no trouble performing his lines in perfectly metrical flow. In Jay-Z's *Decoded*, which attempts to confer a kind of literary status to his lyrics, lines are quite often delineated as syntactic rather than rhythmic units. In our book, however, concerned as it is with rap's syllabic rhythms and rhyme patterns, lines are treated first and foremost as metrical constructs.

14. Quoted in Paul Edwards, *How to Rap 2* (2013), pp. xi and xiii.

15. But see also Mark Costello and David Foster Wallace's *Signifying Rappers* (1990), a brave, brilliant commentary on rap's first decade. Their listing of rap's essential features on pp. 93–97 remains relevant: "(a) No melody besides canonized fragment without progression; (b) A driving, oh-so-danceable 4/4-cut-time 'krush groove,' a pyramidical rhythms-within-rhythms structure. . . . (c) Lyrics that are spoken or

yelled, often rhymed or assonant, but always metered, complicating and complementing the marriage of back-bass, scratches, and drums, creating a dense diachronic rhythmic layering instead of the harmonic or contrapuntal synchronicities that have marked most Western music from Haydn to Heads; (d) A consistency in its deployment of maybe half a dozen themes. . . . (e) An overall aesthetic that mainstream pop critics and performers . . . scorn as shallow and materialistic and self-referential. But one (we opine) is probably the most revolutionary movement in ten dry and formulated years of rock, a movement not without similarities to postmodernism in art, fiction, classical music, poetry. . . . (f) No instruments. Nor even any original notes, I'm afraid."

16. Some metrical theory treats the rhythms of literary poetry also in musical terms. See especially Richard D. Cureton, *Rhythmic Phrasing in English Verse* (1992), where *meter* is defined as a non-linguistic grouping of beats, and *versification*, then, consists of the actual rhythms of the verbal syllable-stream overlaid on this metrical beat—analogous to *flow* in rap. *Prosody* in traditional literary studies is the study of poetic rhythms (meter and versification) irrespective of content, the musicality of poetic language. In contemporary linguistics, however, prosody refers generally to the whole suite of non-denotative features in speech, to include stress, pitch accents, pauses, and tone units; see, for example, Ann Wennerstrom, *The Music of Everyday Speech: Prosody and Discourse Analysis* (2001).

17. See Edwards, *How to Rap*, pp. 4–5. As Brand Nubian's Lord Jamar puts it, "At the end of the day, subject matter is the thing that would really be the meat of what you're doing. A flow is a flow—I can hum a flow right now—[but] the substance to the flow is what's being said. What really makes a flow dope is what's being said within the flow, not just the flow itself." Lateef from Latyrx adds: "The . . . content, is gonna be how it is that people are able to relate to what it is that you're saying. . . . Eminem does subject matter really well, where the song is not about the same shit, and it's fucking crazy. . . . The subject matter is so out there you're really entertained."

18. Edwards, *How to Rap 2*, pp. 1–2. Crooked I's artistic experience supports Evidence's musical priority: "I've sacrificed a lot of ingenious metaphors because it wouldn't fit precisely on the beat how I wanted it to" (p. 2); so does the critical response of Royce D 5' 9" to Jay-Z's "Money, Cash, Hoes": "the song ain't really about nothing, really he's just rhyming. But the thing that catches your ear is the flow—it's the way he rides the beat that makes me like that song" (*How to Rap*, p. 65).

19. "Explicit content" in poetry and drama is rarely literal. In the opening scene of Aristophanes' *Lysistrata*, as the title character begins organizing the women of Athens to deny sex to their husbands in order to put a stop to war, she and a girlfriend engage in this light banter: CALONICE: "My dear Lysistrata, why have you asked the women to meet here? What's going on? Is it something big?" LYSISTRATA: "It's huge." C:

"And hard as well?" L: "Yes, by god, really hard." C: "Then why aren't we all here?" L: "I don't mean *that*! If that were it, they'd all be charging here so fast. No. It's something I've been playing with—wrestling with for many sleepless nights." C: "If you've been working it like that, by now it must have shriveled up." L: "Yes, so shriveled up that the salvation of the whole of Greece is now in women's hands." In Shakespeare's *Twelfth Night* (II, 5), Malvolio, a pompous Puritan who would never speak openly about sex, unwittingly betrays his desires while gleefully identifying his Lady's handwriting in a note he assumes—deluded—to be a love letter rather than the practical joke it really is: "By my life, this is my lady's hand! These be her very **C**'s, her **U**'s, '**n**' her **T**'s, and thus makes she her great **P**'s. It is, in contempt of question, her hand."

It's true, however, that in Chaucer's *Miller's Tale* the effeminate parish clerk Absolon, who has already been identified as extremely squeamish, especially about farts, and who suffers from unrequited infatuation with the Miller's young wife, Alison, ends up *literally* kissing her ass in the dark. She has been happily committing adultery with the manly cleric Nicholas, their lodger, but when pesky Absolon starts wooing her beneath her architecturally incongruous "shot-wyindow" (slit-window), Alison decides it will be a great trick to offer him her butt in lieu of her lips:

> Derk was the nyght as pich, or as the cole,
> And at the wyndow out she putte hir hole,
> And Absolon, hym fil no bet ne wers,
> But with his mouth he kiste hir naked ers
> Ful savourly, er he was war of this.

Here the literal language (*hole, ers*) is dramatically appropriate to the character of the taleteller, a crude blasphemer, and the prolonged anal kiss is itself funny because it contrasts so sharply with the cleric's expectation, his prissiness, and his preference for romantic fantasy-land. But *hole* and *ers,* while crude, were not taboo in Chaucer's day. The word *cunt,* by contrast, is not in *The Canterbury Tales* although the hypersexual Wife of Bath points to it proudly as her *thing* or her *bele chose.* Earlier in the *Miller's Tale,* when "handy" Nicholas first woos Alison, he takes the most direct approach possible:

> As clerkes been ful subtile and ful queynte,
> And privily he caught hire by the queynte

Here the first *queynte* means "quaint," an elegant French (upperclass) term in the same register as *subtile* and *privily.* The second *queynte* means "cunt," obviously, but it doesn't exactly say so—except by word play, in much the same way that *privily* also alludes to Alison's private parts. Since clerics are stereotypically subtle, refined, and reserved, Nicholas's act dashes all such assumptions. The couplet's humor, then, is both linguistic and situational.

Too $hort, one of very few early rappers who indulge in "explicit content," deploys a very *queynte*-like tactic, but not quaintly. In "Female Funk" (1983), he uses a suggestively pitched *funk* almost sixty times to mean either "vagina," "fuck," or both, but he's not really saying it, explicitly. By contrast, 2 Live Crew frequent flaunting of *dick* in their *As Nasty As They Wanna Be* (1989) album is anomalous in its literal explicitness. The word *dick* is actually quite common in recent rap songs, but it almost always occurs in the phrase "on my [or his] dick," as meaning "too close to" or "under the sway of." The "explicit content" is merely metaphorical.

The history of culture displays many shifts on the continuum of linguistic tolerance and intolerance, depending on the relative influences of religious hegemony, emerging political or dynastic interests, the work of creative artists, and ongoing critical responses. One of the most popular courtly poems in the Middle Ages was the *Romance of the Rose,* a love and sex allegory exceeding 20,000 lines. In it, the rose symbolizes the lady, femininity, and, most prominently, the vagina; the pilgrim in quest of the rose carries a staff with a bag. More obviously misogynistic sex metaphors abound: styluses and tablets, plows and fallow fields, hammers and anvils, arrows and shot-windows—in all of which pairings, men are the actors and women are those acted upon. At one juncture, Lady Reason lectures the Lover/Dreamer on explicit content, arguing that words for sex are just words; that male and female genitals, being created by God and necessary for human propagation, are good; and that there's nothing wrong with the names *penis* and *vagina*—why, then, do humans foolishly persist in creating all of these ridiculous metaphors? Early in the fifteenth century, the poet Christine de Pisan attacked the *Romance of the Rose* for its sheer misogyny. Jean Gerson, the chancellor of the University of Paris, attacked the poem because it encouraged idleness and vain pursuits, and because it was obscene, for it named the members of generation (*penis, vagina*). So it goes.

20. Here we can compare these puerile, misogynistic lines of Too $hort in "Don't Stop Rappin'" (1983)—

I like those girls that are real real fine
Thick young tenders, yours and mine
It's not all about getting that steak
Cuz what is a girl without a lot of bank
A bump and a grind and she's on her knees
The way it is now you might catch a disease

—with the more cynically, cruelly misogynistic lines in 2 Live Crew's hit, "Me So Horny" (1989), from *As Nasty As They Wanna Be.* It begins: "Sitting at home with my dick on hard / So I got the black book for a freak to call." Sentiments like these follow naturally:

> It's true you were a virgin until you met me
> I was the first to make you hot and wetty-wetty
> You tell your parents that we're going out
> Never to the movies, just straight to my house
> You said it yourself, you like it like I do
> Put your lips on my dick, and suck my asshole too
> I'm a freak in heat, a dog without warning
> My appetite is sex, 'cause me so horny

This album was ruled without serious artistic value—a condition for obscenity according to the US Supreme Court—in federal court in Ft. Lauderdale, June, 1990. The ruling (a first for rap music) was overturned by the US 11th Circuit Court of Appeals in Atlanta in 1991.

See also Blowfly's "Rapp Dirty" (1980). In the mode of Redd Foxx, Blowfly had strong comedic talent and produced a series of raunchy "party records." His rapping on this track is indeed explicit in its hyperbolic sexual details, but it's all subsumed within the comic genre of the first-person toast: a hapless, reckless black man encounters a transvestite at juke joint, battles the Ku Klux Klan, tears up the place with his truck, and lives to tell the tall tale.

21. "Nigga" in its normatively valorized, somewhat testosteronic sense is well exemplified in The Notorious B. I. G.'s "Big Poppa" (https://www.youtube.com/watch?v=phaJXp_zMYM); the identity is cultural more than personal: "Choppin' Os, smoking la in Optimos / Money, hoes and clothes, all a nigga knows." Two decades later, J. Cole in "Wet Dreamz" (https://www.youtube.com/watch?v=eCGV26aj-mM) can deploy "nigga" to signify a culturally constructed, uncomplicated, would-be libidinous mode of the self ("She had a vibe and a nigga started diggin' it / I was a youngin', straight crushin', tryna play the shit cool") or else one part of a divided self ("But I was scared to death, my nigga, my stomach turnin' / Talking shit, knowing damn well I was a virgin, fuck").

22. Sometimes humans, like other apes—and dogs—self-identify as pack animals. In hip-hop slang, *dog* means good friend or fellow gang member, as in Snoop Dogg's moniker or as in this expression of grief from Bone Thugs-N-Harmony's "Tha Crossroads": "Why they kill my dog, damn, man?" Some male musicians personify their instruments with female names, for example B. B. King's Lucille, and we know an aging jazz musician who refers to his upright bass more generally, but still intimately, as "my bitch."

23. See Lupe Fiasco's "Bitch Bad," quoted in full in a note later in this chapter.

While joining other "conscious rappers" in decrying the use of *bitch* as misogynistic, Lupe also explains its gendered usage—and uses it artfully.

24. Encouragingly, over the past few years the topic of homophobia itself has become increasingly prevalent in the field's artistic discourse, and some rappers have come out as LGBTQ, rallying around the term "homo hop." Openly LGBTQ rappers include Azealia Banks, Mélange Lavonne, Deadlee, and Katastrophe. Meanwhile, some prominent straight rappers like Macklemore have endorsed same-sex marriage, e.g., Macklemore in "Same Love," while Eminem has fallen relatively silent on the subject. In another strand of commentary, J. Cole signals his acceptance in "Villuminati" while also suggesting that the word "faggot" in its historical rap context does not clearly map to that of mainstream culture. J. Cole's lyrics also imply that sensitivity around the word by newer rappers may nevertheless indicate a residual homophobia.

25. By the late 1980s, however, MC styles on both coasts had morphed radically in the direction of hyper-male "gangsta," pimping, and drug-dealing personas, expressed through more aggressive diction and relatively unpredictable rhythms. One of our outside reviewers characterized this performance of male aggression and grandiosity as *desperate,* and indeed, Ta-Nehisi Coates in *Between the World and Me* (2015) has eloquently addressed the underlying traumatic fear pervading black expression in consequence of systematic post-slavery exclusion from the "American Dream" through violence, job, housing, and judicial discrimination. There is much truth in this, but we would argue for a more complex explanation of rap braggadocio. In his exhaustive study of the dozens, *Talking 'Bout Your Mama: The Dozens, Snaps, and the Deep Roots of Rap* (2012), Elijah Wald lists these competing theoretical explanations of this global and pan-historical insult traditions: "The dozens is . . . a puberty ritual . . . training in self-control . . . a cathartic form of group therapy and a valuable social outlet . . . misogyinist hate speech . . . a retrograde expression of African American self-hatred . . . an art at the heart of African American expression" (pp. 169–181). Typically, the aggressive and demeaning components of any rap verse, even in battle rap, are balanced by different and even contrary components, becoming "part of the mix" as it were. For example, Black Thought's recent 97 Freestyle, a ten-minutes-plus video tour de force, contains quite a few widely spaced threats and insults, but the main point is his masterful flow and intricate rhyming. Black Thought's demeanor throughout is that of a serene, omniscient warrior-god.

26. See discussion in the next chapter, Hot Vinyl.

27. Wikipedia currently lists sixty-nine examples of "dirty blues" dating from Ma Rainey's "See See Rider" (1924) to Blind Willie McTell's "Salty Dog" (1956). Many are from female artists. Titles such as "Good Grinding," "Banana in Your Fruit Basket," "Press My Button (Ring My Bell)," "I Need A Little Sugar In My Bowl," "Meat Balls," "My Man Stands Out," and "Sittin' On It All The Time" suggest the range of play-

ful suggestiveness. "See See Rider" puns on *easy rider*, which means lover *and* gigolo or pimp—as well as sexually smooth. The *back door man* is a secretive adulterer, not necessarily one with a certain preference, whereas Sippie Wallace's claim to be a mighty tight woman is clearly anatomical. The "explicit content," then, is either metaphorical and/or synecdochic. The only extant "dirty blues" song that's truly explicit, literally about sex, is the unexpurgated alternative take of Lucile Bogan's "Shave 'Em Dry" (1935)—possibly preserved on the sly by the recording engineers, possibly intended for the "party music" black market:

> I got nipples on my titties, big as the end of my thumb,
> I got somethin' between my legs'll make a dead man come,
> Oh daddy, baby won't you shave 'em dry? (Now, draw it out!)
> Want you to grind me baby, grind me until I cry.

> Say I fucked all night, and all the night before baby,
> And I feel just like I wanna fuck some more,
> Oh great God daddy, grind me honey and shave me dry,
> And when you hear me holler baby, want you to shave it dry.

28. Generally speaking, African American musical themes and styles were not just appropriated by rock and roll; they were sanitized. The de-sexualized translation of Big Mama Thornton's R&B hit "Hound Dog" (1952)—which had already been covered many other white artists working in country and other styles—into Elvis Pressley's "Hound Dog" (1956) is paradigmatic. In the original, Big Mama Thornton evokes the back door man but reduces him to a pesky, snooping hound. The door, the tail-wagging, and the feeding all resonate with sexual double entendre:

> You ain't nothing but a hound dog, been snoopin' 'round the door
> You ain't nothing but a hound dog, been snoopin' 'round the door
> You can wag your tail but I ain't gonna feed you no more

The later version ignores the original's semantic roots and shrinks its metaphorical reference to the hound dog alone. Thus, a powerful and cheeky assertion of personal independence (throwing the gigolo out) is reduced to mere mean-spiritedness. Elvis Presley simply calls his ex-girlfriend an incessant whiner or a weeper, a dog worthless at doing its job, so no friend of his. The eroticism has vanished:

> You ain't nothin' but a hound dog, cryin' all the time
> You ain't nothin' but a hound dog, cryin' all the time
> Well, you ain't never caught a rabbit and you ain't no friend of mine

Both versions are of course twelve-bar blues, formally, but only the original embodies the spirit of the blues. Elvis's version is good for jitterbugging, and that's about it. Ironically, both "Hound Dog" songs were #1 hits, but Big Mama Thornton got only about $1,000 in royalties for hers, while Elvis Pressley made millions. Its phenomenal success (with sales topping 10,000,000) helped Elvis attain the unofficial title, King of Rock and Roll, leaving other worthy claimants such as Chuck Berry in the commercial dust.

29. The number of people behind bars for nonviolent drug law offenses increased from 50,000 in 1980 to over 400,000 by 1997. For a concise, artistic exposition of the failed War on Drugs by Jay-Z and Molly Crabapple, see http://www.drugpolicy.org/facts/new-solutions-drug-policy/brief-history-drug-war-0

30. Normalization is resisted by feminist rappers like MC Lyte and Queen Latifah as well as by "conscious" rappers like Yasiin Bey (Mos Def), Common, Juru, Immortal Technique, and many others.

31. These include Rakim, Q-Tip, Yasiin Bey (Mos Def), Freeway, Brother Ali, and Lupe Fiasco. The Five-Percent Nation, or NGE (Nation of God and Earth) has had a foundational influence on hip hop culture in New York, evident in the lyrics of Nas, Guru, LL Cool J, Big Daddy Kane, Big Pun, and especially KRS-One. See also *The Gospel of Hip Hop: First Instrument presented by KRS-One for the Temple of Hip Hop* (2009).

32. Even as the derogatory term *bitch* has been scrutinized by hip hop scholars and critics, quite a few rappers have denounced its use, often in passing. Lupe Fiasco's "Bitch Bad," however, uniquely articulates a full poetic essay on the topic, and by extension, on the cultural construction of misogyny. Verse 1 details the word's impact on young males:

> Now imagine there's a shorty, maybe five, maybe four
> Riding 'round with his mama listening to the radio
> And a song comes on and a not far off from being born
> Doesn't know the difference between right and wrong
> Now, I ain't trying to make it too complex
> But let's just say shorty has an undeveloped context
> About the perception of women these days
> His mama sings along, and this what she says
> "Niggas, I'm a bad bitch, and I'm bad, bitch!
> Somethin' that's far above average."
> And maybe other rhyming words like cabbage and savage
> And baby carriage and other things that match it
> Couple of things are happenin' here
> First he's relatin' the word bitch with his mama—comma

And because she's relatin' to herself
As most important source of help
And mental health, he may skew respect for dishonor

Lupe now in verse 2 laments the societal damage on young females:

Yeah, now imagine a group of little girls 9 through 12
On the Internet watching videos
Listening to songs by themselves
It doesn't really matter if they have parental clearance
They understand the Internet better than their parents
Now, being the Internet, the content's probably uncensored
They're young, so they're malleable and probably unmentored
A complicated combination, maybe with no relevance
Until that intelligence meets their favorite singer's preference
"Bad bitches, bad bitches, bad bitches
That's all I want and all I like in life is bad bitches, bad bitches."
Now, let's say that they less concerned with him
And more with the video girl acquiescent to his whims
Ah, the plot thickens: high heels, long hair, fat booty, slim
Reality check, I'm not trippin'
They don't see a paid actress, just what makes a bad bitch

When the two mix, there's an unresolvable mismatch:

The little boy meets one of those little girls
And he thinks she a bad bitch and she thinks she a bad bitch
He thinks disrespectfully, she thinks of that sexually
She got the wrong idea, he don't wanna fuck her
He think she's bad at being a bitch like his mother
Momma never dressed like that
Come out the house, hot mess like that
Ass, titties, dressed like that, all out to impress like that
Just like that, you see the fruit of the confusion
He caught in a reality, she caught in an illusion
Bad mean good to her, she really nice and smart
But bad mean bad to him, bitch don't play a part
But bitch still bad to her if you say it the wrong way
But she think she a bitch; what a double entendre!

HOT VINYL

1. The crossing of hip hop rap into audio tapes and records compares with how Homer's oral poetry turned into literature. A unique, real-time, ephemeral performance is converted into a common, anytime, permanent recording of a performance, which itself may be spliced together and edited from multiple takes and remixes. Imagine an amazing illiterate ("blind") poet, a master of epic, the best bard of his day, widely famous, who makes an excellent living performing on demand. He is invited by a rich patron (and for an irresistibly large fee) to perform his masterwork about ancient Greek warriors besieging and conquering the great city of Troy. But this time he must chant his epic not quite the way he normally would, reciting it at a steady pace to a relaxed, attentive, feasting audience; instead, he must deliver it so slowly that a single scribe or group of scribes can copy it accurately.

2. These earliest hip hop hits hit the charts as R&B or Soul singles—even the fourteen-minute "Rapper's Delight." No one outside of New York knew exactly what they were hearing, but it was funky and danceable and *new*! "Rapper's Delight" peaked at #4 on the US Hot Soul chart and #36 on the Billboard Hot 100. "The Breaks" hit #87 on the Billboard Hot 100, but #4 on its R&B chart and #9 on its Dance chart. "Planet Rock" rose to #48, #4, and #3 on these charts, followed by "Looking for the Perfect Beat," climbing to #10, #18, and #36. "The Message" maxed at #62, #4, and #12.

3. Early hip hop artists would have been aware of call and response in African American preaching, in James Brown's songs, and probably also in Jamaican contexts such the Nayabingi chanting tradition represented by Ras Michael, Burning Spear's "Slavery Days" in *Marcus Garvey* (1975), and the work of DJs like U-Roy and Big Youth, whose rapping over dub records was a kind of ongoing "response" to their samples' erased but remembered lyrics.

4. This is the rhetorical figure known as *adunaton* (the impossibility trope): "The rivers will run uphill when I stop loving you."

5. Hominy Grit makes an appearance in Method Man's first rap in the unreleased recording of "The What," cleaned up in *Ready to Die*. As Method responds to Biggie's play on "flapjacks and bacon," his own culinary insult probably alludes as well to this archetype of a backstabbing friend.

6. Almost all of "When the Revolution Comes" imagines a *when*-sequence of topsy-turvy post-revolution situations when current capitalist relationships and cultural phenomena have flipped or vanished. But at the song's very end comes an alternatively prophetic *but until then* clause: "But until then you know and I know niggers will party and bullshit and party and bullshit and party and bullshit and party and bullshit and party. . . . Some might even die before the revolution comes." One of the great ironies of rap history, then, is the cultural and commercial success of the

mafia don lifestyle embraced famously by The Notorious B. I. G. among many others. Biggie's single, "Party and Bullshit," alludes to The Last Poets' phrase, offering an enthusiastic, funny affirmation of the apolitical behaviors decried by them. Ironically, Biggie's wildly successful albums were titled *Ready to Die* (1994) and *Life After Death* (1996), and he was shot dead even before this second release.

7. It is possible but unlikely that purple here might suggest royalty, wealth, spiritual authority, or beauty, as it does in some Western and African historical contexts. The tone of Wonder Mike's quatrain seems to exclude such associations. We need to remember that "Rapper's Delight" appeared three years before Alice Walker's *The Color Purple*. Nor within popular African American or Caribbean cultures is purple included in the complexion palette with red, yellow, and various shades of brown into black. American slavery-based racism works on the binary of "white" and "colored," or alternatively white and black—which can be flipped positively into Black Power and Black Pride—but Wonder Mike's message would seem to be one of cultural inclusion.

8. A sample from another disco hit, Love De-Luxe's "Here Comes That Sound Again" (1979), is used for the musically incoherent intro/outro frame and for the single, brief dance break at 4:36–4:54.

9. As will become abundantly clear, boasting is rap's dominant lyric expression. In relation to MCing generally, boasting serves the rhetorical purpose of commanding attention by claiming to be deserving of it. When Master Gee self-deprecatingly refers to himself as the baby of the group, noting both his third-in-line status and his "small face" and "brown eyes," he immediately parlays this cuteness factor into a boast about how much the ladies like him.

10. Embarrassingly, Hank claims, "But I'm the Grandmaster with the three MCs," as if he were Caz collaborating with the Cold Crush Brothers. If he'd given the matter more thought, he might, like any clever plagiarist, have changed the "three" to "two."

11. The /xxx/ rhythm, exemplified in "while you're sittin' in your seat" (xx/**xxx**/) is rare, and /**xxxx**/ never occurs.

12. In traditional English ballads, those that adhere to strict syllable counts have been referred to as "eights and sixes," but this stanza's brief, early manifestation in rap verses—as well as, later, in rap choruses—exhibits the looser syllable pattern associated with Shakespeare's songs and Old Folk. Lightnin' Rod's deployment of it in *Hustler's Convention* exhibits line lengths comparable to rap verses in the 1990s.

13. See now, however, "Amityville Story," in *Written! The Lyrics of Grandmaster Caz* (2013). This song must have been written after Jay Anson's *The Amityville Horror* was published in September 1977, but was probably inspired directly by the original movie, which appeared in 1979.

14. Master Gee for his part joins in the fun with his own signature scatting:

All I'm here to do Ladies || is hypnotize |
Singin' on n on || on n on on n on |
The beat don't stop until the break of dawn |
Singin' on n on || on n on on n on
Like a hot buttered a pop da pop da pop
Dibbie dibbie pop da pop || pop ya don't dare stop

15. We don't mean to suggest that scatting or the use of nonsense infixes is restricted to the earliest rap, to be replaced by entirely by denotative phrasing in the 1990s. For the–*izz* and–*izzle* infixes, there is a clear chain of influence from Frankie Smith's rap-influenced funk song "Double Dutch Bus" (1981) to Full Force's "Roxanne, Roxanne" (1985) to Snoop Dogg's *Doggystyle* (1993)—now morphed into the phrase *fo shizzle*—to Jay's "Izzo, H. O. V. A." (2001). Das EFX's fast flow on *Dead Serious* (1992), which relied strongly on repetition of–*iggedy*, was platinum popular and influenced the Wu-Tang Clan. Moreover, some current MCs whose verses contain, as is of course normal, nothing but words, nevertheless may compose the "first drafts" of their flow orally, in the form of scatting or mumbling. As Tajai of Souls of Mischief puts it, "[Sometimes my rhythms come] from scatting. I usually make a scat kind of skeleton and then fill in the words. I make a skeleton of the flow first, and then I put words into it. That's where vocabulary comes in—you can make anything fit anywhere" (Edwards, *How to Rap*, p. 114). Vursatyl of Lifesavas composes similarly: "A lot of times when I'm listening to a beat, I hear different patterns—it's almost like math in my mind. And what I try to do is, I'm kinda scatting or mumbling these patterns or those rhythms that are in my mind—then I find words to fit in those patterns. We call that styling, when I really come up with a dope style" (p. 114).

16. Nas has had many emulators, also intent on maximizing rhyme density within maximally extended lines. The linguistic challenges needing to be met to achieve this kind of flow are formidable, and those who attempt it not infrequently find themselves relying on forced rhymes, incoherent syntax, or, in the case of Machine Gun Kelly, a *non sequitur* sequencing of ideas:

Better be **known** I *got* the **throne** || like *I* don't **know** that there's a **king** |
Never grew **up** around a **fam**ily || 'cause I'm **not** a *hu*man **being** |
And *any*one under my **lev**el that's **com**ing in **my** *spot* | for the **top**
Let 'em **have** it | 'cause when **I** leave || the **whole** *world* **drops**
("Invincible," 2011)

17. The Zulu Nation website explicitly states its beliefs in "knowledge, wisdom, understanding, freedom, justice, equality, peace, unity, love, respect, work, fun, over-

coming the negative to the positive, economics, mathematics, science, life, truth, facts, faith, and the oneness of God."

18. With these quandaries in mind as we coded this song, we resorted to two formal criteria to differentiate choruses from the verses. Defining a verse as a group of lines requiring specialized or at least differentiated knowledge to rap, and noting that such lines also featured greater rhythmic variation than others and were uninterrupted by the recorded audience, we classified these as the verses. Those with call and response, having little or no rhythmic variation, we classified as choruses.

19. As documented in Dan Charnas, *The Big Payback: The History of the Business of Hip Hop* (2011).

20. In *There's a God on the Mic* (2001), Kool Moe Dee ranks Melle Mel as the best MC *of all time*, awarding him one-hundred percent grades for "Originality, Substance, Vocal Presence, Live Performance, Poetic Value, Industry Impact, Social Impact, and Lyrics."

21. Genius annotates here that "a *glass jaw* is a term for someone who can't take a punch or is knocked out easily . . . and is tired of being victimized," but adds this comment: "I always thought it was *glass jar*, as in a beer bottle or hard liquor, in reference to alcoholism. Followed by *hear them say, 'you want some more?' Living on a see-saw*: a battle with addiction to alcohol." This plausible alternative hearing seems supported by rhyme-adjective *last* and would also evoke Mel's first image of *broken glass everywhere* in verse 1.

22. Rap verses almost always unfold as a series of couplets, which may be *closed couplets*, containing a completed statement, or *open couplets*, containing just part of an ongoing statement. Closed couplets find closure at the second end rhyme, expressed by a pitch drop and a pause, perhaps marked by a period. Open couplets would never end with a period because their syntax flows right into the next couplet. Closed rap couplets, like Mel's in verse 5 of "The Message," may resemble those in eighteenth-century literary poetry. They are more apt than open couplets to display rhythmic balance and logical dualism, including parallelism. In this couplet from Jonathan Swift's "Description of a City Shower"—

Triumphant Tories and desponding Whigs
Forget their feuds, and join to save their wigs.

—the Tories and Whigs on stresses 2 and 4 of their line are further differentiated by the adjectives *triumphant* and desponding on stresses 1 and 3, so each party occupies half a line. The parallelism continues with the contrast between their divisive "feuds" and their common "wigs." Similar balances occur in Mel's verse 5, beginning with "God is **smiling** on **you** but he's **frowning too.**"

Prior to verse 5, as we've seen, Mel's couplets are much more formally mixed, and include many open couplets. They sound more emotional and less like storytelling. Here we should remember that while MCs and literary poets often speak in couplets, ordinary people do not; so any poet who wants his verse to sound a little less like poetry and a little more like normal speech may want to deploy open couplets. Robert Browning's dramatic monologues purport to be spoken by real or imagined historical characters, and maybe for this reason their couplets are predominantly open. Because a lot of the rhymes aren't followed by pauses, people hearing these lines from "My Last Duchess" may not even know they're in couplets:

> That's my last Duchess painted on the wall,
> Looking as if she were alive. I call
> That piece a wonder, now: Frà Pandolf's hands
> Worked busily a day, and there she stands.
> Will't please you sit and look at her? I said
> "'Frà Pandolf'" by design, for never read
> Strangers like you that pictured countenance,
> The depth and passion of its earnest glance

Browning's speaker is the Duke of Ferrara, a murderer and a smooth operator. His open-ended couplets aid him in projecting an air of confident, sophisticated ease and power. As we've seen, many of Mel's couplets are also open, but to different effect. Like the toxic sensations, dangers, and spiritual breakdowns associated with urban poverty, Mel's couplets are often smeared, suggesting chaos, not order.

23. The tonal clashes in many of Mel's end rhymes anticipate N. W. A. Mel juxtaposes *mind / mankind, stay / alleyway, number-book takers / big money-makers, gamblers / panhandlers, fool / high school*. His most tragically expressive rhyme occurs with hyperstressed *Maytag* followed by *undercover fag*, a weak glide of secondary stresses.

24. Kool Moe Dee adds: "Up until this point, there had been only party hits with lighthearted lyrical content . . . it changed the routine formulas that groups were using on wax. It was the beginning of the end for the round-robin styles of the three-, four-, and five-man groups. Suddenly there were only soloists and duos."

25. Although Kurtis Blow merits credit as the first MC to keep it socioeconomically real, in "Hard Times," "The Message" was the first breakout message record. Rap music has been accused of saying the same things again and again—always with original rhymes, of course—but we should not ignore its openness to thematic innovation and its capacity for quick response. In the context of the emerging AIDS epidemic (and perennial problem of gonorrhea), Kool Moe Dee's first hit, "Go See The Doctor" (1986) dealt frankly and funnily with the importance of safe sex. Salt-N-Pepa's

"Let's Talk About Sex" (1991), without really talking about sex, poked fun at the widespread avoidance and censorship of sex in the media. The songs of N. W. A. and other so-called "gangsta" groups brought controversial and often unappreciated attention to police brutality in the ghetto. Queen Latifah's "U. N. I. T. Y." (1993) became the breakout feminist anthem against disrespect for women, domestic violence, and sexual predation. Lauryn Hill's "Doo Wop (That Thing)" (1995) covered similar themes but pointed out how sexual problems, often shared between men and women, arise from spiritual weakness. In many songs, "conscious" rappers like Mos Def, Talib Kweli, Guru, and Common spoke out against both misogyny and gang violence. More recently, Jay-Z has defended the integrity of the human voice in "D. O. A. (Death of Auto-Tune)" (2009). Kendrick Lamar calls attention to the problem of alcoholism in "Swimming Pools (Drank)" (2012) in his album *good kid, m.A.A.d city*—which tags Alcoholics Anonymous inside of urban insanity. And Macklemore has released "Same Love" (2012), an anthem of tolerance for gays and lesbians. Granted, some of these message records have been, historically speaking, slow in coming, but meanwhile rap music is *always* current in its allusions and conversations. It is worth noting that after the devastation of Hurricane Katrina in 2007, the response from pop, country music, and folk singers was almost non-existent, yet Kanye West, Lil Wayne, Outkast, Snoop Dogg, Mos Def, The Legendary K. O., Public Enemy, and Jay Electronica were on it within days.

BEAT

1. Edwards, *How to Rap*, p. 115, quotes several MCs' views on how their flow responds directly to the beat: "More so than anything else, I'd say that my flow tends to follow the percussion. I'm also a producer, so I realize the important of the percussion section as the backbone of the music, and I usually try to adhere to that" (Akir); "I'm basically trying to be like another instrument on the track. I want to ride it like the baselines riding it, only with words. I want to ride it just like the guitar or the violin or whatever instrument, just riding it" (Gift of Gab, from Blackalicious); "When the music changes, it lets you know what to do and how to change as far as the flow patterns" (Devin the Dude).

2. Twista's spectacular tempo is 144 bpm in "Badunkdunk." When Krayzie Bone raps, his unique style within Bone Thugs-N-Harmony is due partly to his particular quirks of flow (e.g., repeated triplets), partly to his practice of shifting smoothly into 32nds or "doubletime" within a moderate tempo.

3. Edwards, *How to Rap*, p. 127.

4. The ictus is a musical or metrical beat conceived and experienced as a single stroke, from Latin *ictus* = strike, blow, sting. Although even the briefest sounds are

durational, the ictus beat feels percussive and instantaneous. When rappers rap "in the pocket," when drummers drum in perfect time, they are hitting the ictus beat.

5. Dips 2 and 5 are the longest dips by structural consequence. We have also found that dips 1 and 6 tend to be shorter than dips 3 and 4, likely because the risk of missing and cluttering the downbeat is lessened by introducing additional variation in dips 3 and 4.

6. A good discussion of the process—and mystique—of "digging in the crates" can be found in Schloss, *Making Beats*. Although taking samples from previously recorded sounds was the dominant ethos until the emergence of digital sampling by major producers today, live instrumentals and vocals aren't completely new to the rap backdrop beat. Artists like Kurtis Blow, Stetsasonic, and The Roots experimented with the original norms of sampling techniques by using live instruments to fatten riffs in their pre-compiled beat track.

7. Both Dan Charnas, in *The Big Payback,* and Jay-Z, in *Decoded,* acknowledge the qualitative artistic and commercial growth made possible by Rakim's breakthrough flow in *Paid in Full.*

8. Trap music is a subgenre of today's popular Electronic Dance Music (EDM). Trap's origins are misty, however. Each trap song is tagged with the phrase "run the trap," best recognized by fans in Major Lazer's "Original Don (Flosstradamus)" mix. The genre is characterized by a loose snare and a tempo of about 150 bpm, making hip hop's adoption an easy transition. Prominent artists include Bro Safari, Major Lazer, Heroes x Villains, Flosstradamus, and Grandtheft.

9. Since the hip hop beat is embodied in rap poetry, it is theoretically possible to use rap itself as the primary component of a new beat. That's what Canibus enabled listeners to do with his "Poet Laureate Infinity" (2007). This 1,000-line song has five 200-line divisions, each with parallel rhymes, yielding five rap tracks available for remixing. Canibus posted it, along with a virtual synthesizer, on a website which unfortunately has been taken down.

RHYTHM

1. An overview of hip hop's Jamaican lineage, with emphasis on the social history of the Kingston-Bronx nexus, can be found in Jeff Chang's *Can't Stop, Won't Stop: A History of the Hip-Hop Generation* (2005), chapter 2.

2. This shift was decried by "conscious rappers" such as Yasiin Bey (Mos Def) and Talib Kweli, who openly critiqued the exploitation of hip hop culture by big money interests: suddenly in Brooklyn "they paint murals of Biggie / In cash we trust because it's ghetto fabulous." For a thorough exposition of the business of rap, see Dan Charnas's *The Big Payback* (2010).

3. Biggie's title and chorus refrain defy and flip the politically conscious admonition concluding The Last Poets' "When the Revolution Comes" (1970):

When the revolution comes
When the revolution comes
When the revolution comes
But until then you know and I know niggers will party and bullshit and party
      and bullshit and party and bullshit and party and bullshit and party . . .
Some might even die before the revolution comes

4. Traditional metrists use the term *prosody* to describe the rhythms of language irrespective of content, that is, with respect to the contours of their syllable-groupings and pauses. Metrists actually disagree on what constitutes meter. Those like Richard Cureton, who locate the meter in an underlying, non-linguistic, essentially musical beat, refer to the prosodic arrangement of syllables as *versification*, while those who locate the meter in the language itself view versification as the meter.

5. Some rappers like Run-DMC, Del, and Khia space their metrical stresses right on the beat, metronomically, while others like Eminem seldom do so, cultivating a tense, disorienting style, and still others like Rakim and Guru move freely between on-time and syncopated stresses, like good jazz singers.

6. Over time, we've seen a significant increase in the mix of lines in our database that include pauses; when they do occur, however, their rhythms tend to be anchored by medial and terminal pauses. Interestingly, the increase in frequency of extra pauses has not been accompanied by any change in the frequency of caesuras or end stops. Few rappers we analyzed enjamb more than ten percent of lines, and few elide caesuras for more than ten to fifteen percent of lines.

7. This is not to say that there are no two-stress or three-stress lines. Well under five percent of our verse lines have just three beated-stresses and, in some cases, elided caesural pauses, but most of these lines fit rhythmically into 4/4 time by means of an insertion of a long pause following or preceding these stresses. When unaccompanied by an extended pause, they often have tags or choral shout-outs.

8. For an excellent survey of the varieties of musically conventional triplets used by rappers, see Edwards, *How to Rap 2*, pp. 16–28.

9. In Wonder Mike's three-stress / / / [B] lines, a pause always occurs, anomalously, between stresses one and two ("I'm **rappin'** || **to** the **beat**"), whereas in all later metrical lines with single long pauses the midline pause always falls normatively between stresses two and three.

10. We use the term *idiolect* to refer to personal voice. In life and in performance poetry, key factors of personal voice include—beyond physiology, personality, and

family influences—age and regional accent, with vocal timbre being a product of multiple physiological and cultural conditions. But *poetic* idiolect is also a product of dictional, syntactic, and rhythmic habits. To cite a literary analog, in all of Shakespeare's plays no one else but Othello (or Iago, or Juliet, or Cleopatra) sounds like Othello (or Iago, or Juliet, or Cleopatra). This phenomenon argues that style cannot be reduced to performance choices in combination with voice qualities.

11. Ann Wennerstrom summarizes and exemplifies linguistic consensus on the "rules of eurythmy" in *The Music of Everyday Speech: Prosody and Discourse Analysis* (2001), pp. 54–58.

12. These two components of rap, rhythmic regularity and strong semantic emphasis, are shared by all earlier four-beat metrical systems, from Old English verse to Middle English alliterative long-line to early and Old Folk ballads, jingles, nursery rhymes, and blues. Here are some examples, with stressed syllables boldfaced:

þa **com** of **mor**e || under **m**ist-**hleo**þum
Grendel **gon**gan, || **God**es yrre **bær**;
mynte se **man**scaþa || **man**na **cyn**nes
sumne be**syr**wan || in **sele** þam **hean**. (*Beowulf*, 710–13)

(Then came from [the] moor, under mist-hills
Grendel going, God's ire [he] bore
[he] had in mind, the man-scather, of the kin of men
someone to destroy in the high hall)

Ac **Glo**ton was a **gret cherl** || and a **grym** in the **lif**tyng,
And **kough**ed up a **caw**del || in **Cle**mentes **lap**pe.
Is noon so **hun**gry **hound** || in **Hert**ford**shir**e
Dorste **lape** of that **le**vynge, || so un**love**ly it **smaugh**te!
(*Piers Plowman* B, 5.354–5.357)

(But Glutton was great churl and grim in the lifting,
And coughed up a mess in Clement's lap.
There's hound in Hertfordship hungry enough
To dare to lap up that deposit, so unlovely it stank.)

Fee! **Fie**! || **Foe**! *Fum*!
I smell the **blood** of an **Englishman**.
Be he alive || or be he *dead*,
I'll **have** his **bones** to **grind** my ***bread***. ("Jack and the Beanstock")

I'm lookin' **fun**ny in my *eyes* ‖ and I **b'lieve** I'm **fix**in' to *die*
I'm lookin' **fun**ny in my *eyes*, ‖ and I **b'lieve** I'm **fix**in' to *die*
I **know** I was **born** to *die* ‖ but I **hate** to **leave** my **child**ren *cryin'*
(Bukka White, "Fixin to Die")

13. The longest line in our database is from Aesop Rock's "Daylight," with no pause, seven stresses, and twenty-two syllables: "**Fa**thom the **spli**cing of **first** genera-tion **fuck** up or **tri**ckle-down **an**ti-hero **smack**." Here the rhythms are continuously cacophonic, as chaotic as the sense. Compare Eminem's twenty-syllable line from "25 to Life," which displays superb rhythmic versatility: "**Chew** me **up** and **spit** me **out** ‖ I **fell** for this | **so** many **times** it's **ri**diculous." The clichéd parallelism within the a-verse's accusation of emotional disregard is captured by alternating stressed and unstressed syllables and sounds like catalectic trochaic tetrameter, a common and overused Eng-lish poetic meter. The b-verse is split by a pause into two sections, the first one express-ing genuine emotional bewilderment, the second one sounding like exasperated self-talk, with its successive triplet of anapests.

14. Lupe wittily connects the Sphinx's eroded nose with the boxer's broken nose. He assumes that his own rise to the top of the game will be equally spectacular, what-ever the wounds. In the *Pegasus/pheasants* line, he aligns himself with divinity and power, the commercial rap game with ground-dwelling ordinariness. His far-fetched figurative juxtapositions fit within an ambitious thematic program. In verse 1, Lupe's rhymes flow topically from the sense of sight to divinity. Verse 2 opens with devilish play on the root sense of "dumb": rather than "dumbing it down" to the commercial standard, he would be "mouthless" and "soundless"—which of course he is not. His song flows through the senses from eyesight to taste to touch to hearing to olfaction, and his mind's eye becomes transcendent. This intellectualized transcendence recalls the tradition of romantic flight in first- and second-generation Romantic poets.

15. Lamentably, these murals of Biggie have recently been defaced as a part of an "urban renewal" project.

16. In our database, we code caesural pauses as C and potential but overridden caesural pauses as D. We use a similar placeholding alternative at line end: E for end stop and F for performance flow from one line into the next. These codes allow us to compile accurate data on the syllables and pauses comprising lines, half lines, and initial and final dips in each half line. The line's two medial dips are always bounded by [B,R], but the line's other four dips are bounded by [B,R] and [E,F] or [C,D].

17. English four-beat poetry has not always been backloaded. In fact, rap's closest metrical cousin is the strongly frontloaded alliterative long line verse of the fourteenth and fifteenth centuries, which has similar line lengths and conforms to the same metri-cal template. Unlike rap, long line typically has a-verses longer as well as semantically

and syntactically stronger than b-verses, which are often formulaic. The dominant long line alliterative pattern, AA|AX, packs sound play into the a-verse, reduces it in the b-verse, and removes it from terminal position.

And rhyme *per se* is backloaded, unlike alliteration. Alliteration begins on a consonant onset, but rhyme can't begin till the vowel nucleus, after which it can continue to subsume one or more unstressed syllables, where alliteration would no longer be heard. Alliteration is the perfect metrical marker in a front-stressed language, but it becomes less "natural" with the importation of hundreds of French words into Middle English: *interagacioun* rhymes with *soun* but can't easily alliterate with anything else.

The contemporaneous importation of rhyme from French poetics during the fourteenth century changed English listening habits and expectations from Chaucer onwards. Eventually rhyme *occupied* the native four-beat forms. In effect, four-beat came to conform less to musical rhythms and more to English speech rhythms. This must already have been happening linguistically to some extent during the long line period. The phrasal units that make up half lines are often, as in rap, tone units. In alliterative long line then, as in rap today, pitch accents occur just prior to the caesural and terminal pauses even though they are marked differently—by alliteration at position 2 and by *non*-alliteration at position 4. The lack of alliteration at the end of the line was often coordinated by a rhythmic drop and by diminishment of thematic interest— the opposite of what happens in rhyming verse. Some poets like William Langland, however, used non-alliteration to express striking semantic clashes: for example, *Lord of lif and of light, of lisse and of peyne* (where *pain* contrasts sharply with life, light, and joy) or *Kinges and knightes, kaysers and popes* (where the *popes* contrast with the kings, knights, and keisers because of their religious office, yet ironically, all four are worldly potentates. From a hip hop perspective, these non-alliterations are totally ill.

18. Rap's prosodic backloadedness correlates to some degree with its semantics and syntax. Pre-caesural and terminal stress-words tend to be stronger semantically and syntactically than the other two, with the strongest rhyme words ending the line; somewhat less consistently, b-verses tend to be stronger than a-verses—even though their average syllabic length is roughly equivalent. Here in in these lines from Rakim, 1 and 2 mark relatively weak and relatively strong values within and between half lines.

```
x  /  x  x   /  || \  x  x   / x|  x   /      x  x
A gift to be swift, follow the leader, the rhyme will go
noun   phrase  ||   clause          clause
   R       R            B           R (multi)
   1       2            1               2
          1                        2
```

```
/ x x / x   x x  / x x   / x x
```
Def wit the *re*cord that was *mixed* a long <u>time ago</u>
adj. phrase   .rel. clause   phrase
R   R   R   R (multi)
1   2   1   2

19. Triplets have a long history in hip hop, Tupac and Krayzie Bone being among their chief popularizers. In post-2010 rap, sequential triplets have become so pervasive that they have been dubbed "triplet flow." Most demonstrably, this flow can fill entire lines with contiguous syllables ("Versace, Versace, Versace, Versace," by Migos), or it can be more artfully inserted as a rhythmic variation, as in Kendrick Lamar's *DAMN*. Other prominent recent rappers utilizing triplet flow include J. Cole, Lil Wayne, Danny Brown, and Cardi B.

20. Tupac's relative predictability, hinted at here in these two couplets, is corroborated by other metrics such as in which positions he chooses to deploy multis in two and three-syllable dips. The backloadedness of his two-stress multis contrasts sharply with the rhythmic masterwork generated by Lauryn Hill when deploying the same device in "Doo Wop (That Thing)." Her multis contain three rather than two phonetic sequences, and these are successively morphed and expanded into new horizontal and vertical relationships, all of which communicate important social and psychological truths. See our discussion in Rhyme.

21. See Edwards, *How to Rap 2*, pp. 183–5.

RHYME

1. Referring to a unit of rap poetry as a "rhyme" is *synecdoche*: naming a whole by a part (or vice versa). This figure of thought pervades hip hop culture, where rappers often "represent" a region, a city, or a borough. Nas embodies a "New York state of mind" and Lil Wayne claims more broadly, "I am the music." Then too, bling may suggest broader extravagance, women may be disparaged as "hoes" (a subset of females, a focus on just one activity) and the "mic" stands in for the sound system, for performance, for the poetry itself.

2. Blank verse is iambic pentameter without rhyme. It was termed "blank" because it was missing something. This rhyme-less poetry first appeared in sixteenth-century English translations of Homer and Virgil, whose dactylic hexameter verse also lacks rhyme (as does classical poetry generally), but it was especially favored by playwrights like Marlowe and Shakespeare, who realized wisely that rhyme prevented dramatic characters from sounding like real people. John Milton composed *Paradise Lost* in blank verse, and he had this to say about the matter: "The Measure is *English*

Heroic Verse without Rime, as that of *Homer* in Greek, and *Virgil* in Latin; Rime being no necessary Adjunct or true Ornament of Poem or good Verse, in longer Works especially, but the Invention of a barbarous Age, to set off wretched matter and lame Meeter; grac't indeed since by the use of some famous modern Poets, carried away by Custom, but much to thir own vexation, hindrance, and constraint to express many things otherwise, and for the most part worse then else they would have exprest them."

3. As noted elsewhere, Big Boi withholds rhyme at the end of the first verse in "Reset." André 3000 also has some rhyme-less lines in "A Life in the Day of Benjamin André." It's very possible that the occasional avoidance of rhyme will emerge as a future trend in MCing; see Lil B's "Giving Up (Pretty Young Thug)."

4. This statistic represents the majority of rap lines in our database; over sixty percent of the data have between three and four rhymes, with the median line involving three rhymes and two or more rhymes in proximate lines.

5. David Caplan's *Rhyme's Challenge: Hip Hop, Poetry, and Contemporary Rhyming Culture* (2014) is only of broad yet limited relevance here. Caplan's first sentence announces, "We live in a rhyme-drenched era," and he demonstrates this claim not only by considering the daring, innovative rhymes coined by rappers, but by exploring the contexts of rhyme's sudden appeal to hip literary poets, its cynical uses by the advertising industry, and its essential rhetorical problematics. For example, when Supreme Court justices rhyme, they are being purposefully ironic and indeed cheesy; or when defense attorney Johnnie Cochran rhymed in his closing argument at the O. J. Simpson trial ("If **it** [the bloody glove] don't **fit**, you must ac**quit**"), he turned an illogical proposition into effective persuasion. Caplan's sustained treatment of rappers' usage, however, contributes only minimally to hip hop poetics. He treats rap rhyming as daring, inventive doggerel (not unlike the verses of William McGonagall) and observes that it works particularly well for insult and seduction; but his preoccupation with rhyme's relatively obvious affective themes bypasses its fundamental rhythmic functions—how it shapes lines and couplets, how it works in tension with the beat, how it contributes to the ongoing complexity of flow.

6. Historically, biting has been a serious ethical infraction, whether the borrowed material has been a beat or a rhyme. In MC Lyte's "10% Dis" (1988), where the chorus repeats "Beat biter, dope style taker / Tell you to your face you ain't nothing but a faker," Lyte accuses MC Antoinette: "your beat, your rhyme, your timin'—all from me." See also MC Shan's "Beat Biter" (1986), addressed to LL Cool J, and Missy Elliott's "Beat Biters" (1999). In Eminem's early "Biterphobia" with Soul Intent, these lines cast biters as spurs to further creativity:

'Cause biters are fallin' head over heels
In love with every rhyme that I've said over reels

That's how I became paranoid
Chewin' my fingernails, pullin' my hair annoyed
'Cause every time you bit it was deliberate
So I'm forced to hit a little quicker with
An ultimatum I assault and slayed 'em
With rhymes and its ultimatum just to cultivate 'em
Energetic and imaginative,
Pronouns and verbs, predicates and adjectives
Will reach out and grab ya, 9 times outta 10
That's why I'm spilling one-of-a-kind rhymes out a pen

Although the anti-biting code of conduct remains a powerful force in the contemporary hip hop scene (see, e.g., Rugged Intellect's "Biter's Block" [2007]), the issue has been softened and perhaps clouded by an interest in tribute or, more neutrally, quotation and allusion. For example, the self-proclaimed hip hop DJ Pretty Lights incorporates sampled rap verses into his beats in songs like "Sunday School," following in the sampling tradition of other major producers while simultaneously using live instrumentation to fatten his samples.

7. This alludes to one of several variously remembered and interpreted episodes involving Jadakiss, and it typifies the pervasive insider particularity that inflects hip hop discourse. Probably more important, "ask 'Kiss'" puns on "ass kiss," which is completely relevant to Nas's point that Jay-Z needs to apologize.

8. This personalizes Jay-Z's poetics, shifting the focus from rap to rapper, and the expression is oxymoronic: pop is bad, of course, as in the case of "Hawaiian Sophie," while *shit* in hip hop slang often means "excellent material"—but not here.

9. For a relevant and accessible discussion of English stresses, pitch accents, and pauses, see Ann Wennerstrom, *The Music of Everyday Speech: Prosody and Discourse Analysis* (Oxford University Press, 2001), pp. 3–64. Along with the wholesale international export of rap, its poetics have been adopted into languages as diverse as French, Arabic, and Korean, which have different prominence markers than English. One of several methods of rapping in non-English languages has involved the *imitation* of English stress patterns—heard for example in PSY's viral "Gangnam Style" (2012).

10. Strictly speaking, alliterative verse was not simply "replaced" by rhyming verse. Quite a lot of late medieval poetry is heavily alliterative yet also contains end rhyme; metrically too, it seems to waver with uncertainty between a four-beat line and a syllabic line. The nexus of these competing prosodic figures of sound shows up as well in popular sayings which combine both rhyme and alliteration: "eeny meeny miny mo," "hickory dickory dock," and that mnemonic gem of use to all dyslexic handlers of wrenches and screwdrivers, "righty tighty, lefty loosy."

11. Playing the part of Dr. Carter, Lil Wayne says to his heart patient, "Now let me put some more Vocab in your I. V. / Here take this Vicodin"; in other words, to rap well you need a lot of different words and can't be dwelling on your pain. The well-known case of Nas studying the dictionary typifies rappers' efforts to expand their lexical arsenals. See VH1's *Behind the Music* http://www.youtube.com/watch?v=c-hqEAOKkJI

12. IPA symbols for initial English consonants are: [b] *b*ad, [d] *d*id, [f] *f*ind, [g] *g*ive, [h] *h*ow, [j] *y*es, [k] *c*at, [l] *l*eg, [m] *m*an, [n] *n*o, [p] *p*et, [r] *r*ed, [s] *s*un, [ʃ] *sh*e, [t] *t*ea, [tʃ] *ch*eck, [θ] *th*ink, [ð] *th*is, [v] *v*oice, [w] *w*et, [z] *z*oo, and [ʒ] *j*ust. (The only other basic consonant sounds are [ŋ] si*ng* and [ʒ] plea*s*ure.)

13. The early English alliterative poets typically linked words based only on their initial consonants, but they often made an exception of the **s**-clusters, treating [st], [sk], [sp], etc., as distinct sounds. Thus, they deployed at most about thirty different consonant chimes.

14. See in particular the evidence of Mel's clashing stressed, unstressed, and semi-stressed rhyme words in his iconic verse 5 in "The Message," discussed in Hot Vinyl.

15. This was known as *rich rhyme*, and was a device imported from French poetics along with rhyme generally. Especially brilliant is this couplet capping the first sentence of *The Canterbury Tales*:

The hooly blissful martir for to **seke**,
That hem hath holpen whan that they were **seeke**.

Our words for *seek* and *sick* sounded identical in Middle English. Chaucer is saying that the pilgrims seeking the shrine of St. Thomas à Becket are grateful for having been healed, but he also implies through the rhyme, that they are spiritually sick.

16. The standard blues tercet, with a rhyme scheme of AAa, repeats the same line twice, then rhymes on its end word in line 3. Some early ballads display similar patterns of rhyme-inducing line repetition. Such repetition is of course a feature of call and response, so it's not surprising that it recurs in the choruses of rap songs.

17. In the following lines from Lil Wayne's "A Milli," *bitch* is repeated seven times, but although the word's basic meaning remains constant its tone constantly shifts due to changes in context, grammar, and contiguous rhymes:

Never answer when it's private, damn I hate a shy bitch
Don't you hate a shy bitch?
Yeah I ate a shy bitch
She ain't shy no more, she changed her name to my bitch
Haha, yeah, nigga that's my bitch

So when she ask for the money, when you through don't be surprised, bitch
It ain't trickin' if you got it
But you like a bitch with no ass, you ain't got shit

Cee Lo's verse from Outkast's "Reset" contains a particularly effective use of sudden semantic shift. After three consecutive lines end ironically (with the interjection *right* in the sense of "don't you agree?"), a delayed fourth line proffers the straight moral adverbial sense:

Can't live forever, so have some fun, right?
Life's a bowl of candy, you can have one, right?
You can handle if tomorrow never comes, right?
You'll get used to singin' if only for one night,
But I intend to raise two daughters and a son right

18. In describing roaches and rats, Jay-Z's imagery follows Mel's lead ("broken glass everywhere"). Such concreteness is rare in rap lyrics but pervasive in the accompanying videos, which often depict peeling paint, rusty pipes, and overflowing trash cans to authenticate the rapper's underclass status. This pictorial tactic goes back to The Last Poets' first LP jacket, authenticating designs for blues and country singers, and self-promotional photography by Beat poets.

19. It would be a mistake, however, overly to dichotomize oral and literary rhyming. Although traditional literary poets and readers valued the restrictive order of full rhymes, being willing to admit even print-perfect (though not aurally rhyming) *eye rhymes* like *love/prove* into their sonnets and odes while shunning assonantal off rhymes like *love/done*, most modern literary poets, if they rhyme at all, regard full rhymes as passé. The great advantage of off rhymes is that can they make "flawed" connections—connections with disconnections, admitting irony and paradox into the game. The inventor of off-rhyme, Emily Dickinson, well understood its brutally honest lyricism:

I like a look of agony
Because I know it's **true**–
Men do not sham Convulsion,
Nor simulate, a **Throe**–
The Eyes glaze once—and that is Death–
Impossible to **feign**
The Beads upon the Forehead
By homely Anguish **strung**.

Meanwhile many early and contemporary songwriters who specialize in "dignified" forms, like hymns and national anthems, are as fastidious as pre-Modernist literary poets in preferring the decorum of full rhymes.

20. As in Booker White's "Fixin' to Die Blues" ("I'm lookin' funny in my **eyes**, and I believe I'm fixin' to **die**") or in many an early ballad:

> Half o'er, half o'er to Aberdour
> It's fifty fadom **deep**,
> And there lies guid Sir Patrick Spens
> Wi' the Scots lords at his **feet**.

21. Vowels being the cores of all syllables, the small-scale flow from syllable to syllable will be much smoother if the intervening consonants are *voiced* (e.g., **b**, **d**, **v**, **g**) rather than *unvoiced* (e.g., **p**, **t**, **f**, **k**). All vowels involve vibrating vocal chords when spoken normally, but whispering mutes these vibrations. Voiced consonants require vibrating vocal chords, and unvoiced consonants require non-vibrating vocal chords. By way of illustration, sing "amazing grace," where all three syllable boundaries are voiced, then sing "wretch like me," where the boundaries contain unvoiced consonants. Euphony and cacophony each depend largely on this difference.

22. See http://www.youtube.com/watch?v=FStoecoZa88: "I put my *orange, four-inch door hinge* in *storage* and ate *porridge* with *George*."

23. Keith Cowboy and Lovebug Starsky have each been credited with the term's prior use.

24. The seventeenth-century religious poet George Herbert made beautiful use of just such dissonance in "Denial." Up to its end, the fifth and last line of each stanza is an unrhymed and rhythmically flawed fragment: *And disorder, Of alarms, But no hearing* (twice), *Discontented*. The prayed-for spiritual resolution alters the mood tonally though its rhythms, concordant sounds, and concluding rhyme:

> O cheer and tune my heartless breast,
> Defer no time;
> That so thy favors granting my request,
> They and my mind may chime,
> And mend my rhyme.

25. These are grammatically identical Latinate morphemes, all meaning "with." That they range from an unstressed assonance to an unstressed full rhyme to a stressed full rhyme testifies to the thoroughness of Guru's tonal sophistication. Also alliterating on **c** is *'cause*, but it's questionable whether this would be noticed even by a careful listener.

26. The two-plus-two symmetry of these rhyme words also contrast (a) the redundancy of majoring in a major with (b) the progressive activity of making money.

27. Frequency of verbal repetition of course radically affects the quality of chorus rhymes, which are also somewhat denser than verse rhymes. Because choruses are often full of phrasal repetition as well as word repetition, the experience of rhyme echo is even greater than these statistics suggest. Frequency of verbal repetition also shifts rhyme's meta-meaning. In rap verses, each particular full rhyme or assonantal rhyme normally happens just once, whether it occurs in a singular rhyme event like couplet-binding, or in the course of an extensive rhyme chain. In rap verses, therefore, the experience of rhyme is fresh, in process, ephemeral—the opposite of chorus rhymes, where the repeated links are predictable and persistent.

28. The chorus in its longer form begins with this quatrain: "So, lick it now, lick it good / Lick this pussy just like you should / Right now, lick it good / Lick this pussy just like you should."

29. There are of course exceptions. Dido's chorus in Eminem's "Stan" adds a necessarily accumulating feminine pathos—sensitive, domestic, elegiac, grieving—which counters the pathetic, masculine fan worship dramatized in the verses. Drake's chorus in Lil Wayne's "She Will" contextualizes and complicates Wayne's playful erotic philosophizing through its voyeuristic recognition of the role of money, fame, and power in sexual exploitation.

30. It is possible, when listening to certain bars by Kendrick Lamar, to be fooled into thinking it's André 3000. To quote Busta Rhymes, "Yo, which muthafucka stole my flow? Eeny meeny miny moe" ("Woo Hah!! Got You All In Check"). But this jibe misses the point of the current hip hop trend toward tribute, a cultural indicator of the move toward classicism already evident in jazz.

31. Chaucer has one of his more ridiculous lovers rhyme *cinnamome* (mispronouncing *cinnamon*) with *Come hider, love, to me* (misplacing the stress), making the character seem both silly and stupid (meanwhile punning on sin and me). Byron quips in *Don Juan*: "But O ye lords of ladies *intellectual*, / Inform us truly, have they not *henpecked you all?*" In traditional poetics, such rhymes are known as mosaic rhymes because at least one of the two rhyming components is made of small pieces (two or more little words). Prior to the late 1980s, such rhymes were used almost exclusively to create comic effect. They figure broadly in Samuel Butler's mock-heroic *Hudibras* (1678) and in Ogden Nash's light verse. For an excellent exposition of the contributions rappers have made in liberating this kind of rhyming from its generic restrictions, see Baba Brinkman's TED talk: http://www.youtube.com/watch?v=8t4F83aHAXU

32. By the early 1990s, more and more couplets contain rhyme on the down beat, multisyllabic rhyme, rhyme on all four beats, and interlaces of two or more rhymes:

> Now what ya gonna **do** with the boy with **no talent,**
> **Using step** one and **step two** to keep the **show valid?**
> (Del, "Pissing on your Steps," 1991)

> I smoke on the mic like smokin' Joe Frazier
> The **hell raiser, raisin' hell** with the **flavor**
> (Inspectah Deck, "Protect Ya Neck," 1993)

In the following passage, Biggie deploys each of the above techniques, meanwhile extending two of his couplets into tercets:

> **Nigga, blue light, nigga, move like Mike, shit**
> Not to be **fucked with, motherfucker better duck quick**
> 'Cause me and my dogs **love to buck shit,**
> **Fuck** the **luck shit,** strictly **aim,**
> No aspirations to **quit the game**
> **Spit your game, talk your shit,**
> **Grab** *your* **gat, call** *your* **clique,**
> **Pass** that weed, **I got to light one,**
> **All** *them* niggas, **I got to fight one,**
> **All** *them* hoes, **I got to like one.** ("Notorious Thugs," 1997)

33. These rhymes are, in verse 1: <u>friend</u>, <u>again</u>, Benjamins, him, <u>trim</u>, begin, <u>pretend</u>, him <u>again</u>, when, <u>him</u>, then, then, <u>again</u>, sayin', <u>Christian</u>, Muslim, slee-pin', <u>jinn</u>, sin, <u>in</u>, when, <u>spin</u>, <u>trend</u>, Girlfriend, <u>again</u>, <u>genuine</u>, <u>gem</u>, <u>minimum</u>, defendin', 'em, Lauryn, <u>human</u>, been, <u>predicament</u>, million women in, <u>Penn</u>, be in, <u>European</u>, <u>Koreans</u>, <u>again</u>, <u>again</u>, <u>again</u>, <u>again</u>. And in verse 2: <u>men</u>, rims, Timbs, women, Him, men, in, <u>hooligans</u>, offend, <u>yen</u>, pretend, <u>men</u>, men, <u>basement</u>, men, men, <u>men</u>, when, women, <u>men</u>, silent men, -<u>violence men</u>, semen, men, win when <u>within</u>, win when <u>within</u>, win when <u>within</u>, <u>again</u>, <u>again</u>, <u>again</u>, <u>again</u>.

34. These rhymes prepare for and steady the entire multi chain: *dedicated, care, they, waste, case, basement, face, claiming, take, care, they, face, case, late, taking, breaking, hate.* Shifts and variations benefit from small sets: *mother, money, wonder; need and three; four, court, support.* Especially smart is the *Cristal, pretty, did a bid* sequence, carried over from verse 1's memorable *million women in Philly Penn.* Yes, these men are really appealing, at first!

35. This passage, with its increasingly cacophonous, dark, and complicated rhymes, is itself the complex core of verse 2. After verse 1, which offers warnings, encouragement, and sisterhood to the women, Lauryn first "dedicates" this one to the men—not all men, but the main man and his crew "More concerned with his

rims and his Timbs than his women / Him and his men come in the club like hooligans / Don't care who they offend…" No multis yet, just simple, spread out rhymes on men and women. And after our passage, the multis simplify into normal two-part forms, which further simplify into single rhymes. We hear—again, in apposition to men, but not all men, just these "men / The sneaky, silent men, the punk domestic-violent men / Quick to shoot the semen, stop acting like boys and be men." And the verse concludes with moral commentary to a doo wop background: "How you gonna win when you ain't right within? (x3) / Come again, come again, come again, come again." As in verse 1, the structure is chiastic.

36. Lauryn Hill's mastery of rhyme management, her ability to coordinate rhymes with different rhythms, registers, and syntax patterns to say things that need to be said, has influenced many of our more conscious emcees. Her formal impact was immediately evident in Senim Silla's verse 2 in Binary Star's "Reality Check" (2000). He maintains an **I**-vowel end rhyme throughout, packs other **I**-rhymes and contrasting rhymes in his lines, then increasingly blends these into continually shifting multis, varying the rhythm from line to line. What's different is the thematic point. Where Lauryn Hill deploys this technique to explore the sociology, psychology, and ethics of urban sexuality, Senim Silla displays it for the sheer fun of it and to demonstrate his amazing skills.

37. The great alliterative poet William Langland on occasion uses a similar grid patterning to align his alliterative collocations vertically:

Til **G**loton hadde y**gl**ubbed a **g**alon and a *gille*.
His **g**uttes bi**g**onne to **g**othelen as two **g**redy *sowes*

In these two lines with **g** alliteration, the grid matches Gloton with his guts, his gulping of ale with his stomach's rumbling (a g-g sequence!), his gallon (largest bar measure) with greed, and, contrastingly, his little jill (smallest bar measure, "one for the road") with the simile's huge sows.

38. Although the continual triplet syllable structure (strong-weak-strong) offers rhythmic consistency, One Be Lo counters this by shifting primary stress from the first to the third position and by varying the articulation of the "off" syllable between unstressed to secondarily stressed—as well as, occasionally, giving equal stress to both.

39. A precursor of this technique of fourth-through-first-position homophones may be found in verse 3 of Capital D's 1998 "Thinking Cap" ("I'm not content with your content / Tint on your window"), which also contains an impressive cluster of eponymous D-alliterations. Another type of homophonic rhyme innovation is found in verse 3 of All Natural's "Stellar" (2001), where all of the rhymes fall on *over-* or *under-*morphemes.

40. In certain literary forms like villanelles and sestinas, poetic lines also work through the same end-words. In Dylan Thomas's villanelle, "Do not go gentle into that good night," about alternative attitudes toward death, the key words are *night* and *light* ("Rage, rage, against the dying of the light"). In Elizabeth Bishop's "One Art," a villanelle about loss ("The art of losing isn't hard to master"), the key words are *master* and *disaster*. In Bishop's "Sestina," about the grief of an orphan girl living with her grandmother, the key words are *child*, *grandmother*, *house*, *stove*, *almanac*, and *tears*. In these literary poems, the cyclical order and timing of the key words are strictly controlled, which not at all the case in "Hold," but KRS-One's triad of *hold*, *hole*, and *whole* is comparably brilliant.

MODES AND GENRES

1. Rap music continues to be a vessel of political commentary, a function evident in rappers' critique of current events and often expressed in "fuck the institution" responses. This ethos underlies commentary on the police shooting of unarmed black males in Ferguson, manifested in songs like J. Cole's "Be Free" and the Game's "Don't Shoot," as well as pervasive disparaging of the Trump presidency. Less recent political commentary includes songs like Jay-Z's "Open Letter" and "99 Problems."

2. Many early DJs elected to use their skills as an honorific title. Aside from Herc, there were DJ Hollywood, DJ Spinderella, DJ Premier, and others. Probably because MCing was less prestigious than DJing during the early years, we don't find it used much as a title, with MC Shan and MC Lyte among the few exceptions.

3. In Sanskrit-based Indian languages, S can represent [s], [sh], or a retroflex sibilant not used in English. The spelling of KRS's adopted middle name *is* that of the God. In Sanskrit, R is a vowel, so the sequence KRS really does sound out Krishna's root syllable.

4. The logical culmination of this tendency is today's mumble rap, featuring rhythmically monotonous phrasal and verbal repetition, strongly auto-tuned and, in some cases, literally mumbled. For a 10-minute sampler of this popular, stoner dance genre, see "The Evolution of Mumble Rap [2011-2018]" (https://www.youtube.com/watch?v=VuRSOnrwPQA), featuring Future, Migos, Young Thug, et alia, with interspersed critical commentary by the likes of Grandmaster Caz and Snoop Dogg. See also Vin Jay's "Mumble Rapper vs Lyricist" (2019) (https://www.youtube.com/watch?v=1lmpGxQnjqk), a mock battle in which he plays the dual roles of a dull-witted Mumble Rapper strung out on Promethazine cough syrup ("Talkin' 'bout women and chains / Droppin' that shit that be numbin' your brain / It's fuckin' insane and they love it / We ain't gotta rap or noghin'") and a Lyricist defending and embodying traditional techniques: ". . . don't stack the syllables / You have to hit 'em with new

flows. . . . Like where's the word play and the metaphors at? / What y'all make, I could never call rap / Big L, Big Pun, I'ma get 'em all back / And you mumblin' motherfuckers had better fall back."

5. In this song, Tupac's timbre expresses a kind of street grit contrasting with Richie Rich's silkiness.

6. In "Ratha Be Ya Nigga," for example, the three verses become progressively more sexually explicit.

7. In verse 3, Weezy seems to be announcing his immanent retirement from the game about the same time that he's about to pass out:

> Can't nobody save yah
> New Orleans pride and savior
> Nigga this that Carter 5
> I feel like, feel like I'm on my final caper
> Uh, and I'm about to smoke one, pass out, OG kush, hashed out

8. In verse 2, KRS-One asserts his divine status as an avatar by claiming, "I came as Isis" and Moses, Solomon, Jesus, Harriet Tubman, Sojourner Truth, Nat Turner, Marcus Garvey, Bob Marley, and Malcolm X.

> Now I'm on the planet as the one called KRS
> Kickin' the metaphysical, spiritual,
> Tryin' to like get wit you, showin' you, you are invincible
> The Black Panther is the black answer for real
> In my spiritual form, I turn into Bobby Seale
> On the wheels of steel, my spirit flies away
> And enters into Kwame Ture

See also his *The Gospel of Hip Hop: The First Instrument* (2009).

9. The notion of a rapper as prophet or as God on the microphone is hardly exclusive to KRS-One. Many Jamaican rappers (in addition to the Jamaican expat KRS-One), alongside Muslim rappers (e.g., Jay Electronica), assert religious authority. The divine status of the rapper may have originated in an indigenous Jamaican religion known as Kumina. First recorded by the West in the seventeenth century, Kumina was and still is practiced by descendants of the Koromantyn people. When white slave-owners first recognized the religion, it aroused their suspicion because, while the Koromantyn slaves seemed never to collude, they were extraordinarily successful at organizing insurrections. One thought is that Kumina religious practices, like Haitian Voodoo, offered a secret forum in which slaves could cultivate solidarity and even openly criticize the slave-owners without interference. A musical and poetic tradition,

Kumina precedes and somewhat resembles Rastafarianism and, by extension, secular dance hall parties. In Kumina, a chanting religious leader accompanied by a troupe of drummers producing a highly repetitive beat, would direct a trance-like experience. The leader's authority derives from his direct revelation of a truth in stark opposition to the slave-owner's doctrines and practices, and a similar authority is claimed by a Rastafarian teacher or by a conscious rap MC. Whether or not socially conscious rappers are aware of these precedents, they gain credence by claiming to channel God. Their appeal to divine authority lends strong support to their critique of the "system," against whose crimes and immorality they hope to inspire public awareness and political action.

10. According to the annotation in Genius, the third floor in hospitals usually houses cancer and AIDS patients, which would make Weezy exceedingly ill (skillful), but the veracity of this assertion is hardly certain. However, by using the rhyme on *hospitals* Weezy is almost certainly reinterpreting Jay-Z's VA (the state) as Veterans Administration, making Jay-Z an old, wounded vet unlike his own young self.

11. Kendrick also drops the name of Grandmaster Flex in his first line of this song produced by No ID, but probably no insult is intended in that. Instead, "Flex" is invoked as the muse of bomb-dropping.

12. Eminem's interview at the BET network can be found at: http://www.youtube.com/watch?v=3JynehU6pVk. Another response to Kendrick's grand boast (which is always, generically, a highly lucrative career-booster) is to remain silent, above the fray. Big Sean and Jay Electronica, both dissed in this song, chose this course.

13. According to Aristotle's classification of modes, narrative falls between drama and lyric because unlike drama, which is *never* in the poet's voice, or lyric, which is *only* in the poet's voice, narrative is partly in the poet's voice, partly in the voices of his characters. The model here was Homer's epic poetry, full of memorable heroes (and gods and monsters) with very diverse origins, characters, actions, and speech patterns. If Aristotle had instead been responding to Aesop's *Fables*, or fairy tales, or the ballad tradition—or rap narratives—he would have had to rethink his definition. In truth, rap storytelling usually has a lot more in common with a fairy tale, ballad, or comic book episode than with more complex forms like the epic, romance, modern novel, or short story.

Probably the main factor behind the relative simplicity of rap storytelling is song length, itself determined largely by cultural factors. Short songs have been around for millennia, and many kinds of stories work better if they're brief, such as moral fables and bedtime stories. But many earlier cultures produced long chanted narratives. Today, most people today don't have time for novels, have never read an epic, and don't listen to symphonies or operas either. We have short attention spans. We want our stories and songs to be brief. We've been conditioned by market and other cultural forces to accept the brevity of the TV episode, the download, or the blog post as normal. Certainly, the relative simplicity of rap storytelling can't be attributed to its poetic form, for *Beowulf, Sir Gawain and the Green Knight,* and *Piers Plowman* were all composed in very similar four-beat meters. But those poems would have required hours of listening. We won't make time for that.

14. In the final lines of this passage, the rhymes on *robbin, job,* and *stop* are certainly there, but in the context of the over-determinate end-rhymes, they are barely heard.

15. Tech's artistic control over these relatively stark lines is evident too in his welding of the last couplets into an *aaa* quatrain, its frame rhymes on *brothers* and *mother* encapsulating the plot's central problem: the shooter's split loyalties.

16. *Say Word! Voices from Hip Hop Theater,* ed. Daniel Banks (University of Michigan Press, 2011), offers a good introductory anthology of hip hop theater work. Staged productions featuring characters rapping their dramatic roles, needless to say, dislocate rap from its normative venues for lyric performance—club, arena, or studio—and instead use rapping in place of other forms of theatrical speech, such as Shakespeare's blank verse, contemporary stage prose, or the Broadway musical song and recitative. Hip hop theater is often a relatively fringe phenomenon, presented in small venues by repertory companies, for example the critically acclaimed *Vietgone* (2016), or hosted by the New York Hip Hop Theatre Festival, founded Danny Hoch in 2000. The Chicago-based Q Brothers, a DJ and MC team, recently presented their *Othello: The Remix* at the Chicago Shakespeare Theater, at countless schools internationally, and at the Cook County Jail. For a review of this last performance, see http://www.dailymail.co.uk/news/article-2407032/Hip-hop-adaptation-Shakespeares-Othello-performed-prison.html. Other Shakespeare flips include the wildly successful *Bomb-itty of Errors* and Steve Bannon's *Coriolanus* rewrite (just a script).

17. There have been so many rap films that the category has almost become a separate genre: just google 25 Best Rap Films. Some of the films feature rap stars like Ice Cube, Ice-T, Common, Mos Def, and Eminem, but all of them feature "rap themes" like drugs, hustling, police violence, the challenge of coming of age in the ghetto, and often, MCing—as in *8 Mile.* Rap film releases correlate well with rap popularity, and rap films are themselves allied to the media's corporate aims. Just as videos can communicate an ancillary or even dominant sense of the meaning and flavor of a rap song, so rap films can communicate something—more or less true, more or less fictional—about the state of hip hop.

18. See for example the MTV production of *Carmen, a Hip Hopera* (2001), starring Beyoncé in the title role (No Man Can Resist Her), with other cast members including Mekhi Phifer (who costarred opposite Eminem in *8 Mile*), Mos Def, and Wyclef Jean.

19. See especially the dramatic monologues of Robert Browning, such as "My Last Duchess" and "Porphyria's Lover." Browning is often cited as the inventor of the dramatic monologue, but it goes back to Chaucer's *Wife of Bath's Prologue*. In any event, Giles Foden's enthusiastic comparison of Eminem with Browning is of interest: http://www.theguardian.com/books/2001/feb/06/poetry.features

20. All of the various videos of "Stan" feature Dido singing her chorus in living quarters where she interacts with Stan as his girlfriend, so the dominant popular interpretation of her otherwise, disembodied, non-dramatic chorus is just that—yielding three rather than two dramatic characters. The poignant lyricist and the woman screaming in the trunk of Stan's car become one and the same.

21. The references to Eminem's "97 Bonnie & Clyde," in which the speaker kidnaps his daughter and dumps her mother's body into the ocean, and to Uncle Ronnie, who committed suicide after a rejection, both work as disturbing forecasts in the song. Those to Skam and Rawkus merely display the fan's mastery of his idol's discography.

22. Complementing this very early verbal dramatic irony, we hear the sampled splash of Stan's car entering the river not only after verse 2 but following Dido's second intro chorus, less than ten seconds before "at the bottom."

23. Eminem rapping as Stan and Eminem rapping as Slim Shady have distinctly different stress and rhyme patterns over the beat. Stan favors an unconventional rapping pattern, frequently choosing not to rhyme on the four beat (thirty-five percent of his lines don't). In addition, his lines often have unrhyming offbeat stresses, and he frequently packs four extra stresses in the line (fifty percent of his lines do). In contrast to Slim, he rarely makes use of exactly two or three (only six percent of his lines do). While Slim also raps with four extra stresses in a line about fifty percent of the time, he incorporates significantly more rhyme. Unlike Stan, for whom lines either have none, one, or four extra stresses, Slim's stress patterns distribute fairly evenly over no-extra-stress (twenty-five percent), one-extra-stress (sixteen percent), and two-extra-stress (seven percent) lines. These tendencies, coupled with the fact that Stan's rhymes move towards the front of the line and Slim's rhymes move towards the back, produce a substantial rhythmic difference mimetic of each persona's mental state. While Slim's varied style manifests emotional flexibility and genuine concern, Stan's rigidity and extreme rhythmic and rhyming patterns create a tenor of repressed volatility, one in which the rhythms themselves are driving erratically towards the end of the line—just as he does in the end.

24. Paulsen, M, "'Hamilton' Heads to Broadway in a Hip-Hop Retelling," *New York Times,* July 12, 2015.

25. This is historical fiction. Angelica Schuyler had two brothers and was already married when she met Alexander Hamilton.

26. https://genius.com/Lin-manuel-miranda-alexander-hamilton-lyrics

27. We have re-lineated Hamilton's verse from the Genius site in order to preserve not only the rhymes but our Founding Father's strict adherence to the couplet form.

28. Here we evidently disagree with Adam Bradley, who in his *Book of Rhymes* begins his chapter on "Storytelling" (nestled between "Style" and "Signifying") with this sentence: "Storytelling distinguishes rap from other forms of popular culture."

VERSES, SONGS, AND ALBUMS

1. The interplay between the two senses of time resembles that between a melody's focal note or theme and its complementary rhythms and harmonies—each of which may be temporally in sync, syncopated, or modified by augmentation, diminution, or inversion (in relation to the melodic trope). So long as the musical theme retains its defining notes and sequences, it behaves like the rhyme texture of a verse or, sometimes, of a song. Just as the musical themes among individual variations are linked by means of distinctive patterns, the verse's rhyme sound weave seemingly arbitrarily related concepts and their contingent semantic commitments together, regardless of the speed or phrase-grouping in which the relevant themes are delivered. This cerebral experience, coupled with the more corporeally engaging rhythm-plane, is always in juxtaposition with our basic sense of time (*lub-dub*), and produces a new sense of time involving each of the discrete components of the musical experience.

2. Although one might reasonably argue that all rap songs make sense within the context of their culture, we are referring here specifically to normative logical "randomness" or incoherence—or alternatively, expressionistic freedom—which pervades some rap verses, particularly boasts.

3. That is, the kind of freestyle that is not pre-written or recited. An Old School freestyle, by contrast, was normally understood to be a written rap song not intended to be recorded.

4. See the Introduction for references to the essential orality of rap and to the analogy between the recording of "Rapper's Delight" on vinyl and the transcription of oral-formulaic epics—media shifts which immediately opened the poetry up to new styles and structures. A comparison more immediate to hip hop would be the recording in Jamaica of Ras Michael's Nyabinghi drumming and chanting from the 1960s. Its style is highly repetitive, with anaphoristic messages as simple as "Jah Lives," and in a non-vinyl, communal performance environment it might have been sustainable for decades. Once recorded, however, and with future releases in sight, the impulse to sophisticate the instrumentation and the beat (in the direction of reggae) was inexorable, and reggae artists such as Burning Spear and Culture in turn incorporated call

and response into their albums (e.g., on Burning Spear's "Slavery Days," in *Marcus Garvey* [1975], with the repeated call tag, "Do you remember the days of slavery?")

In rap music, the call tag remains a vestige in regional boasts and contemporary posse rap, but is virtually absent from more polished studio productions post-Afrika Bambaataa. Rappers like Ice Cube, Snoop Dogg, and Kendrick Lamar did and still will call out mid-performance for the audience to complete a tag line. So do cypher participants prior to beginning their verses, as heard in Funkmaster Flex's 1997 live freestyle with Biggie, Tupac, Shyiem, and Big Daddy Kane, where Tupac says "Where all my dogs at!" before starting his verse, or in the G. O. O. D. Music cypher on the 2010 BET awards ("Good music, good music, good music"). It is also possible to think of tags like Lil Wayne's "I tell her," opening both verses in "She Will," as the lyrical relics of call and response, with the rapper giving voice to both parts. We may recall that the syntax of each sentence in The Last Poets' "When the Revolution Comes" opens with anaphoristic repetition of the title phrase as a subordinate clause, followed by new and different main clause.

5. Since verses are rapped, not sung, and since rapping is the essential performance style of rap poetry, the term "song" is odd on the face of it, but it suits the genre's essential musicality and conforms conveniently to market norms within the music industry. Considered as musical commodities, hip hop performances are quintessentially songs. As rap migrated from streets and dance halls into recording studios under the supervision of producers, its ephemeral wit was required to fuse with memorable thought, and rapping itself was required to be complemented by choral singing. By way of illustration, Jay-Z's poetic progression from rapper to musical artist can be traced along the timeline from *The Black Album* to *Magna Carta . . . Holy Grail*. In the recent past, there has been some pushback. Kanye West's "New Slaves," for example, omits choruses altogether, leaving more room for the beat.

6. Many of these names are obscure but, overall, they follow a rough chronological order. Keith Wiggens, an original member of Grandmaster Flash and the Furious Five, died of AIDS in 1989, and Scott La Rock, the DJ with Boogie Down Productions, was murdered in 1987. This pairing is indicative: it's not all about homicide. Again, Biggie was shot, but Killa Black died of depression and suicide.

7. As Guru recounts the lives of those who died in the black community, he confronts its utmost possibility, its death, and this confrontation results in his questioning community's values. Verse by verse, Guru pursues what it means to live meaningfully, with substantive commitments. He ultimately argues against a livelihood "outside the system" (i.e., hustling and gang-banging) and for a life devoted to enlightenment.

8. For a similarly conflated analogy between street violence and emceeing, see Ice-T's "Mic Contract."

9. Guru also confronts the philosophical purpose of evil in the world, motivat-

ing it to count in favor of an authentically lived life—like that which he has made for himself using music.

10. Always grounded in the black community, hip hop often remains fixed and even fixated on community myths as well as social conditions, the myth of the invincible dealer or pimp being but one of many. Guru's tactful tactical brilliance here lies in the way he pays homage to this fantasy reality while moving beyond it. If we think of hip hop not simply as community-formed but as resisting the culture surrounding it, then Guru's sequencing of verses makes another kind of sense: by extending centripetally out from the community he resists classic rock, which invariably tries to promote global messages through seemingly "universal" emotions, not those of lived experience.

11. Allusions to the slave trade were a common trope in Old School rap. For Guru, who intends to confront social issues and inspire black impoverished youth into honest livelihood, the slave trade motivates a didactic rhetoric. This bears little resemblance Biggie's non-PC treatment in "Gimme the Loot" from *Ready to Die* (1994):

> Nigga, you ain't got to explain shit
> I've been robbin' motherfuckers since the slave ships
> With the same clip and the same four-five
> Two point-blank, a motherfucker's sure to die
> That's my word, nigga even try to bogart
> Have his mother singing "It's so hard . . ."

Today's references take a stance superficially similar to Guru's but without either his political bite or his sense of decorum. In "Oceans (feat. Frank Ocean)" from *Magna Carta . . . Holy Grail*, Jay-Z actually compares his own socioeconomic position with that of his enslaved ancestors: "I crash through glass ceilings / I break through closed doors." Through the verse, he simultaneously laments his forefathers' suffering as he expresses gratitude for the opportunities and rich rewards available to him. His lament is echoed in the chorus by Frank Ocean as he sings about the brutal slave voyages that brought each of their ancestors to the Americas. To further emphasize his respect to his ancestors and detestation of slavery, Jay-Z distances himself from America's "discoverer" and "Founding Father" yet he pledges his allegiance to a successful rapper because without Biggie, there would have been no Jay-Z ("Only Christopher we acknowledge is Wallace / I don't even like Washingtons in my pocket").

In his role as capitalist historian, Jay-Z avoids Guru's didacticism, praising freedom's opportunities rather than philosophizing about systematic oppression. Kanye West similarly, rather than focusing on questions pertinent to ethics, preaches on crises in consumerism, using Slave Trade allusions in order to gain rhetorical traction. In

"New Slaves," (*Yeezus*, 2013), Kanye attempts a prescriptive takeaway. Criticizing the willing addicts of consumerism as new slaves, Kanye uses history as a forward-looking tool—abstracting enslavement to mean "blind compliance with any authority," human or material.

12. All of the Google citations of "Mary Coleman," "Robert N'Blangio," or "Runy Manuel" [sic] point to this song.

13. For intonational "punctuation," see again Wennerstrom (2001), pp. 17–45. The falling pitch accent means, basically, "I'm done saying what I was saying," and can either invite response or simply conclude a point. If it were punctuated textually, it would take a period.

14. The comma, dash, and periods in Snoop's lyrics here are added by us, unauthorized, intended only to indicate the actual linguistic pauses inside and framing his closed couplets. MCs rarely publish their lyrics, and transcriptions by others typically remain unpunctuated, preserving their non-literary performance mode.

15. Although more complex forms such as the *ababcc* sestet, rhyme royal (rhyming *ababbcc*), the *ababbabcc* octave, and the Spenserian stanza (*ababbcbcc*) have been used as narrative vehicles within the English literary tradition, quatrains have always been the forms of choice for popular ballads, hymns, and stand-alone songs (like "Happy Birthday"). The loosest quatrain form is the ballad stanza rhyming *abcb*, whereas hymns tend to be composed in stricter *abab* quatrains. Occasional *abba* quatrains also exist, but are relatively rare. The monorhyming *aaaa* quatrain is also found in many a ballad and popular song. In world poetry, the quatrain is by far the most pervasive stanza form and musical structure. Crossing linguistic and cultural boundaries, its appeal is fundamentally human.

16. Typography is an index of this difference. Literary quatrains are always printed with white space between them, but couplets are not—except in the case of free verse couplets, which can only be expressed and detected by means of intervening white space.

17. As discussed in Hot Vinyl, *abcb* quatrains are used by Wonder Mike and Big Bank Hank in "Rapper's Delight," and other evidence exists of there having been an acceptable alternative form to four-beat couplets. Having only three stresses (and one beat-length pause) in lines 2 and 4, however, those quatrains differed metrically from the ones used by more modern rappers, which are always comprised of four-beat lines. Rappers like Eve and André 3000 can maintain their flow even as they veer away from couplet rhyming to create extra rhythmic temporalities and delayed thematic links. Wonder Mike and Big Bank Hank sound more like they are rapping stanzas from Old Folk ballads.

18. Vordul's verse in Cannibal Ox's "Painkillers" (2001) begins also with a problem-summarizing quatrain: "Right here <u>trapped</u> in the **box**, thinkin' / <u>Rap's</u> all I **got**, <u>smoke</u>

too much **pot** / <u>Bones</u> with <u>chromes</u> twisted in **knots** / <u>Cold</u> vein with thoughts bubbling **hot**." Here the *aaaa*-organization is somewhat modulated by two internal rhyme sounds, the more dominant of which gives a slant echo to the end rhymes. This off-rhyme in turn controls a second quatrain—not only the end rhymes but numerous internal rhymes as well: "**Stoned** in the bedroom writin' this **poem** / Off the **phone** caught a head rush, **smoke** clouded my **dome** / At the end of my **ropes** writing these **notes** / **Hopin'** to **float** on what is <u>bullshit, pull spliffs</u> **flowin'** to **ghosts**." The problem, obviously, is snowballing addiction.

19. Another key non-rhyme caps line 60: "myself and Big Boi." The point of the phrase may be that Outkast's two emcees "rhyme" with nothing except each other, professionally. A similarly non-rhyming "idea rhyme" at lines 96–97 links André with Erykah Badu at their initial meeting. Backed by the internal rhymes of *singer, thing,* and *similar,* their erotically charged connection is expressed through synecdoche, *her hair* and *my dreads,* not yet uncovered:

And on stage is a singer with something on her hair
Similar to the turban that I covered up my dreads with

20. Over the course of his blistering ten-minute December 2017 freestyle on Hot 97, Black Thought superbly controls the *aaaa* quatrain schema, departing from it only a handful of times: https://www.youtube.com/watch?v=prmQgSpV3fA

21. Considering the prevalence of triadic structures in pop music and the relative abundance of three-verse rap songs—a cultural preference not unusual in other genres, periods, and languages—it may be that humans share a preference for triadic rhythms. Nevertheless, we seem to think more easily in dualities than in simple this-that-and-the-other thing series, or in hierarchies like good-better-best or in dialectical triads of thesis, antithesis, synthesis. Rap songs may be triadic, but they are rarely systematically so, and meanwhile rap lines and couplets are strongly dyadic. Of the two traditional sonnet forms, the two-part Italian option (octave plus sestet), while harder to rhyme in, is more conducive to basic love-logic. It favors processes like quest and discovery, desire and fulfillment, or being lost at sea and finding a safe harbor (in her, she being also the North Star). The English or Shakespearean option, essentially triadic with three quatrains and a concluding couplet, is easier to rhyme in but not so useful to think in. Shakespeare's perfect Sonnet 73 is often used in Intro to Poetry classes to illustrate how his triadic form works, but in fact most of his sonnets display a two-part logic, with the two initial quatrains combining to make a longer initial point, resolved in the final quatrain and couplet.

22. Who gets the last word matters. In "Reality Check," Senim Silla's spectacular chain rhyming seems to trump One Be Lo's superior wit; in "Life's a Bitch," AZ's

impressive flow is overshadowed by Nas's inspirational ethos; in "HYFR" Drake's rhythmic flexibility seems subordinate to Wayne's witty predation.

23. Although Drake's chorus are lineated into twelve lines in Genius and some other internet editions, with these lines constituting a concluding quatrain—

> Do it for the realest niggas in the fuckin' game right now she will, yeah
> Do it for the realest niggas in the fuckin' game right now she will, she will, she will
> Maybe for the money and the power and the fame right now she will, she will, she will
> Do it for the realest niggas in the fuckin' game right now she will, she will, she will

—this passage clearly forms a musical and metrical octave, and we regard one other tag as a line unit, yielding a total of seventeen.

24. Although *pussy-popping* in its earliest usages could refer to the female orgasm, its primary sense in recent slang refers to a stripper's teasing, eventually "orgasmic" dance move. Both senses are at play in this song, of course, symbolically in the dancer's moves and in the spectators' desires and metaphorically as suggested by Weezy in his rhymes, "Eat her 'til she *cry*, call that *wine and dine*."

25. We here follow the common interpretation as expressed by Rap Genius and articulated in a fan-supplied Vimeo video directed by Jeff "Echo" Reyes. However, this song could be interpreted to take place in any voyeuristic setting, say, an exclusive party, or even could be stretched as far as to be an allegory for the rap game and Wayne's place in it.

26. In this respect, "She Will" flips the entire hip hop sub-tradition of party fun and its attendant sexual conquest. The crowd noises, the sounds of whooping or clinking glasses—sounds typically amplified on rap tracks—here are, such as they are, barely audible. She will . . . but maybe she won't.

27. The skit was an integral part of *Hustler's Convention*, providing narrative content and atmosphere to each of the verses. Its skits were both musical and verbal, containing dialogue as well as sound effects. These features often served to articulate an album's thematic delineations. After Jalal's work, however, skits were not popular again until the early to mid-nineties. They returned in De La Soul's 1989 album *3 feet High and Rising*, where they mostly provided comedic effect. But sometimes skits function like mega-samples at the scale of the album (or song), setting a mood or creating a social space for a sequence/series of songs. For example, Kanye West's early work makes use of many skits, and he continued to do so up through *My Beautiful Dark Twisted Fantasy*. Some notable contemporary skit-artists are Outkast, Eminem, Kendrick Lamar, The Roots, Lil Wayne, Drake, and Nicki Minaj. Today, producer

trends are shifting as major artists like Kanye West choose to omit skits from their albums. We theorize this is because the rap audience is far better informed as to the implicit meanings of the lyrical content than it had been in the nineties and also much less likely to purchase concept albums, where skits seem to offer the most rhetorical mileage.

28. Significantly, he contrasts his own virility with everyone else's, but not with Method's: "And niggaz know they soft like a Twinkie filling." At least it's funny.

29. It's worth noting the absence of such luminaries as Melle Mel, Rakim, and Nas from Biggie's history of hip hop, presented in verse as loose reminiscences of a boy turning adult. The Rappin' Duke was a joke act parodying John Wayne in the role of a rapper. Salt-N-Pepa were of course great rappers, but here they seem more like sex symbols in that they end up "up in the limousine" with Heavy D, a minor rapper more famous for his bling than for his rhymes. Most of the other names are those of DJs, but Lovebug Starsky (whose name, incidentally, packs a four-stress b-verse) was an MC primarily known for clowning and party cheerleading. Biggie may here be accentuating the extent to which hip hop has matured, but it may also be that setting himself among *this* set offers a kind of ego boost while also freeing himself from the social responsibility that Mel's name might have invoked. "Party and Bullshit" is particularly relevant in this context.

STYLE

1. Although a single beat pattern underlies most verses, rappers sometimes cover the bridge between two (often thematically related) beat patterns, for example in "Respiration" by Black Star or in "Black Skinhead" by Kanye West.

2. "Amazing Grace" has become so standardized as a spiritual classic associated especially with funerals and memorials that it can be piped by a bagpiper, its words and themes implicit in its melody, accented by the drone pipes. The perverse inverse of "Amazing Grace" crystallized in a rap song is Chief Keef's "I Don't Like," whose "verses" simply repeat the hook's single rhyme and monotonous rhythm. The stoner "rapping" is so predictable, banal, inane, and uninteresting that its theme, a litany of dislikes, cannot develop at all in the course of the song. On his collaboration album *G. O. O. D. Music Presents*, Kanye West in fact treats Chief Keef's "verse" component as a sample, superimposing normatively variable verses over it.

3. Flaunting an academic or technical diction may boost an MC's reputation for rhyming skills, but it's restricted by the need to relate to as broad an audience as possible, including those potentially less learned. In addition, long, sophisticated words can often get in the way of a smooth flow and the illusion of spontaneity. Many rappers, then, consciously strive to balance relatively rare polysyllabic words with com-

mon mono- or disyllabic ones, and particularly revealing in this regard is their use of polysyllabics to anticipate humbler yet more clever rhyme resolutions, in multis formed of common words:

> The new moon rode high in the crown of the <u>metropolis</u>
> Shinin', like who on <u>top of this</u>? (Mos Def, "Respiration")

> So I can rip through the <u>ligaments</u>, put the fuckas in a bad <u>predicament</u>
> Where all the foul <u>niggas went</u> (The Notorious B. I. G., "Warning")

This technique is favored over twin polysyllabic rhyming. Rappers using this technique also exhibit a tendency to load rhyming rhythms into the first line of a given line pair for rhetorical effect. When a pair of lines has three or four rhymes, it is likely that we'll hear an extra stress packed near the end of the first line. This rhythm of rhyme accentuates the second line's end rhyme, effectively turning it into a punch rhyme.

4. At this point, it may be useful to ponder the vast appeal of these objects to various audiences (including white suburban teenagers) during the 1980s, 1990s, and 2000s. It may also be useful to ponder an alternative still-life tradition that proliferated in during the seventeenth, eighteenth, and nineteenth centuries in England and in colonial and postcolonial America: the burnished silver platter piled with shot quail, grouse, pheasants, and hares. Sometimes this platter is depicted on an interior table along with servants or slaves and an attendant, a well-fed setter, looking on. And, not to forget the fruit, it may be useful to ponder our contemporary production of glass grapes, onyx pears, and the like. Who produces and markets these objects? Who buys and displays them? Why? Here we are also reminded of style and its connection to what is known as lifestyle—a potentially fascinating, weird, amusing, and possibly humbling branch of inquiry.

5. Underground rappers are often quick to denounce *wack* MCs making Gs. A particularly outspoken example is Hopsin, who considers himself and many other underground rappers as good as, if not better than, Kendrick Lamar, and says so publicly on Sway's radio show: http://www.youtube.com/watch?v=PTUSJAP15Qc

6. An example of these rappers' Old School counterparts would be Run and DMC, who, while important for the genre's establishment within the mainstream, had redundant styles: between the two of them, in "It's Like That" and "Christmas in Hollis," they use only eleven-line types. *MTV! Raps* promoted them to represent the rap genre over more progressive and sophisticated poets like Melle Mel. In parallel, *New York Times* has recently promoted the poetically minimalistic YG and Sage the Gemini as the faces of rap to come.

7. Not all rappers crave the mainstream. For some, the thematic dumbing down and stylistic conformity are just not worth it. For others, following the flock violates

the self-stylized and empowered ethos of holding the microphone. For a special few like Yasiin Bey, the requirements of celebrity status go against his dedication to artistic collaboration and community representation. And for some who don't "make it," it's just because they didn't make it.

8. As we mentioned in Rhythm, until Rakim's 1987 *Paid in Full* and N. W. A.'s 1988 *Straight Outta Compton,* variation in line patterns depended on varying dip lengths. Even as late as 1984, the Cold Crush Brothers' lines seldom feature extra stresses, extra rhymes, or enjambment. If there were extra stresses at all, they tended to be deployed in the second half of the line, most commonly in the fifth dip.

9. Rhyming off-beat stresses were present though exceptionally rare in early rap. Less than eight percent of our pre-1987 lines feature any of the eight types of rhyming off-beat stress rappers were using at the time. The most common positions for these loaded syllables were in dips three, four, five, and six—likely because they offered a kind of semantic and rhythmic balance to the rhythmically denser a-verse. After 1987, the conventional placement of rhyming off-beat stresses becomes more common, and rappers eventually invented twelve more types of lines that incorporated rhyming off-beat stressed syllables. On the other hand, *unrhyming* off-beat stressed syllables were even rarer prior to 1987, with only one instance appearing in our database. Its positioning between dips three and four suggests that it was used to produce a metronomic line atypical of four-beat meter. Since 1987, however, these lines have become more common, although they seldom occur except where either the extra stress is buffered by one or two unstressed syllables on each side or where neither of the adjacent beated stresses are rhyming (proximally).

10. The normally (over seventy-five percent) short length of these initial dips in early rap corresponds to the integrity of the line and half-line units, which were normally enclosed by pauses. When longer initial dips did occur, they created a strikingly different rhythm, and that is their purpose—to add variety in a minimally varied line. Similar "long" dips serve to vary the flow in *Beowulf* and in some other classical systems of oral performance poetry. Literary critics refer to them as *anacrusis.* In music, we call them *pickup notes.* All such syllables or notes fill the pocket before the initial beat or downbeat, and as such they are typically subject to relatively strict metrical/ musical constraints.

11. Unstressed rhymes are non-existent in pre-1987 rap. Even today, they remain relatively rare: under five percent of post-1987 lines in our database include unstressed rhyme that can confidently be regarded as purposeful. Unstressed rhymes occur accidentally and go unnoticed (e.g., the unstressed assonance in "they remain relatively **rare**"). Even when they are meant to have poetic impact, they remain in danger of not being consciously heard, precisely because they lack stress.

12. Jay-Z's stylistic tendencies have changed decisively over time, as can be

readily heard if we juxtapose "Can't Get Wit That" (http://www.youtube.com/watch?v=pu4UG8uLHZ8) from 1994 with his new work in *Magna Carta . . . Holy Grail*. In the former, Jay-Z sounds very much like a speech-effusive rapper: in the latter, he sounds definitively percussive-effusive.

13. Publishing his *Rap Music and the Poetics of Identity* in 2000, Krims could reasonably argue for the existence of four discrete genres (party rap, mack rap, and jazz/Bohemian rap including "conscious rap"), and reality rap, linking each genre with a particular musical style, flow, and set of topics (pp. 46–92). In delineating these types, Krims admits the existence of hybrid genres such don rap, which fuses the gangsta variety of reality rap with mack rap, and he fully acknowledges the fluidity of these categories. With respect to flow, Krims associates the "sung" style with party rap and with its dumbed-down, R&B-infused cousin, mack rap. Krims characterizes jazz/Bohemian rapping (epitomized by A Tribe Called Quest and De La Soul) as eclectic, infused with both "sung" and "percussive-effusive" styles. Reality rap, according to Krims, is the primary site for edgy, complex, discordant beats as well as for the "speech-effusive" style of flow. Although we regard Krims's taxonomy of genres as outdated, we admire and are indebted to his work on style, especially insofar as it describes the relationships among style, thematics, and cultural function. To quote Lupe Fiasco's song title (quoting Louis Sullivan), "Form Follows Function" (2012).

14. We distinguish battle rapping from freestyling. Freestyle, as it is used over the course of hip hop, has often been misleadingly labeled. We acknowledge the definitional mess and include anything from its early usage in our scope, referring to prewritten verses not on an album, and the contemporary street-cypher usage, i.e., rapping off the dome.

15. Poetic prowess is reflected by even our crudest of stats. If we consider all the theoretical permutations of *parent strings*—which include four-beated stresses (either rhyming or not), an expected caesural pause (either realized or not), and an expected end pause (either realized or not)—these total sixty-four. Within these combinations, however, MCs can also insert rhyme into the dips, giving rise to as many actual combinations as eurhythmy and musical time permit. Using positional rhyme variance as a lens for stylistic versatility, we can focus on three famous rap battlers: Biggie vs. Tupac, Jay-Z vs. Nas (and fighting on the sidelines, Mos Def), and Lil' Kim vs. Nicki Minaj. Biggie dominates Tupac in this realm, deploying eighty different rhyme strings compared to Tupac's measly forty. Biggie uses secondary stresses in all of the dips, and he uses one particularly avant-garde type (the metronomic line) that Tupac never would have used. The Jay-Z, Nas, and Mos Def battle is somewhat less clear cut, partly because after Nas responds to Jay-Z's "Takeover," Jay-Z continues his relentless public attacks despite Nas's clear demonstration of stylistic superiority in "Ether." Not only does Nas appropriate and ridicule Jay-Z's rhymes, but he does so using thirty

more rhyme strings. In so doing, he manages to pack up to three extra stresses in a line, as well as creating an attack-rhythm relying on rhymes before the first beat. Mos Def, meanwhile, demonstrates at least equivalent control to that of Jay-Z, with sixty types of lines of his own. Unlike Jay-Z, but like Nas, he also successfully packs two to three extra stresses per line. The battle between Lil' Kim and Nicki Minaj is even less clear cut, although it is revealing that Nicki Minaj marshals Eminem's assistance in "Roman's Revenge" whereas Lil' Kim raps twin verses of fifty-seven and twenty-nine lines, ironically assisted only by a sample from Nicki Minaj. That said, Nicki Minaj's range of rhyme strings is slightly larger than Lil' Kim's.

16. Melodic rapping, exemplified by Bone Thugs, is not melodic in the normative Western sense. It shares affinities with other chanting traditions such as Gregorian plainsong, Torah recitation, and Vedic chant, where tonal variation is a structural feature of the line itself rather than any line-grouping, such as a quatrain stanza.

17. Here the comedy seems clearly intended, rhetorically, to mitigate the tough personal info Biggie has just volunteered about his parents' separation and his own subsequent sexual "issues."

18. For a demonstration of this claim, YouTube offers several clips of listener-response criticism. Our favorite is: https://www.youtube.com/watch?v=ND63Tbr6_2w

19. Rakim's stylistic departure from his contemporaries is quite readily seen in our statistics. Rakim's "I Know You Got Soul" itself has forty-one different line rhyme patterns (and that's if we *only* count his beated stresses and off-beat stressed rhymes) over the course of just ninety lines. And other differences are in play. Rakim's exemplary use of off-beat stress and unstressed rhyme in the second half of the line (most often in dip 6) is perhaps his greatest innovation: the destabilization of b-verse rules, the manifestation of which can be seen by contrasting Rakim and his predecessors' average dip lengths. As mentioned, Mel's a-verse housed most of the syllables. By contrast, by using pauses in the middle and second half of the line, Rakim was able to pack his second, fourth, fifth, and sixth dips with extra syllables—his second and fourth dips in "I Know You Got Soul" most often contain two syllables, and his fifth and sixth dips, more often than not, hold two. If we simply group this pattern into pairs of duple dips, we see that the dips themselves, on average, are similar in length, but one of the halves of the phrase is significantly more varied. For dip 1 and 2, dip 2 receives more than twice as many syllables. For dip 3 and 4, dip 4 almost always has more syllables. Dips 5 and 6 have similar lengths, but dip 5 receives more syllables. Using this grouping, we see that the rhythmic backloadedness of the syllabic stream in dips 1–4 is compensated by a more evenly loaded dip 5 and 6. This is similar to bebop soloing, where soloing *around* the beat would happen early in the phrase and would be stabilized by a resolving rhythmic trope *in* key, and *in* time with the musical background.

20. MC Ren, Dr. Dre, and Ice Cube all differ somewhat in style, yet each deploys

a percussive-effusive style. Ice Cube, who opens "Fuck Tha Police" deploys an a-verse similar to Rakim's, but makes dips 2 and 5 longer than Rakim does, and by doing so, modifies the emphasis-structure of the b-verse: dip five would be significantly longer and more varied than dip six. This shift meant that b-verse extra rhyming stresses (over three-fifths of which happen in the b-verse) would almost always be heard in the fifth dip. MC Ren, next up in the song, seems to have the most in common with Old School styles, although this may be to contrast Ice Cube. MC Ren's line types are limited, and at most, he adds one extra stress and elides one pause in a line. Dr. Dre, whose verse is arguably the most complex in the song, follows him. Dre's verse frequently has as many as six stresses and six rhymes per line. This ferocious display of rhyme is complemented by a rhythmic consciousness of caesural elision: over twenty-five percent of his lines with four rhymes forego the medial caesura. In combination, 1987 and 1988 would offer sixty-six new types of lines.

21. The impact of these stylistic innovations was so strong that it began a contest between East and West Coast rappers and listeners, who both aimed to claim the percussive-effusive style for their own, leading rappers to stylize themselves further in the future.

22. By 1994, there are 128 types of lines (only accounting for beated stresses and stressed-rhyme) and the fifth dip would continue to have the most extra stresses and rhymes.

23. If there were multiple extra stresses, they would usually fall in dips 2 or 5, suggesting the essential musicality of the rapper's conformity to our innate *sense of beat*. Extra stresses, in effect, compete with the basic rhythm, but never challenge it.

24. For a spectacular example of "speech-effusive" variations that depart distinctly from "percussive-effusive" style, see "Crossroads" by Bone Thugs-N-Harmony. In just that song, Bone Thugs displays 131 different rhyme patterns (again only accounting for extra rhyming stresses and stresses on the beat). If one were to consider as well the rhythmic variation that Bone Thugs achieves with pitch and intonation, this number might multiply as large a factor as two.

25. Run-DMC, for example, rap together in party music. Because they rap together, their patterns are relatively predictable, since they need to keep *in* time together. Additionally, their music's *function*, party jamming, might contribute to this predictability. Their average dip lengths are extremely regular. In "It's Like That," they never have a syllable in dips 1, 3 or 4, and they always have one in dip 5 and 6, and they always have two in dip 2. Just like Run-DMC, when A Tribe Called Quest's Q-Tip and Phife Dawg rap together, they also have extremely regular rhythmic patterning: in "Sucka Nigga," dips 1, 3, and 6 never have syllables, every dip 4 has one, every dip 5 has two, and every dip 2 has three.

26. Slug from Atmosphere has stated, "I don't want to be just another emcee who

rhymes astral projections with gastric infections." His rhythmic tendencies starkly contrast the stereotypical Old School. In "Modern Man's Hustle" and "GodLovesUgly," from *God Loves Ugly*, his average dip lengths from dip 1–6, unrounded, are: 2, 1, 0, 2, 3, and 0 syllables.

27. Kanye West, Lupe Fiasco, and Common dominate contemporary rap style in Chicago, and today's newer Chicago rappers include quickly rising Chance the Rapper (*Acid Rap, Coloring Book*) and Lil Herb, both of whom, however, appeal primarily to college-age fans.

28. Although at first impression the differences appear minute, over the course of the line, the addition of a "half," one, or two average extra syllables has a substantial impact on style. Additionally, the use of averages here reveals just how tricky it is to represent a region as stylistically diverse as New York without compromising the significantly descriptive constituent lines that are used in the calculation of the average.

29. In general, Tupac's flow is significantly less rhythmically varied than Biggie's. He rarely if ever packs more than one extra rhyming stress into a line, and nearly forty percent of his lines have four rhymes (of which seventy percent have no extra rhyming stresses). Most of his variation comes from caesural elisions and enjambment. The result is that Tupac's style can be modeled in about forty templates of stress-rhyme flow. In contrast, modeling Biggie using the same metric produces eighty stress-rhyme templates, many of which include two or more extra rhyming stresses (sometimes even in the same dip). Further, Biggie's lines that do have four rhymes much more frequently have dip-disrupting pauses, unlike Tupac's.

30. Similar problems arise when assessing the correlation between gender and style and race and style. Just as Biggie and Tupac sought to represent their regions, many female rappers try to cultivate a female sound, and others, an androgynous style in which they try to sound like male rappers. It is impossible to group all female rappers together or all male rappers together without skewing the statistics. In similar fashion, most white rappers rap about topics with which they can identify but do not want to be treated as though they were *white rappers*, take for example Macklemore or Eminem.

31. Tupac briefly rapped under the name Makaveli for the album *The Don Killuminati: The 7 Day Theory*. Kendrick claims to have been visited by Tupac in a prophetic dream, and feels that he is Tupac's "spiritual son." For credence to our documentation of this claim: http://www.hiphopdx.com/index/news/id.15954/title.kendrick-lamar-recalls-having-a-vision-of-tupac-shakur-in-his-sleep

32. In the rap community, this remark was particularly inflammatory: the O. G. King of New York was Biggie, succeeded by Nas or Jay-Z, depending on who you think won the Nas vs. Jay-Z battle. Jay-Z does respond to Kendrick's claim (poorly) but Nas does not. But many others in the New York rap community have weighed in,

most impressively seventeen-year-old rapper Stro, who rapped two verses with choruses that ironically repeat: "Look at me, I'm the King of New York! Suddenly, I'm the King of New York!" See: "K. O. N. Y." by Stro.

33. The looseness can be sensed in the live performance. In "Always Shine" on the *Late Show with David Letterman*, we can hear the rapper and musicians conversing rhythmically among themselves during Lupe's solo. See: http://www.youtube.com/watch?v=——-lgL1khi0

34. Many hip hop heads consider the impact of his album to be similar to that of Nas's *Illmatic*. We believe this comparison doesn't hold with respect to stylistic impact, but we agree that *good kid, m.A.A.d city* has indeed upped the ante through its artistic excellence.

35. Just as nineties public boasts incited other rappers to release their own verses on the same instrumental, Kendrick's boast on "Control" elicited a wide range of responses, (noteworthy) among them: Eminem, Stro, Papoose, and King Los.

36. At seventeen when he performed this (as Astro), Stro looked and sounded like a shorty, but he played this to his advantage: "How can he already be so *good*, and so *nasty*?!" Unlike some of his contemporaries, who apply excellent flow to recycled themes, Stro is a prodigy punster and rhetorician, a master of *contemporary* allusion. In this passage, his performance of the *curious/serious* rhyme is especially noteworthy. If pronounced normally, these words would yield a weak off-rhyme on the front syllables; but, borrowing the cross-stress rhyming technique of last-millennium rappers like Ice Cube and Biggie, Stro inflects *curious* on its second syllable, *cur-EE-ous*, and adjusts its phonemes in other subtler ways to make the word accentuate his Jamaican roots. We're already liking it, but when we hear the resolving rhyme we're rewarded by Astro's mastery. It's a cross-inflected, exaggerated *SEE-ri-ous*. This produces a mini monosyllabic rhyme on the core of *curious*, but it also captures playfully (non-seriously) just how serious Stro is as an emcee, as evidenced by his original pun on Siri, the iPhone's monotone artificial genius voice: **Siri**-ous. Stro can sound androgynous like Siri, and he has at his disposal, like Siri, amazing vocabulary-data resources, but unlike Siri, of course, he's human and conscious and altogether admirable. See: http://www.youtube.com/watch?v=lO52JBzCWFU

Discography

"25 To Life." *Recovery*. Eminem. Priority. 2010.

"A Life In The Day Of Benjamin André." *The Love Below*. Outkast. LaFace, Artisa. 2003.

"A Long Way To Go." *Hard To Earn*. Gang Starr. Chrysalis, EMI Records. 1994.

"A Milli." *Tha Carter III*. Lil Wayne. Universal. 2008.

"Aaron Burr, Sir." *Hamilton (Original Broadway Cast Recording)*. Lin-Manuel Miranda, Leslie Odom, Jr., Anthony Ramos, Daveed Diggs, and Okieriete Onaodowan. Republic. 2015.

"Afro Blue (feat. Erykah Badu)." *Black Radio*. Robert Glasper. Blue Note Records. 2012.

"Ah-Yeah." *KRS-One*. KRS-One. Jive. 1995.

"Album of the Year (Freestyle)." *Album of the Year (Freestyle)—Single*. J. Cole. Dreamville, Roc Nation, Interscope. 2018.

"All Falls Down (feat. Syleena Johnson)." *The College Dropout*. Kanye West. Def Jam, Roc-A-Fella. 2004.

"Always Shine (feat. Lupe Fiasco and Bilal)." *Black Radio*. Robert Glasper. Blue Note Records. 2012.

"Bad M. F." *PTSD—Post Traumatic Stress Disorder*. Pharoahe Monch. W. A. R. Media, INgrooves. 2014.

"Barry Bonds (feat. Lil Wayne)." *Graduation*. Kanye West. Roc-A-Fella, Def Jam. 2007.

"Big Poppa." *Ready To Die*. The Notorious B. I. G. Bad Boy Records. 1994.

"Bitch Bad." *Food & Liquor II: The Great American Rap Album, Pt. 1*. Lupe Fiasco. 1st & 15th, Atlantic. 2012.

"Black Friday (Explicit)." *Black Friday*. Lil' Kim. IRS South Records. 2011.

"Black Radio (feat. Yasiin Bey)." *Black Radio*. Robert Glasper. Blue Note Records. 2012.

"Break The Bank." *Oxymoron*. ScHoolboy Q. Interscope, Top Dawg. 2014.

"Broken Again." *PTSD—Post Traumatic Stress Disorder*. Pharoahe Monch. W. A. R. Media, INgrooves. 2014.

"Brother Hominy Grit." *Hustlers Convention*. Lightnin' Rod. Celluloid Records. 1973.

"Buddah Lovaz." *E. 1999 Eternal*. Bone Thugs-N-Harmony. Ruthless, Relativity. 1995.

"Build Ya Skillz (feat. Busta Rhymes)." *KRS-One*. KRS-One. Jive. 1995.

"Cabinet Battle #1." *Hamilton (Original Broadway Cast Recording)*. Christopher Jackson, Daveed Diggs, Lin-Manuel Miranda, and Okieriete Onaodowan. Atlantic. 2015.

"Can't Hold Us (feat. Ray Dalton)." *The Heist (Deluxe Edition)*. Macklemore and Ryan Lewis. Macklemore LLC, ADA. 2011.

"Chi City." *Be*. Common. Geffen. 2005.

"Children's Story." *The Great Adventures Of Slick Rick*. Slick Rick. Def Jam, RAL. 1988.

"Christmas In Hollis." *Greatest Hits*. Run-DMC. Arista. 2002.

"Christmas Rappin'." *Special Gift*. Kurtis Blow. Mercury MDS-4009. 1979.

"Coppin' Some Fronts for the Set." *Hustlers Convention*. Lightnin' Rod. Celluloid Records. 1973.

"D. R. E. A. M. (feat. Talib Kweli)." *PTSD—Post Traumatic Stress Disorder*. Pharoahe Monch. W. A. R. Media, INgrooves. 2014.

"Damage." *PTSD—Post Traumatic Stress Disorder*. Pharoahe Monch. W. A. R. Media, INgrooves. 2014.

"Dance With the Devil." *Revolutionary, Vol. 1 (Bonus Edition)*. Immortal Technique. 1st edition: Self released Viper Records; Fontana, Nature Sounds. 2001.

"Daylight." *Daylight—EP*. Aesop Rock. Definitive Jux. 2002.

"Definition." *Black Star*. Black Star. Rawkus. 1999.

"DNA." *DAMN*. Kendrick Lamar. Aftermath, Interscope, Top Dawg. 2017.

"Don't Stop Rappin' (feat. Eightball and MJG)." *Can't Stay Away*. Too $hort. Jive. 1999.

"Doo Wop (That Thing)." *The Miseducation Of Lauryn Hill*. Lauryn Hill. Ruffhouse. 1998

"Double Speak (featuring Iomas Marad)." *Vintage*. All Natural. All Natural, Inc. 2005.

"Drop It Heavy." *D. I. T. C.—Diggin' In the Crates*. Showbiz and AG. Tommy Boy Records. 2000.

"DUCKWORTH." *DAMN*. Kendrick Lamar. Aftermath, Interscope, Top Dawg. 2017.

"Dumb It Down (feat. GemStones and Graham Burris)." *Lupe Fiasco's The Cool*. Lupe Fiasco. 1st & 15th, Atlantic. 2007.

"Ed." *O.G. Original Gangster*. Ice-T. Sire. 1991.

"Eht Dnarg Noisulli (feat. The Stepkids). "*PTSD—Post Traumatic Stress Disorder*. Pharoahe Monch. W. A. R. Media, INgrooves. 2014.

"Electric Relaxation." *Midnight Marauders*. A Tribe Called Quest. Jive. 1993.

"Ether." *Stillmatic [Limited]*. Nas. Ill Will, Columbia. 2001.

"FEEL." *DAMN*. Kendrick Lamar. Aftermath, Interscope, Top Dawg. 2017.

"Fight For Your Right." *Licensed To Ill*. Beastie Boys. Def Jam. 1986.

"Fight the Power." *Fight the Power—Single*. Public Enemy. Motown. 1989.

"Fixin' to Die." *Bob Dylan*. Bob Dylan. Columbia. 1962.

"Flava In Ya Ear (Album Version)." *Project: Funk Da World*. Craig Mack. Bad Boy, Arista. 1994.

"Four Bitches Is What I Got." *Hustlers Convention*. Lightnin' Rod. Celluloid Records. 1973.

"Fresh, Wild, Fly & Bold (Mega Mix)." *Fresh, Wild, Fly & Bold*. The Cold Crush Brothers. Ol' Skool Flava. 1995.

"Fresh, Wild, Fly & Bold (Party Acapella)." *Fresh, Wild, Fly & Bold*. The Cold Crush Brothers. Ol' Skool Flava. 1995.

"Fuck Tha Police (Explicit)." *Straight Outta Compton: 20th Anniversary*. N. W. A. Geffen. 1988.

"Gimme The Loot." *Ready To Die (The O. G. Edition)*. The Notorious B. I. G. Not on label—Promo. Unreleased.

"Gin & Juice." *Doggystyle*. Snoop Dogg. Death Row Records. 1993.

"GodLovesUgly." *God Loves Ugly*. Atmosphere. Rhymesayers Entertainment. 2002.

"Got Money (feat. T-Pain)." *Tha Carter III*. Lil Wayne Cash Money. 2008.

"Grit's Den." *Hustlers Convention*. Lightnin' Rod. Celluloid Records. 1973.

"Hamhock's Hall Was Big." *Hustlers Convention*. Lightnin' Rod. Celluloid Records. 1973.

"Hard Times." *Hard Times*. Kurtis Blow. Mercury. 1980.

"Heartbreakers (Instrumental)." *Fresh, Wild, Fly & Bold*. The Cold Crush Brothers. Ol' Skool Flava. 1995.

"Heartbreakers (Mega Mix)." *Fresh, Wild, Fly & Bold*. The Cold Crush Brothers. Ol' Skool Flava. 1995.

"Heartbreakers (Vocal Mix)." *Fresh, Wild, Fly & Bold*. The Cold Crush Brothers. Ol' Skool Flava. 1995.

"Heat." *Like Water For Chocolate*. Common. MCA. 2000.

"Heroin Addict." *PTSD—Post Traumatic Stress Disorder*. Pharoahe Monch. W. A. R. Media, INgrooves. 2014.

"Hit Em Up." *Hit Em Up—Single*. 2Pac. Amaru, Death Row, Interscope, Jive. 1996.

"Hold." *KRS-One*. KRS-One. Jive. 1995.

"Hound Dog." *The Essential Elvis Presley (Remastered)*. Elvis Presley. RCA. 2006.

"I Know You Got Soul." *Paid In Full*. Eric B. and Rakim. 4th & B'way, Island. 1987.

"I Used To Love H. E. R." *Resurrection*. Common. Relativity. 1994.

"Immortal." *4 Your Eyez Only*. J. Cole. Dreamville, Roc Nation, Interscope. 2016.

"In Memory Of . . ." *Moment Of Truth*. Gang Starr. Noo Trybe, Virgin. 1998.

"Invincible (feat. Ester Dean)." *Lace Up (Deluxe Version)*. Machine Gun Kelly. Bad Boy, Interscope. 2012.

"It's Like That." *Greatest Hits*. Run-DMC. Arista. 2002.

"Izzo (H. O. V. A.)." *The Blueprint*. Jay-Z. Def Jam. 2001.

"Jazzy Sensation (Bronx Version)." *Looking for the Perfect Beat 1980–1985*. Afrika Bambaataa and The Jazzy 5. Tommy Boy, Rhino, Atlantic Records. 1981.

"Jesus Walks." *The College Dropout*. Kanye West. Def Jam, Roc-A-Fella. 2004.

"Just What I Am (feat. King Chip)." *Indicud*. Kid Cudi. Wicked Awesome, GOOD, Republic. 2012.

"Keep Floatin' (feat. Wiz Khalifa)." *Best Day Ever (5th Anniversary Remastered Edition)*. Mac Miller. Rostrum. 2011.

"Keep Ya Head Up." *Greatest Hits [Disc 1]*. 2Pac. Amaru, Death Row, Interscope, Jive. 1993.

"Kush." *The Leak—EP*. Lil Wayne. Cash Money. 2007.

"Let's Talk About Sex." *20th Century Masters—The Millennium Collection: The Best of Salt-N-Pepa*. Salt-N-Pepa. Next Plateau. 2008.

"Life's A Bitch (feat. A. Z.)." *Illmatic*. Nas. Columbia. 1994.

"Little Weapon (feat. Bishop G and Nikki Jean)." *Lupe Fiasco's The Cool*. Lupe Fiasco. 1st & 15th, Atlantic. 2007.

"Live at the Barbeque (feat. Nas)." *Breaking Atoms*. Main Source. Wild Pitch, EMI. 1991.

"Losing My Mind (feat. dEnAuN)." *PTSD—Post Traumatic Stress Disorder*. Pharoahe Monch. W. A. R. Media, INgrooves. 2014.

"Love Is Blind." *Let There Be Eve: Ruff Ryders' First Lady*. Eve. Ruff Ryders, Interscope. 1999.

"LOYALTY. (feat. Rihanna)." *DAMN*. Kendrick Lamar. Aftermath, Interscope, Top Dawg. 2017.

"Mathematics." *Black On Both Sides*. Mos Def. Elektra. 1999.

"Me So Horny." *The 2 Live Crew's Greatest Hits*. The 2 Live Crew. Lil' Joe Records. 1989.

"Mic Contract." *O. G. Original Gangster*. Ice-T. Sire. 1991.

"Mister Bill." *Fresh, Wild, Fly & Bold*. The Cold Crush Brothers. Ol' Skool Flava. 1995.

"Modern Man's Hustle." *God Loves Ugly*. Atmosphere. Rhymesayers Entertainment. 2002.

"Moment (feat. Lil Wayne)." *Rise of an Empire (Deluxe Edition)*. Young Money. Young Money, Cash Money, Republic. 2014.

"Moment of Clarity." *The Black Album*. Jay-Z. Roc-A-Fella, Def Jam. 2003.

"Monster (feat. Jay-Z, Rick Ross, Nicki Minaj, and Bon Iver)." *My Beautiful Dark Twisted Fantasy [Explicit]*. Kanye West. Def Jam, Roc-A-Fella. 2010.

"My Neck, My Back." *Nasty Confessions.* Khia. Vanguard. 2002.

"N. Y. State of Mind." *Illmatic.* Nas. Columbia. 1994.

"Notorious Thugs (feat. Bone Thugs-N-Harmony)." *Life After Death.* The Notorious B. I. G. Bad Boy Entertainment. 1997.

"Number One with the Fun." *Fresh, Wild, Fly & Bold.* The Cold Crush Brothers. Ol' Skool Flava. 1995.

"Nuthin' But A G Thang (feat. Snoop Dogg)." *The Chronic.* Dr. Dre. Death Row, Interscope, Priority. 1993.

"Old School Love (feat. Ed Sheeran)." *Old School Love (feat. Ed Sheeran)—Single.* Lupe Fiasco. 1st & 15th, Atlantic. 2013.

"One Mic." *Stillmatic.* Nas. Ill Will, Columbia. 2001.

"One More Chance/Stay With Me (Remix)." *Notorious.* The Notorious B. I. G. Bad Boy. 2009.

"Painkillers." *The Cold Vein.* Cannibal Ox. Definitive Jux. 2001.

"Party and Bullshit." *Party and Bullshit—Single.* The Notorious B. I. G. Uptown. 1993.

"Paul Revere." *Licensed To Ill.* Beastie Boys. Def-Jam. 1986.

"Pissin' On Your Steps." *I Wish My Brother George Was Here.* Del Tha Funky Homosapien. Elektra. 1991.

"Planet Rock." *Looking for the Perfect Beat 1980–1985.* Afrika Bambaataa and The Soul Sonic Force. Tommy Boy, Rhino, Atlantic Records. 1982.

"Post Traumatic Stress Disorder." *PTSD—Post Traumatic Stress Disorder.* Pharoahe Monch. W. A. R. Media, INgrooves. 2014.

"Press Rewind." *Both Sides Of The Brain.* Del The Funky Homosapien. Hieroglyphics Imperium Recordings. 2000.

"Protect Ya Neck." *Enter The Wu (36 Chambers).* Wu-Tang Clan. Loud. 1993.

"Punk Rock Rap (Party Mix)." *Fresh, Wild, Fly & Bold.* The Cold Crush Brothers. Ol' Skool Flava. 1995.

"Punk Rock Rap (Punk Rap Mix)." *Fresh, Wild, Fly & Bold.* The Cold Crush Brothers. Ol' Skool Flava. 1995.

"Punk Rock Rap (Punk Rock Mix)." *Fresh, Wild, Fly & Bold.* The Cold Crush Brothers. Ol' Skool Flava. 1995.

"Put It On." *Lifestylez ov da Poor & Dangerous.* Big L. Columbia. 1994.

"Rap God." *The Marshall Mathers LP 2 (Deluxe).* Eminem. Aftermath, Interscope, Shady. 2013.

"Rap History." *Keep Right.* KRS-One. Grit. 2004.

"Rapid Eye Movement (feat. Black Thought)." *PTSD—Post Traumatic Stress Disorder.* Pharoahe Monch. W. A. R. Media, INgrooves. 2014.

"Rapper's Delight." *The Sugarhill Gang.* The Sugarhill Gang. Sugar Hill Records. 1980.

"Raspberry Fields." *The Cold Vein.* Cannibal Ox. Definitive Jux. 2001.

"Raw (Remix)." *Long Live the Kane.* Big Daddy Kane. Cold Chillin', Warner Bros. 1988.

"Reality Check (feat. One Be Lo and Senim Silla)." *Masters Of The Universe.* Binary Star. Subterraneous Records. 2000.

"Reset (feat. Khujo Goodie and Cee-Lo)." *Speakerboxxx.* Big Boi. LaFace, Artisa. 2003.

"Respiration." *Black Star.* Black Star. Rawkus. 1999.

"Roman's Revenge (feat. Eminem)." *Pink Friday (Deluxe Version).* Nicki Minaj. Young Money, Cash Money, Universal Motown. 2010.

"Satisfied." *Hamilton (Original Broadway Cast Recording).* Original Broadway Cast of *Hamilton* & Renée Elise Goldsberry. Atlantic. 2015.

"Scream." *PTSD—Post Traumatic Stress Disorder.* Pharoahe Monch. W. A. R. Media, INgrooves. 2014.

"Screaming Target." *Screaming Target.* Big Youth. Gussie, Jaguar, Trojan. 1972.

"Sentenced to the Chair." *Hustlers Convention.* Lightnin' Rod. Celluloid Records. 1973.

"Set It Off." *Long Live the Kane.* Big Daddy Kane. Cold Chillin', Warner Bros. 1988.

"Set It Off." *Set It Off (Music From the New Line Cinema Motion Picture).* Organized Noize and Queen Latifah. Elektra, Wea. 1996.

"Shave 'Em Dry II." *Shave 'Em Dry—The Best of Lucille Bogan.* Lucille Bogan. Columbia, Legacy. 2004.

"She Will (feat. Drake)." *Tha Carter IV [Deluxe Edition].* Lil Wayne. Young Money, Cash Money, Republic. 2011

"Sidefx (feat. Dr. Pete)." *PTSD—Post Traumatic Stress Disorder.* Pharoahe Monch. W. A. R. Media, INgrooves. 2014.

"Slavery Days." *Marcus Garvey.* Burning Spear. Island. 1975.

"Spoon." *Hustlers Convention.* Lightnin' Rod. United Artists Douglas Records. 1970.

"Sport." *Hustlers Convention.* Lightnin' Rod. United Artists Douglas Records. 1970.

"Stan." *The Marshall Mathers LP.* Eminem. Aftermath, Interscope. 2000.

"Stand Your Ground." *PTSD—Post Traumatic Stress Disorder.* Pharoahe Monch. W. A. R. Media, INgrooves. 2014.

"Straight Outta Compton." *Straight Outta Compton: 20th Anniversary.* N. W. A. Ruthless, Priority. 1988.

"Sucka Nigga." *Midnight Marauders.* A Tribe Called Quest. Jive. 1993.

"Tab Open." *Tab Open—Single.* Sam Adams. 1st Round Records. 2009.

"Takeover." *The Blueprint.* Jay-Z. Def Jam, Roc-A-Fella. 2001.

"Tha Crossroads." *E. 1999 Eternal.* Bone Thugs-N-Harmony. Ruthless, Relativity. 1996.

"The Bones Fly from Spoon's Hand." *Hustlers Convention.* Lightnin' Rod. Celluloid Records. 1973.

"The Break Was so Loud, It Hushed the Crowd." *Hustlers Convention.* Lightnin' Rod. Celluloid Records. 1973.

"The Breaks." *Kurtis Blow*. Kurtis Blow. Mercury. 1980.

"The Cafe Black Rose." *Hustlers Convention*. Lightnin' Rod. Celluloid Records. 1973.

"The Corner (feat. The Last Poets)." *Be*. Common. Geffen. 2005.

"The Jungle." *PTSD—Post Traumatic Stress Disorder*. Pharoahe Monch. W. A. R. Media, INgrooves. 2014.

"The Message." *The Message*. Grandmaster Flash & The Furious Five. Rhino. 1982.

"The Questions." *Like Water For Chocolate*. Common. MCA. 2000.

"The Rape Over." *The New Danger*. Mos Def. Rawkus, Geffen. 2004.

"The Real Slim Shady." *The Marshall Mathers LP*. Eminem. Aftermath, Interscope. 2000.

"The Recollection Facility." *PTSD—Post Traumatic Stress Disorder*. Pharoahe Monch. W. A. R. Media, INgrooves. 2014.

"The Recollection Facility, Pt. 2." *PTSD—Post Traumatic Stress Disorder*. Pharoahe Monch. W. A. R. Media, INgrooves. 2014.

"The Recollection Facility, Pt. 3." *PTSD—Post Traumatic Stress Disorder*. Pharoahe Monch. W. A. R. Media, INgrooves. 2014

"The Revolution Will Not Be Televised." *Pieces of a Man (Deluxe Edition)*. Gil Scott-Heron. Flying Dutchman. 1971.

"The Shit Hits the Fan Again." *Hustlers Convention*. Lightnin' Rod. Celluloid Records. 1973.

"The What." *Ready To Die (The O. G. Edition)*. The Notorious B. I. G. Not on label—Promo. Unreleased.

"This Is The Carter." *Tha Carter*. Lil Wayne. Cash Money, Universal. 2004.

"Time2." *PTSD—Post Traumatic Stress Disorder*. Pharoahe Monch. W. A. R. Media, INgrooves. 2014.

"U. N. I. T. Y. (1993)." *Black Reign*. Queen Latifah. Motown. 1993.

"Warning." *Ready to Die*. The Notorious B. I. G. Bad Boy, Atlantic. 1994.

"We Ain't (feat. Eminem)." *The Documentary*. The Game. Aftermath. 2005.

"Weekend." *Fresh, Wild, Fly & Bold*. The Cold Crush Brothers. Ol' Skool Flava. 1995.

"We're Gonna Need a Little Scratch." *Fresh, Wild, Fly & Bold*. The Cold Crush Brothers. Ol' Skool Flava. 1995.

"What They Gonna Do Part II (Bonus Track)." *The Blueprint 2: The Curse*. Jay-Z. Roc-A-Fella, Def Jam. 2002.

"When the Revolution Comes." *The Very Best of the Last Poets*. The Last Poets. Charly Records. 2005.

"Woo-Hah!! Got You All In Check." *The Coming*. Busta Rhymes. Elektra. 1996.

"Work." *Moment Of Truth*. Gang Starr. Noo Trybe, Virgin. 1998.

"Work It." *Under Construction*. Missy Elliott. Goldmind, Elektra. 2002.

"Yvette." *Fresh, Wild, Fly & Bold*. The Cold Crush Brothers. Ol' Skool Flava. 1995.

Index

Note: Artists with stage names are alphabetized by stage name, e.g., Queen Latifah.